Infant and Toddler Development *from* Conception *to* Age 3

WHAT BABIES ASK OF US

Mary Jane Maguire-Fong
Marsha Peralta

Foreword by J. Ronald Lally
Afterword by Ed Tronick

TEACHERS COLLEGE PRESS
TEACHERS COLLEGE | COLUMBIA UNIVERSITY
NEW YORK AND LONDON

Published by Teachers College Press, 1234 Amsterdam Avenue, New York, NY 10027

Cover Photos (left to right): Justin Takeoka, jacoblund / iStock by Getty Images, Robert M. Chiles, Jillian Rich

Text Design: Lynne Frost

Library of Congress Cataloging-in-Publication Data

Names: Maguire-Fong, Mary Jane, author. | Peralta, Marsha, author.
Title: Infant and toddler development from conception to age 3 : what babies ask of us / Mary Jane Maguire-Fong, Marsha Peralta ; foreword by J. Ronald Lally ; afterword by Ed Tronick.
Other titles: Infant and toddler development from conception to age three
Description: New York, NY : Teachers College Press, [2019] | Includes bibliographical references and index. |
Identifiers: LCCN 2018034183 (print) | LCCN 2018047669 (ebook) | ISBN 9780807777381 (ebook) | ISBN 9780807761083 (paper : acid-free paper)
Subjects: LCSH: Infants—Development. | Toddlers—Development.
Classification: LCC HQ774 (ebook) | LCC HQ774 .M237 2019 (print) | DDC 612.6/54—dc23
LC record available at https://lccn.loc.gov/2018034183

ISBN 978-0-8077-6108-3 (paper)
ISBN 978-0-8077-7738-1 (ebook)

Printed on acid-free paper
Manufactured in the United States of America

26 25 24 23 22 21 20 19   8 7 6 5 4 3 2 1

To Ryan, Mariah, and Ettalyn, who helped me discover anew
the world through the eyes of infants

— Mary Jane Maguire-Fong

In deep appreciation of those whose love brought me into being.
To my beloveds and those yet to be—may these words be medicine.
And for Mr. Z, whose being inspired me to do more.

— Marsha Peralta

Contents

Foreword J. Ronald Lally vii

Preface ix

1 Infants and Toddlers: How We See Them 1

Connection 1
Participation 2
Belonging 4
Meaning-Making 5
Companionship 6

PART I. CONCEPTION THROUGH BIRTH 9

2 From Stardust to Birth 11

Development and How it Unfolds 11
Phases of Prenatal Development 15
Birth Status and Prematurity 17
Development of the Nervous System 19
Environmental Exposure: Impact on Prenatal Development 23

3 Labor and Birth 27

A Cascade of Hormones Orchestrates Birth 27
The Body Prepares for Labor 28
Labor 29
Optimal Birth Care 36
From Research to Policy to Practice 40

PART II. NEWBORNS AND RESPONSIVE CARE 43

4 Newborn Care 45

Skin-to-Skin Contact 45
The Baby's Microbiome 46
Seeking Safety 47
Responsive Care 50

5 Synchrony in Care: Infant Feeding and Meals 54

Lactation and Feeding: A Perfect Match 54
Complementary Food 59
Infants' Active Participation in Meals 61

6 Synchrony in Care: Rhythms of Sleep 63

Sleep Patterns and Brain Development 63
Where Infants Sleep: Cultural and Historical Context 66
Making Decisions about Infant Sleep 67

PART III. BABIES MAKING MEANING 71

7 How Babies Communicate 73

Language Begins in the Womb 73
Babies as Language Detectives 74
In Dialogue with Others 78
The Roots of Reading Begin in Infancy 82
Language Milestones and Cause for Concern 84
Sharing Stories 85

8 How Babies Move 86
Fetal Movement 86
Newborn Movements 87
Reaching and Grasping 88
Rolling and Sitting 90
Locomotion 91
Freedom to Move 93
Movement: The Social and Cultural Context 93

9 How Babies Learn About People 95
The Biological Urge to Play 95
Young Infants' Social Play 96
Older Infants' Social Play 100
Social Responsiveness: When Concerns Arise 102

10 How Babies Learn About Objects 104
What Infants Know About Objects 104
How Infants Build Concepts in Play 108
Play Space as Context for Learning 121

PART IV. WIDENING THE LENS 123

11 Belonging 125
Learning by Pitching In 125
Detecting Goals and Intentions 127
Sharing 129
Caring 130
Living Within the House Rules 131

12 How the Light Gets In: Coping with Adversity 134
Body Is Home for Life 134
Companionship 135
Traumatic Harm 138
Healing Happens in the Body 143

13 What Babies Ask of Us: Baby-Friendly Policies 146
Pre-Conception 146
Gestation and Pregnancy 147
High-Quality, High-Value Mother–Baby Care 148
Paid Family Leave 154
Affordable, Quality Infant Care 155
Meaning-Making Through Infants' Eyes 158

Afterword Ed Tronick 161
References 163
Index 174
About the Authors 182

Foreword

OF ALL THE BOOKS on infancy I have read over the many years of my professional life, I have never experienced one that more clearly and purposefully communicates, in direct and easily understandable language, the day-by-day development of infants and the essential role adults play in the optimization of that development. On every page of *Infant and Toddler Development from Conception to Age 3: What Babies Ask of Us,* Mary Jane Maguire-Fong and Marsha Peralta demonstrate their passion for transforming the findings of hundreds of research studies, on many topics, into a path that readers can easily follow. Their commitment to communicating in a way that lets readers arrive at a deep understanding of how infants operate, how infants change and grow, and what infants need from those who care for them shows in their choice of words and examples. Their intention to truly get through to the reader what they have uncovered from their in-depth study of infant research is quite evident. They are convinced that how adults understand and treat an infant directly affects the rest of the child's life and influences the evolution of the species. They want to share this conviction with all who come in contact with their book and want to make this information as available and understandable as possible. The authors' understanding of the development of the human infant from pre-conception to age 3 is impressive. The information shared about how adults can support optimal development through this magical period of growth is both wise and based on the most current research available. This book is not just someone's opinion on how babies should be cared for. It is a carefully put together presentation of the needs of infants for support from all parts of society. It spells out in detail the role that parents, families, child care providers, neighborhoods, cultures, governments, and—when necessary—specialists in both prevention and compensatory services need to play to give infants the necessary experiences to successfully master building the foundation for their life's journey.

The book begins with a reasoned argument of how important it is to have the most accurate view of how infants are wired and how they develop based on the most up-to-date science available. This is important because how we view the child's capacities dictates how we treat them. For instance, if we think a child is a "blank slate" coming into the world, we will treat them very differently than if we think a child comes into the world with temperamental distinctions in reaction to what they experience. The first chapter orients the reader to the most current research-based view of what makes infants tick.

Maguire-Fong and Peralta's major contributions are the presentations on the period of life from conception to delivery and newborn care. The authors paint a picture of the power and wisdom of our bodies to prepare us for and get us through the birth experience, along with great advice for dealing with the institutions involved in the birth experience. Of particular importance is the message to surrender and listen to natural instincts to guide one through this time period. It is my opinion that Chapters 2 through 4 are "must reads" for anyone considering having a child. The research cited and interpreted in Chapters 5 through 11 makes clear how development progresses in its various domains. This portion of the book helps the reader understand the underlying structures that are gradually built through the first 3 years of life and how, for the human infant, most of that building takes place in relationship with trusted adults. This section of the book also includes the identification and naming of the skills, concepts, and structures being built. For a new parent or caregiver, just reading the names of these developments can make visible what is going on in the child's life and help the adults become more attuned to their child's learning. I also found helpful the suggestions given for environmental and experiential interactions that caregivers can offer children to match their developing skills, concepts, and structures.

As the book ends, we find two chapters that present issues of adversity and how to deal with it. Presented is information about the frequency of adverse childhood experiences and their negative impact on development, including the debilitating effects for young children of experiencing trauma without adults available to provide support. I found that the measured mix of strategies given the reader to help children regulate their stress through the use of both trained professionals and trusted caregivers was quite insightful. The final chapter deals with the adversity infants face in American society due to lack of appropriate attention to their early environments and experiences by federal, state, and local policies and practices that seem to not take into consideration the important information contained in this book. We as a society must do better in giving infants what they ask of us. It is in everyone's best interest. This book goes a long way to help us understand why.

J. Ronald Lally
Co-Director
Center for Child & Family Studies and Program for Infant/Toddler Care
WestEd
San Francisco, California

Preface

THERE IS an astounding volume of information on every topic considered in this book. The challenge is to differentiate and describe the most relevant research in order to deepen our understanding of infants and their needs and to expand our capacity to see the entirety of the human infant. Although it is impossible to convey the full array of human sensibilities and competencies that are present in a baby right from the start, we have tried to gently tug at the veils of misperception, assumptions, and projections that mask the infant before us. We have tried to bring to life treasures from decades of multidisciplinary research that points us to a more complete view of the human infant.

The narrative presented in this book taps key areas of study to help readers reflect on how they see babies, and perhaps begin to see babies with new eyes (Beatty, Stranger, Beatty, & Gerber, 1984). Babies arrive with biological expectations for the environment they hope to find and the care they seek. It is from this perspective that we tackle the question voiced in the title, "What do babies ask of us?"

This book charts the story of babies' journey, from pre-conception to 36 months. To point the way on this journey, we have tapped the wisdom of luminaries, including researchers and practitioners Heideliese Als, Beatrice Beebe, Nils Bergman, T. Berry Brazelton, Jerome Bruner, Magda Gerber, Patricia Kuhl, Loris Malaguzzi, Jaak Panksepp, Bruce Perry, Emmi Pikler, Barbara Rogoff, Louis Sander, Daniel Stern, Colwyn Trevarthen, Ed Tronick, and D. W. Winnicott. Each has sought to understand the experience of being a baby by spending time with them, seeing them in context—with those who love and care for them—encountering them anew, and imagining what the world is like when seen through their eyes and experienced through their minds and bodies.

Companionship is an evocative theme for the authors of this book. We have worked together as colleagues, as friends, and now as partners in writing. We each bring a distinct personal and professional background, but we have derived mutual benefit from sharing our nascent ideas with one another. The seeds of a decades-long conversation that gave rise to this book began with the topics of pregnancy and birth. Neither of us were mothers yet, but we shared stories in anticipation of the changes parenthood would bring. In time we discovered a common and deep interest in the earliest period of development, prenatal and the first 3 years. There were times when we were too busy to talk, gathering experiences "in the field," as mothers and professionals. Yet those early sparks of curiosity always ignited as we shared insights and ideas about infants and the power they had in our lives. As companions to each other's ideas, we have studied and learned together. We have observed and listened in on many infants and the important adults in their lives as they play and interact. We have done so against a background of constant study of infant development, of how learning happens in the early years, and of infant–parent mental health. We invite readers to join us as companions on this journey, to observe and listen closely to experiences they have with babies. Our hope is that this book can serve as a guide in making meaningful sense of infants' development from pre-conception through the first 3 years, and as a guide in caring for them.

Human infants are amazingly competent, yet vulnerable, reliant on others for warmth, protection, and safety. They cannot exist outside of a relationship of care, and it is this relationship that is explored in this book, with each chapter a distinct lens for examining a unique aspect of development. We use the term *infant* interchangeably with the term *baby* to refer to infants from birth to 3 years of age, and at times we speak of young infants, mobile infants, and older infants, with the latter also being described as toddlers if they have reached the point of using locomotion. There are many involved in infant care. We use the term *parent* to refer neither to biological nor gender-related factors but to describe the caregiver who is emotionally meeting the demands of parenting. We use the term *mother* when appropriate, for example, when speaking of the birthing mother. Occasionally we reference a generic infant, and we have tried to reference each gender in equal measure, as best we can.

We are deeply appreciative of pioneers in the field of infant–parent mental health, including Beatrice Beebe, T. Berry Brazelton, Peter Fonagy, Alicia Lieberman, Joy Osofsky, Alan Schore, and Ed Tronick. Others have helped us understand what it takes to heal the effects of trauma on children and their families. These include Bruce Perry, Bessel van der Kolk, Kristie Brandt, Connie Lillas, Daniel Siegel, Stephen Porges, and our colleagues in the Napa Infant–Parent Mental Health Fellowship/University of Massachusetts, Boston, Postgraduate Certificate Program.

To Lynne Frost, Sarah Biondello, and Susan Liddicoat, whose thoughtful editorial work helped us find our way, and to the families who so generously gave us permission to use photos of their infants in this book, we extend our deepest gratitude. Many colleagues and friends have been a source of wisdom, counsel, and inspiration in this work, including wise women Donis Eichhorn, Betsy Hiteshew, Elizabeth Jones, and Andrea Steffens.

Finally, there are those who put wind in our sails by unceasingly advocating for the rights of babies and their families, and to them we will be forever grateful for their work—J. Ronald Lally, Peter Mangione, Carlina Rinaldi, and Marcy Whitebook. This book is an attempt to honor their work and to keep infants, their families, and those who serve them at the center of policy initiatives to make the world a better place for babies.

CHAPTER 1

Infants and Toddlers

How We See Them

There is no such thing as a baby. . . . A baby cannot exist alone, but it is essentially part of a relationship. —D. W. Winnicott (1964, p. 88)

WHO IS the baby you know? What images come to mind? Perhaps you imagine a newborn baby—soft, moist, melting into the curve of your arm. Or maybe your image is of an enticingly chubby infant, with beckoning smile, or one with a grimace, whose cry alerts. Maybe your thoughts lead to joyful bursts of upright movement, an infant whose bright, inquisitive eyes seek something of infinite interest. Or perhaps the baby you imagine peeks at you with wary eyes, reluctant to engage. Or the eyes might seem empty, a baby unaware, caught in a blur of surrounding sensations.

As they transition through gestation, birth, and on into the first 3 years, babies cross paths with a great many people. How babies are seen, that is, how we imagine them to be, influences how we treat them in the moment, but more significantly, it matters for how we treat them and care for them in the long run. How we see babies has profound influence over the care we give them, day in and day out, how we teach them, how we guide them, how we usher them beyond the first 3 years, and how we as a society formulate policies and services that impact their lives.

This book is an invitation to take a close look at how we see babies, to sharpen our understanding of what babies know, how they feel, how they relate with others, and how they learn. It draws on a wide array of scientific studies. These studies shed light on babies' competence and their biological expectation for care. Decades of research focusing on infancy provide clear evidence that infants arrive at birth far more conscious, more aware, more inquisitive, and more capable than we ever imagined in the past (Gopnik, 2009).

Babies have much to teach us, and the most important task for us in caring for babies is to listen to them well. This means observing carefully as they express themselves through actions, gestures, expressions, and vocalizations—babies' first modes of communication. From an array of disciplines, this book gathers evidence about babies' ways of knowing, feeling, communicating, and moving, and presents it as an invitation to bring into sharper focus the lens through which we see babies.

Each chapter in this book tells the story of what researchers are learning about infants in a particular domain of development. Although these domains are teased apart to examine each area of research, they remain woven together with strong threads to convey the story of infant development from conception through the first 3 years. These threads capture key aspects of what babies seek and what they ask of us—connection, participation, belonging, meaning-making, and companionship. Woven together, these themes narrate a story of infant development that deepens our understanding of who infants are, what they seek, how they think, and how they feel, giving practical answers to the orienting question of this book, "What do babies ask of us?"

CONNECTION

The quote that introduces this chapter captures an idea key to research on infancy. British pediatrician and psychoanalyst D. W. Winnicott (1965) identified the vital necessity of babies being emotionally, socially, and at times, physically connected to others, advising, "Whenever one finds an infant, one finds maternal care, and without maternal care, there would be no infant" (p. 38).

Over the course of his long career, Winnicott worked with many thousands of mother–child pairs, most of whom were poor. He recognized that all infants are born with unique and individual potentials that they bring to the relationship. One of Winnicott's important contributions is that these potentials can only be realized when there is a responsive, holding environment provided by what he described as "a good-enough mother" (1965, p. 144). "Good-enough," in Winnicott's view, is a mother who is positively preoccupied with her child, and who adapts her behaviors fairly extensively to the needs of the baby, gradually stepping back to allow infants' competencies to take hold as they emerge over the first year.

Winnicott described with profound insight the emergent "self" as it forms in infancy and how infants expect a responsive other. He articulated the tragic sense of loss when an as-yet-unformed being has no responsive other, no attuned or attentive person, no container, no "holding" environment. Winnicott understood the nature of such infant agony and suffering and used his insight to build therapeutic bridges into the profound isolation that ensues, and to examine how this loss can lead to behavioral patterns that last a lifetime.

Winnicott's image of infants was in marked contrast to prevailing views in psychology, where the popular description of infants was as a "blank slate," or "tabula rasa," implying an organism with limited and undifferentiated motor and perceptual abilities. From this perspective, infants were seen as idle recipients of care, rather than active participants in care or active contributors to the relationship of care.

Not until research began to incorporate an ethological approach to infancy did this perspective begin to change. Ethology is the study of behavior with emphasis on the behavioral patterns that occur in natural environments. Leading proponents of this perspective were theorists and researchers John Bowlby (1982) and Mary Ainsworth (Ainsworth, Blehar, Waters, & Wall, 1978). They described how the infants' dependent status causes them to seek the caregiver for the benefits of nourishment, protection, and survival, but equally important, for social engagement. Their work deepened understanding of the importance of the caregiving environment, particularly the social environment, for the formation of the infant. They used the term *attachment* to describe how infants, from birth, seek and form an intimate relationship with one person, whom they identified to be most often the mother. The idea that human infants build a bond of attachment designed to ensure their protection and care heralded an exciting new era in infancy research.

PARTICIPATION

New procedures for studying infants made it possible to gather measurable data on infants' relationships with those caring for them and infants' competencies. Researchers devised ways to measure precisely what infants were capable of seeing, smelling, tasting, and hearing. This research evolved beyond exploring infants' sensory capacities to include experiments that measured their social capacities as well. In experiments recording simple moments of face-to-face interaction between infant and adult, infants imitated the facial expression of the adult, demonstrated their acute sensitivity to small changes in language sounds, and showed a keen awareness of changes in facial expression or intentional movements of the adult partner in a social exchange (Tronick, 2007). Contrary to what was once thought, infants were seen to be highly aware of what was occurring around them, quite good at predicting patterns of interactive behavior in social situations, and motivated to actively participate in interactions with others.

This research challenged the presumed image of infants as immature, undifferentiated, unknowing beings. A new image of infants emerged, one of competent beings actively participating in care, and primed by their biology to be in relationship with others. Some of the most revealing research with infants and their caregivers used microanalysis of film and video to shed light on infants' awareness and their ability to communicate with others. This technique captures communicative events that occur in less than a second, imperceptible in real time. Using split-screen photography, with one camera on the baby and one on the caregiver, researchers use the camera as a "social microscope" (Beebe, 2014, p. 4), slowing down the movements of infant and caregiver to detect, through frame-by-frame analysis, synchronous patterns of movement. Beatrice Beebe, a master in conducting such research, describes her findings as:

> remarkably beautiful moments, such as both partners rising up and up into glorious sunbursts of smiles. [This type of recording] also reveals very disturbing moments, such as maternal anger or disgust faces, or infants becoming frantically distressed or frozen in

> alarm. . . . We can see the moment-by-moment dialogue between the two. (p. 4)

This type of research shows clearly that infants' movements, vocalizations, and expressions are linked, in synchrony, with those of the caregiver, and that at some level, babies are aware of, responding to, and adapting to subtle shifts in the behavior of the other.

It is this dynamic awareness and participation on the part of the baby and the caregiver that result in caregiver and baby co-regulating the level of arousal (Trevarthen, 2015), meaning that the affect of one influences and potentially changes the affect of the other. Researcher Daniel Stern (2000) used the term *affect attunement* to describe how this synchrony continues to evolve with development, becoming more complex. The 11-week-old infant in Figure 1.1 smiles in synchrony with the smile of her Grandma, matching expressions and vocalizations.

In Stern's words, it is as if those caring for infants "enter into and swim with the dynamic flows" (2010, p. 79) generated by the babies' expressions and movements. Adults behave with an intuitive familiarity, entering into a hidden biological synchrony of social engagement with the baby's dynamic movements. In their behavior, infants express their level of pleasurable or upset arousal and give clues as to where their behavior is tending. Stern describes the ease with which this synchronous attunement occurs across modalities of expression: "Parents use their facial expressions, vocalizations, gestures, and movements to adjust the strength of their stimulation from moment to moment while playing. They are like a 'sound–light show' for the infant" (p. 77). This intuitive synchrony of rhythmic interaction is explored in Chapters 7 and 9, with respect to synchrony in gestures, expressions, vocalizations, and playful social interactions.

FIGURE 1.1. Synchrony in Care

A biological and physiological synchrony between infant and caregiver also exists. This biological synchrony can be seen in relationships established around feeding and sleeping. The supply of breast milk, for example, and the composition of breast milk adjust in response to infants' sucking, a physiological synchrony between mother and baby. These synchronous changes assure that infants receive a full complement of nutrients, protection against disease, and the energy needed to grow and survive.

Theorists of child development have long debated whether newborns and very young infants are active participants in social exchange, aware of and responsive to expressions and feelings of others (Reddy, 2008). Some have suggested that it is only toward the end of the first year that infants appear to be aware of what others might be thinking. Some have assumed that throughout the first 2 years infants are egocentric, that they cannot see the perspective of others. Students of child development have long been taught that infants and toddlers exist in an egocentric stage of development, not yet capable of seeing others' point of view, a perspective made popular by theorist Jean Piaget (Ginsburg & Opper, 1988). Piaget proposed that infants and young children move through distinct stages of cognitive development, and he described infancy as the *sensori-motor* stage. From this perspective, sensori-motor "knowing" means infants are limited to what they can experience through their senses and through movement of their bodies, rendering them as yet incapable of thinking about what others might be feeling or thinking.

Clever experiments with newborns and young infants have revealed the fallacy of seeing infants as simply sensori-motor creatures, however (Meltzoff & Moore, 1977; Reddy, 2008; Trevarthen & Delafield-Butt, 2017). Studies show infants' acute sensitivity to the communicative cues of others. Infants have been found to be highly aware of facial expressions, of intonations of the voice, and of gestures and patterns of how people move. Rather than being egocentric, some

FIGURE 1.2. Feeling the Experience of the Other

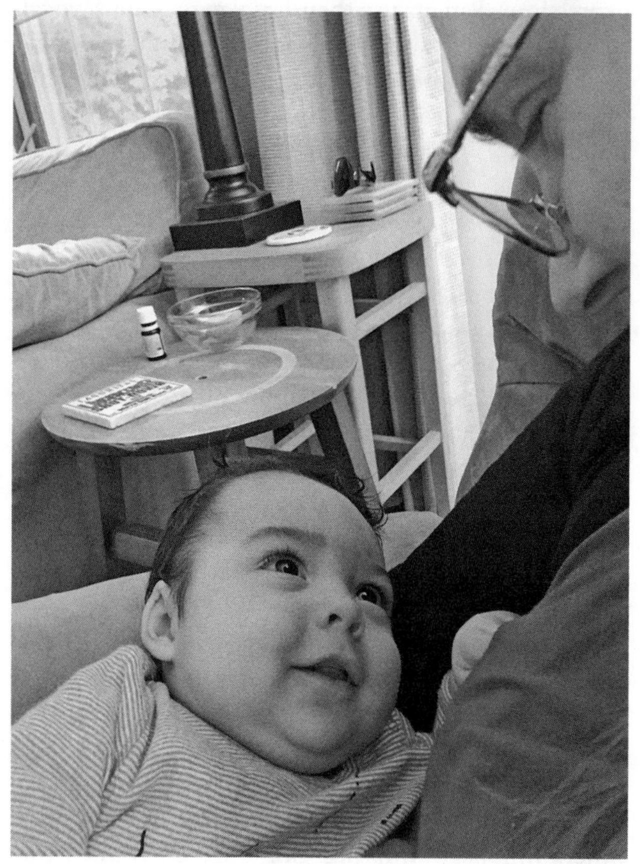

Photograph by Robert M. Chiles

argue that infants are *altero-centric,* which Bråten (2007) describes as the innate capacity to experience what another person is experiencing, or what has been described as *intersubjectivity* (Trevarthen & Aitkin, 2001). A growing body of research has begun to show that infants are capable of participating in synchronous, reciprocal, social-emotional exchanges (Figure 1.2).

With the grace of a dancer, infants are biologically prepared to move through layers of interactive attunement with those who provide nurturing care. This innate capacity to participate in another person's experience is key to understanding babies.

BELONGING

Babies are born with a biological expectation to be protected, nourished, and kept safe and warm, factors common to all mammals and key to survival. Relative to other mammals, however, human babies are very dependent. For example, other mammals, such as cows and goats, give birth to babies capable of standing, walking, and nursing immediately following birth. Baby humans are much more dependent on the care of others. Almost a year of such care is required before infants can independently stand and walk. They have a biological expectation that they will be met at birth by someone who will nourish them, protect them, and keep them warm. This biological expectation primes them to reflexively seek others at birth and to exhibit proximity-seeking behavior, with respect to the caregiver, in the years that follow.

Babies' behavior is not only motivated by their biological expectations, but it is also a reflection of their cumulative experiences, from conception forward. As with all living creatures, the behavior we see in infants is informed by the human capacity to adapt to experi-

A CLOSER LOOK

How Babies "Are" and What They Expect in Care

- Consider a baby's experience *at birth.* Perhaps you have your own memories of giving birth or being close to someone giving birth. Reflect on how the image we hold of infants might influence birth practices. If babies are seen as immature, undifferentiated, unknowing beings, requiring nothing more than basic physical care, what birth practices might be common, and what policies related to birth might be created? If babies are seen as aware, as competent seekers of information, as being sensitive to what occurs around them, what birth practices might you expect to see, and what policies would follow?
- Consider a baby's experience *after being born,* in the period called the neonatal period. Neonatal care varies across communities and cultures. Reflect on your experience with neonatal care or your ideas about that care. If newborns are seen as competent, sensitive, and aware, what care might they be expecting? Does the infant care you experienced or the infant care you know meet such an expectation? If newborns are seen as not-yet-knowing, as unaware, and as essentially incompetent and needy, what might be the conditions under which infant care is provided?

ences. Babies' cumulative experiences impact their physiology, that is, their bodily functions and their parts, including respiration, digestion, elimination, and stress response. When babies' biological expectations are met in fairly consistent ways—that is, when they are protected, nourished, and made to feel safe and warm—babies feel "good," meaning their physiological systems are well supported by the care they receive. In contrast, when babies' biological expectations are not met—that is, when the care they seek is absent or neglectful—babies' physiological systems are forced to adapt in ways that over time might compromise health and well-being (Perry, Pollard, Blakley, Baker, & Vigilante, 1995). Individual differences among babies, therefore, may represent distinct adaptations to the fetal environment to which the baby was exposed and to the postnatal environment that the baby encounters (Lester, 2010).

MEANING-MAKING

Developmental psychologist and theorist Jerome Bruner (1990) describes how infants make meaning out of their experiences, as they read others' communicative gestures and expressions and relay their own communicative gestures and expressions in return. Researcher Ed Tronick (2015) describes the marvel of this feat, drawing on inspiration from Bruner's concept of humans as meaning-makers:

> Infants are active makers of meaning. They do not simply receive meaning. . . . When Bruner referred to all humans—infants and children included—as makers of meaning, he chose the word "makers" carefully. Those who "make" things are not passive, but active creators of something new. Humans must (yes, must) make meaning about the world and themselves. To fail to do so is a psychic catastrophe. The infant bangs a block or a spoon and, as Piaget told us, the infant makes a sensori-motor meaning that both are the same—"bangable." The action is the meaning. A few short months later, for the same infant, one of these objects is for eating and the other is for building. The meaning made has changed; the actions have changed. The meaning the infant makes changes how the infant is in the world—how she makes sense of the world and herself in it. (p. 168)

Tronick goes on to point out that infants' early meaning-making is done without language and without symbols, yet it is still very powerful, continuing throughout development, growing more complex and coherent.

In describing how infants learn in interaction with others, researcher Colwyn Trevarthen (2015) explains that "Humans have evolved to enjoy making meaning" (p. 410). Infants' innate capacity to detect the perspective of others and to engage in synchronous participation with others propels their learning. A baby who has not even reached her first birthday, for example, can be seen imitating the behavior of caregivers, like spoon-feeding a doll, using the same gestures and expressions experienced when being spoon-fed herself. Such moments highlight a critical aspect of how infants learn. Much of what infants learn comes through eager participation in what happens around them. Infants participate *virtually* by watching with focused attention what they see caregivers do and listening with focused intent to what they hear them say (Rogoff, 2011). Even when caregivers are unaware of it happening, infants are participating virtually, capturing what goes on around them, learning as virtual participants in care, and in time taking initiative to pitch in and contribute to what is going on.

During moments of engaged participation in care, infants not only feel and make meaning of their own experience, but they also feel and make meaning of the experience of others. For example, an infant engaging in face-to-face play sees the other's smiling face and might imitate it in some way, with a rise of the eyebrows, a brightening of the eyes, or a widening of the mouth. In addition to this sensori-motor engagement, the infant is engaged emotionally. The infant feels not only the "motion" of the moment but also the "emotion," relayed back and forth between infant and other.

Infant researcher and theorist Daniel Stern (2010) was one of the first to explore deeply the experience of being a baby. He argues that a key aspect of how infants make sense of such close interpersonal encounters is the dynamics of the exchange, that is, the level of activity, power, intensity, urgency, and force in movement—what he termed *vitality*. His research demonstrates that infants are primed by their biology to focus on dynamic features, including how people and things move but also how they emote or show force or intent. From this inherent awareness, infants create meaning. They interpret the power and force of energy, that is, the power and force of perceived motion.

Stern argues that infants are primed to take note of the vitality of both generalized and specific movement, like micromovements of a smile or a nod of the head.

Any movement traces a contour in time. Infants are biologically prepared to notice these contours, what Stern (2000, 2010) describes as "vitality contours." Very young infants notice these vitality contours, for example, the muscles of the mother's mouth moving up or a rise of her eyebrows. Infants attribute feelings and meaning to these dynamic changes. Stern argues that it is *how* something is experienced that is most significant for babies, not *what* or *why.*

To illustrate this, Stern suggests imagining the sensation that comes to mind upon hearing the words *exploding, surging, accelerating, swelling, fading, drawn out, disappearing, fleeting, cresting, hesitant, graceful.* Each relays a dynamic contour. It is this vitality contour that infants experience in everyday life. Infants experience the dynamics of moment-by-moment encounters, lasting no more than seconds, within caregiver–infant interactions, described by Stern (2010) as:

> the force, speed, and flow of a mother's gesture; the timing and stress of a spoken phrase or vocalization; the way the baby breaks into a smile and opens up his face or the time course of decomposing the smile and closing the face back down; the manner of shifting position; the time course of lifting the eyebrows when interested and the duration of their lift; the shift, the flight of a gaze. These are examples of the dynamic forms and experiences of everyday life. (p. 75)

Babies are biologically prepared to watch the dynamics of movement, most notably movement of the human face (refer to Figures 1.1 and 1.2). The dynamics of some movements make infants feel "good" and want to engage with others, and the dynamics of other movements make them feel "bad" and want to avoid others. Infants interpret some dynamics as calming, evoking a feeling of goodness. They interpret some dynamics as concerning, a feeling of fear or grief (Perry, 2014a). It is in the dynamics of their exchange with babies that parents and caregivers help infants regulate arousal of emotional states.

The late gifted pediatrician, researcher, and teacher T. Berry Brazelton (2006) spent a lifetime helping parents and clinicians to take a new look at infants as competent communication partners and makers of meaning. As noted earlier, at a time in history when newborns were still regarded by doctors, educators, and clinicians as not-yet-aware, essentially "blank slates," Brazelton documented the extraordinary behavioral repertoire of the newborn, demonstrated how competent newborns are as interaction partners, and helped those caring for babies see newborns' innate capacity to self-regulate and to interact with others. His work changed the way pediatricians and scientists saw, thought about, and understood babies (Lester, 2010; Lester & Sparrow, 2010). Brazelton created an internationally recognized program called *Touchpoints,* designed to help parents and those caring for infants to see infants as competent interactive partners and to foster belief in their own competence in being with babies and reading their subtle, yet powerful cues.

COMPANIONSHIP

Even as newborns, infants begin life "with an eagerness to share meaning in the pleasure of activity with friends" (Trevarthen, 2017, p. 18). Infants' inherent biological intelligence is readily seen at birth, as infants seek warmth, nutrition, and nurturance through companionship. Trevarthen and Delafield-Butt (2017) describe babies as "intuitively sociable, seeking affectionate relations with companions who are willing to share the pleasure and adventure of doing and knowing with 'human sense'" (p. 17).

Pawl and St. John (1998, p. 1) offer sage advice in their titling of an essay on caring for infants, "*How* you are is as important as *what* you do." The authors elaborate:

> Babies are born utterly motivated to engage in social interaction. . . . [This] changes the way we look at babies. When we really understand that their prime motivation is to interact, to be with another human being, then it casts all the things we do with babies and for babies in a different light. Whatever we are doing, the central thing for them is that we are with them, engaged with them. That is what is important to them and that is what we need to remain aware of. How we are being with them. How we are being together. This is the issue. (p. 3)

To be mindful of "how we are with babies" means respecting what each baby brings to the interaction, as an inquisitive, seeking, meaning-making being. This means listening to infants and paying attention to what messages they relay to us through their movements, expressions, gestures, and vocalizations. This is not hard to do. In fact, loving parents do this intuitively, as do experienced infant–toddler teachers, yet it is too frequently overlooked in advice focused primarily on *what* to do with babies.

Researchers Condon and Sander (1974) were among the first to study infants' acute sensitivity and responsiveness to caregivers' communications. They recorded the movements of the baby in relation to the communication and behavior of the parent. Sander (2008, p. 180) and Tronick (2007, p. 414) describe these as "moments of meeting," when the caregiver recognizes or sees the baby and simultaneously the baby recognizes that she is being seen. The caregiver adapts his actions to those of the baby and the baby adapts her actions to those of the caregiver. By adapting to each other in this way, the caregiver's presence, or "being" with the baby, helps the baby to organize herself in a more coherent way than she was able to do before. Sander describes such recognition within relationships of care as being critical to an infant's development.

How babies experience moments of being cared for by companions influences what they learn about others and influences how they care for others and care about others. Infants get many opportunities to *virtually* feel how others are feeling. They experience this in what they see, in how they are touched, and in what they hear as they are subjected to care. It is this learning that is evoked later in life as they care for others in need or in distress. Such moments will elicit care that resembles the care given them as infants.

As internationally recognized early childhood educator Carlina Rinaldi (2006) advises, "The search for meaning begins from the moment of birth. . . . Children ask us to share the search with them. We are asked to be the child's traveling companion in this search for meaning" (p. 21). What *do* babies ask of us? How do we see our role as traveling companion to the meaning-making infant? The chapters that follow, organized into four parts, provide resources in support of answering these questions.

PART I

Conception Through Birth

PART I focuses on development from conception through birth. Chapter 2 provides an overview of conception and prenatal development, with attention to how experiences during gestation impact development. Chapter 3 explores babies' biological expectations for birth and their active participation in the birth process, bringing to fruition the preparation under way during gestation.

CHAPTER 2

From Stardust to Birth

Our bodies are made of the burned-out embers of stars that were released into the galaxy in massive explosions long before gravity pulled them together to form the earth. These remnants now compose essentially all the material in our bodies. —Karel Schrijver and Iris Schrijver (2015, p. 1)

POETS AND SCIENTISTS have long been inspired by stars in the night sky. According to astrophysicists, tons of cosmic dust fall to Earth each year, comprised of oxygen, carbon, iron, and other elements that eventually find their way into living beings. The human body is composed of these primary atoms, making the story of human development fascinating and complex. Humans truly are made of stardust. Scientists have employed incredible advances in technology to unravel the mysteries of the story of human development. This chapter tells one aspect of that story, the journey from pre-conception to a single-cell organism to a 37-trillion-cell human infant. To establish a clear understanding of the first stage, the first act, in the story of becoming a baby, this chapter presents an overview, not an exhaustive description, of prenatal development. It is this story that serves as a foundation for the chapters that follow, where the narrative of development continues through the first 3 years.

DEVELOPMENT AND HOW IT UNFOLDS

Human development is the result of the dynamic interplay between biology, behaviors, and the environment, more simply described as the interaction between nature and nurture. Nature, in this context, refers to our genetic inheritance from each biological parent. Much like a blueprint, genes provide molecular instructions used in the construction of cells, tissues, and organs. Each cell has a nucleus at its center, within which are chromosomes and genes (Figure 2.1). Genes give direction to somatic, nerve, and reproductive cells about where to go, what to become, and how to behave. Nurture, in this context, refers to the environment surrounding the organism. The blueprint (genetic instructions) is realized through environmental supports.

The period prior to birth is largely invisible, taking place deep within the human body. Growth from conception to birth is exponential and dynamic. Once shrouded in mystery, it was accessible only through the imagination. With advancements in technology and methods, scientists have charted new terrain in resolving some of the mysteries of this early and complex period of development. Influences prior to conception play a role as well. Since some of the material described in this chapter may be unfamiliar to readers, Figure 2.2 provides a list of terminology and definitions pertinent to prenatal development.

FIGURE 2.1. Chromosomes and Genes

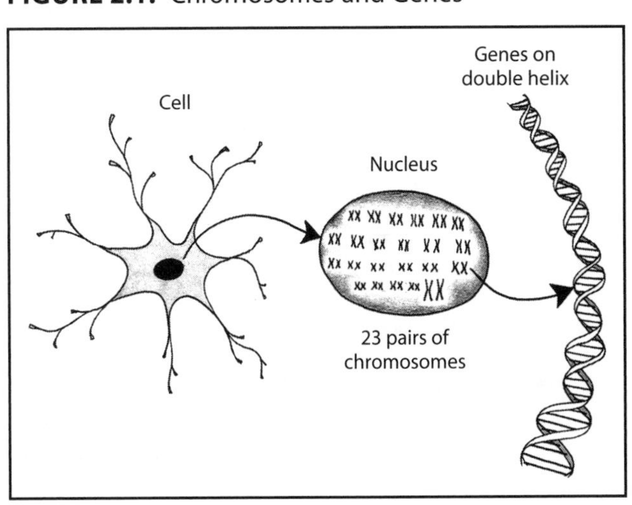

FIGURE 2.2. Prenatal Development Terms

Amniotic sac: membranes holding fluid surrounding the developing fetus; sometimes called "bag of waters"
Cells: basic building blocks of all living things
Chromosome: An entire chain of DNA along with a group of stabilizing proteins
DNA: double-stranded genetic material, referred to as a *double helix,* made up of molecular pairs, G–C (guanine–cytosine) and A–T (adenine–thymine)
Epidemiology: study of disease in large populations
Epigenetic markers: chemical tags on the DNA that change the expression of the gene
Epigenome: chemicals above, around, or on the DNA that affect its function but not its sequence
Fallopian tubes: two narrow ducts that transport the egg to the uterus
Gametes: reproductive cells, the sperm (male) and ovum or egg (female)
Genes: basic units of heredity on the chromosome; made up of nucleic acids (DNA or RNA)
Genome: a person's entire DNA complement
Motility: ability for the sperm to move well through the female reproductive system
Neurogenesis: generation of neurons
Neurons: specialized cells designed to transmit information throughout the body
Nucleus: center of the cell; contains genetic material (DNA)
Oocytes: immature eggs
Ova (*singular* ovum)/Eggs: female reproductive cells
Ovaries: where eggs are held
Placenta: temporary organ that connects fetus to uterine wall to facilitate nourishment and much more
Somatic cells: all cells in the body except the gametes and neurons
Sperm: single male reproductive cell (often used to refer to multiple sperm cells)
Spermatogenesis: process of creating sperm from stem cells
Spermatozoa: male reproductive cells
Synaptogenesis: generation of synapses
Term: a biologic continuum of development from 37 to 42 weeks of gestation (outcomes improve in later weeks)
Testicles: testes and the epididymis, where the spermatozoa mature
Umbilical cord: conduit between the fetus and placenta
Uterus/Womb: pear-shaped female reproductive organ
Zona pellucida: transparent thick layer surrounding ovum

Genes and the Epigenome

The ultimate product of the instruction code (or DNA) within a gene is largely dependent on experience (Siegel, 2015). Experience influences the actions of special molecules that sit on the surface of the gene. Through the action of these molecules, experience determines how the gene will be expressed. These special molecules make up the epigenome. *Epi-* means "on" or "above," so these special molecules are called the epigenome. The epigenome is not part of the genetic code (DNA), but is composed of tags (or markers) that either turn off (i.e., silence) genes or turn on (i.e., activate) genes (Figure 2.3). These markers encode gene-regulating signals over time and occur as a result of environmental exposures such as smoking, diet, pollution, and war.

If the genome is the blueprint, the epigenome is the construction team. This team follows the blueprint but incorporates the unique contributions of experience into how that blueprint is realized. To take the metaphor further, every house within a neighborhood may have a similar floor plan, but each house has a distinct color and style according to the choices made by the homeowner.

Epigenetics is the study of the process by which gene activity is changed without changing the DNA (the genetic code). This is a relatively new field of study, one that holds potential to identify which genes have markers that increase risk of physical and mental diseases such as cancer, Parkinson's disease, and schizophrenia. Epigenetic research is providing insight into how the reproductive cells carry information across generations, meaning grandparents have much more influence on their grandchildren's lives than was once thought.

Longitudinal studies have tried to determine the impact of epigenetic markers on health and disease. In 1992, researchers began to follow 14,000 parents and

FIGURE 2.3. Epigenome with Marker

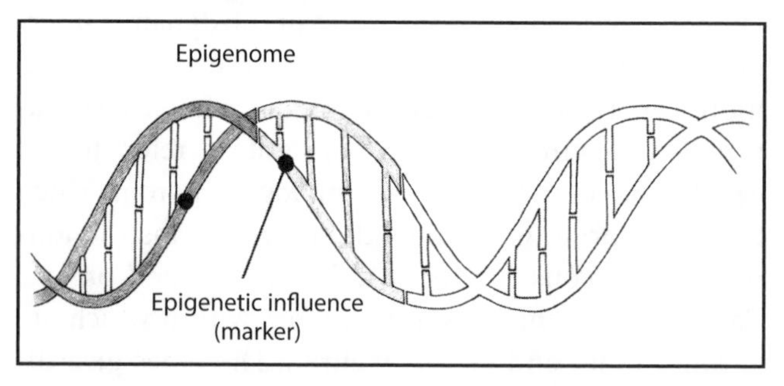

their children to detect the influence of prenatal and early life habits of grandparents on descendants' health and development (Pembrey, Saffery, & Bygren, 2014). They found strong correlations between men beginning to smoke before 11 years of age and obesity rates in their sons, which in turn correlated with shortened lives. Grandmothers who smoked had grandsons heavier at birth and through childhood, even if the mothers did not smoke.

Food supply of ancestors, measured by records of famine, also appears to affect the longevity and mortality rate of the grandchildren (Cloud, 2010; Pembrey et al., 2014). Those who lived through cycles of feast and famine experienced changes in their epigenome that caused an epigenetic transfer of information from one generation to the next. However, feast and famine triggered a different effect in each gender. If a female prenate experienced famine while in the womb, her descendants two generations later were more likely to show significant negative health outcomes. In contrast, the critical time of exposure in males was not prenatally, but in childhood. When a male child experienced famine, that child's descendants two generations later were at risk for significant negative health outcomes. For each gender, there appeared to be a different window of vulnerability. These vulnerable periods are specific to times when the reproductive cells are reading environmental signals. Female prenates are sensitive to outside influences during gestation, when their eggs are forming. In males, the sensitive period is prior to the onset of puberty, when their sperm are forming.

This research suggests that grandparents' life experiences have an impact on the health and well-being of their grandchildren at the point when the grandparents' reproductive cells are most sensitive to epigenetic effects (Figure 2.4). Pembrey et al. (2014) refer to these measurable patterns of epigenetic transmission as transgenerational.

Simply put, this research underscores the genetic legacy from one generation to the next. Environmental conditions of parents and grandparents are influencing how genes are expressed, through the epigenome. The developmental period when ancestors are most sensitive to these conditions is when reproductive cells are alert and reading the environment. In the maternal line, this is when one's mother or grandmother was in the womb (Figure 2.4). In the paternal line, this is when one's father or grandfather prepared to enter puberty.

FIGURE 2.4. Epigenetic Change Across Generations

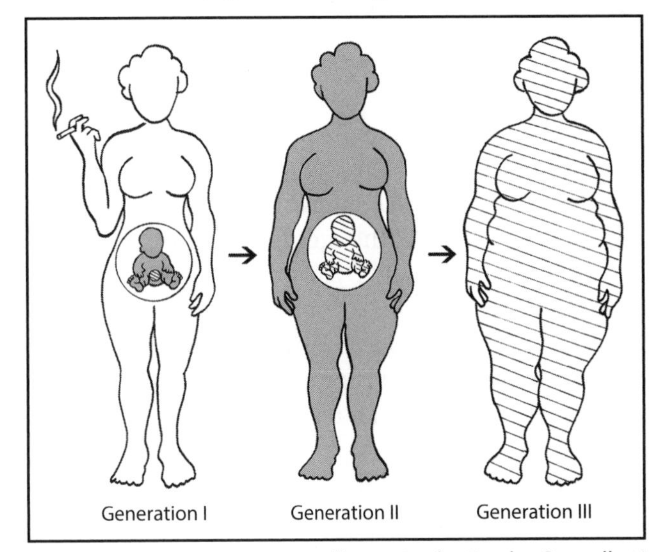

Illustration by Sandra Cappelletti

"Young parents-to-be, therefore, have a responsibility to all their heirs to take care of their physical and mental health during pregnancy and after" (Fogel, 2009a, pp. 140–141).

Cells and How They Work

The biological transformation from a single cell to a 37-trillion-cell human baby, with functioning organs, skeletal structures, and complex physiological processes, seems nothing short of miraculous. Once mature, the human body will hold 50–100 trillion cells. As defined in Figure 2.2, cells are the basic functional units within the body. There are different types of cells—gametes, somatic cells, and neurons. Gametes are the specialized reproductive cells. Somatic or body cells include skin, bone, muscle, and organ cells. Most of the body is made up of somatic cells. Neurons are specialized cells that make up the nervous system.

In the way a body has life-maintaining functions, cells do as well. The cells take in nutrition, digest and distribute it, eliminate waste, use electrical charges to communicate with other cells, and secrete hormones. Almost every cell has a nucleus, which holds genetic material (refer to Figure 2.1). The nucleus organizes the flow of input and output within the cell. Cells are able to read their environment, assess information, and then select appropriate responses to maintain survival (Hauser-Cram, Nugent, Thies, & Travers, 2014; Lipton, 2005).

Fertility and Conception

Gametes are the sexual reproduction cells—sperm in the male and egg in the female. The process of development is different for each type of gamete. The egg (or ovum) is the largest cell in the human body. The sperm is the smallest. The eggs form during prenatal development. By 6 months gestation, all of the eggs a female will ever produce are fully formed. However, these immature eggs are not yet primed for reproduction. They will not be ready until a girl enters puberty.

The creation of sperm, or spermatogenesis, begins in male puberty and continues until the end of life. To maintain optimal health, sperm require specific temperature control (close to 93 degrees F.). This is about 5 degrees cooler than the rest of the body. To maintain this temperature, sperm are sequestered in the scrotum outside of the body core. One factor that contributes to low sperm production is higher scrotum temperature, sometimes attributed to tight apparel. If this is the root cause, wearing looser apparel is a relatively easy adjustment.

FIGURE 2.5. Conception and Implantation

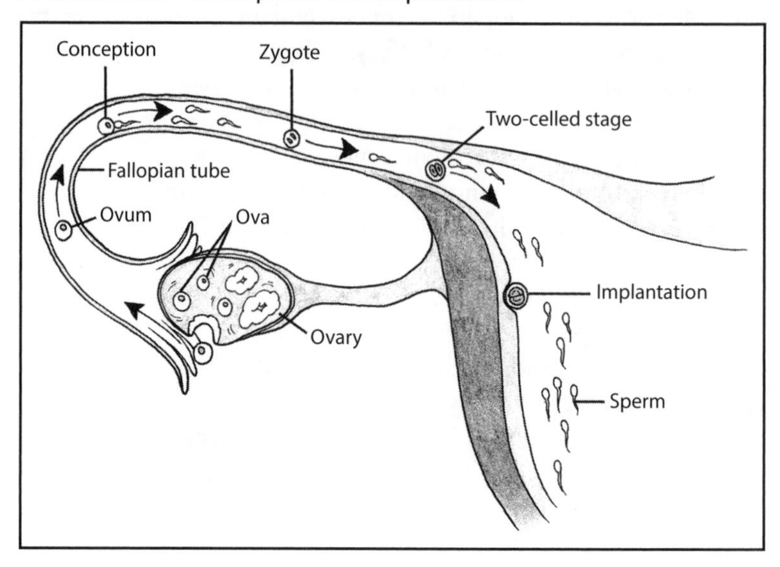

The immature eggs that form prenatally are called oocytes. By the time a young girl has entered puberty and begins to menstruate, the eggs have matured and are called ova. Near the end of a menstrual cycle, the pituitary gland secretes a hormone that begins the ripening process of a single ovum. As it ripens, a protective follicle, or sac, surrounds the ovum (Figure 2.5). As this follicle puffs up, it begins to protrude out of the ovary. The egg will emerge from this follicular sac. This ripening and release of the egg is the process of ovulation. Ovulation ultimately results in either menstruation (cyclical shedding of the uterine lining) or pregnancy (which utilizes the uterine lining for nourishment). Thus, female fertility is cyclical, coming in monthly waves. Most of the time, the ovary releases one egg during each menstrual cycle. A typical pattern for women is the release of 350–450 eggs during their reproductive life.

Once the egg is released, the fingerlike fronds at the end of the fallopian tube pulse gently, pulling the egg into the tube. Tiny hairlike protrusions in the tube, called cilia, slowly guide the egg along. Back at the ovary, the follicle from which the egg emerged relays a hormonal signal that causes the uterine wall to begin to build up nutrients and blood. This nutrient-rich material will serve as nourishment if a pregnancy occurs. If pregnancy does not occur, the lining and ovum are discharged.

The other player in this story, the sperm, undergoes a separate developmental journey. During the onset of puberty, males begin to produce hormones that stimulate a massive production of spermatozoa in the testes. Males can generate as many as 2 million sperm cells per day in a lifetime. Thus, male fertility is steady, not cyclical. During ejaculation, anywhere from a few million to 200 million sperm are released. However, only a small fraction, no more than a third, will be healthy enough to reach the egg (Hauser-Cram et al., 2014). The fluid released from the penis during ejaculation is a combination of sperm and seminal fluid, or semen. Semen is produced by the prostate and seminal vesicles.

These descriptions may make the process of reproduction seem very mechanical. It may be helpful to step back and remember that most conceptions take place as part of a human exchange between two individuals. The physical, psychological, emotional, and spiritual contexts vary from person to person, culture to culture, and even sexual encounter to sexual encounter. Some individuals are conceived in love, some "by accident," and still others in less than optimal circumstances. Each beginning has its own features, which to varying degrees are etched into our cells, tissues, and perhaps even our epigenome.

Understanding how the human body adapts to and carries forward experiences—through the cells, organs, and tissues—may lead to better health care for both genders in the childbearing years. There is a growing consensus that gestation is a time when the embryo and fetus "read signals in the maternal internal environment" to prepare for survival in the outside world (Weinstein, 2016, p. 48).

Most sexual encounters do not occur during periods of female fertility. Most of the time, the opening to the uterus, the cervix, is protected by a hardened plug of mucus. During fertile periods, this mucus becomes thinner and more viscous. The slippery nature of the mucus makes it easier for the spermatozoa to slide through and enter the uterus. The rhythmical contractions of the vagina and uterus assist with propelling the sperm further into the uterus. A relatively small number of sperm cells, perhaps a million, enter the uterus. Researchers think that the physical obstacles the sperm encounters in the uterus are nature's way of selecting for well-formed, superior, and more functional sperm cells. As one researcher said, "The female needs to separate the studs from the duds" (Ted Tollner, personal communication, September 8, 2008). Reproduction and fertility scientists have identified several different types of sperm, leading them to wonder if each sperm type has a different purpose. Some sperm may play the role of facilitating the movement of more robust sperm, or those with better form and more motility.

A phalanx of sperm moves upward in the uterus toward the fallopian tubes. Perhaps fewer than a hundred sperm enter the fallopian tubes, and only a small fraction of those will reach the egg. The fallopian tubes are narrow, and their interior is lined with epithelial folds that create nooks and crannies. Many sperm are caught in these nooks and do not progress further. It is important to note that since only one ovary releases an egg in each menstrual cycle, sperm entering an empty fallopian tube will be unsuccessful in locating an egg.

The journey of the sperm cells is long and arduous. Some sperm tire, while others get stuck in the epithelial folds. For those still on the move, the egg comes to their assistance. Biologists have discovered that sperm get a chemical boost from the egg to draw them closer. The cell membrane surrounding the egg releases progesterone, which in turn stimulates the sperm's tail to move more rapidly. This action propels the still robust sperm to follow the trail toward the egg. Only about a dozen or so sperm make it to the egg. This small group of sperm surrounds and attaches to the membrane of the egg. At the top or head of each sperm cell is an enzyme capsule, which interacts with the fluid membrane of the egg. The egg "reads" the chemical signature of the sperm to determine which one to select. Through a set of biochemical changes, the egg allows entry to the best match (Fogel, 2009a; Hauser-Cram et al., 2014; Tsiaras, 2002).

Once the sperm is completely immersed in the egg, the sperm head separates from the tail. A clear membrane encircling the egg (the zona pellucida) quickly changes electrical charge, which causes the other sperm to move away. Within 5 minutes a stronger protective barrier encircles the egg, "safeguarding the unique mix of parental genes" (Tsiaras, 2002, p. 42). Each gamete (sperm and egg) carries half of the parent's genetic instructions (the DNA) in their 23 chromosomes (refer to Figure 2.1). When these chromosomal pairs line up and reconnect in an entirely unique configuration, this is considered the moment of conception. The remaining sperm will dissolve and be released through the vagina (Fogel, 2009a; Hauser-Cram et al., 2014). The fertilized egg, referred to as a zygote, will travel a few days before implanting in the uterine wall.

What happens next, during the full period of prenatal development, is not simply maturation. Development, from this point forward, is a *dynamic* process marked by a complex set of interactions between the developing organism, the mother's body, and the surrounding environment. The womb environment varies from one baby to another and is responsive to the mother's bodily systems and to her environment. The developing fetal–maternal system changes moment by moment in response to these physiological conditions.

PHASES OF PRENATAL DEVELOPMENT

Prenatal development from the time of conception to the completion of implantation is called the germinal phase. The germinal phase transpires in approximately the first 2 weeks. The next period is the embryonic phase, which ends at week 8. The period of development from week 9 through the end of gestation is called the fetal phase (see Figures 2.6 and 2.7).

Germinal Phase: First 2 Weeks

Healthy conceptions take place in the fallopian tube. Conceptions that occur in other locations will not survive. A conceptus is not yet a pregnancy. Much more has yet to happen before the pregnancy begins. For counting purposes, the moment of conception is considered day 0. The fertilized egg, or zygote, divides to

FIGURE 2.6. Counting Time: Prenatal Phases

Embryonic–Fetal Perspective: Phases	Mother's Perspective: Trimesters
• Germinal Phase (0–2 weeks) • Embryonic Phase (3–8 weeks) • Fetal Phase (9 weeks until birth)	• First Trimester (1–12 weeks) • Second Trimester (13–28 weeks) • Third Trimester (29–42 weeks)

become a two-celled organism. It then proceeds to divide quickly, each cell identical to the next during this early phase. In a couple of days it will begin to resemble a mulberry, which is why at this stage it is called a morula, Latin for mulberry. Around the 4th day, it will move out of the fallopian tube and float in the uterus. During days 5–6, the organism grows in complexity and becomes a blastocyst. The blastocyst begins to differentiate into three structures. One will become the embryo, another will become the amniotic sac, and the last will become the placenta.

FIGURE 2.7. Prenatal Development in Weeks

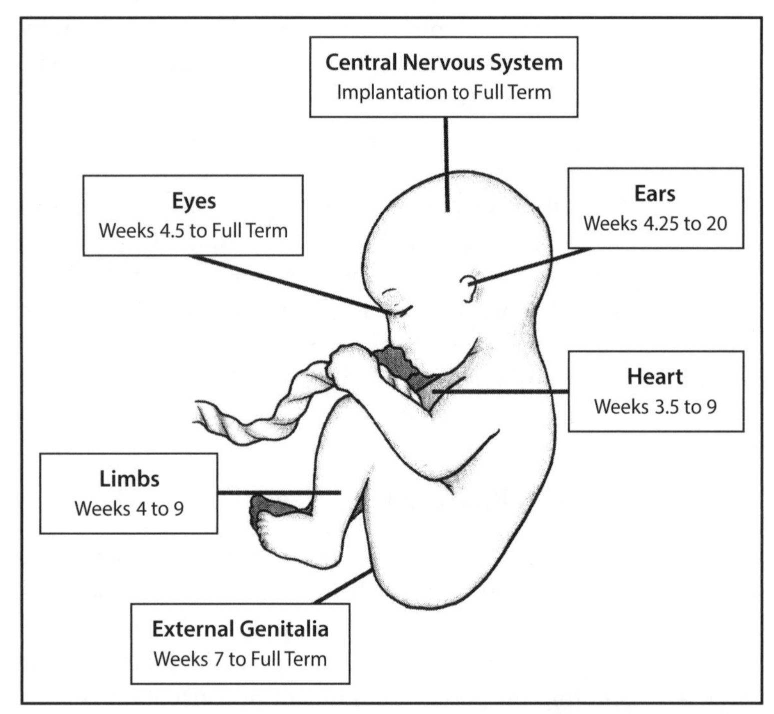

Illustration by Sandra Cappelletti

During days 6 and 7, the blastocyst will attach and burrow into the uterine lining in search of nutrients (Fogel, 2009a). This process is called implantation and will be complete by day 9. Implantation stimulates the release of a group of hormones called human chorionic gonadotropin (HCG). The presence of this substance in urine is used to detect pregnancy in lab tests. Many conceptions never actually implant in the wall of the uterus. Of those that do, a percentage will dissolve or not properly embed in the uterine lining. Successful pregnancies resulting in live births make up only about one-third of all conceptions.

Embryonic Phase: 3 to 8 Weeks

Implantation in the uterine wall, and the subsequent release of hormones, is the beginning of maternal–fetal physiological connection and communication. This marks the first moment a woman may detect physical changes. Some women will not have any physical indication of pregnancy until the first menstrual cycle has been missed. In either case, implantation initiates a robust cascade of hormonal changes marking the onset of gestation.

The cell mass (embryonic disk) that will become the embryo goes through a complex set of changes in a very short time. This disk has three layers: the endoderm, the mesoderm, and the ectoderm. The endoderm forms into any organ system that has linings, such as the digestive, urinary, and respiratory systems. The mesoderm will become connective tissue, fluids, muscles, bones, and the reproductive system. The ectoderm layer will become the brain, central nervous system, sense organs, skin, and teeth (Fogel 2009a; Lipton, 2005).

By the end of the first month, a group of heart cells has clumped together to form the heart muscle, which begins to beat rhythmically (refer to Figure 2.7). By week 8, the embryo is about 2 inches long, with about half of its weight in the head. Resources are directed to the growth of neural tissue, which will become the neural tube, spine, and brain. By around week 9, all of the major organs are formed and in place, with one exception, the genital organs.

The placenta is a complex and unique organ, coming into being for a short period and ceasing to exist after the birth. This critical yet transitory existence makes it unlike any other human organ. The placenta grows throughout pregnancy to support the growth of the fetus. The establishment of the maternal blood supply to the placenta is usually complete between weeks 18 and 20 (Hauser-Cram et al., 2014). Nutrients and oxygen pass from the maternal bloodstream to the fetus through the placenta and umbilical cord. Waste materials are moved from the embryo through the cord to the maternal bloodstream to be eliminated. While it is common to think of the placenta as a filter, blocking any harmful molecules from passing through, this is a myth. It is now understood the placenta has far less capacity to filter than once thought. Researchers have identified a surprisingly rich set of physiological fetal–maternal interactions. These dynamic, reiterative, and two-way communications are facilitated through the placenta and umbilical cord throughout gestation (Wadhwa, Entringer, Buss, & Lu, 2011). In essence, the placenta assumes an active role, adapting to the maternal environment and programming the fetal experience in utero (Myatt, 2006).

Fetal mouth and limb movement begin near the end of the embryonic period, even though the mother may not be aware of it until later in pregnancy. Fetal movements are jerky and irregular at first. However, over time they will become more rhythmic and coordinated as the rhythms of the heart and nervous system grow and organize (Fogel, 2009a; Gilkerson & Klein, 2008).

Fetal Phase: 9 Weeks to Birth

The fetal phase, which begins at 9 weeks, marks a period of significant brain development in the fetal phase. The major organs grow and prepare for the work they will do once outside the womb. The external genitalia becomes visible by around the end of the first trimester (week 12), although at this point it is too early to determine gender.

During the 4th month, the fetus grows larger. Up to this point, the uterus has rested within the pelvic basin, but this changes as the fetus enlarges. The mother may be able to feel the upper edge of her uterus just beneath her naval. Sometime in the 4th month mothers may begin to feel the "quickening," the first detectable movements of the fetus. It has been described as a sensation of butterfly wings fluttering. Depending on the mother's body type and the position of the fetus, some mothers may not feel this quickening until 20 weeks. Fetal movements are important to the development of the body and the nervous system, building strength and coordinating nerves with muscle and organ systems. Chapter 9, focusing on the development of movement patterns, provides a more detailed description of fetal movements.

Substantial growth in the nervous system takes place around 20 weeks gestation. The most important function of the brain is to ensure survival, so if these neural circuits are not well organized the fetus will not survive. By about 24–25 weeks, the fetus reaches the "age of viability" (Hauser-Cram et al., 2014, p. 89). This is the age at which a preterm newborn may survive outside the womb with the support of medical technology, such as a fully equipped neonatal intensive care unit. Birth at this early stage has greater risk of poor outcomes, including the inability to survive, even with medical support. Survival rates increase with each week of gestation, yet even when premature babies survive, many have lifelong health vulnerabilities as a result of early birth.

In the last month of gestation, the fetus adds about half of its birth weight, including substantial brain growth. By 40 weeks the skin is smoother, and most prenates will have hair on their heads. The final burst of prenatal growth focuses on the brain and accounts for additional weight gain in both mother and baby. A healthy fetus will continue to store fat and practice breathing throughout these last weeks. Along with the additional weight, women may experience fatigue, discomfort, and/or swelling in the final weeks of pregnancy. Abdominal weight may feel more burdensome. Pregnant women may experience relief from pressure with massage or by immersing themselves in water, although this may not be possible in all pregnancies. As the due date approaches, placental functioning and amniotic fluid levels are monitored, assuring all is well.

Most women prepare for birth physically and mentally. Many report becoming more sensitized to considering the needs of the baby-to-be. This prenatal preoccupation is necessary to the development of capacities mothers will need in the first weeks of newborn care (Klaus, Kennell, & Klaus, 2012, p. 173).

BIRTH STATUS AND PREMATURITY

Figure 2.8 charts birth weight and term status. Up until 2012, being born at "term" indicated birth anytime from 3 weeks prior to until 2 weeks after the estimated due date (American College of Obstetricians and Gynecologists [ACOG], 2013). Increasingly, researchers

FIGURE 2.8. Birth Weight and Term Status

Birth Weight	Term Status
The average weight for a full-term newborn is 7.5 pounds.	Term is a range from 37 to 42 weeks.
• Low Birth Weight (LBW) is less than 5.5 pounds. • Very Low Birth Weight (VLBW) is less than 3.5 pounds. • Extremely Low Birth Weight (ELBW) is less than 2.3 pounds.	• Pre-Term Birth (PTB) is birth before 37 weeks. • Very Pre-Term Birth (VPTB) is birth from 28 to 32 weeks. • Extremely Pre-Term Birth (EPTB) is birth before 28 weeks.

Source: ACOG (2013); Hauser-Cram et al. (2014).

have found that newborn health outcomes vary depending on the timing of birth *within* this 5-week span, with "term birth" inclusive of early-, full-, and late-term births. The new ACOG designations are as follows:

- ***Early term:*** from 37 to 39 weeks
- ***Full term:*** from 39 to 41 weeks
- ***Late term:*** from 41 to 42 weeks
- ***Post-term:*** 42 weeks and beyond

Full-term babies typically have a healthy weight, which predicts better health outcomes. Babies born pre-term typically have a low birth weight (LBW). Some full-term babies are LBW as well, and are considered small-for-gestational-age. The new ACOG

A CLOSER LOOK

Global Campaign to Address the Epidemic of Prematurity

An internationally coordinated effort by doctors, nurses, and public health professionals has been working to address the global epidemic of premature birth. The March of Dimes led this effort in the United States with the 2003 launch of their Prematurity Campaign (March of Dimes, PMNCH, Save the Children, & WHO, 2012). The campaign has two goals:

1. To raise awareness about the impact of prematurity
2. To reduce the rates of premature births in the United States and improve the odds that every baby can have a healthy full-term birth

Beyond education and advocacy, the March of Dimes is working to improve the experiences of families and premature babies when they are in the neonatal intensive care unit.

There are many reasons for pre-term births, some more complex than others. There may be genetic factors. Some early births are the result of inaccurate due dates, resulting in induction of labor or surgical births before the baby is ready. Other contributing factors have to do with the health of the mother. Improving the quality of health care prior to, during, and after each pregnancy will help to reduce the number of pre-term births and improve the health outcomes for all babies. Health outcomes are best when babies are born at term. No external structure can replace the support that the womb provides in the last days and weeks of gestation, especially for the brain and nervous system (see Figure 2.9). The March of Dimes efforts are designed to make pregnancy safe for the baby and mother.

FIGURE 2.9. Gestational Brain Growth

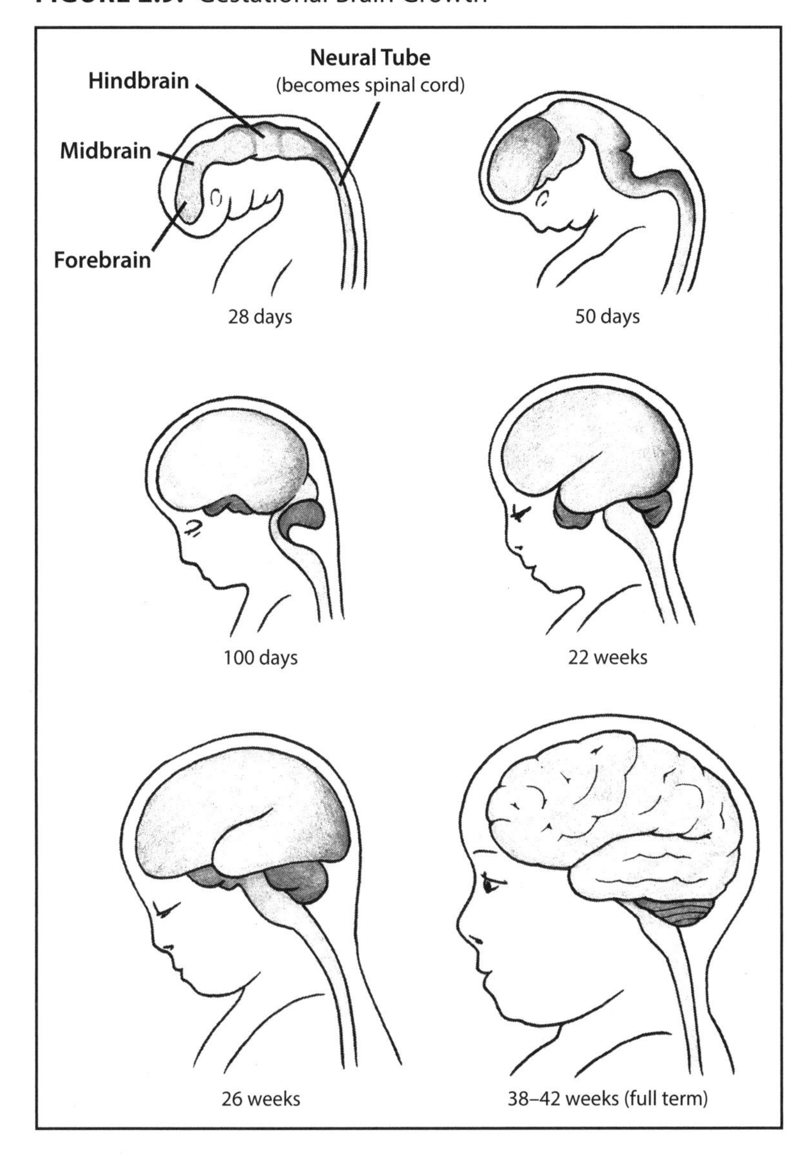

descriptions reflect a more nuanced understanding of the difference that a few days gestation can make.

Adequate maternal weight gain is very important to healthy prenatal development. A woman's individual health status, including weight and body mass index (BMI) before conception, will determine the recommended weight gain during pregnancy. The American College of Obstetricians and Gynecologists (2013) recommends that a woman whose weight is in the normal range for her height, and whose body mass index is between 18.5 and 24.9, should gain between 25 and 35 pounds.

Premature birth is birth that happens before the baby is ready to be born. When a baby is born prior to the end of 37 weeks, that baby is premature. Being born early means that many systems in the body have yet to complete the final "finishing off" phase of development. These babies may have health problems that require longer hospital stays than full-term babies. A large study (46 million births) published in *Obstetrics & Gynecology* found that babies born between 39 and 41 weeks have better outcomes than those born during weeks 37 or 38 (Reddy et al., 2011). When babies are born early, the process of neuronal growth and development is not complete.

Prematurity has real-life implications for the physical, psychological, cognitive, and emotional capacities of the premature baby. Prematurity is also the number one cause of death of babies in the United States (Wadhwa et al., 2011). Premature babies who survive often have lifelong health problems, including cerebral palsy, cognitive disabilities, respiratory illness, and sight or hearing loss. Babies born too soon are more likely to have feeding problems because coordination between the muscles, nerves, and sensory systems involved in sucking, swallowing, and breathing has yet to occur. At full term, the respiratory system is ready for breathing air. Babies born early may experience breathing problems such as apnea, or periodic breathing, which can be dangerous.

DEVELOPMENT OF THE NERVOUS SYSTEM

The brain begins to grow very early in gestation. A thin line, called the primitive streak, is visible between days 15 and 18. This will grow into the neural tube, which will close in a zipper-like fashion, from the midpoint toward the two ends, top and bottom. Once the tube closes, it triggers the start of cell proliferation and differentiation. By the end of the 4th week, this closure is complete. The structures of the spinal cord and brain grow upward, building layer upon layer. This is the core of the nervous system, of which there are two major components: the central nervous system (CNS) and the peripheral nervous system.

The CNS is an amazingly efficient network for transmitting messages (Tsiaras, 2002). When complete, it connects the deep brain with nerve endings throughout the body, with connections to skin, muscles, organs, and bones. This growing network of connections continues to grow throughout gestation. By about 20 weeks, these nerve fibers extend throughout the fetal body and are beginning to form protective, insulating covers known as myelin sheaths. These insulating covers facilitate communication throughout the organizing organ and muscular systems, making it more efficient. The formation of myelin sheaths is a process called myelination. Myelination begins in gestation, but it takes many years to complete (Hauser-Cram et al., 2014).

FIGURE 2.10. Neuron and Synapse

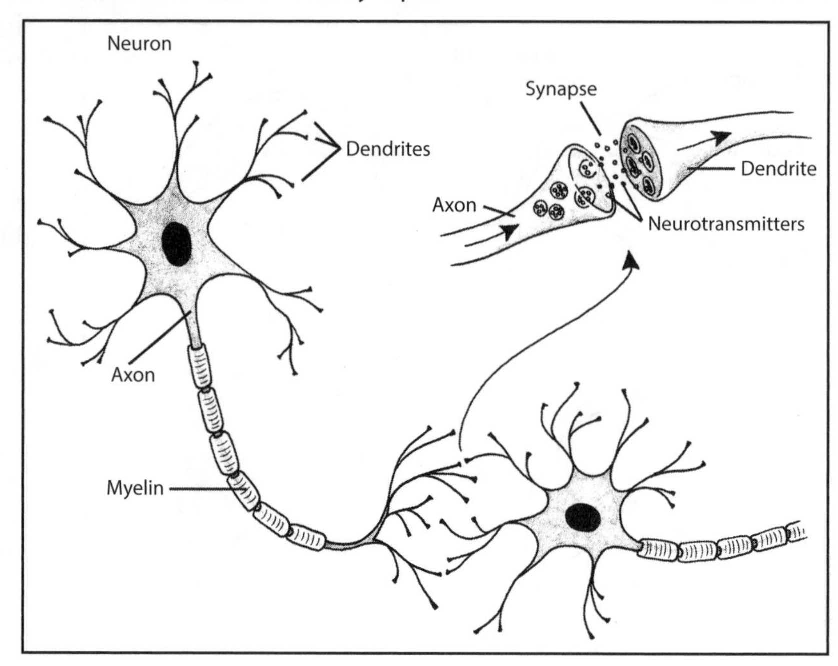

The other branch of the nervous system, the peripheral nervous system, has two components: the somatic nervous system and the autonomic nervous system. The somatic system relays sensory information throughout the body, routing it through the spinal cord. The somatic system is a major conduit for information about what is happening in the peripheral, or far away, regions of the body back to the brain and CNS. The somatic nervous system, as with every other system in the body, is building and organizing itself while the fetal systems it innervates are beginning to develop and function. The process can be likened to building an airplane while it is in flight.

The other component of the peripheral nervous system, the autonomic nervous system (ANS), is central to ensuring survival. The ANS holds important biological processes that regulate basic functions during gestation. Once the baby is born, the ANS operates beneath conscious awareness (Hauser-Cram et al., 2014), allowing focus on daily interactions and routines.

Neurons: Building Blocks of the Brain

The appearance of the primitive streak foreshadows the development of the brain. The rate of growth from the neural tube to a functioning complex human brain is unparalleled. At birth, the newborn brain has 100 billion neurons that serve as the building blocks of the nervous system and 10 trillion support cells called glial cells. Neurons are similar to other cells with one key difference. They are specialized to convey information throughout the body.

The proliferation and differentiation of neurons is a key feature of prenatal growth. Neurons comprise about 10% of the cells in the brain, and glial cells comprise the other 90%. Glia insulate neurons and keep them together (Hauser-Cram et al., 2014). The process of creating neurons is called neurogenesis. In the prenatal period, millions of neurons are traveling in waves along the fibrous path of the glial cells en route to specific locations. These neurons will differentiate according to their genetic instructions to serve unique functions. Once in place, neurons begin to communicate with one another to form an integrated messaging network, a community of neurons working together. These communities cluster together to form neural networks, eventually becoming larger regions, or neighborhoods in the brain.

In fetal life and thereafter, neurons are forming connections with other neurons to convey information. They transfer information through synapses, which are connections that form in the gap between one neuron and another. The rapid growth of synapses is called synaptogenesis. As illustrated in Figure 2.10, each neuron has a cell body, out from which extend two types of fibers. One is called an axon and the other a dendrite. Synapses form when a positive electrical charge travels down the axon toward the gap between the neurons. This action stimulates the release of chemicals called neurotransmitters into the gap, and these neurotransmitters carry the charge into the neighboring neuron. The receptors on the dendrite of that neuron recognize and translate the incoming neurotransmitters. This complex action occurs millions of times in the process of creating, building, and wiring the brain.

In periods of proliferation, a surplus of cells and connections develop. Those synaptic connections used more often, for example those connected to oxygenation or blood flow, will become stronger with use. Those cells and connections used less often will atrophy or be "pruned." The maxim "use it or lose it" describes this process succinctly.

Neural Networks and Brain Regions

The neural networks of the central nervous system connect to create coordinated working groups, or brain regions—the lower, middle, and upper parts of the brain. Paul MacLean (1990) described distinct neural regions as making up a three-part brain, which he termed the "triune brain" (see Figure 2.11). The triune brain consists of the brainstem (lower), the limbic region (middle), and the cerebral cortex (upper). These regions form in sequence, from more primitive structures in the lower brain to more complex structures in the upper brain. Because neurodevelopment is sequential, developing from more primitive structures to more complex ones, the upper frontal regions of the brain are not fully mature until an individual's mid-twenties. During the earliest phases of development, all areas of the brain are "wiring up," connecting in increasingly complex ways (Siegel & Hartzell, 2013). The brain organizes from the bottom up (brainstem), the back to the front, the inside out, and the simplest to the most complex (cortex) (Ludy-Dobson & Perry, 2013; Siegel, 2015). Every stage of growth is built upon the foundation that preceded it.

Brainstem. The deep circuits of the brainstem regulate the flow of energy and basic physiological functions that maintain life. The brainstem regulates moment-by-moment functioning of the cardiovascular, respiratory, metabolic, and temperature regulation systems. Since these functions are essential for survival, the brainstem must be established during the first trimester in order to support fetal development. After birth, this region is responsible for important newborn capacities. These include breathing, eating, sleeping, waking, and crying, as well as detecting hunger, wetness, temperature, and pain (van der Kolk, 2014).

FIGURE 2.11. Three Neural Regions: Cortex, Limbic, Brainstem

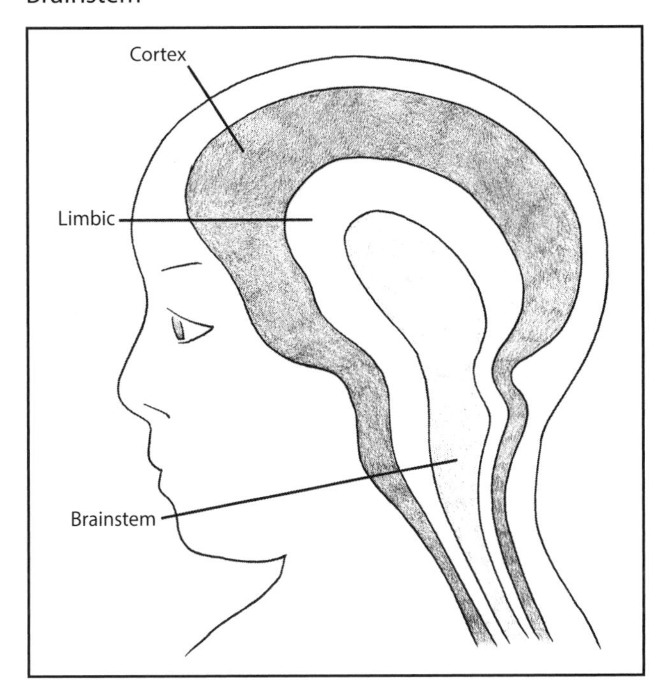

Specific neural networks in this area are responsible for survival and protection and include those that relay a set of reactions known as fight–flight–freeze–faint. Stephen Porges (2011) uses the term *neuroception* to describe how these networks are wired to detect and respond to danger or threat. This specialized response circuit is part of the autonomic nervous system and will play an important role in regulation of physiological and emotional states once the baby is born (Siegel, 2015).

Limbic Region. Above the brainstem is the limbic region of the brain (refer to Figure 2.11). The limbic region is sometimes called the emotional brain, as it houses brain structures that have to do with emotions, feelings, and affective memory (Siegel, 2015; van der Kolk, 2014). These structures and their neural networks include the hippocampus and amygdala, both of which connect to the prefrontal cortex (Figure 2.12). The limbic system is also responsible for the forming of bonds of attachment and facilitates healthy reliance on parents for safety and security. The limbic region serves as a mediator, linking to other areas of the brain and integrating the functions of the brainstem with those of the cortex (Fogel, 2009a; Siegel, 2015).

The limbic structures that facilitate emotion and memory are growing during the second trimester

FIGURE 2.12. Key Structures in the Developing Brain

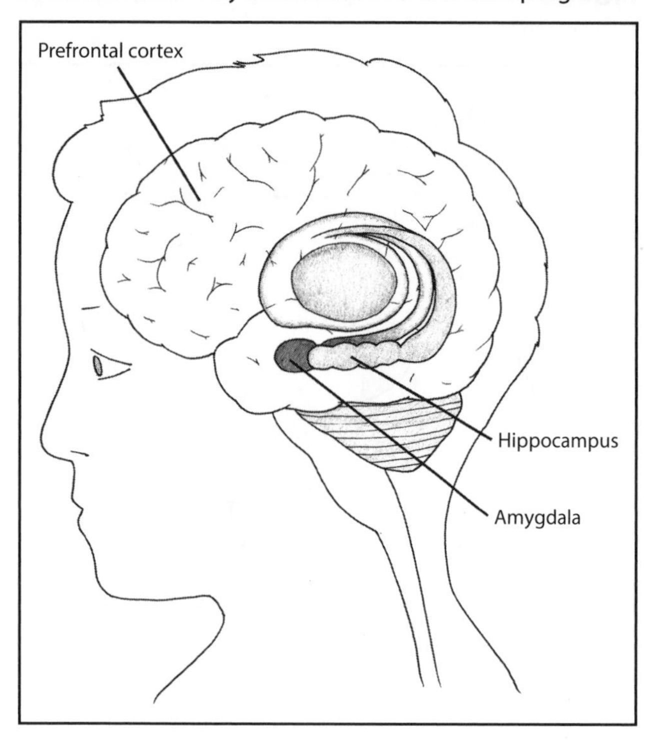

(Fogel, 2009a). This growth coincides with parents' increasing awareness of prenatal movement. Many parents report spending more time during the second trimester imagining the qualities of the baby-to-be.

Each structure within the limbic region is instrumental in the meaning-making function of the brain (Siegel, 2015; van der Kolk, 2014). The amygdala is responsible for registering strong emotions like fear, anxiety, and anger. The amygdala can be thought of as the alert or alarm system of the brain and is functional late in gestation. During strong emotional responses, activity in the amygdala increases. This sends inhibitory signals out to the hippocampus and cortex. The hippocampus plays a role in organizing and categorizing experiences. When the hippocampus is inhibited, processing and categorizing function is dampened.

The brainstem and the limbic area, including the structures within the limbic area, are responsive to the emotional and physical experiences of the mother. Through the physiological connection of the umbilical cord, the mother's emotions and stress responses are transmitted directly to the developing prenate. These early emotional experiences are held in neural networks dedicated to body-based and emotional memory, networks that precede language development. This means that early emotional experiences are held as body-based memory, incorporated into fetal neural structures.

Cortex. The upper area of the brain is called the cerebral cortex, or neocortex. This is the last region of the triune brain to develop in gestation. The cortex undergoes an especially robust growth spurt in the last weeks of pregnancy. This burst of neuronal growth is optimal when completed inside the womb, rather than outside, in a hospital intensive care unit. The cortex is responsible for complex processing that involves reasoning, perception, and creative thought (Siegel, 2015). In order to maximize surface area, the cortex folds over to create hills and valleys. This layering allows for complex interconnections between differentiated areas, which facilitates more neural and cognitive complexity. As the brain grows itself outward and upward, the last region to fully mature is the area of the cortex near the front, known as the prefrontal cortex (refer to Figure 2.12). This is the slowest growing area, not reaching full maturity until the mid- to late twenties. It is responsible for planning, action, and executive function.

Wholeness and Integration. Integration and coordination is a key part of healthy development. Neural networks have unique characteristics and are linked to other networks through long axonal fibers, just as electrical and communication lines connect neighborhoods.

These three areas of the brain—the brainstem, the limbic area, and the cortex—are embedded within one another, each successive system incorporating the one below. The deeper areas of the brain regulate physiological states, including those that operate to preserve and protect, such as the stress response systems. The middle or limbic area plays a role in emotions, memory, and meaning-making (Siegel, 2015; van der Kolk, 2014). At birth, the upper area, the cortex, is still underdeveloped, requiring experience to wire up neuronal connections. As the brain grows in response to experiences inside and outside the womb, neural wiring lays the foundation for important capacities, such as emotion regulation, self-awareness, and empathy. The prefrontal cortex, as it grows, is thought to play a vital role in coordinating information and neural activity within the three neighborhoods in the brain (Siegel, 2015).

If development is robust and healthy, the brain reflects that. Conversely, if there are nutritional deficits or environmental insults, there will be gaps in connectivity. Optimal health throughout the system requires healthy development in each neural neighborhood. Early experiences establish neural circuitry upon which subsequent growth and development is built (Perry, 1997; Perry et al., 1995). The brain is responsive to experience throughout life; however, experiences in the first years have "disproportionate power in shaping the brain" for better or worse (Ludy-Dobson & Perry, 2013, p. 29).

FIGURE 2.13. Epigenetic Modulation

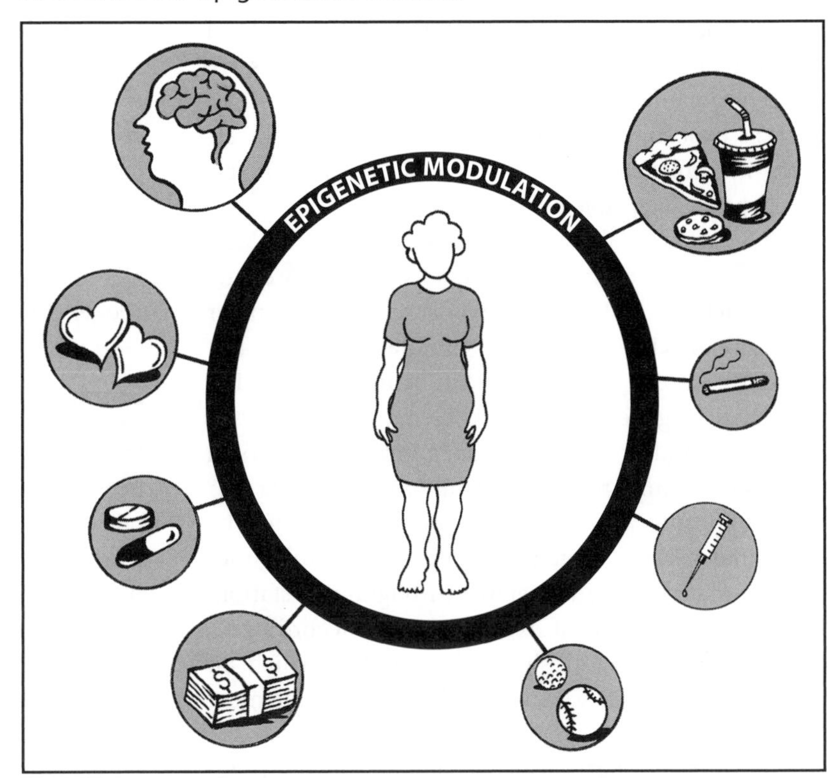

Illustration by Sandra Cappelletti

ENVIRONMENTAL EXPOSURE: IMPACT ON PRENATAL DEVELOPMENT

There are many factors that will influence the development of the prenate during gestation. Research has revealed that the developing prenate has the capacity to read signals in the maternal environment (Shonkoff, Boyce, & McEwen, 2009; Weinstein, 2016). Prenates improve their chance of survival when they can prepare for and adapt to the conditions into which they will be born. Shonkoff et al. (2009) state that as early as "the first weeks after conception and continuing into early infancy, the immature human 'organism' 'reads' key characteristics of its environment and prepares to adapt" to what the world offers (p. 2257). That world may offer safety and nourishment, or fear and peril.

Fetal brain development is a dynamic and complex process, responding to the conditions of its environment. As the brain builds tissue, cells, and connections, this all takes place within the mother. The emotional and physiological experiences of a fetus are to a large degree determined by the experiences of the mother—her daily nutrition, exercise, stress levels, and emotional life. Through the umbilical cord, the mother and fetus exchange information about the surrounding environment, along with nutrient-rich blood. Epigenetics has demonstrated how important the biological mother's life is in influencing the developing prenate (Figure 2.13). Environmental factors affect the father's genetic contribution as well. The male gametes (sperm) are affected by poor diet, substance use, high heat, and exposure to environmental toxins (Donkin & Barres, 2018).

The power of the maternal–fetus biological connection should not be underestimated. As Sandman and Davis (2012) state: "Fetal exposures to intrauterine conditions including elevated stress hormones increase the risk for a spectrum of health outcomes, depending on the timing of exposure, the timetable of organogenesis, and the developmental milestones assessed" (p. 1). Therefore, for the prenate, there is no other option but the mother. He cannot ask for "another womb" or seek out another umbilical cord through which to get nourishment. The prenate depends on the mother and the surrounding care network for a "good enough" if not optimal, environment (see Figure 2.13). This includes a healthy lifestyle, things a pregnant woman can strive for, such as adequate nutritional intake, exercise, and sleep. On the other hand, there are experiences one has little control over, such as exposure to pollutants or events such as war, violence, or extreme weather (floods, hurricanes, etc.).

Exposure to substances, events, disease, and stress affects the prenate via direct and indirect routes. Direct entry is through diffusion from the mother's blood vessels to the fetal bloodstream. Indirect routes include physiological changes in the placenta or in the mother, which in turn will have an effect on the prenate. These physiological alterations include an increase in blood pressure or a decrease in oxygen. Some exposures are entirely out of the awareness of a pregnant mother, such as exposures to unidentified toxins in work settings, in public water systems (e.g., lead), or in the air (perhaps undetectable by odor).

There are several factors to consider when thinking about negative or harmful impacts on the prenate. These include the timing of exposure, the amount or dose of exposure, and genetic vulnerabilities. The last of these—genetic conditions—can be discussed with a physician or genetic counselor. Genetic sensitivity to substances and/or stress hormones varies from person to person. Timing refers to critical or sensitive periods when exposure may have more power to harm. The brain and nervous system are so central to full functioning that they are vulnerable throughout gestation. The dose or amount of exposure varies according to substance. A dose threshold, the point at which an amount will have impact, should be based on the most recent research.

The "precautionary principle" applies during pregnancy, meaning it is better to err on the side of precaution whenever possible. When the future health and wellbeing of children are at stake, it may not be wise to wait for scientific certainty before taking a preventative or protective approach.

Alcohol

Alcohol consumption is associated with low birth weight, premature birth, miscarriage, and still birth. Alcohol use is the leading behavioral cause of congenital anomalies or birth defects. Even moderate use can cause developmental problems. The effect on the mother is that alcohol slows down her central nervous system. The cognitive effects on the fetus can range from subtle to profound cognitive deficits. Prenatal exposure to alcohol increases the risk of abnormal growth, structure, and functioning of organs and the brain. Fetal alcohol syndrome (FAS) is a condition that has lifelong impacts. Those diagnosed with FAS often have learning disabilities and severe cognitive deficits, including attention, memory, problem solving, and speech challenges. Children born with FAS have facial malformations as well. A lesser condition is fetal alcohol exposure (FAE). Babies born with FAE do not generally have the facial features associated with FAS, however, they can have neurobehavioral problems such as hyperactivity, learning and memory deficits, attention problems, and lower intelligence scores. According to the March of Dimes (2016), there really is *no safe time* for alcohol consumption during pregnancy. In addition, research shows that *no safe level* of alcohol consumption during pregnancy has been established (Gilkerson & Klein, 2008). Pregnant women can best protect the developing prenate "by eliminating all alcohol consumption until after their babies are born" (Fogel, 2009a, p. 137).

Smoke

Smoking tobacco or marijuana during pregnancy has been "shown to cause respiratory problems, birth complications, growth retardation, antisocial behavior and learning disabilities in early childhood" (Fogel, 2009a, p. 137). All smoking decreases oxygen and nutrition to the fetus. Specifically, nicotine has a negative effect on the prenatal brain. Maternal smoking results in babies who are at greater risk for colic, gastrointestinal distress, asthma, and childhood obesity. These newborns are also more prone to irritability and are more difficult to soothe. Maternal smoking is also correlated with low birth weight and preterm deliveries. When both parents smoke, the rates of LBW double.

Passive smoke exposure is equal to direct exposure and causes respiratory problems in those exposed. When a nonsmoking pregnant woman is exposed to secondhand or thirdhand smoke, her respiratory system is affected, which in turn affects the oxygenation of the developing prenate. Secondhand smoke refers to smoke that is inhaled from another person's burning of tobacco or marijuana, whether burned in paper cigarettes, pipes, or other devices.

Thirdhand smoke refers to residue (small particles) from secondhand smoke that sticks to indoor surfaces, including hair, clothing, furniture, carpets, and walls. It persists in the environment and can be activated by brushing against the fiber or surface to which it is attached. Such residue contains lead, arsenic, and carbon monoxide. Open windows may give the illusion of nonexposure, but they do not safeguard against exposure to toxic particles. Even relatively low levels of thirdhand smoke can disrupt cell function and adversely impact health. Researchers have discovered cellular, mitochondrial, and DNA changes as a result of exposure to thirdhand smoke (Bahl, 2015).

All smoke inhaled directly into the lungs will deprive the prenate of adequate oxygen supply. Marijuana introduces a powerful psychoactive compound, tetrahydrocannabinol (THC), to the developing brain. Patterns detected in marijuana-exposed prenates include differences in newborn sleep and crying behaviors, and deficits in attention, impulse control, and problem-solving (Gilkerson & Klein, 2008). Research on marijuana has not been funded adequately. However, scientists have documented the negative impact of marijuana on the teen brain, which is also undergoing a growth spurt. The findings of the impact of marijuana on the teen brain have resulted in recommendations to eliminate marijuana use until the brain has fully matured, about 25 years or older. If science points to harmful effects during adolescence, when the brain is undergoing massive change, surely it makes sense to eliminate marijuana use during gestation, when the brain is forming. It is best to apply the precautionary principle and err on the side of caution, suggesting that no safe level of marijuana use during pregnancy has been established.

Substances

There are many substances that have negative impacts on the developing fetus. These include prescription and over-the-counter medications, as well as recreational or street drugs. Experts advise pregnant women to not take any drugs unless explicitly advised by a physician (Fogel, 2009a). Pregnant women should consult with their physicians about the potential risks associated with any prescriptions they may be using. Doctors can best evaluate the costs and benefits of medications for mothers and developing prenates.

About 5% of pregnant women use addictive substances. Cocaine is one of these. Most women experience normal cardiovascular changes in pregnancy; however, using cocaine will magnify these changes, risking serious blood pressure issues. Cocaine may cause migraines and seizures and disrupt healthy development of the placenta, which may seriously jeopardize the pregnancy. Cocaine use is associated with prematurity, LBW, shorter newborn length, and smaller newborn head circumference (Wendell, 2013). Newborns who have been prenatally exposed to cocaine exhibit more stress behaviors, restlessness, irritability, tremors, and abnormal reflexes. These infants may have impaired attention and arousal regulation, as well as differences in memory capacity (Gilkerson & Klein, 2008).

Opioids are a class of drugs that include prescription medications like fentanyl, codeine, morphine, oxycodone, and hydrocodone. Heroin is an illegal opioid. The legal drugs in this category are prescribed for pain relief, but they can lead to dependency or addiction. The effect of opioids on pregnant women include reduced body temperature, slower breathing, and reduced mental functioning. The effect on the fetus includes decreased nutrition, depressed breathing activity, altered brain waves, irregular blood sugar levels, and increased risk of stillbirth (Gilkerson & Klein, 2008). Opioid-exposed babies are more likely to be born early, to be LBW, and to have smaller heads and congenital anomalies. They also are at greater risk for complications during pregnancy. Once born, these babies remain at risk for health and developmental issues. They may exhibit withdrawal behaviors and have more irritability, tremors, seizures, and other symptoms associated with opioid addiction. They are more likely to have behavior and conduct problems and poor ability to focus attention. Infants born with gestational opioid exposure are at much greater risk for sudden infant death syndrome (SIDS) (Gilkerson & Klein, 2008).

Substance use is best understood from a biopsychosocial framework, which identifies how substance use is often a response to unresolved or unrecognized *adverse childhood experiences* (ACEs). These childhood experiences include abuse, neglect, and household dysfunction. The science correlating the number of early adverse events with later self-medicating behaviors is very strong. Despite the short-term relief that substances may provide, they are not effective at resolving the pain and suffering or root causes of childhood difficulties. Becoming pregnant may motivate some women to get into treatment programs and face these early issues before they become parents. While the motivation may be there, treatment programs are neither as comprehensive nor as accessible as the need requires. Substance use affects women and men across all levels of education and socioeconomic status. Pregnancy is a critical time, when the right support and interventions can make the greatest difference in the lives of families. Health-care providers need training to recognize these moments and resources to provide pathways to health to those ready to make the commitment.

Substance use that continues, or begins again, after birth will have serious impacts on the newborn (Gilkerson & Klein, 2008). Studies show that addicted parents spend more time seeking out drugs and, as a result, are less likely to attend to the immediate needs of their newborn. The consequences of this are dire, the results impacting newborns physiologically and psychologically for many years.

Stress

The effect of stress on the body destabilizes regulatory functions, which can cause physiological, mental, and, in some circumstances, psychological impacts on the fetus. Even in the best of circumstances, pregnancy is a time of change and stress. Life is filled with everyday stress, such as having a work deadline or planning an event. This type of challenge may be positive, in that completion of a task brings a sense of accomplishment and competence. Such low-level stressors cause brief periods of elevated heart rates or hormone levels in the mother. Low-level stressors like these may even have a positive influence on the development of the prenatal nervous system, because part of the work of the prenatal period is to establish a healthy, adaptive stress response.

When stress levels rise to the level of being unmanageable, this affects the mother and the prenate. Elevated levels of stress and anxiety may affect the prenate's developing nervous system. Stress hormones course through the mother's body and are distributed through the blood into the placenta and umbilical cord. Studies show that babies who were exposed to maternal stress during gestation show patterns of increased crying and fussiness, as well as difficulties with regulation and social behavior (Fogel, 2009a).

Stress triggers a cascade of responses often beneath conscious awareness in the mother's own nervous system. When feeling unsafe or under threat, the stress response system is activated, causing changes in hormones, blood pressure, heart rate, and respiration. When these states are very intense and/or unrelenting in the mother, it can affect not only the development of the fetal nervous system but other fetal organ systems as well. When such stress is prolonged during gestation, the health outcomes for the prenate may be lifelong. More important, extended stress during gestation may disrupt healthy newborn behaviors critical to the formation of strong bonds of attachment. This, in turn, disrupts maternal care behaviors. These gestational neurobiological changes can profoundly impact ongoing newborn care and put in jeopardy the support that babies expect, need, and deserve.

THE PRENATAL JOURNEY—from stardust to zygote and beyond—transforms essential elements of life that cascade onto the Earth into tissue and bone and in time into a fully formed being, prepared for birth. Shaped by the many forces in play during gestation, a unique being will be born into a particular family and a particular culture. Gestation prepares each baby to participate in the next journey, from inside to outside, the journey of birth. As described in the next chapter, birth continues the journey from stardust to new life, preparing the newborn to connect with awaiting companions who will usher the baby into a new and ever-widening world.

CHAPTER 3

Labor and Birth

All of us have special ones who have loved us into being.
—Fred Rogers, Emmy Lifetime Achievement Award speech (1997)

THE ACT OF GIVING BIRTH is hard-wired into the mother's brain and body. It is an innately instinctual act refined across millions of years to ensure the best outcomes for mother and baby (Buckley, 2015). Birth encompasses much more than simply the baby's exit from the womb. Birth is a process that originates at conception, continues through gestation, proceeds through the contractions that effect labor and delivery, and culminates in the moments and hours that follow. This chapter explores birth from the baby's perspective, being born, and from the mother's perspective, giving birth, and describes the physiological synchrony that ties the two, as they co-navigate a highly instinctual and hormonally guided journey.

The period prior to birth, during birth, and in the first hours and days that follow is known as the perinatal period. What transpires prenatally impacts birth, what occurs during birth impacts what occurs when baby and mother first meet, and what happens in the first moments of meeting significantly shapes how the baby comes to know the world and how the baby will develop. Deeper understanding of what transpires physiologically between baby and mother during the perinatal period prompts a closer look at birth practices, from the onset of labor, to the intense process of birth, to the way mother meets baby in the first minutes, hours, and days.

A CASCADE OF HORMONES ORCHESTRATES BIRTH

Birth is an intense, rewarding, and exquisitely paced experience for which mammalian mothers and babies are well prepared physiologically. In a well-orchestrated pattern, mother and baby experience physiological changes that prepare them for the spontaneous onset of labor. These include a cascade of hormones to help them withstand the intensity of labor contractions, to reduce stress and the perception of pain, and simultaneously to evoke pleasure and mutual affection.

As illustrated in Figure 3.1, some hormones advance the progress of labor by triggering strong uterine muscles to contract, stretch, and open, and these hormones are synchronized with a release of other hormones that ease the perception of pain. Some hormones slow the progress of birth, while others prepare pathways and receptors for what follows (Buckley, 2015). A cascade of hormones, in an elegantly timed sequence, provides the perfect elixir to support mother and baby as they prepare for and engage in labor, delivery, birth, and the period that follows.

Oxytocin, commonly called the hormone of love, plays a role throughout gestation. Oxytocin helps initiate labor and assures labor progress. Surges of oxytocin stimulate the uterine muscles to contract, thereby facilitating the baby's descent and birth. A peak in oxytocin as the baby is born helps the baby initiate breastfeeding. Oxytocin, which evokes feelings of affection and love, helps baby and parent build strong bonds of attachment. Another hormone, prolactin, often referred to as the mothering hormone, prepares the mother for breastfeeding and simultaneously evokes a surge of tender maternal nurturance.

Endorphins, considered hormones of pleasure, contentment, and euphoria, course through the mother and baby throughout labor, delivery, and the period that follows. Endorphins are natural analgesics, pain relievers, and are key to reducing stress and the perception of pain during labor contractions. Endorphins not only ease the perception of pain, but they also bring a

FIGURE 3.1. Cascade of Hormones During the Perinatal Period

LATE PREGNANCY AND EARLY LABOR

Rise in hormones and receptor systems prepares for:

Efficient labor and birth
Efficient lactation and bonding/attachment
Fetal well-being in labor and newborn transition

↓

ACTIVE LABOR

Hormonal processes prepare for:

Effective postpartum contractions and hemorrhage prevention
Healthy newborn transition
Breastfeeding and bonding

↓

BIRTH AND THE HOURS THAT FOLLOW

Physiologic birth and skin-to-skin contact promote:

Hormone release that may reduce hemorrhage risk
Initiation of mother–newborn bonding
Preparation for successful establishment of long-term breastfeeding

Source: The Hormonal Cascade of Childbearing. National Partnership for Women & Families (2015). www.NationalPartnership.org

sense of calm and needed strength while undertaking intense work. Endorphins peak as delivery nears, and this surge of endorphins prepares baby and mother to experience supreme pleasure at the moment of birth.

Catecholamines are another category of hormones that play a key role toward the end of gestation, as well as during the period immediately before and after delivery. Catecholamines, which include epinephrine (adrenaline), are considered to be "fight-or-flight," energizing hormones. They prepare the baby's lungs for breathing, give baby and mother strength and stamina during labor and delivery, reduce the amount of oxygen the baby's brain requires during contractions, and ensure that baby and mother are alert and excited when they meet at birth.

THE BODY PREPARES FOR LABOR

During pregnancy (see Figure 3.2), the cervix, a short, muscular, neck-shaped ring in the bottom of the uterus, remains tightly closed and firm to the touch, despite the growing pressure of the full weight of a mature baby. Near the end of gestation, the cervix begins to change in preparation for the baby's descent out of the uterus. The firm connective tissue of the cervix begins to relax, loosen, thin, and pull back. A plug of thick mucus that has sealed the cervical opening throughout pregnancy is expelled in the hours leading up to the onset of labor.

In the final weeks of pregnancy, the uterus moves from a state of quiescence to activation, in preparation for contractions. Throughout pregnancy, secretions of the hormone progesterone keep the muscles of the uterus "quiet" by inhibiting contractions. As pregnancy nears term, increases in the hormone cortisol help convert progesterone to estrogen (Slater & Lewis, 2011). Estrogen, an activating hormone, has the opposite effect of progesterone. It signals uterine muscles to contract, that is, to tighten and release in regular waves. Muscles in the upper part of the uterus tighten to push, while muscles in the lower part of the uterus simultaneously relax and release. Both actions, tightening and releasing, help babies move toward delivery. As the inhibitory control over the muscles of the uterus is removed, mothers often feel a tightening and a few contractions in the days leading up to the onset of labor.

Oxytocin stimulates effective contractions and plays a key role in the onset of spontaneous labor. As pregnancy nears an end, levels of oxytocin in the mother's blood increase, as do the number of oxytocin receptors throughout the mother's body (Amis, 2014). This assures optimal stores of oxytocin to effect labor progress. A rise in oxytocin toward the end of pregnancy also prepares the mother's mammary glands for lactation and breastfeeding.

In the final days of gestation, babies experience a beneficial surge of oxytocin as well. Animal studies show a surge of maternal oxytocin moving through the placenta in the 24 hours that surround spontaneous onset of labor (Amis, 2014). This surge of oxytocin enters the baby's brain through the still immature blood–brain barrier. A buildup of oxytocin in the baby's system is considered a factor in helping the baby withstand the intense physical compression of uterine

FIGURE 3.2. Anatomy of a Pregnant Woman

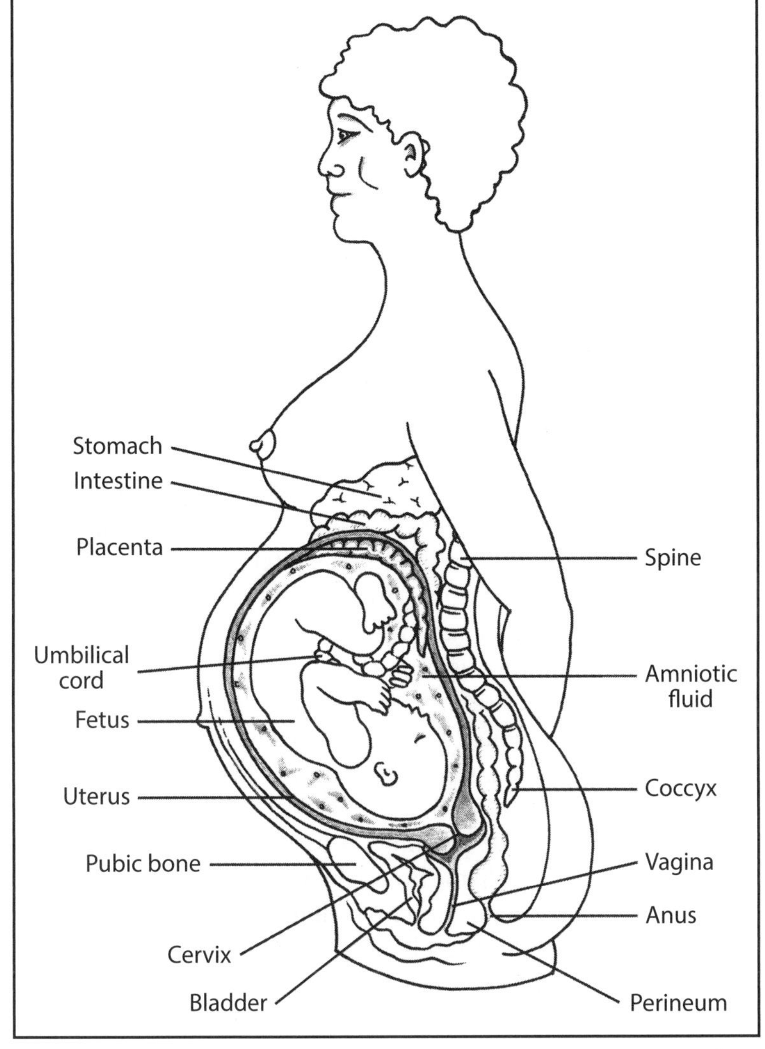

Illustration by Sandra Cappelletti

contractions. Oxytocin also reduces the amount of oxygen the baby's brain requires, thereby protecting the baby's brain during contractions (Buckley, 2015).

With surges of oxytocin come releases of endorphins. Endorphins are key to helping mother and baby cope with the intensity of labor. Levels of endorphins and endorphin receptors increase gradually and are very high near the end of gestation. Endorphins and their receptors prepare pain-relieving pathways in mother and baby (Buckley, 2015). These pathways minimize the perception of pain and help mother and baby adapt to the stress of labor contractions.

Studies show that women who exercise regularly during pregnancy have higher levels of endorphins when they go into labor and report less labor pain than those who do not exercise regularly (Varrassi, Bazzano, & Edwards, 1989). This peak in endorphins and endorphin receptors at the physiological onset of labor provides mother and baby with a "pregnancy induced analgesia" (Buckley, 2015, p. 97). When labor begins spontaneously, and when mothers have exercised regularly throughout pregnancy, mother and baby have optimal stores of endorphins to help them manage the intensity of labor contractions.

Another hormone, prolactin, increases in early pregnancy and helps the mother's body adapt to the physiological changes that occur during pregnancy, including preparing for breastfeeding, reducing stress in mother and fetus, and promoting growth. Late in pregnancy, prolactin production increases in the lining of the uterus, considered to be a factor in the onset of labor (Buckley, 2015).

Prolactin is present in the amniotic fluid, which not only surrounds the baby but also fills the fetal lungs. Prolactin helps prepare the fetal lungs for breathing (Buckley, 2015). Catecholamines play a role in preparing the lungs as well. They help to reduce the fluid present in the fetal lungs as gestation nears an end (Buckley, 2015). Prior to birth, a neural circuit develops between the baby's pituitary gland, the adrenal gland, and the hypothalamus, and this circuit causes the release of cortisol. Cortisol helps the baby's lungs and other organs mature (Buckley, 2015; Romano & Lothian, 2008).

Spontaneous onset of labor contractions at the end of gestation signifies a physiological readiness for birth on the part of baby and mother (Romano & Lothian, 2008). Normally, this readiness triggers labor to begin spontaneously between 37 and 42 weeks of pregnancy (Simkin, 2013). With the spontaneous onset of labor, both the baby and the mother have in place the supports they need to take on the work before them.

LABOR

The term *labor* refers to the process of giving birth to a baby and a placenta. Labor involves six key events (Simkin, 2013):

1. Contractions of the uterus, the largest and strongest muscle in the woman's body
2. Softening, thinning, and dilation of the cervix
3. Spontaneous breaking of the amniotic sac, the body of waters that surround the baby
4. Rotation and molding of the baby's head to fit through the pelvis
5. Descent of the baby from the uterus through the vagina and pelvis
6. Birth of the placenta

Prelabor

In the last weeks of gestation, the baby's head descends to, or even partially through, the pelvic inlet (Figure 3.3). This is called *lightening.* This descent causes a change in the shape of the mother's abdomen, often described as the baby "dropping into position." The optimal position for the baby within the mother's pelvis is head-down, with the face toward the left or right side of the mother's body. These positions are called *left occiput anterior,* or *right occiput anterior,* respectively (see Figures 3.3 and 3.4).

A less comfortable and less desirable position is when the back of the baby's head is toward the mother's back, with the weight of the baby and the baby's spine pressing on the mother's spine. This position, called *occiput posterior,* can be painful for the mother and can slow labor. Towards the end of gestation, a care provider can tell the baby's position by palpating the mother's abdomen. To help the baby turn from an occiput posterior position to an anterior position in the final weeks of gestation, some care providers suggest periodically taking a hands-and-knees position; sitting on or leaning forward over an exercise ball, knees lower than hips; or standing and leaning against a table (Figure 3.5). Such positions flex the pelvis to give the baby room to turn to an anterior position. They may also bring relief if there is intense discomfort from the baby pushing on the mother's back.

Most occiput posterior babies, if they have not yet turned to an anterior position at the onset of labor, do so during labor, but this may take time. In rare situations, a baby is in a breech position late in pregnancy. This means a baby is lying across the pelvis, is bottom down with legs up, or has one or both feet down. A breech position makes it harder for the baby to turn while moving through the pelvis, making birth more complicated. Globally, common practice is to attempt to turn a breech baby manually through carefully monitored, gentle pushing on the lower abdomen or exercises that help the breech baby turn. If the baby remains in a breech position following such attempts, most care providers, rather than attempt a vaginal delivery, recommend surgical delivery through an incision in the abdomen, a procedure called cesarean section (Cunningham et al., 2018). A cesarean delivery can be lifesaving in some complicated births.

Labor is usually preceded in the last weeks of pregnancy by hours or days of "prelabor" contractions that

FIGURE 3.3. Descent Through the Pelvis

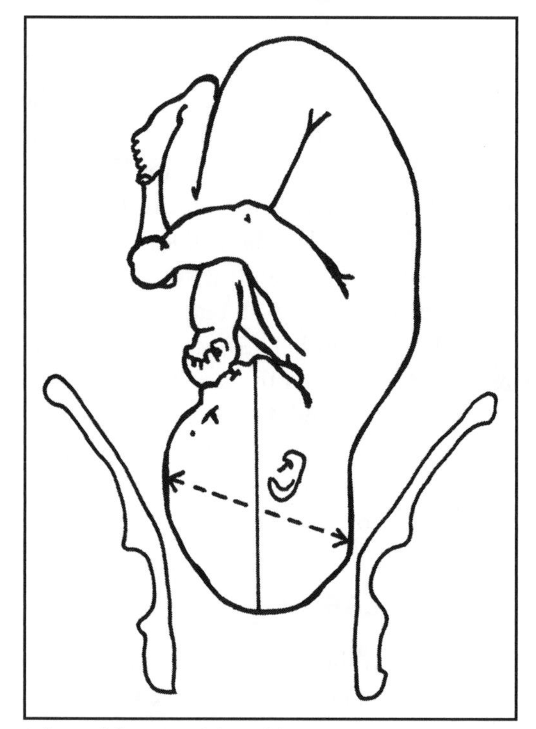

Adapted from World Health Organization (2017c).

FIGURE 3.4. Left and Right Occiput Anterior Positions of the Fetal Head

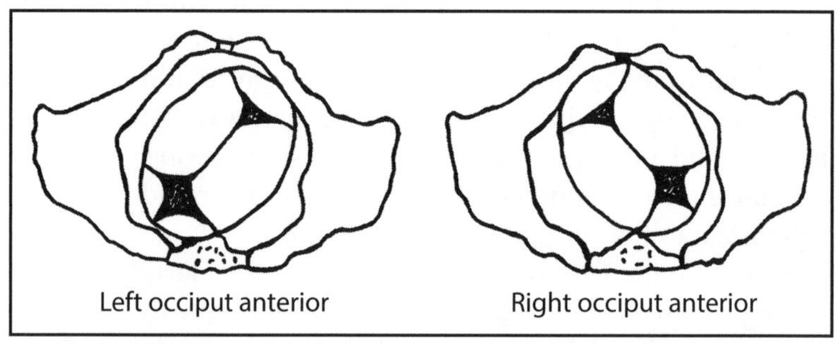

Adapted from World Health Organization (2017c).

FIGURE 3.5. Positions That Relieve Back Labor and Help Reposition the Baby

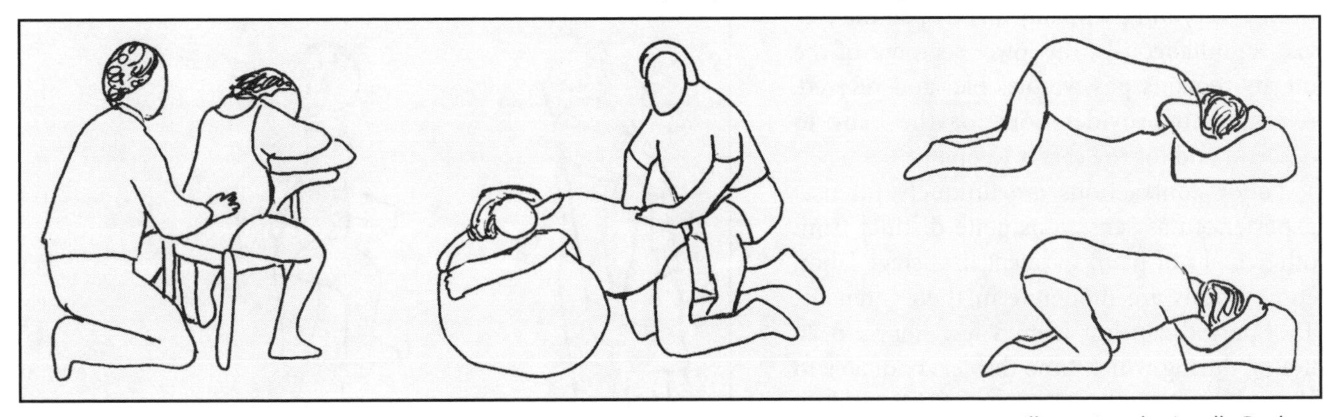

Illustrations by Janelle Durham

occur off and on or can even be regular, constant, and strong. Prelabor contractions, often called Braxton-Hicks contractions, are shorter, less frequent, and less intense than those of active labor, and they do not progress, that is, they do not get longer, stronger, or closer together. Prelabor contractions help the cervix reposition and remodel in preparation for the baby's descent. The cervix, which points toward the mother's back during pregnancy, moves forward as labor nears. It also becomes extremely soft to the touch. This softening is sometimes referred to as cervical *ripening.* As the cervix ripens, it thins and shortens (effaces), from about 4 centimeters long (0% effaced) to less than 1 centimeter long (100% effaced), becoming paper-thin. Figure 3.6 illustrates this transformation.

First Stage: Latent Phase

Once the cervix is fully effaced, it begins to dilate open, eventually reaching full dilation at 10 centimeters. Dilation of 1–3 centimeters may occur before the woman shows signs of labor. When labor contractions show a pattern of becoming longer, stronger, and closer together, a woman is said to be in the latent first stage of labor. This is a period of time characterized by intense uterine contractions, variable changes of the cervix, including some effacement, and a slow progression of dilation up to 5 centimeters (World Health Organization [WHO], 2018b).

During a labor contraction, the top portion of the uterus actively firms, tightens, and contracts, a move-

FIGURE 3.6. Effacement and Dilation of the Cervix

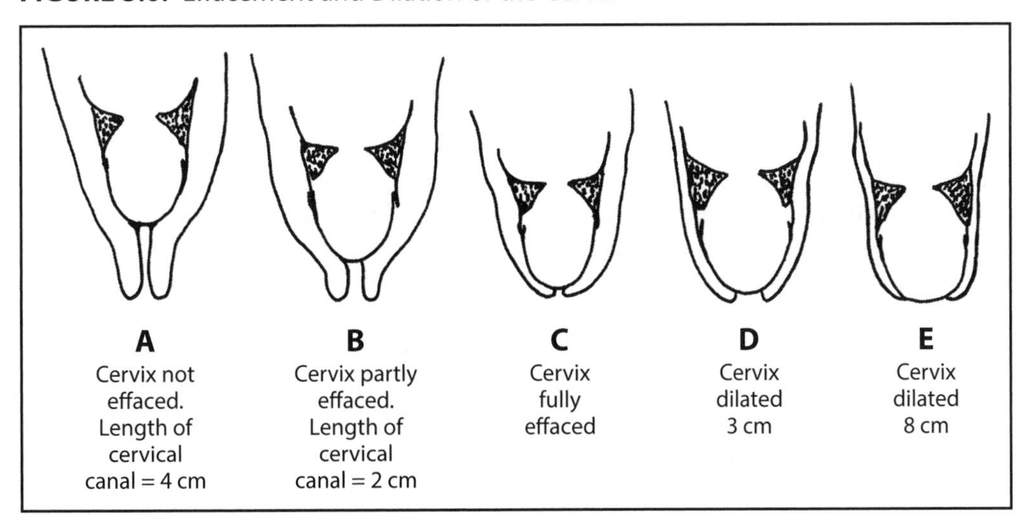

Adapted from World Health Organization (2017c).

ment that pushes the baby downward to help thin, efface, and eventually dilate open the cervix. Simultaneously, the lower segment of the uterus remains passive, flexible, and relaxed, releasing to provide room for the baby to descend and for the cervix to open.

Labor contractions are uniquely intense, experienced as sensations quite distinct from other types of pain. In latent first-stage labor, contractions are moderate in their intensity. This period can last from a few hours to 20 hours, during which time the cervix dilates to about 3 centimeters (Lothian, 2014; Simkin, 2013). Dilation is usually quite slow at first, and it is not uncommon for labor to stop and start several times (Gaskin, 2003). A pause in labor contractions provides an opportunity for a quick replenishing nap.

In this early stage of labor, mother and baby work in hormonal synchrony to thin and dilate the cervix. The pressure of the baby's head pushing down on the cervix during a uterine contraction helps the cervix dilate. This pressure also sends a signal to the mother's pituitary gland to release more oxytocin, which further stimulates strong uterine contractions. As oxytocin increases, endorphins increase, helping mother and baby withstand the pressure of contractions. These surges of oxytocin also protect the baby against low oxygen, thereby reducing stress on the baby (Buckley, 2015).

As with almost all mammals, human mothers are often restless during the early phase of labor, jostling, wiggling, and turning to help the baby maneuver into an advantageous position (Gaskin, 2003). When free to move, a woman in labor will naturally move, walk, and often assume an upright position, which uses the force of gravity to help the baby move head down into the pelvis. Figure 3.7 illustrates possible positions for being active during labor, including standing, walking, sitting on a birthing ball, or leaning on a person or a surface. Women who are free to move during contractions have shorter labors, receive less intervention, report less perception of pain, and describe more satisfaction with their childbirth experience as compared to women who remain in recumbent or supine positions during labor (Adachi, Shimada, & Usui, 2003).

FIGURE 3.7. Positions for Being Active During Labor

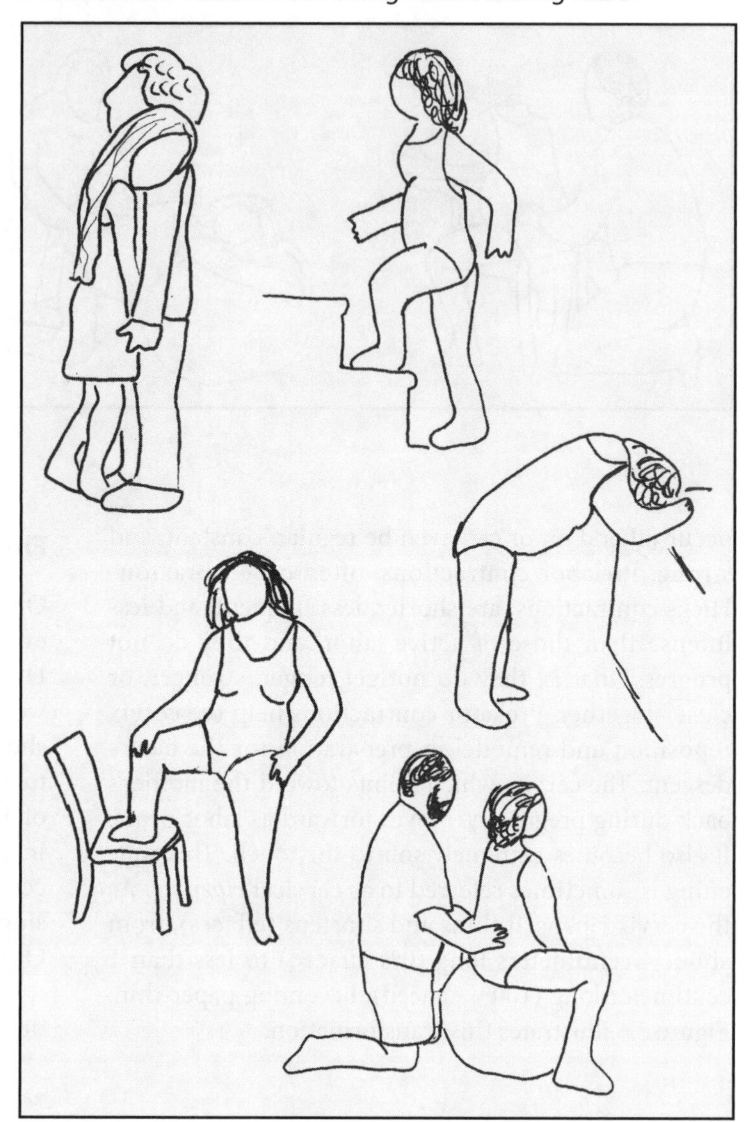

Illustrations by Janelle Durham

Mothers planning to deliver in a hospital or birthing center are advised to experience the progressive contractions of early labor in the comfort of home, with continuous support of close companions. In familiar surroundings, the mother can more easily relax, feel comfortable, and experience a sense of safety. Feeling safe, in itself, facilitates the release of oxytocin to help labor progress (ACOG, 2017a). In contrast, when mothers do not feel safe or when their surroundings feel unfamiliar or invasive, their systems release catecholamines, hormones that cause contractions to slow or cease. This is true for all mammals. Catecholamines serve to protect offspring by slowing labor in the face of threat (Romano & Lothian, 2008). Recommended practice for women who plan to deliver in a hospital is to remain at home until dilation has reached 4–6 centimeters (ACOG, 2017a).

A CLOSER LOOK

Baby's Descent and Birth—A Beautifully Choreographed Dance

As babies gain weight near the end of term, the spacious environment becomes more compressed. To fit into the diminishing space, the baby nestles into a tighter position, usually with legs and arms held close to the body. Babies use their limbs and head to push against the powerful uterine walls, waking up the muscles and building strength in preparation for life on the outside. Babies who are already head down will "drop" into the pelvic inlet (Figure 3.8A). This simply means the head is further into the pelvic basin.

The pelvic *inlet* is widest from side to side, as illustrated in Figure 3.8B. The pelvic *outlet* is widest from top to bottom, that is, from pubis to coccyx, as illustrated in Figure 3.8C.

Ideally, when the baby drops into the pelvis, his body is turned to face the mother's side. This position aligns the widest part of his head to pass through the widest part of the mother's pelvic inlet (Figure 3.8D).

The baby's head makes contact with the cervix and exerts pressure on it, which helps stimulate uterine contractions. The baby's rhythmic pressure on the cervix stimulates rhythmic action of the baby's heart and lungs, preparing for the act of breathing. Using the helpful force of strong contractions, the baby pushes his head regularly and slowly through the pelvic inlet. He compresses his body by flexing his head, dropping chin to chest, which eases his passage.

As the baby's head approaches the narrower pelvic outlet, he uses the force of contractions to turn it toward the mother's spine, thus aligning the widest part of his head with the widest part of the pelvic outlet (Figure 3.8E). Contractions that get longer and stronger help him push his head through the pelvic outlet.

The curve of the baby's sacrum allows him to extend his neck, and in sync with the mother's strong pushing, the crown of his head and then his full head slide through the vaginal opening. In this position, his shoulders are aligned with the widest part of the pelvic inlet, easing the passage of his shoulders through the widest part of the pelvic inlet. However, to fit his shoulders through the widest part of the pelvic outlet, he must make a final turn. He turns toward the mother's side, a move called *restitution* (Figure 3.8F). This allows his shoulders to pass through the pelvic outlet and be born—first the anterior shoulder, followed by the posterior shoulder. With the force of his mother's intense pushing, he slips the rest of his body through and is born.

FIGURE 3.8. A. Baby in Position to Be Born. **B.** Pelvic Inlet, Widest from Side to Side. **C.** Pelvic Outlet, Widest from Top to Bottom. **D.** Baby Aligned to Fit Through the Pelvic Inlet. **E.** Baby Aligned to Fit Through the Pelvic Outlet. **F.** Restitution.

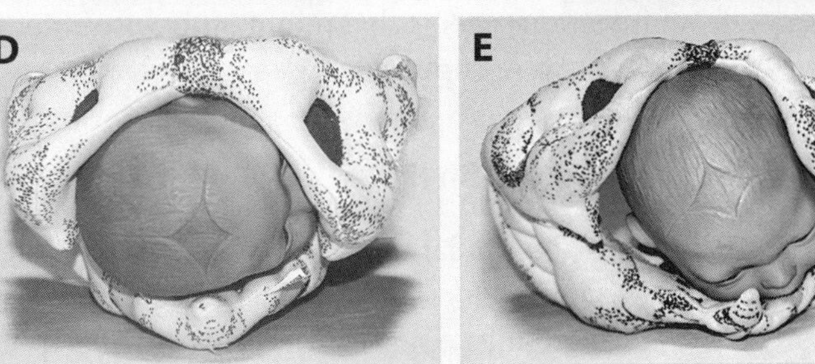

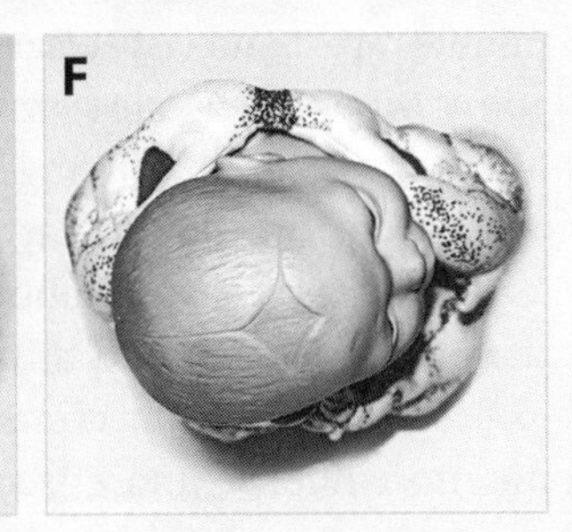

Photographs by Jerry Hitchcock

FIGURE 3.9. Positions for Active Relaxation or Resting During Labor

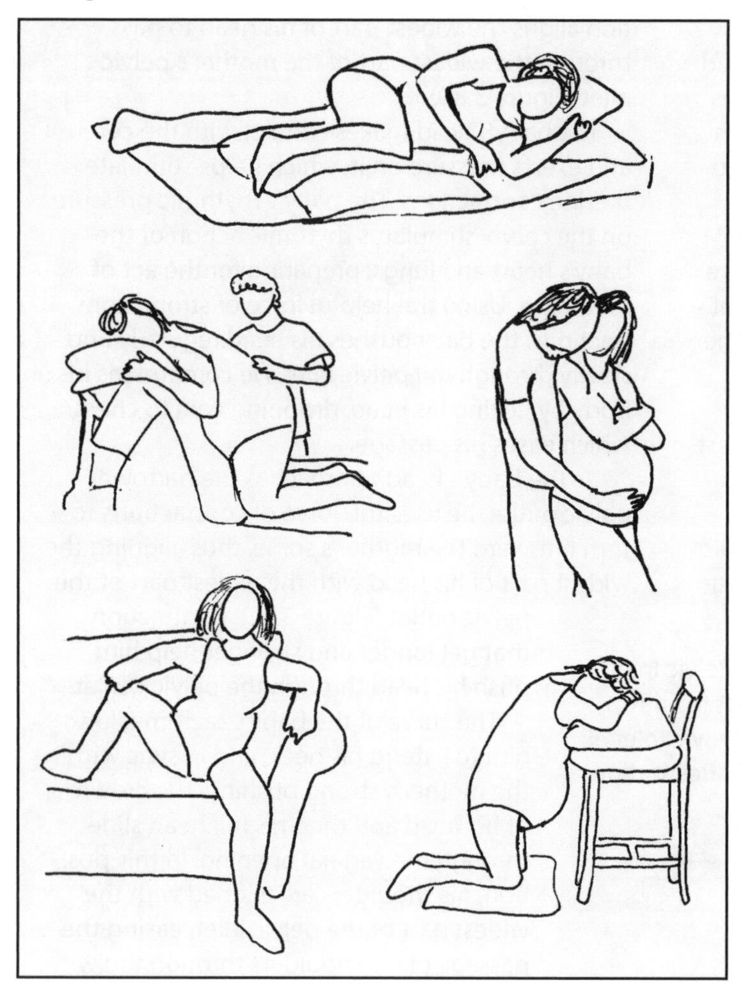

Illustrations by Janelle Durham

For generations, women have garnered the strength they need to endure the intensity of labor contractions. Women's physiology primes them with surges of perfectly timed hormones that give them the power to cope with the discomfort and intense sensations of birth. They also find comfort in a range of strategies that use relaxation, rhythm, and ritual (Simkin, 2013) to reduce the perception of pain. These include passive relaxation, both during and between contractions, for example, remaining still, with limp limbs, while breathing slowly and deeply, as well as active relaxation, like swaying, rocking, and slow dancing (Figure 3.9). Chanting or singing rhythmically, or even moaning, employs rhythmic breathing and a slow release of the breath, which is effective in calming and relaxing. A personally meaningful ritual, repeated with each contraction, provides another way to relax and move through a contraction.

Between contractions, gravity-neutral positions, as depicted in Figure 3.9, allow the mother to rest, conserve energy, and relax. The baby benefits as well when the mother relaxes between contractions, because this relieves pressure on the placenta, which increases the flow of blood to the baby and thereby protects the baby against low oxygen.

The amniotic sac that holds the water that surrounds the baby usually breaks on its own in late labor. Until then, this fluid-filled sac provides baby with a liquid environment within which to rotate and move. The cushion of water inside the amniotic sac also reduces the impact of contractions on the umbilical cord. When the amniotic sac is intact, the umbilical cord, which holds blood vessels carrying oxygen to the baby, floats freely. An intact amniotic sac keeps the baby's oxygen supply from being restricted by the intense pressure of contractions. In addition, an intact amniotic membrane protects mother and baby from infectious agents that might otherwise enter if the membrane were ruptured.

First Stage: Active Phase

As contractions grow more intense and become more closely spaced, the cervix dilates to an opening of 3 centimeters or more, marking a transition to a more active phase of labor. To determine this transition, a companion can time and chart contractions to gauge labor progress. Active labor is generally considered to be the point when the mother experiences in an hour at least 12–15 contractions that are 4–5 minutes apart and last at least 1 minute, commonly called the 4-1-1 or 5-1-1 rule (Simkin, 2013).

The progress of labor speeds up during the active phase. As the mother transitions from early labor to active labor, the cervix dilates from 3 to about 6 centimeters. To exert the pressure needed to thin and fully dilate the cervix to 10 centimeters, the contractions of active labor become more intense, more frequent, and last longer, a minute or more.

Second Stage: Birth

A turning point in labor occurs as the cervix dilates the last 1–2 centimeters and the baby begins to descend through the fully open cervix. This turning point is called *transition.* Transition contractions come with an uncontrollable urge to bear down, that is, to catch the breath, grunt, and strain or breathe out forcefully. Although at their maximum intensity at this point in labor, transition contractions serve an important role—helping the baby push her head through the cervical opening. Transition demands strength and stamina from the mother, who feels a sudden and intense pressure in the vagina as the baby's head passes through the cervix. Mother and baby are supported by a flood of catecholamines. These hormones give the strength and stamina needed to accomplish the hard work of pushing the baby into the world (Simkin, 2013).

Once the cervix fully dilates to 10 centimeters, the mother is supported in her pushing efforts to help the baby move through the cervix, the pelvis, and out through the vagina. First, the baby's head passes through the cervix. This leaves the uterus fitting loosely, rather than snugly, around the rest of the baby's body. To effectively push the baby fully through the cervix, the uterine muscles must tighten once again around the baby. For most women this occurs during a welcome pause in contractions. This resting phase lasts from 10 to 30 minutes and ends with a return of strong uterine contractions.

The mother's pushing and bearing down helps the baby descend fully through the cervix. The urge to do so is uncontrollable in unmedicated mothers. Although once a common practice, there are no data to support a policy of directed pushing in unmedicated births, that is, giving women direct instructions for how and when to push during this phase of labor (Romano & Lothian, 2008). Mothers who receive an epidural, however, must rely on the care provider to tell them when to push and when to rest. Epidurals reduce both catecholamine and oxytocin levels, so pushing the baby out may be harder and take longer for mothers who have had an epidural.

The mother's vagina stretches, and the pelvic bones flex to accommodate the baby's descent. The pelvis is made up of separate bones held together with flexible ligaments, and the coccyx, at the tip of the spine, is hinged, allowing the mother's pelvis and lower spine to open and expand to accommodate the baby's passage. The baby helps as well, by tucking the chin and rotating to find a path of least resistance through the pelvis. In a normal delivery, the baby moves through the pelvis at an angle, aligning the oval shape of her side-lying head with the widest oval opening of the pelvis (see Figure 3.3). The cranial bones of the baby's skull gradually shift and mold to fit through this tight space.

In most births, the baby's head becomes momentarily visible through the vaginal opening as the mother bears down, but then slips back and disappears, only to appear again as the next contraction peaks. As the mother bears down strongly during contractions and the baby presses hard on the perineum, the perineum stretches to accommodate the baby's exit.

Upright positions like standing, kneeling, or squatting (Figure 3.10) help the mother take advantage of

FIGURE 3.10. Possible Positions for Birth

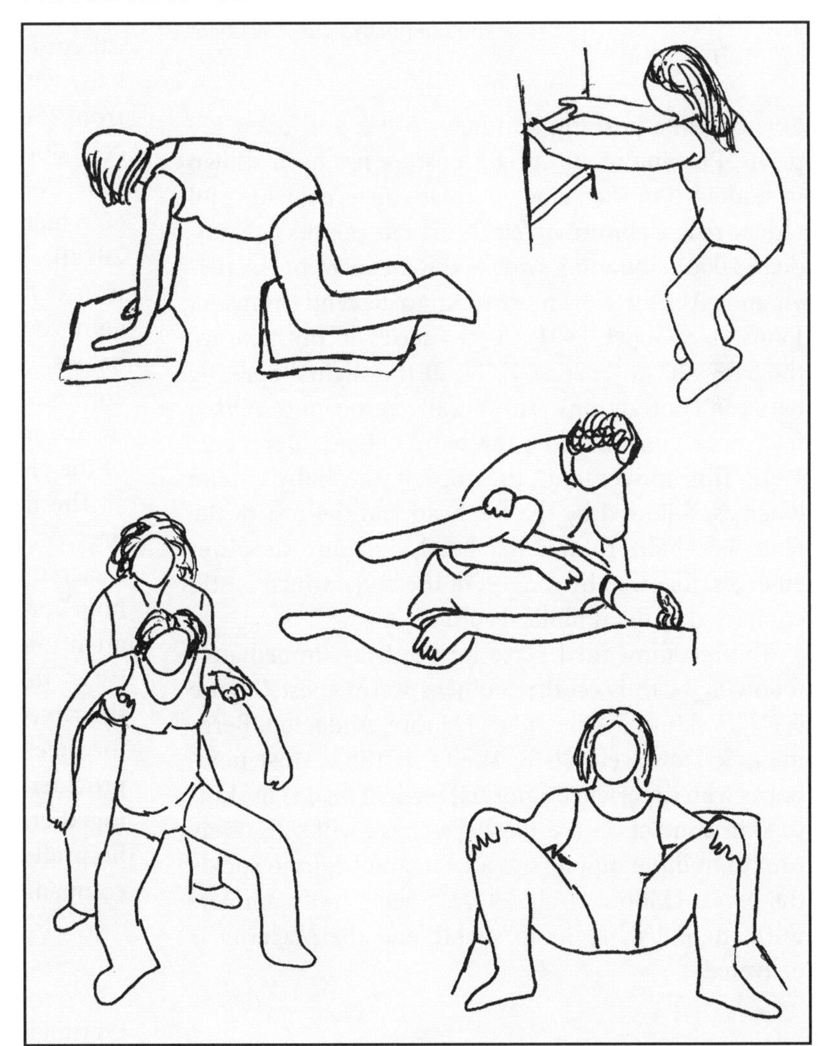

Illustrations by Janelle Durham

FIGURE 3.11. Skin-to-Skin in First Hour

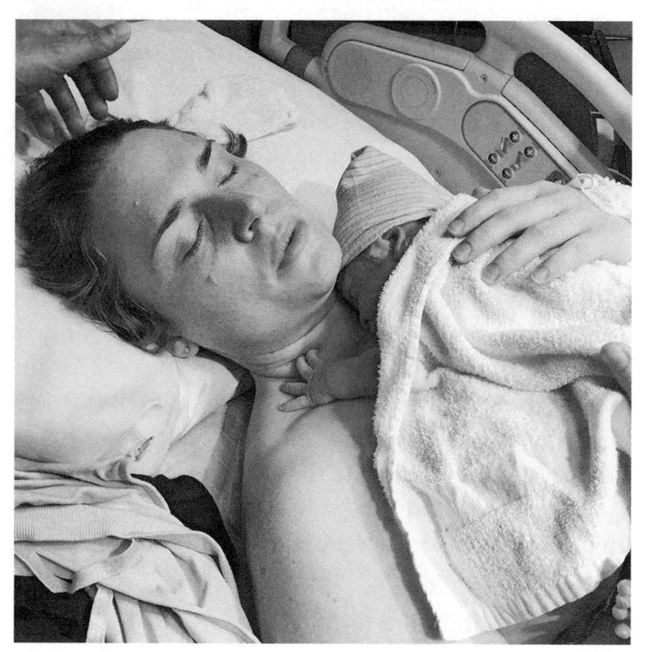

Photograph by Robert M. Chiles

gravity while pushing and help to flex and open the pelvis. Pushing in an upright posture has been shown in studies to shorten labor, decrease maternal pain, and reduce risk of abnormal fetal heart rate (Gupta & Nikodem, 2000). Squatting widens the diameter of the pelvis and gives the baby more room to descend (Johnson, Johnson, & Gupta, 1991). After a series of contractions, the baby's head remains visible at the vaginal opening between contractions. This is called *crowning*. With a few more contractions, the baby extends her neck. With this movement, the top of the baby's head emerges, followed by the forehead and the rest of the face. The baby rotates her head, and one shoulder emerges, followed by the rest of the body, which is still connected to the umbilical cord.

The recommended place for the baby immediately following birth is on the mother's warm chest (Figure 3.11), in skin-to-skin contact (Moore, Anderson, Bergman, & Dowswell, 2012; WHO, 2018b). Most newborns who experience a normal birth, if placed in skin-to-skin contact on the mother's chest, will reflexively root to find the nipple, self-attach, and begin to suckle the breast (Moore et al., 2012). Birth is not complete until the baby begins to suckle and the placenta is delivered.

Third Stage: Delivery of the Placenta

Delivery of the placenta is considered the third stage of birth and occurs a short time after delivery of the baby. Baby and mother are still biologically connected until the placenta is released from the uterine wall. As mother and baby await delivery of the placenta, the newborn remains in a liminal phase, between total dependency and nascent interdependence. When mother and baby experience this period in quiet, calm, and safe surroundings, they experience a physiological release of hormones that facilitate delivery of the placenta, without need for intervention (ACOG, 2017b; Bergman, 2014; Goer & Romano, 2012). A surge of oxytocin stimulates milder uterine contractions that release the placenta from the uterine lining (Hastie & Fahy, 2009). The placenta is delivered in a rush of dark, red blood, about 15–20 minutes after the baby emerges.

Once the placenta is delivered, the baby's warm, oxygenated blood flows passively through the umbilical cord from the placenta to the baby, providing the baby with a full supply of blood. The blood that flows from the placenta to the baby through the umbilical cord during this period increases the baby's blood volume by as much as 30%, providing the baby with a 60% increase in red blood cells (ACOG, 2017b; WHO, 2014b). This surge of blood protects the baby against iron-deficiency anemia, a condition that can seriously compromise development. For both term and preterm babies, it is recommended that cutting the umbilical cord be delayed until after pulsation of the cord ceases or, at a minimum, at least 30–60 seconds after delivery of the placenta (ACOG, 2017b).

The first moment of meeting marks an extraordinary, precious time for the family. Many experience it as a sacred time, referring to the first hour as "the golden hour" or the "magical hour," when the baby and parent are primed to get to know one another. The vast majority of full-term babies do not require removal from their mothers in the first hour, preserving it as a time for meeting. In most births, it is appropriate for care providers to take a step back and allow the family time together. As will be explored in Chapter 4, in the first hour after birth, mother, newborn, and other intimate companions are primed hormonally to fall in love.

OPTIMAL BIRTH CARE

Optimal care along the birth continuum is considered by birth professionals to be the least use of interven-

> **A CLOSER LOOK**
>
> **The Birth Sanctum**
>
> Respecting the physiology of mother and baby throughout the birth continuum means cultivating what has been characterized as a sanctum for birth, described by Hastie and Fahy (2009) as "a homelike, private, warm, dimly lit environment that feels physically and emotionally safe for the woman" (p. 92). A birth sanctum requires the presence of loving and trusted familiars. Planning for who this will be—that is, who will be present and available in the period immediately following birth—is an important part of preparing for birth. Whether health-care professional, family member, or friend, each brings potential to shape how baby and family will experience their first moments of meeting.

tions that result in the best outcomes for mother and baby. Goer and Romano (2012), referring to optimal care for healthy women experiencing uncomplicated labor, use the term *physiologic* care, which they describe as "the use of supportive care practices and low-technology techniques that facilitate the normal biological process of childbirth" (p. 3). Physiologic care, supporting the mother's body in ways that allow labor to progress, is increasingly understood to be best practice for uncomplicated births. In cases of complicated pregnancies or complex medical needs, increased monitoring or medical intervention may be needed, but physiologic approaches are used when possible. True physiologic care includes specific guidelines, skills, and practices "predicated on the degree to which care can hinder or promote the cascade of hormones that optimizes postpartum physiologic and psychological functioning in mother and baby" (p. 387). The World Health Organization (2018b) describes recommended care throughout labor and birth as

> Respectful maternal care—which refers to care organized for and provided to all women in a manner that maintains their dignity, privacy, and confidentiality, ensures freedom from harm and mistreatment, and enables informed choice and continuous support during labour and childbirth. (p. 3)

Continuous Labor Support

A guiding principle in physiologic birth care is that birthing mothers have continuous personal support throughout labor and birth. Birth requires relaxation of inhibitions and the ability to surrender to what is physiologically under way in the body. A mother can do this most readily when in the company of people who can support her, listen to her, and respect her dignity and autonomy. This can include friends or family, but it can also include professionals who take on this role. The key factor in assuming this critical role is that the support be continuous from the onset of labor to the final stage of birth.

If friends or family members are chosen to fill this role, it is important to consider that being present at a birth is such an extraordinary experience that the "wow factor" may override one's ability to be fully involved in serving the birthing mother. For this reason, trained professionals, called doulas, can be used to serve as a childbirth assistant. *Doula* is a Greek word that refers to an experienced woman who helps other women. The term has come to mean a woman who provides consistent and continuous emotional, physical, and informational support before, during, and just after childbirth (Klaus et al., 2012). This support includes a range of comfort measures, emotional support, and assistance in conveying the birthing woman's wishes to others (see Figure 3.12).

Most doulas are trained either in formal certification programs or through apprenticeships. They typically know the childbirth educators and curriculum in their service area, have positive working relationships with local hospitals and birthing centers, and have attended many types of birth. This depth of knowledge and experience allows the partner, or chosen friend or family member of the birthing woman, to be present without taking on the burden of what can be an unfamiliar, stressful role for which they may have minimal preparation. With a doula present, fathers and partners do not have to take on the full role of childbirth assistant. They are free to fully enjoy their role as family member or friend, giving emotional support to the laboring mother.

Sometimes, conditions arise during pregnancy and/or labor that require specific medical attention, including increased monitoring during the period approaching birth. When this occurs, the presence of a doula, or someone who provides continuous labor support, may be even more beneficial than under normal conditions.

FIGURE 3.12. What a Doula Provides—Three Pillars of Labor Support

Emotional	Physical	Informational
Reassurance Encouragement Praise Positive reframing Caring measures Mirroring Help to couples with fears/doubts Debriefing after birth	Soothing touch Massage Creation of calm surroundings Assistance with water (tub, shower) Monitoring of temperature Warm/cold packs Assistance with walking or repositioning	Guidance through labor Comfort techniques Help as labor progresses Evidence-based options Explanation of medical procedures Help to partner in understanding what is occurring in the labor

If the medical need has been identified prior to labor, a doula can help prepare the mother and family for what may come and will be able to support them during and after labor.

There is much supporting research for the effectiveness of mothers having continuous personal support throughout labor and birth, with improved outcomes for mothers and babies. This evidence includes increased spontaneous vaginal birth, shorter duration of labor, reduced use of analgesia, decreased cesarean and instrumental vaginal births, and fewer mothers reporting negative feelings about the birth experience (Bohren, Hofmeyr, Sakala, Fukuzawa, & Cuthbert, 2017). Based on a large body of research, the World Health Organization (2018b) and the American College of Obstetricians and Gynecologists (2017a), together with the American College of Nurse-Midwives and the Association of Women's Health, Obstetric and Neonatal Nurses, recommend continuous personal support for the mother during labor and birth.

As labor begins, it is not uncommon for women to express concern about their ability to withstand the intensity of labor contractions. When mothers know about the birth process and are informed about ways to relieve pain without medication, they can successfully manage labor without suffering and without medication. There are many effective nondrug pain-relief methods that are easy to perform and safe for baby and mother. These include active movement, position changes, taking a warm shower, immersing in a warm tub of water, massage, acupuncture, breathing and relaxation exercises, and access to aids such as a rocking chair, birth ball, squatting bar, hot packs, and cold packs (Jones et al., 2012; Simkin, 2013). Continuous emotional support from a companion of choice is key to the effectiveness of such pain management strategies.

Avoiding Routine Interventions

A mother's body is well equipped to move through the instinctively guided process of mammalian birth. Just as the heart rhythmically beats to circulate blood through the body and the lungs rhythmically inhale and exhale to bring needed oxygen, the mother's body knows how and when to give birth, through the rhythmic contractions of the uterus and the body's cascade of hormones. Being fully informed about the physiological process of giving birth, respecting its elegant synchrony, and avoiding unnecessarily disrupting that synchrony are key to optimizing birth outcomes.

However, there are times when medical intervention is necessary when giving birth. A medical intervention is a procedure or treatment done to find, prevent, or correct problems. When a problem arises during labor, there may be a need for medical intervention. Interventions make sense when the mother and care provider agree that there are medical benefits to intervening that outweigh potential risks. Interventions do not make sense if done routinely, when not medically needed. However, despite the absence of a medical reason for intervention, in many birth settings, interventions have become routine, standard practice.

All interventions carry risks. Unnecessary intervention can disrupt labor and make birth less safe and more difficult. Most interventions disrupt the physiological cascade of hormones that support mother and baby during the progression of labor and birth. Of particular concern is that one intervention will often launch a sequence of further interventions. Such a sequence of interventions frequently ends in surgical birth (Lothian, 2014).

It is not uncommon for women to be offered an intervention that circumvents spontaneous onset of labor. Instead of waiting for labor to begin spontaneously, labor may be induced by artificially rupturing the membrane of the amniotic sac. This procedure is called an *amniotomy.* There are medical reasons for inducing labor—examples being a significant decrease in amniotic fluid, a small-for-gestational age baby, or hypertension (Gaskin, 2003)—but the American College of Obstetricians and Gynecologists (2017a) recommends against inducing labor unless it is medically indicated. Because 70% of women in labor reach full dilation with the membrane of the amniotic sac intact, there is no evidence to support the practice of amniotomy unless medically indicated. For both mother and baby, an amniotomy disrupts the beneficial release of hormones that facilitate labor, breastfeeding, and attachment. Undergoing an amniotomy sets the stage for a continuous series of medical interventions, including intravenous lines, electronic fetal monitoring, and infusion of pain medication, all of which carry risk of birth complications and cesarean section (Romano & Lothian, 2008).

When contractions do not progress, a common intervention is to give the mother an infusion of Pitocin, which is a synthetic version of oxytocin formulated to stimulate labor. However, use of Pitocin increases the risk of other interventions, including use of forceps or vacuum extraction during delivery, cesarean delivery, and episiotomy (a small surgical cut in the perineum). Over time, Pitocin reduces the sensitivity of the mother's oxytocin receptors, thereby reducing the mother's response to oxytocin and raising the risk of maternal hemorrhage after birth (Buckley, 2015). The long-term effect of interfering with the oxytocin system in mothers and babies is still unknown (Buckley, 2015).

Inducing or speeding up labor may have unintended consequences. Administering Pitocin when a baby is in the process of finding an optimal line of passage through the pelvic bones may result in sudden and rapid contractions that push the baby into an awkward position within the pelvis. This in turn may make labor more painful for the mother and ultimately may require painful interventions. At other times the mother grows profoundly anxious or becomes thoroughly exhausted. In such situations, the mother may choose to request pain medications, most often an injection of an epidural anesthesia agent. With an epidural, the mother remains awake and alert but feels no sensation in her lower body. The epidural injection blocks the nerve impulses from the lower segment of the spine, numbing the body below the waist. The drug used in an epidural is a local anesthetic, but it is often delivered in combination with opioids or narcotics to decrease the required dose of the local anesthetic. The drug is injected through a catheter into a small area of the mother's back surrounding the spinal cord.

With an epidural, the mother feels no pain, but there are significant consequences for labor. Epidurals slow the progress of labor, which in turn increases the likelihood that Pitocin will be used. With an epidural, a

A CLOSER LOOK

Inducing Labor

In a national survey, more than 40% of women who gave birth in hospitals reported that their care provider had tried to induce their labor (Declercq, Sakala, Corry, & Applebaum, 2013) before their bodies and their babies had initiated the process. Some inductions are prompted by a desire to schedule the birth at a time convenient for the care provider or the parent, and some are prompted by the desire to speed labor progress. However, the risks to the baby are considerable. Rupturing the membrane in an amniotomy removes protection for the baby's umbilical cord, putting the baby's oxygen supply at risk. Once the protective cushion of water is gone, the force of contractions can pinch the umbilical cord between the baby's head and the opening of the cervix, restricting the baby's oxygen supply. An amniotomy also disrupts the cascade of hormones that prepare the baby for labor and delivery, including those that prepare the baby's lungs for breathing. This puts the newborn at higher risk for respiratory problems (Buckley, 2015).

mother may not feel the labor contractions and is therefore unable to rely on her own sensations to relax into and support the work of the contractions. During the second stage of labor, she will have to rely on others to direct her as to when to push and bear down to support the baby's descent.

An epidural interferes with the beneficial cascade of hormones that support labor, birth, and the sense of well-being of baby and mother as they first meet. The nerve blocking effect of an epidural disrupts an important feedback loop between the nerves in the cervix, the nerves in the pelvic floor, and the pituitary gland, which secretes oxytocin. As a result, the amount of oxytocin secreted into the mother's system sharply declines, restricting access to oxytocin for both mother and baby. Because oxytocin facilitates effective contractions, uterine contractions become less powerful and labor slows.

Epidurals require continuous electronic fetal monitoring, often accompanied by a precautionary intravenous hook-up to accommodate the administration of Pitocin. Both interventions restrict the ability of the mother to freely move and change positions. Restricting the mother's freedom to move during labor is, in fact, an intervention in itself, as it compromises the baby's efforts to rotate into position for delivery (Ondeck, 2014) and compromises the mother's ability to find positions that facilitate labor.

A common intervention is use of an electronic fetal heart monitor designed to identify babies in distress. The electronic fetal heart monitor measures the heart rate and rhythm of the baby, either intermittently, by pressing a handheld listening device against the mother's abdomen, or continuously, by strapping a listening device to the mother's abdomen. If used continuously throughout labor, the mother may not be able to get out of bed. Despite recommendations to the contrary, in many care settings, it has become standard practice to use continuous electronic fetal monitoring. Evidence shows that continuous electronic fetal monitoring in low-risk pregnancies does not lead to a healthier baby, but in fact increases the likelihood of a sequence of further interventions, including cesarean delivery (Devane et al., 2017).

Another intervention is called an *episiotomy,* a small cut in the vaginal opening. Episiotomies were once a routine intervention. They were intended to reduce tearing of the vaginal opening during delivery, despite the fact that most such tears heal without adverse outcomes. Studies show insufficient evidence for recommending routine episiotomy (ACOG, 2016; WHO, 2017c). An episiotomy actually makes recovery from birth more difficult, intensifying and prolonging postpartum pain (Goer & Romano, 2012). An episiotomy also risks weakening the muscles in the perineum, putting the woman at risk of ongoing incontinence. Massaging the perineum, either prior to the onset of labor or during the second stage of labor, can stretch the perineum to reduce the likelihood of tearing. Placing warm compresses on the perineum during the pushing phase of labor does this as well.

Labor involves a complex interplay of naturally occurring processes. Altering this interplay can unleash a sequence of medical interventions, all of which hold a degree of risk to the health and well-being of baby and mother. Figure 3.13 provides suggestions for how to avoid unnecessary interventions during labor and birth.

A CLOSER LOOK

Freedom to Move During Labor

When birthing women are free to move during labor (see Figures 3.7 and 3.9), they will instinctively choose a variety of movements to cope with the intense sensations of labor pain. They might stand, walk, rhythmically sway, lean forward, or assume a hands-and-knees position. By responding to their own body cues, women find the right position at the right time. Studies show, however, that routine use of intravenous lines and electronic fetal heart monitors restricts how women can move during labor. As a result, the majority of women giving birth in hospitals spend most or all of their laboring time in bed, often lying back in a supine position (Declercq et al., 2013).

FROM RESEARCH TO POLICY TO PRACTICE

Although research should inform policy and practice related to birth, statistics show otherwise. According to the World Health Organization (2015), cesarean sections are medically necessary in only 10% of births. In

FIGURE 3.13. Avoiding Interventions During Labor and Birth

Instead of . . .	Many women can benefit from . . .
Being admitted early to the birth facility	Going to the birth facility once in active labor (about 6 centimeters dilation)
Using continuous electronic fetal monitoring (EFM) during labor	Listening to the baby's heart tones at intervals with a handheld device (Doppler or fetal stethoscope)
Laboring without continuous support	Having continuous labor support, for example, from a doula
Using IV lines, with no fluids by mouth	Drinking clear liquids
Using a procedure to rupture the amniotic sac	Leaving amniotic sac intact, to break spontaneously
Laboring while lying down in bed	Staying upright and moving around in labor
Using epidural and other pain medication	Using various drug-free pain relief measures
Pushing and giving birth while lying down	Giving birth in whatever position is most comfortable
Pushing when 10 centimeters dilation is reached, rather than waiting for the urge to push	Resting while the baby descends and waiting for the urge to push
Following staff-directed coaching to push	Once fully dilated, pushing when feeling the urge to push

Source: Professional Recommendations to Limit Labor and Birth Interventions: What Pregnant Women Need to Know. National Partnership for Women & Families (2017). www.NationalPartnership.org

the United States, however, cesarean deliveries account for, on average, 32% of total births (Martin, Hamilton, Osterman, Driscoll, & Drake, 2018). Several factors contribute to this high rate, including a high incidence of women being anesthetized by using an epidural. In the United States, 61% of all mothers have an epidural, which brings risk of further intervention, including cesarean delivery.

Organizations worldwide are calling for renewed support for birth practices that allow a mother's innate physiology to guide the progress of birth. The World Health Organization (2018b) cautions that the growing knowledge on how to "initiate, accelerate, terminate, regulate, or monitor the physiological process of labour [has led to] . . . increasing medicalization of childbirth processes, [which] tends to undermine the woman's own capability to give birth and negatively impacts her childbirth experience" (p. 1). During most births, time can be thought of as an ally, rather than an enemy, because with time, many problems in labor resolve (Simkin, 2013). As described in Chapter 2, recommendations for determining when a pregnancy reaches term have been updated (ACOG, 2013). In addition, the World Health Organization recommends eliminating the benchmark that has been used for decades—that every labor progress at the same rate, 1 centimeter of dilation per hour—as a means of determining whether labor is progressing normally. In recognizing that this rate may be unrealistic for some women, WHO recommends that this factor alone not be a routine indication to accelerate delivery through administration of Pitocin or by cesarean.

A CLOSER LOOK

Birth Story

What do you know about your birth, or the moments that followed? Who was there to greet you? Were birth stories shared in your family? Narratives about birth may or may not be woven into family history—perhaps a function of time, tradition, perceived propriety, or association with loss and sorrow. When birth is portrayed as a joyous first meeting, it creates a spark of delight in a child's eyes. But whatever the circumstances, it can be revealing to discover the story of one's birth. Doing so may draw generations together in surprising new ways and illuminate how the experience of being born and giving birth can resonate and inform patterns that last a lifetime.

The World Health Organization (2018b), as well as the American College of Obstetricians and Gynecologists (2016, 2017a), recommends against routine amniotomy and episiotomy. Both entities recommend the presence of a companion of choice for the mother throughout labor and birth; intermittent monitoring of the baby's heart, rather than routine use of an electronic fetal heart monitor; oral fluid and food intake during labor, rather than use of an intravenous drip to satisfy fluid requirements; and freedom to move and change positions during labor.

These policy recommendations, based on stringent research, have the potential to transform labor and birth. Because recommendations based on scientific findings often take many years to be fully implemented, it is critical that families be fully informed with respect to birth care, using reliable, up-to-date, and trustworthy sources as they make decisions that keep the baby in mind.

PART II

Newborns and Responsive Care

PART II focuses on newborns and their care, with attention to an amazing physiological synchrony that exists between babies and those who provide their physical and emotional care. Chapter 4 takes a close look at babies' and mothers' biological expectations during the first hours and days of care, including how the environment that greets the baby supports these expectations. How newborns and young infants seek nourishment, warmth, and protection from caregivers is explored, with description of the social engagement nervous system and the role of responsive caregiving. Chapter 5 looks at the inherent biological synchrony between baby and mother during lactation and breastfeeding, and Chapter 6 focuses on this synchrony with respect to patterns of sleep and decisions that face families with respect to infants' sleep.

CHAPTER 4

Newborn Care

The first sound that every human hears is the sound of the mother's heartbeat in the dark lake water of the womb. This is the reason for our ancient resonance with the drum as a musical instrument. The sound of the drum brings us consolation because it brings us back to that time when we were at one with the mother's heartbeat. That was a time of complete belonging. —John O'Donohue (1997, p. 70)

AS DESCRIBED in Chapter 1, human infants are born notably dependent on others for a relatively long period. At birth, they go in search of these "others," and for most babies, this search leads to caring companions prepared to accompany them in the journey that follows. This chapter explores the newborn period, when babies first meet those who will provide their care. It examines babies' biological expectations for care and gives an overview of how those caring for babies are primed to meet these expectations in the first minutes, hours, and days following birth.

SKIN-TO-SKIN CONTACT

A newborn transitions from a dark, relatively quiet, water-filled environment to an air-filled environment saturated with new sights and sounds. In the womb, the baby was protected, warm, nourished through the placenta, and surrounded by familiar sounds—the mother's heartbeat, pulsing blood, and echoing voice. In many respects, newborns seek a continuation of what they had in the womb—what is described by Montagu (1994) as "a womb with a view" (p. 2). Skin-to-skin contact immediately after birth is the baby's expected environment and the biological norm among mammals (Bergman & Bergman, 2013). Based on convincing evidence, skin-to-skin contact immediately following delivery is recommended practice for all births, including babies born at term, those born prematurely, and those born through cesarean (ACOG, 2017a; Conde-Agudelo, Belizán, & Diaz-Rossello, 2011; WHO, 2014a).

Primed with catecholamines that flood the baby's system at birth, a newborn is alert, physiologically excited, and prepared to seek nourishment and warmth. If, immediately after birth, a dry, naked newborn is placed prone on the mother's bare chest, covered as needed with a warm blanket, the newborn reflexively nudges his body toward the breast. As the newborn's cheek is stimulated by the touch of the mother's skin, this triggers a reflex called rooting. Rooting, turning the head in the direction of the touch, helps the baby search for and find the breast. With bobbing head and mouth reflexively opening and closing, the newborn finds the nipple and latches on, which triggers another reflex, suckling—drawing the nipple and its surrounding areola and underlying breast tissue deeply into the infant's mouth, forming a sealed cavity around the nipple, and compressing the breast in rhythmic waves to draw milk into the infant's mouth. Suckling is a strong motion that triggers a surge of oxytocin in the mother. Oxytocin helps calm mother and baby, helps to minimize maternal bleeding, and stimulates the uterus to contract in order to shear the placenta away from the walls of the uterus.

When newborns are placed on the mother's warm body in skin-to-skin contact immediately after delivery, this contact alone triggers secretion of oxytocin. As described in Chapter 3, oxytocin floods mother and baby with a feeling of goodness, and it also opens blood

A CLOSER LOOK

Optimal Care of the Newborn

Strategies for optimal care of the newborn include, but are not limited to, the following:

- Place the newborn on the mother's body right after birth, and maintain continuous skin-to-skin contact between mother and newborn for at least the first hour after birth. If the mother's condition does not allow for this, provide continuous skin-to-skin contact with the father, partner, or another birth companion (Figure 4.1).
- Perform routine assessments, such as the Apgar, while the newborn is in skin-to-skin contact with the mother.
- Delay all nonurgent procedures, such as measuring, weighing, or bathing, until after the first 1–2 hours following birth.
- Encourage breastfeeding in the first hour after birth, and provide support or assistance as needed.
- Encourage frequent skin-to-skin contact during the first week after birth.

vessels in the mother's chest, increasing the temperature of her chest by several degrees (Cunningham et al., 2018). Babies lying skin-to-skin with the mother experience a radiating source of welcome heat (Bergman, 2014). This is beneficial because, immediately after birth, epinephrine—which energizes the baby to stay warm and to regulate heart rate, breathing pattern, and heart rate—drops steeply in the baby. Babies in skin-to-skin contact are able to counter the impact of this drop by stabilizing body temperature, breathing, and heart rate through contact with the mother's body. Another benefit of skin-to-skin contact for the baby includes a more stable blood sugar level (Moore et al., 2012). Newborns, including those born prematurely, when held skin-to-skin, cry less and stay warmer than newborns placed in warming cribs (Bystrova et al., 2003). Skin-to-skin contact helps newborns reserve their limited stores of energy for feeding and growing.

FIGURE 4.1. Skin-to-Skin Contact in the First Hours and Days

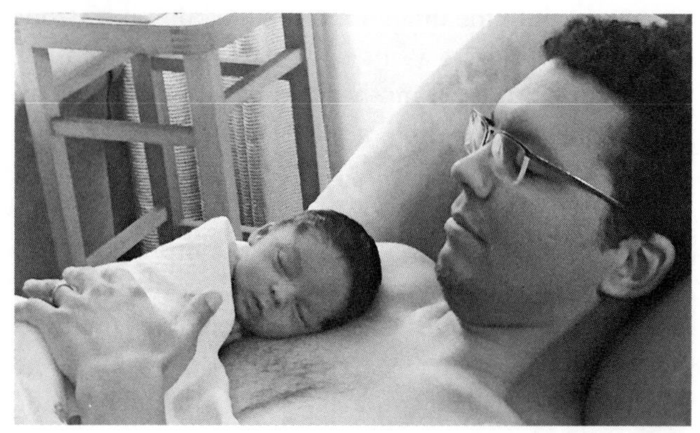

Photograph by Robert M. Chiles

THE BABY'S MICROBIOME

Once the membrane that contains the amniotic fluid breaks, infants are exposed for the first time to a rich world of organisms that play a primary role in lifelong health and well-being. This mix of organisms is called the microbiome. The *human microbiome* is the collective term for all of the microscopic organisms, called microbes, that live on and in the human body. The microbiome includes organisms such as bacteria, viruses, fungi, and protozoa. Only a small number of microorganisms are harmful, considered pathogens. Most microbes are harmless, and many are beneficial to humans. Some microbes live on the skin; some occur in the mouth, eyes, ears, and lungs; and an important group live in the gut. Microbes play a key role in digestion and in developing the immune system, topics explored more deeply in Chapter 5.

During gestation, the baby is exposed to beneficial microbes through the placenta, amniotic fluid, and umbilical cord blood. The greatest exposure to beneficial microbes, however, occurs once the protective amniotic membrane breaks and the baby is bathed in the *Lactobacillus* bacteria that have proliferated in the mother's vagina, in preparation for breastfeeding. Babies are exposed, as well, to a wide variety of other microbes as they move through the vagina. By eating nourishing food like fresh fruit and vegetables, as well as high-fiber and fermented foods, a pregnant woman builds up a rich reservoir of microbes to be passed on to the baby.

As soon as the amniotic membrane breaks, which usually occurs when the baby is moving into and through the vagina, the mother's microbes quickly populate the baby's skin, ears, nose, eyes, and mouth. When he exits the vagina and slips past the perineum, head facing the mother's back, the baby is exposed to microbes from the mother's gut. These microbes include a bacterium that supports the baby's digestion. As he begins to breathe air and to touch the mother's skin, he gathers other beneficial microbes. And as the baby lies skin-to-skin and begins to suckle, he is colonized by more than 700 species of microbes, including some that help with digestion and some that will protect the baby from harmful bacteria.

A baby's exposure to the mother's microbiome and to the microbiome of the surrounding environment plays a key role in establishing the baby's immune system. In the days and weeks that follow birth, babies acquire more microbes as they breathe new air, touch new things, and mouth new things. The microbiome to which the baby is first exposed creates set points in the baby's immature immune system, in effect teaching the baby's immune system how to distinguish friend from foe—that is, helpful microbes from hurtful microbes (Harmon & Wakeford, 2017). Throughout the baby's first year, these microbes continue the work of training the baby's immune system.

If breastfed, the baby receives a diverse array of beneficial microorganisms, none of which can be replicated in the contents of formula. Thirty percent of the beneficial bacteria in a baby's intestinal tract come directly from mother's milk, and an additional 10% come from the skin on the mother's breast (Pannaraj et al., 2017). Babies who continue to breastfeed even after they begin eating solid food continue to reap the benefits of a growing population of gut bacteria associated with better health. Scientists believe that the diversity and growth of a baby's gut microbiome stabilizes sometime between 1 and 3 years of age.

The microbiome is altered in babies delivered by cesarean. In a cesarean delivery, the baby is removed from the uterus through an incision in the mother's abdomen. As a result, the baby does not pass through the vagina as happens in a vaginal birth. The baby's microbiome is still colonized by microorganisms, but it is not the full complement the baby would otherwise acquire from the mother's vagina and gut (Lif Holgerson, Harnevik, Hernell, Tanner, & Johansson, 2011). With an emergency cesarean section, if the amniotic sac has broken prior to surgery, the baby will reap the benefit of *some* exposure to vaginal microbes.

Researchers suggest that an altered microbiome may explain the link between cesarean birth and an increased risk of asthma, Type 1 diabetes, obesity, and celiac disease (Dietert & Dietert, 2012; Harmon & Wakeford, 2017). There is much as yet unknown with respect to the baby's microbiome, but evidence points to a relationship between the baby's microbiome, the baby's lifelong health, and the health status of future generations (Dietert & Dietert, 2012).

A CLOSER LOOK

The Microbiome—Passed Generation to Generation

When a mother gives birth vaginally and when she breastfeeds, she passes on colonies of essential microbes to her baby, the same microbes that her mother passed on to her. For babies born vaginally and breastfed, this mix of microbes spans female ancestry for generations. The microbiome of the baby resembles that of the mother, the grandmother, and the great-grandmother. Researchers describe the transmission of these beneficial microorganisms as "seeding and feeding" the baby's system with a colony of microbes adapted over generations to meet the distinct conditions experienced by the baby's ancestral mothers (Harmon & Wakeford, 2017).

SEEKING SAFETY

Birth was once thought of as a time of separation, a cutting of the tie between baby and mother. Standard practice in hospitals was to remove the baby to a separate newborn nursery. This practice has begun to change, as research has highlighted the importance of proximity for both mother and baby following birth (Bergman, 2014):

> A human will never be as alert as after a vaginal birth: noradrenalin wakes up the brain and is 10 times higher at birth than ever again (Lagercrantz & Bistoletti 1977). High levels of noradrenalin activate the lungs and, more importantly, ensure early bonding with the mother (Ross & Young 2009). The mother's smell (Porter 1998), contact and warmth 'fire' a pathway from the baby's amygdala to its frontal lobe (Bartocci et al. 2000), which connects the newborn's emotional and social brain circuits (Nelson & Panksepp 1998). Whilst genes have made this possible . . . , the experience of a mother's constant and uninterrupted physical presence makes it happen (Hofer 1994). (p. 1)

Social Engagement

When the baby emerges and is placed on the mother's abdomen or chest, the full focus of the mother's attention is on the baby, and in most cases, the baby is alert and attending to the mother. In the period immediately following birth of the baby and leading up to delivery of the placenta, maternal oxytocin increases in response to the smell and touch of the baby, especially during breastfeeding. As oxytocin floods the mother's brain, it triggers profound feelings of love for her infant. A peak in endorphins after delivery alleviates stress in mother and baby, but just as important, it activates the reward center of the brain, increasing the sense of reward and pleasure in connecting with each other (Buckley, 2015).

Endorphins are also present in the initial secretions of breast milk. This generates in the suckling baby a sense of satisfaction and pleasure in the experience of breastfeeding. As mother and baby gaze at each other, each experiences a release of oxytocin, helping them fall in love. Oxytocin, together with prolactin, which is released in the mother as the baby suckles, builds in the mother a fearless urge to protect her baby. Prolactin also reduces anxiety and tension, sensitizes the mother to the baby's nonverbal cues, and helps in the production of milk.

Since infants cannot survive on their own, they need a caregiver to help them find nourishment, warmth, and protection. They also rely on others for help in regulating the flow of energy to internal body organs, which are immature and adjusting to life outside the womb. Mother Nature, in her wisdom, adapted the human nervous system with a special neural circuit not found in other vertebrates. This special neural network gives humans the capacity to access other people for regulatory support. This neural circuit is called the *social engagement system* and is a branch of the autonomic nervous system.

As described in Chapter 2, the autonomic nervous system develops prenatally and regulates metabolism and basic physiology. It does this through distinct neural circuits. One neural circuit, called *parasympathetic,* promotes functions related to rest and restoration of vital organs and conservation of bodily energy. A second neural circuit, called *sympathetic,* promotes increased metabolic activity to deal with challenges from outside the body. Some organs of the body are innervated by each of these circuits, which allows them to readily shift the flow of energy to meet internal and external needs. For example, when the body is preparing for a challenge, the sympathetic system causes the pupil of the eye to dilate, letting in more light; the heart to beat faster; and the sphincter muscles to tighten. These changes prepare the body for action. In contrast, the parasympathetic neural circuit constricts the pupil of the eye, slows the heart, and relaxes sphincter muscles.

In times of danger, the parasympathetic system acts to "immobilize" the body for safety, in essence to slow down metabolism or to disengage from outside stimulation. In contrast, the *sympathetic* system acts to "mobilize" for safety, for example to fight or flee. Newborns cannot fight or flee; however, they *are* able to sense danger, just like all humans, through neuroception (described in Chapter 2). Through neuroception, the body perceives and assesses whether situations or people are safe or unsafe. If a situation feels unsafe, humans are able to access a third branch of the autonomic nervous system, the *social engagement* circuit. When in danger, humans seek safety by communicating with or engaging with others, behaviors supported by the social engagement neural circuit.

The social engagement system keeps babies connected to and protected by caregivers. This circuit originates in the brainstem and connects muscles of the face, eyes, and middle ear directly with muscles that wrap around the heart, gut, and other internal organs. If a baby is cold, hungry, tired, or in some way feeling unsafe, the baby's sympathetic nervous system activates and the baby flails arms or legs, cries, or shows signs of anxiety. The baby seeks comfort by looking for the mother, reaching for her, nestling into her body, and beginning to suckle. In doing so, the baby activates the social engagement neural circuit. As the baby sees, hears, and feels the mother, neural impulses travel from the baby's eyes, skin, and mouth to the heart and other organs, slowing the baby's racing heart and relaxing the muscles that cause pangs of hunger. The social engagement circuit has the power to override activation of the sympathetic nervous system. In essence, it "puts the brakes on" the aroused system. Porges (2011) describes this action as "safety trumps fear" (p. 195).

The social engagement branch of the autonomic nervous system is rooted in the brainstem with direct connections to the limbic area, described in Chapter 2 as the emotion center of the brain. As the baby suckles or sees and feels the touch of the caregiver, the baby's neuroception signals "safety," and by virtue of the direct connection to the limbic area, both baby and caregiver "feel good." As babies develop over the course of the first 6 months, they show improved abilities to spontaneously engage with others and to be soothed by others (Porges, 2011). This is largely a function of improved connectivity of the social engagement neural circuit.

From their earliest encounters, babies assess the world as to whether they expect it to be a safe place or a threatening place. If a baby is handled roughly, her neuroception codes this as a threat and signals "danger." The baby responds to this signal by seeking comfort from the caregiver. If the caregiver is absent or avoidant, the baby begins to cry, grows agitated, and her heart may begin to race and her skin may flush. These are all signs of activation of the sympathetic neural circuit. When a baby shows these signs of distress, a responsive caregiver responds with a soft voice, a touch, or a caring look. The baby senses this and calms, with heart rate and skin color returning to normal.

A classic experiment by researcher Ed Tronick (1989) used an experiment called *Still Face* to capture the power of the social engagement system. In this experiment, a mother is asked to play with her baby in a face-to-face situation while a camera records the mother's face. Another camera simultaneously records the baby's face. Several minutes of play are recorded before the researcher prompts the mother to adopt a still face, that is, to cease smiling and playing with her infant and to look down.

Babies in these situations sense danger. They show alarm, they gesture or scream in protest, and they may reach with their bodies in a desperate attempt to get the mother to look back. These are all signs of activation of the baby's sympathetic neural circuit. When none of this works, most babies respond to the stressful situation by activating the parasympathetic neural circuit. They seek safety by reducing contact—averting their gaze and looking away from the caregiver. They begin to self-soothe, perhaps fingering their hands or rocking back and forth, as a means of restoring a sense of calm. After a few minutes, the mother is prompted to look back, engaging once again the baby's social engagement neural circuit. Immediately, the baby calms, shows relief, and resumes interactive play with the mother.

The baby's physiological disorganization is striking in the still face portion of the experiment, but equally striking is how quickly the baby recovers once the engaged connection with the mother returns. There is a rupture in the social interaction, but a quick repair once the mother resumes actively engaging with the baby.

Tronick (2007) describes this as *mutual regulation,* when the feelings and states of the caregiver, relayed through the social engagement neural circuit, influence the feelings and states of the baby, and vice versa. In a typical pattern of interaction, sometimes caregiver and baby are in sync with each other, and sometimes they are not. Tronick emphasizes that it is the overall pattern of rupture followed by repair that matters. This pattern of rupture and repair helps the baby learn that losing contact with the caregiver occasionally is not cause for alarm.

Prematurity, illness, or neglect may dampen the developmental trajectory of the neural networks that make up the baby's social engagement system. Of concern is the emotional separation that occurs when a mother experiences postpartum depression or when there is a pattern of inconsistent or unreliable care in the first year. Babies who lack access to the regulatory support of a comforting, reliable caregiver either remain anxious and hyperaroused for long periods or attempt to manage dysregulation by reducing their exposure to outward stimulation, avoiding eye contact, turning away, looking down, or self-soothing by sucking fingers or thumb or compulsively rocking (Schore, 2001; Tronick, 2007). With too much activation of the stress response system, babies experience lasting impairment of their ability to regulate basic bodily functions, such as digestion and elimination, and an impaired ability to manage stress (Porges & Furman, 2011).

Attachment

Over time and in response to patterns of care, infants build an expectation that experiences with others will either make them feel good or make them feel bad. Studies demonstrate that early life patterns of everyday care—such as how much a baby is held, when she is fed, or how she is responded to when crying—establish expectations in the baby for how she will be treated in relationships with others. These expectations endure over time and establish a pattern of behavior commonly described as either a secure or an insecure bond of attachment (Ainsworth et al., 1978). Babies who experience responsive, reliable care tend to exhibit a secure bond of attachment to caregivers. Babies who experience inconsistent, unreliable care tend to exhibit an insecure bond of attachment.

Some have described this response as "'States' become 'traits'" (Perry et al., 1995, p. 271). When early life patterns set up a secure bond of attachment, babies expect harmonious interactions with those who provide care. For securely attached babies, their social engagement system serves them well, and they are able to use the caregiver as a protective and reliable safe harbor (Powell, Cooper, Hoffman, & Marvin, 2013). For insecurely attached babies, their social engagement system fails to bring them comfort and help, so they avoid or reject the caregiver in time of need, their biological expectation for care and nurturance violated. For them, the caregiver is a source of distress or anxiety, and their options are limited. They either remain in a state of anxiety, hyperaroused and "mobilized" with an activated sympathetic system, or they "immobilize" with an activated parasympathetic system. They turn inward and away from the caregiver, avoiding contact in a desperate attempt to self-soothe (Perry et al., 1995).

A CLOSER LOOK

What Babies Expect in Care

Researchers devised an experiment to shed light on infants' expectations as to being comforted by others (Johnson, Dweck, & Chen, 2007). They recruited 14-month-olds and assessed the status of each baby's attachment relationship with the parent, whether insecure or secure. First the babies watched a simple animated screen, where they saw two shapes, a short oval and a tall oval, standing next to each other. The animation began. The short oval followed the tall oval to nearby stairs, and upon reaching the stairs, the sound of a baby's cry was played, at which point the tall shape hopped onto the stairs, while the short oval remained stuck at the bottom. The babies saw this scene over and over until they tired and looked away.

Then the researchers showed the scene again, followed by two distinct actions. In the first, the tall oval, upon hearing the baby's cry, descended the stairs to stand next to the small oval. In the second, the tall oval, upon hearing the cry, continued up the stairs and moved away from the small oval. The researchers measured how long the baby looked at each scene.

Babies, like adults, tend to look longer at things that seem odd, curious, and unexpected. The secure babies looked longer at the scene where the tall oval moved away upon hearing the cry, whereas the insecure babies looked longer at the scene where the tall oval moved toward the short oval. Researchers interpret this as evidence that at a very young age, babies have learned to expect patterns of care—be it responsive or avoidant.

RESPONSIVE CARE

Over the course of the first 6 months, the dance of social engagement between infant and caregiver becomes more intricately defined, and by the end of the first year, babies and caregivers relay and recognize symbols, such as a wave of the hand or the pointing of a finger, in a synchronous social exchange (Tamis-LeMonda & Bornstein, 1994).

Reading Cues and States

The behavior of a baby, largely nonverbal, can be read as either a message of "approach/engage " or a message of "avoid/disengage," that is, either "Please come close" or "Please go away." Figure 4.2 lists some of the cues babies relay as signs of either engagement or disengagement, some subtle and some potent (Sumner & Spietz, 1994).

Another way babies convey their readiness to engage socially with others is through clear changes in behavioral state. A *state* is defined as an organized pattern of recurring physical and physiological responses related to an infant's level of arousal or activity (Fogel, 2015; Nugent, Keefer, Minear, Johnson, & Blanchard, 2007; Wolff, 1966). Researchers have identified six infant states that can be readily observed (see Figure 4.3). Identifying a baby's state has implications for successfully caring for babies. For example, if a baby is in an alert state, it is hard to entice the baby into a sleep state; or if a baby cries vigorously, it is hard to engage the baby in an activity; or if a baby is in quiet sleep, it is hard to arouse the baby (see Figure 4.3). Sleep states will be explored more fully in Chapter 6, with a discussion of infants' developing sleep–wake patterns.

A baby in a quiet alert state is processing stimulation from the environment and will often orient to a source of stimulation, for example, turn in the direction of a ringing bell or in the direction of the parent's voice. In

FIGURE 4.2. Cues of Engagement and Disengagement

Engagement Cues	Disengagement Cues		
Brow raising	Back arching	Whining	Lips compressed
Eyes wide and bright	Coughing	Withdraw from alert to sleep	Head lowering
Face brightens	Crawling or walking away	Straight arms along side	Hiccups
Hands open, fingers slightly flexed	Cry face	Cling posture	Join hands
Head raising	Crying	Dull-looking face/eyes	Look away
Babbling	Fussing	Eyes blink	Pout or pucker face
Smiling	Halt hand	Eyes clinched	Rapid wrist rotation
Facing gaze	Lateral head shake	Facial grimace	Self-clasp
Smooth, cyclic movements	Maximal lateral gaze aversion	Finger extension	Shoulder shrug
Feeding sounds	Pale/red skin	Brow lowering	Sobering
Talking	Pulling or pushing away	Gaze aversion	Tongue show
Giggling	Saying "no"	Hand behind head	Turn head
Turning head to caregiver	Spitting or spitting up	Hand to eye, ear, or mouth	Whimpers
Mutual gaze	Tray pounding	Leg tense	Wing palm
Mutual smiling			Wrinkled forehead
Reaching toward caregiver			Yawn

Source: Adapted from Sumner and Spietz (1994).

FIGURE 4.3. Infant States

Infant State	Identifying Features	Implications
Quiet Sleep (deep sleep)	Eyes closed, still; no spontaneous movement; regular breathing; may startle or show sucking bursts	Hard to wake; if aroused, quickly resumes sleep
Active Sleep (light sleep or rapid-eye-movement [REM] sleep)	Eyes closed with rapid eye movement visible beneath lids; irregular breathing; spontaneous startles, sucks, or movements; brief crying sounds	Less difficult to wake; not ready to feed
Drowsy	Eyes semi-alert, may be open or closed; variable activity level; irregular breathing	Easier to wake, but needs time to fully awaken before feeding
Quiet Alert	Eyes alert, with bright look; minimal motor activity; regular breathing	Attentive and willing to participate in feeding, talking, or play
Active Alert	Eyes open, not bright; considerable motor activity; respiration irregular; may have periods of fussiness	Signals a need; hard to engage in sustained interaction; left on own, may self-console
Crying	Intense cry vocalization; increased motor activity; elevated or irregular breathing rate; grimace	Strong signal of need; may either self-console or signal need for help

a quiet alert stage, babies are paying attention, in essence, responding and arousing to stimulation that enters through eyes, ears, or skin.

Infants have different kinds of cries that reflect different kinds of stress. Crying is accompanied by a pattern of actions that include expressions, movement of arms and legs, and changes in skin tone, patterns of breathing, and muscle tension. Together with the acoustic features of the cry, these behaviors provide cues that can be read by caregivers as indications of the baby's discomfort or distress.

Sometimes, among normally developing infants between birth and 2 months of age, a sudden onset of inconsolable crying appears, particularly in the late afternoon and evening. The crying peaks in intensity very quickly and has a piercing and unchanging pitch. This is referred to as *colic.* During an episode of colic, babies may tighten their muscles and draw limbs in close, or they may stiffen arms and legs. Their faces redden, and they may hold their breath momentarily (Lester, 2005). Colic is distinct from simply excessive crying, which is not uncommon as babies move through their first 6 weeks, when crying tends to increase.

Infants' sensitivities to stimulation may be a factor in colic. For some infants, their sensitivity may allow them to quickly amplify the cry to a level that is hard to regulate. It is noteworthy that when Western societies are compared to hunter-gatherer societies—where newborn infants are carried in a sling or a pouch, breastfed frequently, and kept in almost constant contact with the caregiver—babies cry with similar frequency, but since the cries among hunter-gatherers are attended to quickly, babies sustain the cry for a much shorter period (Fogel, 2015). Studies show that when caregivers are generally slower to respond to infants' cries, the infants show a pattern of persistent crying (Papousek & von Hofacker, 1995). This suggests that when infants are not tended closely or are fed on a rigid schedule with no regard for hunger cues, their sustained cry not only amplifies and intensifies, but also triggers secretion of stress hormones, a possible factor in colic. It is noteworthy that mothers who experienced high levels of stress during pregnancy were three times as likely to have a colicky infant (Søndergaard et al., 2003).

Respectful Interactions

The coordination of behavior that occurs between infants and caregivers during intimate moments of care has a defining influence on how infants think and interpret events, how they use symbols to communicate, how they regulate strong feelings, and how they begin to assess good from bad (Feldman, 2007). In the 1940s, an insightful pediatrician named Dr. Emmi Pikler (1994) recognized this phenomenon and developed a philosophy of respectful infant care. She urged those caring for infants to see them as subjects worthy of respect, rather than as objects in need of care. She saw infants as active, competent participants in care. She urged caregivers to carefully read babies' states and cues and to invite babies to actively participate in the everyday routines of care.

For example, with a baby whose diaper needs to be changed, a caregiver reaches toward the baby with outstretched arms and says, "Come, I'm going to take you to the table to change your diaper. Are you ready?" The caregiver pauses, giving the baby a chance to respond with a gesture, facial expression, or vocalization. Or a baby whose face is in need of wiping hears, "I'm going to wash your face. This is a warm cloth. I'll let you touch it first with your fingers." The baby then feels a soft, damp, warm washcloth touching the skin of his hand. Or a baby who is being dressed hears, as the caregiver holds up a shirt, "Now it's time to put your shirt on. Are you ready? You can help me. Which arm goes in first?" Each encounter is an invitation, rich in language, gesture, and pauses. Pauses are important, as they give the baby a chance to respond, with a reach, a look, or a simple turn of the head.

Key to the idea of respectful infant care is that babies, when treated with respect, learn that their communications are valued, and in turn, they communicate with more vitality and precision. When denied such respect, they do the opposite. They reduce the effort they put into the interaction, and the communication falters. As described by Magda Gerber (2002), a colleague of Pikler and founder of the organization called Resources for Infant Educarers (RIE), "This is the difference between being understood and misunderstood. Being understood creates security, trust and confidence. Being misunderstood creates doubt both in oneself and in one's own perceptions" (p. 63).

In a respectful approach to infant care, the learning is reciprocal. Baby and caregiver learn from each other as they participate in care. To engage reciprocally requires a willingness to watch, listen, and patiently pause and reflect before acting, in effect, "What do I notice? What is the baby telling me through gaze, posture, or movement?" At times, it might mean asking,

A CLOSER LOOK

Respectful Diapering

Reflect on this diapering episode as an invitation to the baby to respectfully participate in the experience:

> "I think you are ready for a diaper change. Am I right?" says Corey's caregiver, who squats next to 3-month-old Corey lying on a blanket. He looks up at her. She reaches toward him with her arms and says, "Time to pick you up and change your diaper. Let's go." Corey reaches toward his caregiver, and she gently picks him up and carries him to the diapering area. As she lays him on the diapering table, she says, "I think you will feel good having a dry diaper. This is the wet one." She pauses to let him see the wet diaper before she drops it in the waste receptacle. "Now I'll wash your bottom. Remember how yesterday you lifted your bottom?" she says, gently patting his legs. Corey looks at her intently and begins to kick his legs. "You remembered! Time to lift your legs. Now we can put on the new diaper."

with an expectant attitude, "I don't know what you feel or want from me in this moment, but I am going to listen while you tell me in your own way." An "asking, expectant" communication creates time and space for each to inform the other about what should come next (Gonzalez-Mena & Eyer, 2012; Lally, 2011).

The care babies receive during meals, diapering, and preparing for sleep influences not only their health and well-being but also what they learn and how they feel about themselves and others. It is not always easy to figure out infants' nonverbal communication and to know with certainty the baby's feeling, desire, or intention. However, if we trust that we can learn from the baby in equal measure to that which the baby learns from us, then babies will guide us in knowing what to do (Brazelton, 2006).

CHAPTER 5

Synchrony in Care

Infant Feeding and Meals

From the day she is born to her first birthday, breastfeeding gives baby the very best start to life. And the benefits reach far into the future.

—1,000 Days (thousanddays.org/the-issue/why-1000-days/)

SYNCHRONY refers to a relationship that occurs in time, a temporal relationship. Feldman (2007) describes the synchrony that occurs between infant and parent as a process of "co-creating not only a shared relational moment but a shared biology" (p. 330). Scientists measure synchrony by observing the behavior of babies and their caregivers, but also by recording underlying physiological processes, including rhythms of breathing, release of hormones, and patterns of sleep, and by comparing simultaneous recordings of these biological processes.

Co-constructing shared biological rhythms can be traced to the third trimester of pregnancy (Mirmiran & Lunshof, 1996), when important physiological systems begin to organize, such as the system that regulates the heart rate or the system that works as a biological clock, producing circadian rhythms that regulate daily sleep–wake cycles. This biological synchrony is also seen immediately following birth, with respect to lactation and patterns of sleep. This chapter explores the synchronous relationship that exists between baby and mother with respect to lactation and feeding.

LACTATION AND FEEDING: A PERFECT MATCH

Lactation and infant suckling reflect a complex and fascinating biological synchrony between the newborn and the mother. A lactating mother's milk is perfectly matched to what her infant needs. Researcher Katie Hinde (2013) describes this synchrony as follows:

> Imagine a magic potion. This potion includes all of your calories and hydration for the day. It has fatty acids for your brain, amino acids for your muscles, and essential vitamins and minerals for your cellular processes. This potion provides immunoglobulins to protect you from pathogens and [it contains] hormonal cues about your mother and the environment. This potion delivers bacteria that colonize your gut and then continues to provide specialized nutrients for those beneficial bacteria. Oh, and one last thing, your mom makes it just for you. This magic potion, of course, is milk. (p. 187)

Mother's milk reflects an intricate physiological negotiation between mother and infant. This negotiation begins prenatally, as noted in Chapter 3, when mammary glands develop in response to fetal signals. It continues after birth, as maternal milk production increases and decreases and the composition of milk changes in response to signals relayed through the infant's suckling.

The composition of mammalian milk is specific to each species and provides the perfect blend of nutrients needed for that species to grow and survive within its ecological niche and developmental trajectory. As compared to human infants, some mammals, like cows and goats, give birth to offspring that mature rapidly (Figure 5.1). To support this rapid growth and maturation, their milk is high in protein. In contrast, human infants grow more slowly over a longer period and depend longer on those caring for them to provide nourishment, so human milk is lower in protein. Human milk is also higher in sugars, to nourish the relatively large and very active human brain. The milk of some mammals, like

FIGURE 5.1. Baby Goats, Relative to Baby Humans, Mature Rapidly and Require a Different Milk Composition

arctic seals, is high in fat in order to quickly build a thick layer of body fat to maintain warmth in very cold climates (Hinde & German, 2012).

Infants' Active Role in Feeding

Newborns are biologically prepared to take an active role in lactation and feeding. As described in Chapter 4, an array of reflexes facilitates newborns' participation in feeding. These reflexes include rooting, suckling, swallowing, and extrusion. The rooting reflex, stimulated by a touch to the baby's cheek, helps the newborn find the breast and to latch efficiently onto the nipple. Latching onto the nipple is facilitated when the baby is positioned so that her lips latch asymmetrically, with more areola (the tissue that surrounds the nipple) covered by the lower jaw than by the upper jaw (see Figure 5.2).

The suckling reflex is a combined action of the lips, gums, fat pads of the cheeks, and the tongue. As the baby suckles, the lower jaw drops, the gums form a pressure seal around the nipple (Figure 5.2), and in a rhythmic front to back motion, the tongue expresses milk from the nipple by pressing it against the hard palate. Fluid in the mouth triggers the swallowing reflex. The suckling reflex comes under voluntary control around 2–3 months of age. To keep solids from entering the digestive system prematurely, newborns have an extrusion reflex, which thrusts the front of the tongue forward, pushing solids out of the mouth, thereby protecting the infant's still-maturing digestive

FIGURE 5.2. Latching onto the Nipple

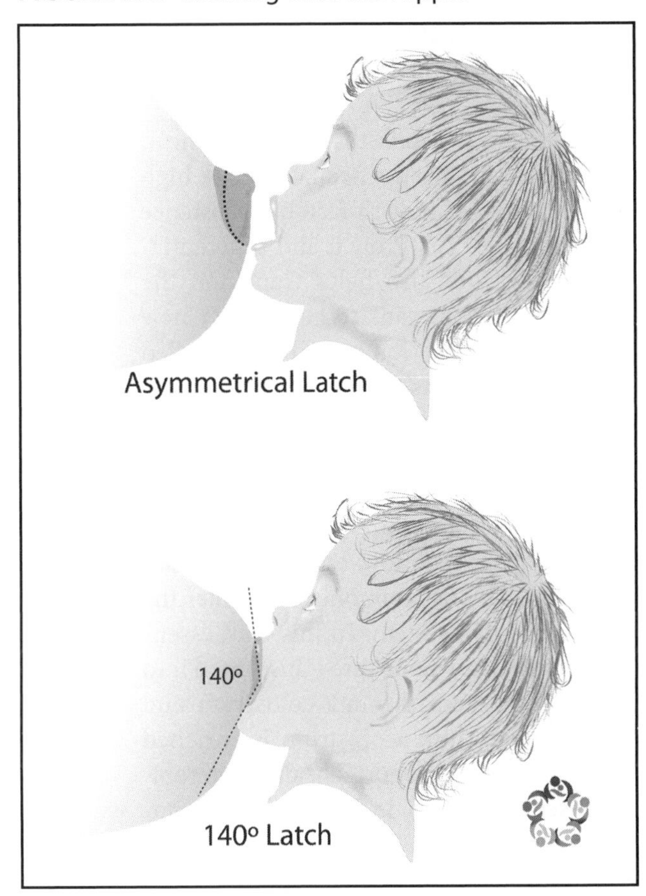

Used with permission of Lactation Education Resources

system. Not until midway through the first year will an infant's stomach be prepared to digest solid food.

Composition of Mother's Milk

During pregnancy, high levels of progesterone inhibit lactation. Progesterone and estrogen levels drop abruptly in the days following birth, and this rapid decrease, in the presence of high prolactin levels, results in milk synthesis. The pituitary gland, no longer inhibited by progesterone and estrogen, releases pulses of prolactin 7–20 times in 24 hours, and greater amounts during sleep (Wambach & Watson Genna, 2016). Prolactin stimulates the mammary epithelial cells to produce milk. Lactogenesis proceeds in stages and begins in midpregnancy as the mother's mammary glands prepare for the production of colostrum, a substance designed to nourish the baby in the first few days. Colostrum is yellowish in color, distinct from the white milk that will follow. Colostrum is perfectly adapted to be the first substance to enter the newborn's digestive system. It protects the baby from infections, prepares the baby's digestive organs, and organizes the baby's metabolic health.

Relative to the milk that will come next, colostrum supplies the neonate with a high concentration of growth factor, a substance that stimulates cell growth and differentiation. Colostrum also helps transition the baby's digestive organs to begin their new work. While in the womb, a substance called meconium protects the lining of the intestines. Once the baby is born, colostrum serves as a laxative to remove the meconium layer.

Infants' intestines are permeable, meaning substances can move easily into circulation in the bloodstream once they enter the baby's digestive system. In this way, essential maternal hormones are transported into the baby's system through colostrum and later through milk. Colostrum is enriched with factors that support a healthy microbiome (see Chapter 4), including the community of organisms present in the baby's intestines that help to establish the infant's immune system. This is important because, in addition to the maternal microorganisms beneficial to the baby that enter the baby's system, an array of environmental microorganisms that are potentially harmful to the baby can also enter. This puts newborns, whose immune systems are relatively immature, at risk. Colostrum plays a further important protective role in that it is enriched with factors that engulf and destroy harmful bacteria that could make the baby ill.

FIGURE 5.3. Breastfeeding and Hormones of Lactation

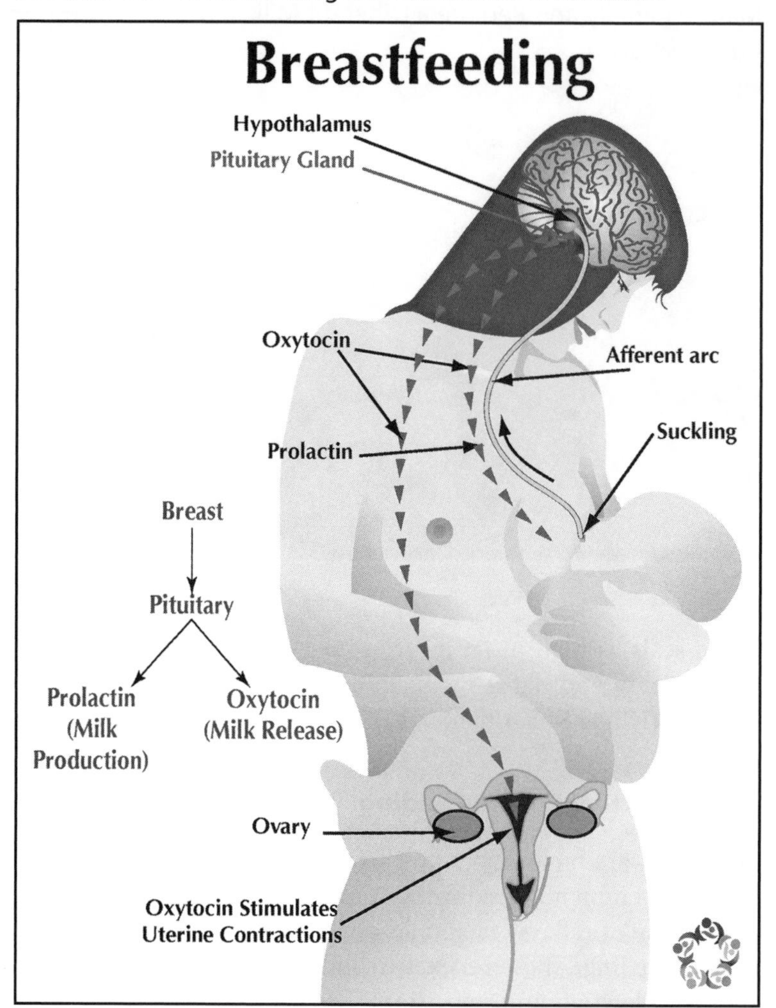

Used with permission of Lactation Education Resources

Milk Production: A Mother–Infant Synchrony

During pregnancy, the hormone prolactin stimulates mammary tissue to prepare for the production of milk. Milk secretion is blocked during pregnancy by the action of the hormones progesterone and estrogen. After the baby is delivered, the levels of progesterone and estrogen fall rapidly, unblocking prolactin, and the secretion of milk begins.

A baby's suckling stimulates sensory nerve endings located in the areola of the breast (see Figure 5.2). These sensory neurons relay a signal to the hypothalamus, using a neural circuit called the afferent arc (Figure 5.3). In response, the hypothalamus releases prolactin and oxytocin into the pituitary gland, where they move into the blood (Lawrence & Lawrence, 2015). Prolactin stimulates milk synthesis and secretion, and oxytocin causes a reflexive ejection of milk from the cells of the mammary gland. Commonly called the "letdown reflex," this enables the milk that has been produced in the breast to flow to the nipple.

Whenever a baby suckles the breast, the level of prolactin in the mother's blood increases, stimulating cells in the mother's mammary gland to secrete milk (see Figure 5.3). During the first few weeks, the more a baby suckles and stimulates the nipple, the more prolactin receptor sites are created, and the more prolactin is

FIGURE 5.4. Alveoli

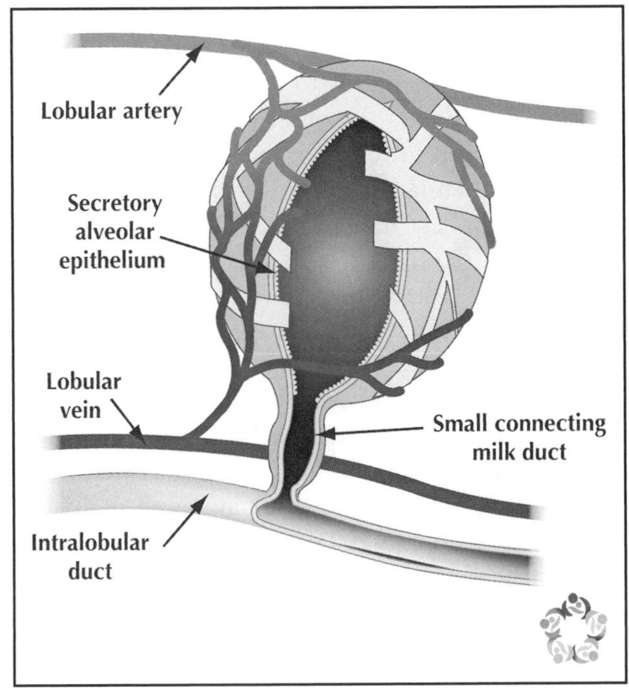

Used with permission of Lactation Education Resources

released into the mother's system. This increases the mother's milk production capacity.

Because more prolactin is produced at night than during the day, breastfeeding at night is especially helpful in the first weeks to ensure an adequate milk supply. To the mother's advantage, prolactin has a relaxing effect on the mother's system, thereby helping her fall back to sleep, even if breastfeeding at night. In the early weeks and months, mothers frequently produce more milk than the baby needs, most likely an adaptation that assures sufficient milk for twins or triplets. Over the first few months, the mother's body adjusts milk production to fit the baby's needs. Suckling also affects the release of other hormones that are involved in suppression of ovulation and menstruation, so frequent breastfeeding can help to delay a new pregnancy.

Milk is produced in the mammary gland of the breast within structures called alveoli (Figure 5.4). There are many alveoli, each connected to a duct (intralobular duct) that carries milk to the nipple. The inner wall of the alveoli (secretory alveolar epithelium) is lined with milk-producing cells that have receptors for the hormone prolactin. These receptors capture prolactin from the blood (lobular artery) and move it into the cell to stimulate the synthesis of milk. The prolactin level is highest about 30 minutes after the beginning of feeding, so its most important effect is to make milk for the next feeding.

Lactation is controlled by a synchronous physiological relationship between baby and mother. A mother will, for example, experience the oxytocin-induced letdown reflex when her baby suckles, but also when she simply touches, smells, or sees her baby; when she hears her baby cry; or even when she lovingly thinks of her baby. Although prolactin enables milk secretion, prolactin does not control the amount of milk produced. That control lies with the baby. The amount of milk produced is a function of how much the baby suckles. The amount of milk produced in each breast is controlled by how much milk the baby removes from that breast.

Breast milk has a special inhibitor that supports ongoing, synchronous regulation of milk production. As the breast reaches full capacity, this inhibitor stops the cells in the alveoli from secreting more milk (Wiessinger, West, & Pitman, 2010). Once the baby removes milk from the breast, the inhibitor is removed, and secretion of milk resumes. The presence of this inhibitor assures that the amount of milk produced is determined by how much the baby consumes.

Human milk is composed of a mix of sugars, proteins, fats, and minerals perfectly blended for what each baby needs. The concentration of fat changes from the beginning to the end of a feeding. At the start of a feeding, the concentration of fat is lower than at the end, because as milk flows through the intralobular duct (Figure 5.4), fat globules accumulate and stick to the walls of the duct. Not until the end of the feeding, as the breast empties, are these fats delivered, much like a fatty dessert delivered toward the end of a meal. If an infant only partially empties the full breast, the milk consumed has a lower proportion of fats. This low-fat feeding causes the infant to be hungry again sooner and to cry or fuss to elicit another feeding. Because this next feeding is more closely spaced, the breast is less full and has a higher proportion of fat to assure that the baby receives the full complement of nutrients.

Of concern is when parents are encouraged to feed babies on a rigid schedule, putting at risk this natural physiological synchrony between baby and mother. When milk accumulates in the breast, milk production slows, so delaying nursing in an attempt to stay on a set schedule runs the risk of decreasing the milk supply.

Protective Factors of Breastfeeding

Human milk contains antibodies that protect infants from disease. The protective value of human milk extends even beyond the point when a baby is weaned. A review of research comparing breastfeeding to formula feeding concludes that breast milk is associated with decreased risk of a wide variety of diseases, including diabetes, multiple sclerosis, sudden infant death syndrome, childhood cancer, cardiovascular disease, obesity, allergies, and asthma (Wall, 2013).

The components of breast milk are much more complex than once thought. Rather than being something that can be easily duplicated and replaced by a manufactured infant formula, breast milk contains an amazing variety of complex sugars called oligosaccharides, and in humans, the variety is exceptional. Babies do not digest these oligosaccharides for their sugar content. Instead these sugars pass through the stomach and small intestine and make their way to the large intestine, where bacteria thrive. The oligosaccharides in breast milk provide food for a very specific kind of bacterium that lives in the human gut. As long as this particular bacterium has a supply of oligosaccharides to consume, it outcompetes other gut bacteria, keeping them in check. In essence, these "good" bacteria starve out the "bad" bacteria. These beneficial bacteria, as they consume oligosaccharides, also produce a particular kind of fatty acid that is a favorite food for still other beneficial bacteria and that guide the infant's cells in using energy and mounting an immune defense. These helpful bacteria also help ward off dangerous bacteria that cause diarrhea, a common cause of infant death (Bode, 2012; Gura, 2014).

Researchers emphasize that human breast milk should be recognized for its immune protection properties as much as for its nutritional purpose (Gura, 2014). Other components of human milk, particularly fatty acids, have been related to cognitive functioning and vision. Scientists have also begun to look closely at the microbiome of the baby's gastrointestinal system for clues related to obesity. Differences in oligosaccharide composition in mother's milk can produce either an increase or a decrease in an infant's body fat as a function of the particular sugars present in the baby's gut (Alderete et al., 2015).

Lactation also has protective benefits for the mother (Dieterich, Felice, O'Sullivan, & Rasmussen, 2013). After birth, the baby's suckling releases oxytocin from the mother's pituitary gland. As described in Chapter 4, oxytocin signals the breasts to release milk to the baby, but it simultaneously causes the uterus to contract, which is important in reducing hemorrhaging and returning the uterus to its pre-pregnancy state. Breastfeeding delays the onset of the mother's menstrual cycle and lowers risk to the mother of iron-deficiency anemia. The act of producing milk is a metabolic process that requires 200–500 calories a day, thereby reducing risk of abnormal weight gain. Breastfeeding has also been found to reduce maternal risk of various cancers, heart disease, and osteoporosis (Wall, 2013).

Breast milk alone meets the nutritional needs of full-term infants of normal birth weight during their first 6 months, assuming the mother was well nourished during pregnancy and remains well nourished while nursing (WHO, 2003). As a global public health recommendation, the American Academy of Pediatrics (2012) and the World Health Organization, in conjunction with the United Nations Children's Fund (WHO & UNICEF, 2014), advise that infants be exclusively breastfed for the first 6 months to achieve optimal growth, development, and health.

Breast Milk Substitute: An Imperfect Match

According to WHO (2003), "Exclusive breastfeeding from birth is possible except for a few medical conditions. . . . Virtually all mothers can breastfeed provided they have accurate information, and support within their families and communities and from the health care systems" (p. 8). Not all mothers choose to or are able to breastfeed. In resource-poor settings, some mothers may not produce enough breast milk to provide adequate nutrition to their babies. Women with certain health problems, including mothers who are malnourished or have a drug or alcohol problem, may be advised to not breastfeed. In such cases, infant formula is a suitable substitute, despite the fact that it is not equivalent with respect to protective factors related to health and development (Wall, 2013). It is worth noting that even for women infected with HIV, WHO and UNICEF (2016) recommend exclusive breastfeeding for the first 6 months, with introduction of complementary foods thereafter, as well as continued breastfeeding.

Within the broader recommendation that "Breast is best," WHO (2003) provides guidelines for feeding infants who are not breastfed and instead are fed with a suitable infant formula. Use of infant formula requires careful attention to clean and sterile preparation and storage, especially if using a powder or liquid concentrate. The safest option is to prepare fresh formula prior to each feeding and to consume it immediately, in order to prevent the growth of bacteria in the formula. If advance preparation is the only option, it is advised that formula be prepared in individual bottles, cooled quickly, refrigerated, and discarded if not used within 24 hours. Chilled bottles of formula should be warmed in a container of warm water, rather than in a microwave, as microwave heating can create hot spots that risk scalding the infant's mouth. If not consumed within 2 hours, warmed formula should be discarded.

Safe, Responsive Feeding

Babies relay distinct cues as to their readiness to feed. Early cues are subtle and later cues are more intense. Early cues include wiggling and moving arms or legs, rooting, and bringing fingers to the mouth. These early cues are followed by fussing, squeaky noises, restlessness, and intermittent crying. Late cues include a full cry, often with an aversive screaming pitch, and changes in skin tone (Wambach & Riordan, 2016). By watching for the early cues, caregivers can assess an infant's readiness for feeding and begin to engage with the baby prior to him having to relay readiness through more pronounced cues.

If an infant struggles or cries during a feeding, caregivers should pause and wait to offer food until the infant calms. A swallow is timed to coincide with a momentary holding of breath, which seals off the trachea, and if an infant struggles or cries during feeding, there is a risk that this process will be interrupted, with food slipping down the trachea rather than the throat. Paying attention to the cues that an infant gives is key to helping young infants self-regulate their ability to participate in feeding. Some cues convey a readiness to feed or to engage in interaction, while others convey a desire to disengage from interactions (see Figure 4.2). For example, an infant might show disengagement cues, such as yawning, facial grimacing, arching, or a rapid change of state. These cues are signs that the infant needs a period of rest as a means of self-regulating. When caregivers see such cues, instead of playing with or attempting to feed the baby, it may be better to comfort the baby to assist him in self-regulation, for example by swaddling, holding, or rocking. Conversely, if the baby is alert and shows sucking, mouthing, smiling, or smooth movements, these are cues of engagement, signs that the baby is in a well-regulated state and ready for interaction or feeding.

During the first 6 months, infants enjoy being held in the caregiver's arms while being fed. When caregivers focus their full attention on the baby, as they feed the infant in arms, they invite the baby to join in a responsive ritual. By talking to the infant and punctuating the talk with respectful pauses, signaled by the baby's cues, caregivers give infants the opportunity to experience the ebb and flow of conversation. The time spent feeding an infant is the perfect time for a dialogue between infant and caregiver, often wordless, yet rich in the exchange of feelings and ideas.

A caregiver might be tempted to lay a baby in a crib and prop a bottle in order to accommodate a feeding, but such a practice risks liquid pooling in the baby's mouth, posing a choking hazard. It also puts the baby at risk of tooth decay, because any sugars contained in the retained liquid can begin to decay existing and erupting teeth. An additional concern is risk of ear infection, because liquids pooling in the baby's mouth will flow readily from the back of the throat into the ear canal, where they enter the middle ear and become a perfect medium for harmful bacteria.

COMPLEMENTARY FOOD

During the first 6 months, breast milk alone meets the nutritional needs of full-term infants of normal birth weight. After 6 months, as breastfeeding continues for up to 2 years of age or beyond, complementary food is added to meet nutritional needs (WHO, 2003, 2017a). From safe, nutritionally adequate, complementary food, an infant extracts key nutrients (e.g., iron, essential fatty acids, and protein) and calories, and from continued breastfeeding, an infant receives an ongoing source of nutrients and immune support in preventing disease.

At 6 months of age, small amounts of complementary food can be offered, increasing in quantity as the child gets older, while still maintaining frequent breastfeeding. If an infant is consuming more or less breast milk than average, the amount of complementary food will need to be adjusted up or down. For breastfed babies, the amount of breast milk consumed is always an estimate; thus, the amount of food to offer is based on responsively reading babies' cues as to satiation. Because infants' needs vary depending on breast milk intake and variability of growth rate, it is wise not to be overly prescriptive about the amount of complementary food to offer. Infants recovering from illness or living in environments where energy expenditure is high may require more energy and more food than an average that works for others.

Although the appropriate number of feedings of complementary food depends on the type and the amount of food offered, the recommendation for the average healthy breastfed infant is two or three times per day at 6–8 months of age and three or four times per day at 9–24 months of age, as well as additional nutritious snacks that are usually self-fed, convenient, and easy to prepare (WHO, 2016). Examples of such snacks are a piece of fruit or bread with nut paste (WHO, 2017b). If the child is no longer breastfed, more frequent meals may be required.

Preparing the Meal

Good hygiene and proper food handling diminish the risk of exposing infants to disease. The incidence of diarrheal disease peaks during the second half of the first year of infancy, the period when intake of complementary food increases. Contamination of food is a major cause of such infections. The World Health Organization (2007) suggests the following guidelines for safe preparation and storage of infant food:

- Wash the caregiver's hands and the child's hands before preparing food or eating.
- Store foods safely and serve foods immediately after preparation.
- Use clean utensils to prepare and serve food.
- Use clean cups and bowls when feeding infant.
- Avoid the use of feeding bottles that are difficult to keep clean.

Food Consistency. The maturation of muscle systems in the region of the mouth and throat, along with the gradual emergence of teeth, enables infants to chew, sip, and swallow solid food. Somewhere between 4 and 6 months of age, infants lose the extrusion reflex, which protects newborns from choking. Once the extrusion reflex subsides, infants are able to hold solids in the mouth. The neuromuscular system of the mouth matures to allow infants to close their mouth over the spoon, scrape food from the spoon with their lips, and move food with sufficient force from the front to the back of their mouth (Satter, 2000).

The first complementary foods that infants are prepared to take must be pureed. The consistency and variety of pureed food can be increased as infants' requirements and abilities change. As they develop, infants begin to move the jaw muscles up and down in a more circular, munching motion. Their teeth also begin to emerge. These advances allow infants to chew food, marking readiness for mashed, semisolid, and eventually solid foods. These changes coincide with the infant's ability to get into a seated position independently, a posture that facilitates swallowing.

Midway through the first year, the muscles of the hand develop to enable a voluntary grasp. Initially, a baby grasps objects using fingers together in opposition to the palm, like the action of a mitten, making it possible for infants to scoop up small portions of food. Gradually, the muscles coordinate to enable a neat grasp, using the index finger in opposition to the thumb. This occurs on average around 8 months of age, a point when infants enjoy finger foods that they can pick up and carry to the mouth themselves. Infants are still developing control of the jaw muscles used to transfer food smoothly from side to side without a pause (Satter, 2000), so finger foods that may cause choking, such as rounds of sausage or whole grapes, which could become lodged in the trachea, should be avoided.

By 12 months, most infants are ready to eat the same types of food as others in the family, keeping in mind the need for nutrient-rich food. There is some evidence that there may be a critical window for introducing "lumpy" solid food, in that keeping infants too long on a diet of semisolid food may increase risk of feeding difficulties later on (Northstone, Nethersole, & Avon Longitudinal Study of Pregnancy and Childhood Study Team, 2001). Of further concern, although feeding commercially prepared pureed and semisolid baby foods might save time, they are rarely cost-effective as the primary source of complementary food for infants. Local, fresh, soft fruits, vegetables, and starches can be easily mashed or pureed for the baby, with minimal cost and time.

Food Selection and Fortification. Infants grow rapidly in the first 2 years, and this creates very high nutrient requirements per unit of body weight. Given the relatively small amount of solids consumed by an infant between 6 and 24 months, the food consumed must be very high in nutrients. Breast milk contributes substantially to the total nutrient intake between 6 and

24 months of age, particularly for protein and many vitamins. It is, however, relatively low in several essential minerals, such as iron and zinc. Infants must get these minerals from complementary food or from food supplements.

There is much variability in diets of complementary foods, as an infant's diet is dependent on a variety of factors, including family tradition and what foods are locally available. Experts agree, however, that plant-based complementary foods by themselves may be insufficient to meet the dietary need for certain micronutrients (Wall, 2013). They advise including meat, poultry, fish, or eggs daily. Dairy products like cheese, yogurt, and dried milk mixed with other foods are a good source for some nutrients. However, consumption of cow's milk prior to 12 months of age should be avoided, as it is associated with fecal blood loss and low iron.

Infants should not be given sugary drinks and soda. These have low nutrient value and decrease the child's appetite for nutritious foods. Fruit juice, with its high sugar content, is no longer recommended for infants younger than 1 year of age (Heyman et al., 2017), as it increases the risk of dental caries; in addition, due to fruit juice's lack of protein and fiber, it can predispose a child to inappropriate weight gain, either too little or too much. After 1 year of age, fruit juice may be used as part of a meal or snack, but it should not be sipped throughout the day.

FIGURE 5.5. Reading Infant Cues

INFANTS' ACTIVE PARTICIPATION IN MEALS

Whether being nursed, fed with a spoon or cup, or introduced to feeding themselves as they develop hand and finger dexterity, infants are prepared to be active participants at mealtime. Initially, they seek participation with a look, a reach, or an open mouth. At the point when infants are introduced to complementary food for the first time, typically around 6 months of age, some infants may be able to get into and hold a seated position on their own, making an infant feeding chair a comfortable option, yet others may not. Until infants have developed the muscular ability to come into a seated position on their own, a more comfortable posture for them to participate in feeding without concern for balance is to be held in arms, supported on the caregiver's lap (Figure 5.5). In Figure 5.5 the father holds his daughter as he offers her a spoon of food. He pauses until she sees the spoon and opens her mouth in readiness. To respectfully invite an infant's participation in the meal, a caregiver can touch the spoon of food gently to the lips, pause for a cue of readiness, such as opening the mouth, and then move the spoon close to allow the baby to use her lips to scrape food from the spoon.

As finger dexterity improves, infants delight in holding a spoon themselves or holding a cup or glass to drink. Once the infant can form a seal with the muscles of her lips around the edge of a cup, she is ready to begin to drink liquids from a cup. Doing so efficiently takes practice, so it helps to avoid using infant drinking cups with lids perforated with an opening, as these require sucking, rather than sipping, a completely different muscular action.

How infants participate in meals changes across infancy. In the first 6 months, their cues are at times subtle—a turn of the head in a newborn, for example—and at times potent—a persistent reach of the arm in a 5-month-old. Being mindful of how infants ask to participate is key, as is adapting care to find respectful ways to accommodate an infant's request without compromising the care. The atmosphere around feeding can be calm or chaotic, depending on how this is done.

In the 1940s, in the aftermath of World War II, Hungarian pediatrician Emmi Pikler (1994), whose philosophy of respectful infant care was described in Chapter 4, established an orphanage called the Pikler Institute. The following is a description of how caregivers respectfully include infants in a feeding at the Institute (Chahin, 2017):

They will hold each child in a similar way and offer the spoon or cup also in a similar manner. It will be the child's rhythm that dictates when he's ready for another spoonful or sip, and the caregiver adapts to this flow. By being attentive to the cues, the caregiver will come to know when he is finished and stop the feeding at his slightest indication. The two feeding principles introduced at the Pikler Institute are that new foods are always introduced gradually and that there should never be a spoonful more than what the child wants. Even as a young infant, the caregivers will hold him in a way where both his arms are able to move freely, thus inviting cooperation when he is ready to help in holding the bottle or cup. . . . It is important for the child [and the caregiver] to have . . . the pleasure of unhurried time together. (p. 49)

Within this perspective, infants are seen as subjects, with feelings and intentions, rather than as objects in need of care. Caregivers are urged to respect infants' attempts to communicate and to participate in the meal, an example of a principle described in Chapter 1 in addressing infant care, "*How* you are is as important as *what* you do" (Pawl & St. John, 1998, p. 1).

CHAPTER 6

Synchrony in Care
Rhythms of Sleep

Parents have fantasies and ambivalent feelings, hopes, and fears about the new infant and their new role and identity as parents. Whereas the newborn is unregulated at birth because of the immaturity of its nervous system, the parents are physically and emotionally dysregulated. This state of disequilibrium may prepare the parents to be open to the infant's way of being and to be able to engage more readily with him or her in the task of self-regulation. —J. Kevin Nugent et al. (2007, p. 49)

AS WITH FEEDING and nutrition, sleep involves a synchronous developmental process that undergoes changes in the infant's first year. Newborns spend up to 70% of their time asleep and stay awake only for brief intervals (Nugent et al., 2007). Whereas adults seem to need somewhere between 7 and 9 hours of sleep daily, newborns, on average, sleep 16–18 hours per day, more or less evenly distributed across day and night and often in 2- to 3-hour spurts. By the end of the first year, this has dropped to a range of 10–15 hours a day, with most sleep occurring at night (Galland, Taylor, Elder, & Herbison, 2012).

Some of this pattern of change can be attributed to the fact that newborns have small stomachs, and that they digest breast milk quickly, so waking every 2–3 hours accommodates their hunger. As infants' digestive systems mature, they consolidate sleep cycles and the length of their sleep period increases (Parmelee, Wenner, & Schulz, 1964). By 3 months of age, some babies begin to sleep through a nighttime feeding for a stretch of up to 5 hours, but many do not. By 5 months of age, about 50% of babies have started to sleep for an 8-hour stretch some nights (Henderson, France, Owens, & Blampied, 2010) but, in general, babies do not sleep all night every night until they are close to a year old.

SLEEP PATTERNS AND BRAIN DEVELOPMENT

As described in Chapter 4, infants show six distinct behavioral states, including the state of drowsiness and two sleep states, active (or light) sleep and quiet (or deep) sleep (see Figure 4.3). To make sense of the sleep patterns of infants, it is worth reflecting on the sleep pattern of adults. During sleep, adults cycle through distinct stages. Each stage has a characteristic pattern of respiration, eye movement, and brain activity. We begin with light (active) sleep, when we drift in and out of sleep. In light sleep, we are easily awakened by something as simple as a sudden muscle contraction. Eye movements can be detected in light sleep, but they cease as we enter deep (quiet) sleep, which is characterized by no eye movement or muscle activity. It is very hard to awaken someone from deep sleep, and when this happens, most people feel groggy and disoriented. Deep sleep transitions to light sleep, characterized by rapid, irregular, and shallow breathing; jerky and rapid eye movements; increase in heart rate and blood pressure; and limp limb muscles. This light sleep includes what is referred to as rapid-eye-movement (REM) sleep. It is during REM sleep that people often report having dreamed. A complete cycle through these stages takes about 90–110 minutes.

Newborns' Sleep–Wake Cycle

Newborns, like adults, move through stages of sleep, but their cycling pattern differs (Anders, Goodlin-Jones, & Zalenko, 1998). It is shorter, lasting 50–60 minutes, with a different order of sleep stages. Newborns' sleep cycle begins with drowsiness and drooping eyes and proceeds to light (active) sleep, when eyelids flutter and breathing becomes irregular. Hands and limbs are flexed, and muscles may startle or twitch, with occasional fleeting smiles or even short bursts of sucking motions. The stage of light sleep lasts relatively longer in infants than in adults: Infants take a long time to move into deep (quiet) sleep. When grimaces and twitches cease, breathing becomes regular and shallow, and muscles of hands and limbs completely relax, dangling loosely, infants have entered deep sleep. From deep sleep, they return to light sleep, where the cycle begins again. Infants cycle through light and deep sleep multiple times a night, and as they pass from deep to light sleep, they awaken easily, especially if hungry or uncomfortable.

With their 50- to 60-minute sleep cycle, young babies are vulnerable to waking every hour. A light touch or soft, rhythmic voice can ease the baby through this vulnerable period and preclude their waking completely. Some babies, if aroused, settle back to sleep on their own, while others need help, be it a soft touch or voice or an opportunity to nurse. Such regulatory support from caregivers helps babies learn how to navigate these sleep transitions on their own, without waking and crying. When parents learn to recognize the signs of light (active) sleep and deep (quiet) sleep (refer to Figure 4.3) in their infant, they can use these signs as helpful clues to determine the best time to transition the baby from one sleeping place to another without arousing the baby.

Benefits of Light Sleep

Compared to 2-year-olds and adults, newborns spend twice as much time in light (active) sleep, about 50% of their total sleep time (Anders, Sadeh, & Appareddy, 1995; Nugent et al., 2007). This pattern accommodates newborns' need to eat every 2–3 hours. Arousing from light sleep is much easier than arousing from deep (quiet) sleep, so there are distinct advantages to newborns of spending more time in light sleep than in deep sleep.

The predominance of time spent in light sleep also supports the work of their rapidly growing brains (Tarullo, Balsam, & Fifer, 2011). During REM periods of light sleep, a newborn's brain actively processes information acquired while awake, discarding what is not needed and consolidating what is needed into long-term memory, in effect stimulating growth of neural circuits. To provide for this, blood flow to the brain increases during light sleep and the cortex continues to be active, an indication of higher-order learning under way. This is not the case during deep sleep.

Considering the rapid growth trajectory of the baby's brain, from 25% of the adult size to 75% of the adult size in the short span of 2 years, this distinct sleep–wake pattern, working night and day, is thought to be a factor in building new neural pathways. Animal studies show that active sleep facilitates synapse formation, neural plasticity, and the formation of neural circuits that influence memory and learning. Findings from studies of human infants suggest a similar pattern (Hupbach, Gomez, Bootzin, & Nadel, 2009), in that neonates with higher levels of active sleep and lower total sleep time, when tested at 6 months of age, had higher scores on the Bayley Mental Development Index (Gertner et al., 2002). Since newborns spend up to 70% of their time asleep and have shorter sleep cycles, it follows that infants are most likely taking in what they are learning while awake, and then, as they move through stages of sleep, are consolidating it as different types of memories (Tarullo et al., 2011).

Parents of newborns who wake every 2–3 hours desperately seek a satisfying night's sleep. Understandably, they are often swayed to try a variety of sleeping devices or training regimes designed to get young babies into a deep sleep without arousing during the night. Although more time spent in deep sleep may sound appealing to the tired parent, for babies it could be disastrous if they find themselves unable to arouse when cold, hungry, or unable to breathe. Key to making decisions about how to assure adequate sleep for parent and baby alike is understanding the infant sleep cycle and the critical roles that light sleep and shorter sleep cycles play in building the baby's brain and facilitating arousal when needed—thereby keeping the baby safe.

It is comforting to know that during the months following birth, the forebrain matures and exerts greater control over the brainstem and cortical regions to organize sleep–wake rhythms. Sleep episodes become longer and more continuous (Mirmiran, Maas, & Ariagno,

2003). Infants begin to organize their sleep–wake states to reflect a sleep pattern aligned with the sleep pattern of the parents. Over the course of the first year, infants increase the total sleep cycle length, decrease light (active) sleep, increase deep (quiet) sleep, and develop a clear circadian rhythm (Mirmiran et al., 2003).

Sensory Proximity and Safe Sleep

Parents of newborns play an important role in babies' organization of sleep–wake states, beginning in utero. During the third trimester of pregnancy, distinct active and quiet sleep states can be detected in the fetus. These budding sleep states vary by time of day and are influenced by the mother's heart rate, stress level, body temperature, and daily activities, all of which signal the fetus to begin to establish a circadian rhythm.

At birth, the direct connection to the mother's biological sleep–wake cycle ends. In a different way, however, babies remain dependent on their parents for assistance in regulating sleep–wake states, as well as heart rate, breathing, and temperature. Babies do this by keeping in touch with the parent through physical proximity. As explored in Chapter 4, proximity to the parent has a physiological regulatory effect on the baby, and this continues whether awake or asleep. Babies who sleep separate from the parent do not have access to this regulatory support. Of concern is that they are sleeping in an environment for which they may not be biologically designed. Most sleep researchers agree that, to sustain regulatory support, mothers and babies should sleep in sensory proximity to each other throughout the early months (McKenna, Ball, & Gettler, 2007).

In studies of infants co-sleeping (i.e., sharing the same sleep surface with a caregiver), there is a 28% increase in light sleep and a 47% decrease in deep sleep, as well as a significantly longer total sleep time, in infants co-sleeping, as opposed to those sleeping alone (Ball, Ward-Platt, Howel, & Russell, 2011; McKenna et al., 2007). Researchers conclude that babies who sleep in close proximity to the caregiver are more likely to experience signals that arouse them slightly, such as breathing sounds, touch, chest movements, and exhaled carbon dioxide. This slight arousal is beneficial in that it keeps babies from remaining for long periods in deep sleep and gives them practice arousing from deep sleep. Being able to arouse from deep sleep may be a powerful defense against respiratory collapse, which can be lethal.

A CLOSER LOOK

Proximity and Infant Sleep

To study the impact of proximity during sleep, infant sleep researchers recorded physiological and behavioral data in pairs of breastfeeding infants and their mothers. They did this in various sleep settings (Ball et al., 2011; McKenna et al., 2007). In one setting, mother and baby slept apart. In another, they shared the same sleep surface, called co-sleeping. Notable in this research is that mothers who slept next to their babies assumed, on their own, the same position, lying on their side facing the baby, with the babies nestled in the curve between the mother's arm and knees. In this position, babies co-sleeping had only to move or vocalize slightly, and the mother aroused and adjusted closer to the baby or began to feed the baby. Babies placed in a crib that was separated from the mother aroused and moved actively, as if searching for the breast, but the mother did not hear or respond to the baby until the baby cried and became distressed. With proximity to the baby, the mother is able to pick up the baby's signals quickly, meaning less distress, crying, and risk of arousal for the baby.

These studies also monitor physiological responses of mother and infant. Those co-sleeping show significant physiological synchrony, with more overlap in arousals and sleep stage of baby and mother (Mosko, Richard, & McKenna, 1997). Researchers suggest that babies sleeping in close proximity to the mother are using multiple sensations to synchronize and expedite their respiration—the sounds of the mother's inhalation and exhalation, the sensation of the rising and falling of her chest, and the exchange of air exhaled by one and inhaled by the other.

Sleeping in close sensory contact with the mother gives the baby a protective edge against a rare phenomenon called sudden infant death syndrome, once referred to as crib death. SIDS, an unexplained lethal episode apparently occurring during sleep, is most prevalent in infants between 1 and 4 months of age (American Academy of Pediatrics Task Force on

Sudden Infant Death Syndrome, 2016). A baby sleeping in close sensory proximity to the mother can better regulate the baby's still immature physiology by accessing the parent's mature physiology. In effect, the respiration, heart rate, and body temperature of the parent help the baby maintain regular breathing, heart rate, and body temperature—and arouse if any of these systems fail.

Most young infants have the ability to take a strong gasp of air to resume breathing if breathing were to cease while sleeping, yet some babies may have a defect that makes them vulnerable and puts them at greater risk of not being able to resume rhythmic breathing. Although the exact cause of SIDS is still unknown, the convergence of three conditions appears to lead to death from SIDS, these conditions being a vulnerable infant, a critical developmental period, and outside stressors. Figure 6.1 illustrates the convergence of these three conditions in what is called a *Triple Risk Model.*

FIGURE 6.1. Triple Risk Model

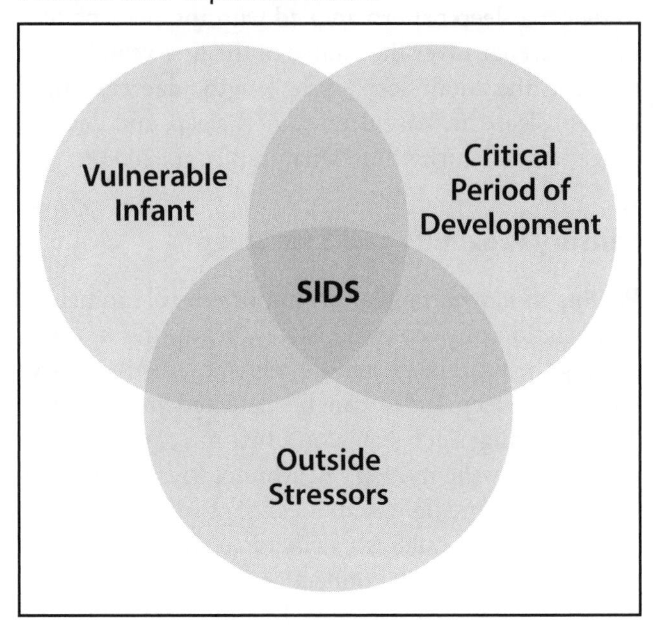

Sensory proximity during infant sleep, especially in the first 6 months, minimizes infant stress, with reduced sleep disruption and reduced bouts of crying. A baby sleeping in close proximity to the mother, when hungry and awoken from sleep, has only to move or vocalize slightly to arouse the mother, who moves closer to feed the baby. Babies sleeping at a distance from the sleeping mother emit the same early hunger cues, and with no response, resort to fussing and crying to arouse the mother, a situation that is disturbing and stressful for both (Ball, 2006; McKenna et al., 2007).

A CLOSER LOOK

SIDS and Shared Breath Control

Respiration of humans is more complex than that of other primates. Infants begin to breathe at birth, yet their respiratory system is still immature. Breathing is initially strictly automatic, that is, controlled out of the brainstem. Somewhere near 2 months of age, infants start to voluntarily control breathing, for short periods, in order to facilitate more complex vocalizing and speaking. Speaking requires a momentary interruption of automatic breathing, voluntarily changing the pattern of air flow, air pressure, and air release, while still breathing automatically, exhibiting essentially shared respiratory control.

The months when infants transition to shared respiratory control coincide with the period when infants are most vulnerable to SIDS, from 1 to 4 months of age. Researchers suggest that this developmental transition may be a factor in causing SIDS (McKenna et al., 2007). Anthropologists who study sleep patterns in primates point to the fact that speech is not present in primates other than humans, nor is SIDS. The complexity of the human respiratory system may put some human newborns at risk of some type of breathing control error during this transitional period.

WHERE INFANTS SLEEP: CULTURAL AND HISTORICAL CONTEXT

In the overwhelming majority of cultures around the world today, infants sleep together with their parents (McKenna, 2016). This can take many forms, such as sleeping in a bassinet positioned next to the parent's bed, in an infant's hammock slung above the mother's, or in an adult bed with the caregiving adult. In each setting there is a sensory link assuring that baby and caregiver can communicate through tactile, visual, auditory, olfactory, or kinesthetic and/or vestibular senses.

It is only in the past century and only in specific parts of the world that this arrangement has changed.

The practice of placing infants to sleep in separate quarters from the parents is largely limited to Western, industrialized societies. Within the United States, the incidence of co-sleeping varies greatly. Across ethnicities, African American families report the highest incidence of co-sleeping, followed by Hispanic families, with Caucasian families reporting the lowest incidence (Dieterich et al., 2013).

The shift from shared sleeping to separate sleeping came about largely as a result of childbirth moving from home to hospital. The practice of giving birth in hospitals started when anesthesia became available for labor and delivery, a change seen mostly in industrialized countries (Ball & Russell, 2012). Initially, the anesthesia used in hospitals incapacitated the mother, so in response, newborn nurseries were created. The care and feeding of newborns was transferred from the mother, still sedated by anesthesia, to the hospital nurse, who oversaw newborns in rows of cribs. Despite a reduction in the use of narcotics during labor and delivery, separation of mothers and infants in newborn nurseries has become standard practice in many parts of the world.

Simultaneously, childrearing approaches aimed at tightly scheduling infants' meals, sleep, and activity became popular (Ball, 2006; Ball & Russell, 2012). Parents were told to feed infants at 4-hour intervals and never at night. The goal was to train babies into a schedule that worked best for the adults doing the care, as well as to instill obedience and fortitude in babies. To implement such a scheduled approach to infant feeding and care, parents were advised not to cuddle and comfort in response to babies' cries, as doing so was seen as "spoiling" the child. During this same period, a movement in psychology called *behaviorism* popularized similar attitudes toward infant care, urging parents to separate from their babies at night to encourage children to be independent and self-reliant. The popularity of these approaches coincided with the development of scientifically designed infant formula that was marketed as a replacement for mother's milk. These ideas still inform prevailing assumptions about infant care.

This same period saw other changes in lifestyle and infant care. As parents began to have babies sleep in rooms separate from the parents, doctors advised putting babies to sleep in a prone position, that is, stomach down, as this position elicits deeper sleep. In addition, more women began smoking during and after pregnancy. It was in this context, in 1963, that SIDS was first described as a medical syndrome, with no known cause.

Research reveals a range of factors that may put babies at risk of SIDS, the most significant being putting infants to sleep in a prone position (Mitchell et al., 1992). This finding overturned decades of pediatric sleep advice to sleep babies prone, and a campaign known as Back to Sleep was launched, in which parents were advised to put babies to sleep supine to reduce the risk of SIDS.

Researchers are still investigating the complexities of newborn sleep with respect to infants' still immature physiological systems and sleep safety. Some express concern with the public health recommendation to put all infants to sleep in a supine position, due to the fact that supine sleep may elevate stress and disrupt sleep cycling, conditions that could have as-yet-unknown consequences on the formation of neural networks in the rapidly growing infant brain (Bergman, 2014). Although supine sleep reduces the risk of SIDS when applied to the whole population, it is still unknown what impact this policy may have on the infant's developing brain.

Although the SIDS rate has reduced markedly as a result of the response to updated recommendations, SIDS remains a leading cause of infant death from 28 days to 1 year. Recent findings identify sensory proximity as a key factor in SIDS prevention. Public health recommendations regarding infant sleep practices now include keeping the baby close during the first 3 months of life, when the risk of SIDS is greatest (American Academy of Pediatrics Task Force on Sudden Infant Death Syndrome, 2016).

MAKING DECISIONS ABOUT INFANT SLEEP

Sensory proximity during this sensitive period assures that parents can hear, respond to, and reach for the baby (McKenna, 2016). Proximity can mean sleeping the baby in a cot by the side of the parent's bed, so the parent can hear and respond to the baby, but it can also mean sharing a sleep surface with the baby, for example in the same bed or in a cot that extends out from the bed surface (Figure 6.2). Such proximity assures that when the baby moves or cries, the parent can hear and respond before the baby starts to cry or become distressed, without having to get up. It is significant that in many Asian societies, even in industrialized societies such as Hong Kong and Japan, SIDS deaths

FIGURE 6.2. Same-Surface Option for Bed Sharing with Infant

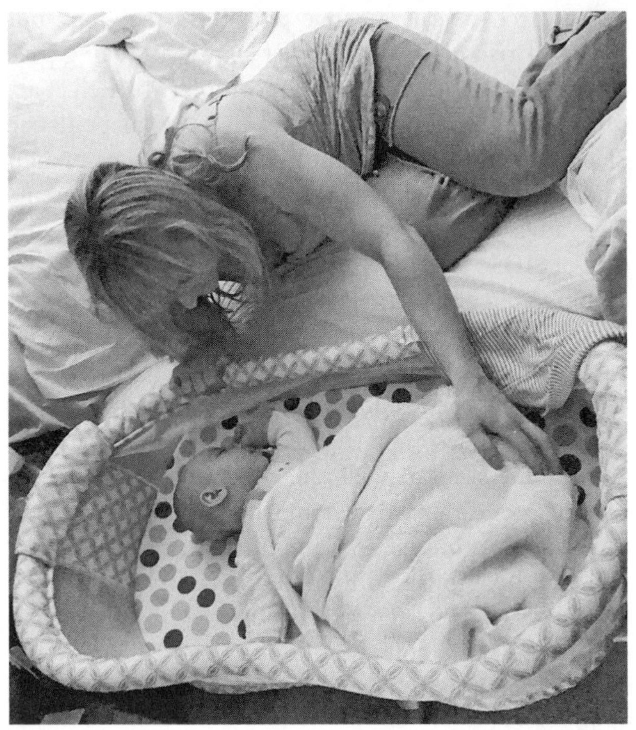

Photograph by Justin Takeoka

FIGURE 6.3. Same-Surface Bed Sharing with Infants: Conditions for Safe Sleep

Co-sleeping requires the following conditions be met:

- Babies placed on their backs to sleep
- A firm, non-quilted sleep surface
- Night clothes without strings or ties
- Long hair tied up
- No soft objects, such as pillows, loose bedding, or heavy covers that could cover the baby's face or head
- Baby not dressed too warmly
- Baby never left alone on an adult bed
- A smoke-free environment
- No pets in the bed
- No space between the bed and the wall where the baby could roll and become trapped
- A mattress that fits tightly against the headboard and footboard, or alternatively, no bed frame

Adults co-sleeping must commit to:

- Not smoking
- Not consuming sedatives, medications, alcohol, or any substance that causes altered consciousness or marked drowsiness
- Not putting baby to sleep on a couch, chair, bean bag, or recliner, whether alone or with anyone else
- Not co-sleeping if ill or tired to the point of it being difficult to respond to the baby
- Not sharing a bed with a baby less than a year old if older siblings who do not understand the risk of suffocation share the same bed

occur at a fraction of the rate found in Western societies (McKenna et al., 2007). In these societies, co-sleeping is considered common practice until babies are weaned, and sometimes long after.

The list of precautions in Figure 6.3 guides parents in making decisions about safe sleep practices with babies in the first year of life. Babies rely on their caregivers to make sure that their sleep surface is safe and that the surrounding environment is safe, including factors related to the adults with whom a baby shares a sleep surface (Volpe, Ball, & McKenna, 2013). Studies of breastfeeding mothers and babies who routinely bed-share show a pattern of sleeping close together on the mattress surface away from pillows, facing one another with the baby supine, level with the mother's breasts. Mothers adopt a protective position, curled around the baby, with an arm above the baby's head and knees bent below the baby's feet (Ball & Klingaman, 2007). Mothers who do not breastfeed but who bed-share with the baby do not appear to automatically assume this protective sleep position, a finding that suggests that, for those not breastfeeding, a safer way to assure sensory proximity is a three-sided same-surface crib attached to the parent's bed (refer to Figure 6.2).

Because babies grow quickly in the first months of life and have very small stomachs, they need to feed around the clock to meet their nutritional needs. As babies' stomachs and intestines grow, they can go for longer periods between feedings and begin to consolidate sleep cycles, running two or more sleep cycles together into a longer period of sleep. These longer periods of sleep may fall in the daytime or during the night, but as babies' circadian rhythm matures, the consolidated sleep becomes nighttime sleep and begins to align more comfortably with parents' sleep patterns.

By 3 months of age, about 70% of babies have begun to consolidate their nighttime sleep, although this may take months to even out and become a regular pattern (Peireno, Algarín, & Uauy, 2003; Rivkees, 2003). Even then, "sleeping through the night" may simply mean sleeping for a 5-hour stretch. For parents of young babies, nighttime awakenings can be disturbing and discouraging. At some point, many parents of young infants become frustrated with disruptions to their own sleep, and without a good understanding of how their infants' bodies are moving through a developmental process of consolidating sleep cycles, they grow concerned that they should be doing something to remedy the situation.

Many frustrated parents seek ways to train their babies to sleep through the night, based on the misguided assumption that babies will not learn to sleep through the night of their own accord. Strategies to "sleep train" babies abound, most of which are designed to extinguish what the parents see as an undesirable sleep pattern, the predominance of light sleep rather than deep sleep, which results in more frequent arousals. The goal in sleep training is to get babies to sleep through the night, in a pattern better matched to adult sleep patterns.

Sleep training strategies teach parents to use various methods to get babies to self-soothe in a crib without assistance in order to sleep for prolonged periods without awakening. While on the surface this appears to be what is happening as babies begin to sleep through the night, it is important to understand the consequences of altering infants' developmentally normal sleep patterns. Encouraging young babies to sleep longer or more deeply than is normal for their stage of development—that is, to spend more time in deep sleep, from which they may encounter difficulty arousing on their own—may increase their risk of SIDS (McKenna, 1990, 2016; McKenna et al., 2007).

Although most studies find that sleep training can alter a baby's behavior, there is no evidence to suggest that these changes last and some concern as to their long-term effect on babies. While it may appear that babies learn to fall asleep, they also learn that their appeals for help in co-regulating their immature physiological systems go unheeded (Blunden, Thompson, & Dawson, 2011; Feldman, 2007). Although infants appear to self-soothe through sleep training, what they may actually be doing is activating the parasympathetic branch of their stress response system, causing them to shut down physiologically. As described in Chapter 4, frequent activation of the stress response system may result in lasting impairment of a baby's ability to regulate basic bodily functions and an impaired ability to manage stress (Porges & Furman, 2011).

A large, systematic review of infant sleep studies (Douglas & Hill, 2013) concluded that sleep training with infants in the first 6 months of life did not improve outcomes for mothers or infants and risked unintended outcomes, including increased amounts of problem crying, premature cessation of breastfeeding, worsened maternal anxiety, and, if the infant is required to sleep either day or night in a room separate from the caregiver, an increased risk of SIDS. Indeed, babies' behavior is malleable and can be shaped to desired ends, but there may be a cost in doing so (Ball, 2006).

Families find sleep patterns that work for them and should not assume there is one right way or that they

A CLOSER LOOK

Sleep Training and Infant Stress Levels

A study of infants 4–10 months of age undergoing a hospital-based sleep training program charted stress levels in infants and mothers (Middlemiss, Granger, Goldberg, & Nathans, 2012). Infants undergoing the sleep training ceased crying at bedtime by the third night of the program, but their stress, measured by the stress hormone cortisol, remained elevated, at the same point it was the first night of the program, when they were crying frantically. Although the babies' behavior changed, that is, their crying stopped, their physiological state remained alarmed. Their biological rhythms were no longer coupled with those of the mother. On the first night of the program, infants and mothers registered high levels of stress, but by the third night of sleep training, the infants' stress levels remained high while the mothers' stress levels had dropped, a marked disruption of the biological, regulating synchrony between infant and parent.

should be locked into rigid notions about where a baby should sleep, for how long, or with whom. Respecting infants' biological cues and working to establish synchrony in biological rhythms optimizes parent–infant sleep. Many families around the world never question the issue of where a baby sleeps. Cultural rules or assumptions specify the normal place for infants to sleep within a given society. This might be a cot or crib in a room prepared especially for the baby, or a futon on the floor alongside the mother, or strapped to the mother's body in a sling (McKenna, 2016). Because environments for infant sleep vary widely across families, public health recommendations for where babies sleep are made on the basis of enhancing infant safety and maintaining infant well-being, which includes support for breastfeeding and building secure bonds of attachment.

PART III

Babies Making Meaning

PART III provides a look at how babies make meaning in multiple ways. Chapter 7 explores how infants pay close attention to the dynamics of conversation and how this leads to acquisition of language. Chapter 8 focuses on how infants figure out the complexities of movement, both small muscle movement like reaching and grasping, and large muscle movement like crawling and walking. Chapter 9 provides a look at how infants make sense of people and how they use playful interactions to do so. Chapter 10 examines how infants build ideas and concepts within everyday play, as they learn about the physical world, the world of objects and events.

CHAPTER 7

How Babies Communicate

A world lies hidden behind each human face. . . . Something more than the person looks out. Another infinity, as yet unborn, is dimly present. . . . The human face is the meeting place of two unknowns.

—John O'Donohue (1997, pp. 41–42)

We speak with more than our mouths. We listen with more than our ears.

—Fred Rogers (2002, p. 116)

YOUNG INFANTS are acutely aware of and observant of the world around them, both the inanimate physical world of objects and the animate social world of people. They actively scan and focus on things in their surroundings, and they seek out facelike patterns (Turati, Simion, Milani, & Umiltà, 2002). When given a choice of objects to look at, they prefer things that contain curves rather than straight edges and things that have high contrast (Fantz & Miranda, 1975), features found in the human face. Newborns respond differently to a person talking with them than they do to an object held before them. Newborns can hear and locate sounds, and they are more responsive to voices than to nonvocal sounds (Muir & Field, 1979). They respond best to sounds in the range of the human voice (Eisenberg, 1976) and show a preference for their own mother's voice (DeCasper & Spence, 1991).

These findings provide clear indication that newborns notice and respond differentially to people and that they are prepared by their biology to seek others and to pay attention to others, as companions in communication. This chapter recounts the story of how infants experience conversation, how they figure out the complex code of language, and how their early language competencies lead to success in learning to read and write.

LANGUAGE BEGINS IN THE WOMB

The story of infants' language development begins in the womb. By 14 weeks gestation, the structures of the vestibular system mature. The vestibular system is the sensory system related to balance, spatial orientation, and the coordination of movement with balance. Scientists track what fetuses are sensitive to by monitoring fetal heart rate. Near-term fetuses show different heart rate patterns when the mother is walking as compared to when the mother is resting (Cito et al., 2005). These findings suggest that prenatal rhythmic stimulation—through such things as maternal walking, rocking, or swaying—plays a significant role in fetal development (Provasi, Anderson, & Barbu-Roth, 2014). It most likely establishes an innate sensitivity to rhythmic patterns that sets a foundation for beginning to understand the rhythmic cadence of language.

At about 30 weeks gestation, as brain regions that control hearing mature (Trevarthen, 2011), fetuses show sensitivity to sound. The womb is a fairly quiet place, with the internal sounds of the womb consisting of the rhythmic sounds that arise from maternal respiration and maternal and fetal heartbeats. Fetuses respond to the mothers' heartbeat and to external stimuli (Porcaro et al., 2006), such as voice, speech, song, and music.

Although speech is muffled when perceived inside the womb, the rhythm of speech and the contours of pitch are preserved (Moon, Lagercrantz, & Kuhl, 2013). From about 30 weeks on, the fetus is exposed to a stream of words in normal conversation, with the most prominent voice that of the mother. The mother's voice evokes a response in the fetus as early as 32–34 weeks gestation (Kisilevsky & Hains, 2011). Near-term fetuses not only detect and respond to the maternal voice (Voegtline, Costigan, Pater, & DiPietro, 2013) but they also distinguish their mother's voice from the voice of a female stranger (Kisilevsky et al., 2003). With precision, the fetal brain is encoding the rhythmic patterns and pitch contours heard in utero, laying a foundation for language.

BABIES AS LANGUAGE DETECTIVES

Given the language environment of the womb, it should not be surprising that newborns respond to spoken language and that they are particularly sensitive to the voice of the mother. Infants are innately prepared to listen intently to spoken language. They detect subtle differences in consonants, vowels, rhythmic timing, and intonation. Newborns recognize and prefer familiar speech sequences that their mothers' recited aloud during the last week of pregnancy (DeCasper & Spence, 1986), and babies just 2 days old can discriminate the language used by their mother during pregnancy from a foreign language (Moon, Panneton-Cooper, & Fifer, 1993). When exposed to two different foreign languages, newborns can discriminate one from the other based on features like melody, intensity, and rhythm (Nazzi, Bertoncini, & Mehler, 1998). When newborns hear recordings of two distinct sets of vowels, those used in English but not in Swedish, and those used in Swedish but not in English, they can distinguish the difference (Moon et al., 2013). This heightened awareness of the distinctions in language sounds, a skill that originates in utero, prepares infants, through their biology, to join in the act of communicating (Nagy & Molnar, 2004).

In Sync with Others

For their initial conversations, infants rely on exchanges of gestures, movements, looks, and expressions. Newborns' readiness to engage in communicative exchanges has been shown in innovative experiments in which newborns watch as an experimenter gazes at them and then sticks out his tongue. Slowly, in response, each newborn sticks out his tongue in imitation of the experimenter, revealing newborns' innate capacity to notice and imitate expressions and facial movements they see in others (Meltzoff & Moore, 1977; Nagy & Molnar, 2004). Infants not only imitate what they see but they also imitate what they hear. In the first hour after birth, infants will imitate vocal sounds, such as the vowel /a/ (Kugiumutzakis, 1999). Infants steadily build on this imitative capacity, and by 2 months of age they show evidence of imitating basic emotions, such as joy and sadness (Field, Woodson, Greenberg, & Cohen, 1982).

Babies are extraordinarily communicative. Over the course of the first few months, they develop a full array of facial expressions that they use to communicate with others. Observant caregivers intuitively pick up on this capacity and respond in synchrony to the many subtle shifts in babies' gestures, expressions, movements, and vocalizations (Papousek & Papousek, 1977). In turn, babies read and respond to the subtle shifts in facial expressions, vocalizations, direction of gaze, and head position of caregivers. Long before speaking their first words, infants actively participate in an interactive, nonverbal social dialogue (Trevarthen, 2011).

To capture these social dialogues, researchers use two cameras, one recording the face of the parent and the other the face of the baby, as they interact face-to-face. When played in slow motion, each recording captures moment-by-moment changes that occur during the interaction. A comparison of the two recordings in a split-screen view shows how the actions of one influence the actions of the other, in a back-and-forth exchange of information relayed through subtle, split-second delivery of cues between the body of the baby and the body of the parent.

These recordings show clearly that newborns are *correspondence* detectors (Beebe, Cohen, & Lachmann, 2016), that is, they make facial movements or hand gestures progressively similar to those observed in the person they watch. To detect these correspondences between self and other, babies use proprioceptive feedback. Proprioception refers to the ability to sense stimuli arising within the body regarding position, motion, and equilibrium. Through proprioception, babies match what they *experience* through senses of vision, hearing, or touch with what they *feel* as they move the muscles of their eyes, face, or hands.

How the action of one corresponds to the action of the other can be seen in Figure 7.1, a series of still shots pulled in sequence from a video recording. Each of the baby's expressions corresponds to the expression of the adult with whom she is interacting in that moment of exchange. Correspondence of vocalizations occurs, as well, when caregivers match their voice to infants' vocal contours, pitch, and rhythm. For example, a baby's vocalization rises sharply in pitch and, in turn, the

FIGURE 7.1. Grandma and Riley (11 Weeks Old) Act in Correspondence with Each Other

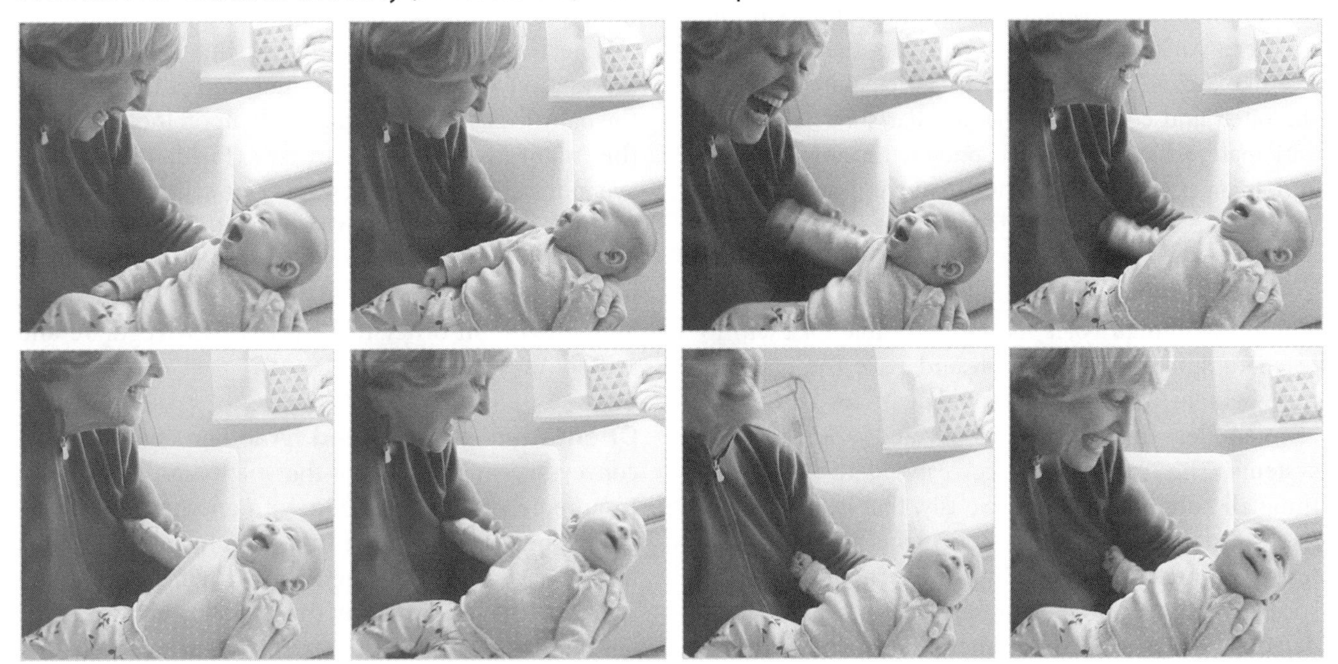

caregiver's voice rises in pitch. When infant and caregiver co-create patterns of correspondence, the infant, as well as the caregiver, "feels felt." This could be translated to mean, "She gets me. She's on my wavelength" (Beebe et al., 2016).

Frame-by-frame analysis of how newborns move in correspondence to the boundaries between language sounds has led to new understanding of how infants acquire language. Researchers (Sander, 2008) describe language acquisition as a system of interpersonal communicative exchanges, with infants and caregivers detecting and responding to patterns in language sounds, gestures, movements, and expressions.

Attunement: The Musicality of Speech

Researcher Colwyn Trevarthen describes infant–caregiver communication as "the musicality of interaction" (1999, p. 185). He cites a video study of a 5-month-old who was born blind and who listens and responds as her mother sings her a song, one she has heard her mother sing many times before. In a frame-by-frame analysis of the recording, researchers chart the baby's hand movements with the lyrical changes in the mother's voice. The baby moves her left hand up, in precise correspondence to the mother's voice rising in pitch. As the mother's voice lowers at the end of a phrase, the baby's hand lowers. Trevarthen compares the baby's

A CLOSER LOOK

Newborns in Sync with Language

Researchers Condon and Sander (1974) recorded the movement patterns of infants lying in a crib while two adults talked next to the crib. In microanalysis of the audio and visual sound tracks, the researchers detected a distinct synchrony between the patterns of adult speech and the patterns of infant movement. In a frame-by-frame analysis, they showed that infants' movements of head, eyes, shoulders, arms, hips, legs, fingers, and toes started, changed, or stopped in synchrony with the patterns of speech the infants were hearing. The infants were detecting and responding to each distinctive articulated speech sound. This synchrony was not found if the infants heard only disconnected nonspeech sounds. This synchrony at microsecond levels between the movements of the newborn and the human speech heard nearby was recorded in infants as young as 12 hours old.

hand motions to those of a conductor leading an orchestra, with the baby moving in synchrony with the mother's voice. Noteworthy is the fact that the baby, just like a conductor, appears to anticipate changes in the pitch and contour of the familiar song. The baby anticipates what is about to happen in the familiar song and changes the direction of her moving hand a fraction of a second before the point in the song when the mother changes her pitch.

Babies' acute sensitivity to the oscillation of sounds within the human voice makes it possible for them to listen to spoken conversation and yoke the patterns they hear to the rhythmic movements of their own arms and legs, using their auditory and proprioceptive systems. This cross-modal correspondence is something all humans do unconsciously, that is, they move in correspondence with the movements and vocal patterns of others. Infants' ability to detect pattern in the speech, gestures, and the movements of others includes detecting patterns of contingency, that is, a relationship of order and sequence. For example, when infants frequently hear two sounds spoken back-to-back, they develop an expectation of contingency, that is, that the second sound predictably follows the first, an "if-then" contingency.

Modes of Communication

Babies let us know what they feel, what they like and dislike, and what they want. They also let us know when they are surprised, wary, or sad. They do so in a language more akin to music and dance than to spoken words or signs. Their first conversations are revealed in gesture, movement, vocalization, and expression. Infants communicate feelings, likes, dislikes, and desires through the direction of the gaze, orientation of the head, facial expression, changes in vocal intonation or rhythm, and movements of the torso, arms, and hands (Beebe et al., 2016).

Gaze—Seeing and Being Seen. When interacting in a face-to-face position, infant and caregiver tend to gaze directly at each other. This gives the infant a clear sense of being seen. However, there are points in the interaction when each partner looks away, and these moments are important as well. Infants tend to engage the gaze of the caregiver in cycles, looking at the caregiver's face for a period of time, looking away, and then looking back (Stern, 1971). Looking away can be interpreted to mean, "I need to pause," as a means of regulating, that is, calming down. Such a pause can be seen in Figure 7.1.

The heart rate of infants during a face-to-face interaction tends to be elevated immediately before the baby looks away. Immediately upon looking away, the infant's heart rate decreases (Field, 1981). Gaze aversion is an important aspect of self-regulation, a means of coping when overstimulated. When a baby breaks the gaze, a sensitive caregiver will lower the level of stimulation offered (Brazelton, Koslowski, & Main, 1974) in order to help the baby regulate and self-soothe.

Orientation of the Head. Another behavior that conveys intent or interest is the orientation of the head. In an episode of interaction with another person, an infant spends most of the time with his head oriented face-to-face with the interaction partner. An infant spends a smaller portion of time, about a quarter of the episode, with his head oriented 30–60 degrees to either side (Beebe et al., 2016). This signals that the infant is beginning to disengage but is still monitoring the conversation partner through peripheral vision (refer to Figure 7.1). By turning 90 degrees from center, the infant averts his gaze completely, sending a clear signal of disengagement. An even stronger signal of disengagement can be seen when an infant not only averts his gaze but also arches his back and pushes away with his torso.

An infant might momentarily turn her head to the side and avert her gaze, a brief disengagement that signals a pause in the conversation (refer to Figure 7.1). This pause gives the infant a chance to regroup or to calm herself before looking back and resuming the interaction. Sometimes a conversation partner fails to see or respect these pauses and actively pursues the baby's gaze, despite the fact that she has tried to disengage. If there is a pattern of moving toward the baby, chasing after the baby's averted gaze as she turns to avoid contact, a severe breakdown in interactive communication can result (Beebe et al., 2016).

Expression of Emotion. Another powerful communication signal is an infant's facial expression. For example, infants show interest by slightly opening or widening the mouth in a way that is distinct from a smile (Figure 7.2). Less common is an evocative variation of expression of interest depicted by a fully opened mouth, without a hint of widening or smiling (Beebe et al., 2016). Sometimes the expression of interest

FIGURE 7.2. Expression of Interest

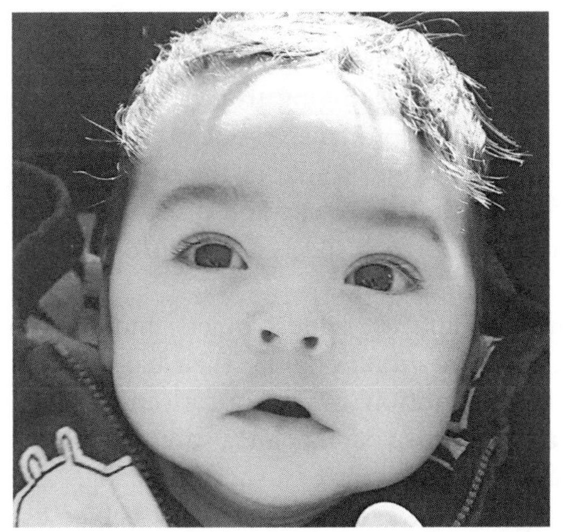

Photograph by Robert M. Chiles

FIGURE 7.3. Transforming Expressions of Emotion

Photographs by Carol Grivette

transforms into a smile. Infants' smiles vary by degrees, and these variations convey meaning. A low smile, as depicted in the top two photos in the series in Figure 7.3, has only slightly upturned corners of the mouth and little or no mouth opening. A high smile (see Figure 7.4) has medium to large mouth opening and upturned corners. Negative facial expressions are also seen in degrees, from low to high, including a grimace with compressed lips, a frown, a pre-cry face, and a cry face, variations of which are depicted in the bottom four photos of Figure 7.3.

Emotion is also communicated through vocal affect. Vocal affect increases and lowers in a bell-shaped curve. For example, a caregiver might convey approval by saying to the infant, "Good!" What the infant hears, in this utterance, are vocal sounds that arc up and down, following the contours of a bell-shaped curve. In contrast, if the caregiver says, "No!" to the infant, as a prohibition, the infant hears vocal sounds that fall rapidly from high to low, as if down the right side of a bell-shaped curve (Fernald, 1992, 1993). Infants notice these vocal contours and register either joy upon hearing "Good!" or dismay upon hearing "No!"

Babies pay close attention to the affective messages relayed through facial expressions, and they mirror what they see while interacting directly with others. Together, baby and caregiver work to match or approximate each other's positive-to-negative affective

FIGURE 7.4. High Smile

Photograph by Wenn Madigan

changes, increasing and decreasing in response to what they read in others (Beebe et al., 2016).

Touch. Another communication mode for babies is touch. The first sense to emerge in utero is touch, and babies are born with an acute sense of touch. The human embryo responds to touch, particularly around the mouth and the soles of the feet, from the second month of gestation (Nugent et al., 2007). Newborns read and respond to touch, which provides a primary source of information from the outside world. Touch is relayed through the skin, the largest sense organ of the body. Nerve endings in the skin relay sensations of touch to the brain. Touch a baby's foot, for example, and an area of the brain associated with the muscle systems of the foot is activated.

A baby's hand grasp provides an opportunity for tactile communication between caregiver and infant, as caregivers spontaneously provide their fingers for infants to grasp. Such tactile exchanges soothe the infant and also serve to inhibit random motor activity. Young infants soothe themselves through self-touch and, in so doing, self-regulate. When excitement or stress overtakes a baby, it is not uncommon to see the baby finger or mouth her hands, as a way to calm herself (Figure 7.5).

Infants gauge their responses to others through information they acquire through a look but also through touch. A rough touch is a signal that alerts the baby to potential harm or danger, while a gentle touch soothes and signals a sense of calm. Touch manifests in a wide range of types, ranging from affectionate to playful to rough and to intrusive. Each type of touch communicates a distinct signal to the baby—to feel good, to feel bad, to turn away and disengage, or to turn toward and approach (Beebe et al., 2016).

FIGURE 7.5. Self-Touch to Soothe

Photograph by Robert M. Chiles

Reach. Just as adults use hands, fingers, and arms to communicate, babies do the same. Their hands are in nearly constant motion during social encounters. Babies' hand motions signal an awareness of the rhythms and vocal patterns of a social exchange, and they also signal babies' excitement. How babies use their hands in relation to the reach can signal intention or desire. For example, an outreached arm with open palm is a gesture that conveys a desire to get or hold an object. In contrast, an outstretched arm with wrist bent up and fingers splayed up communicates a desire to disengage or avoid contact.

THESE SUBTLE SHIFTS of hand or arm movement, direction of gaze, orientation of the head, or intonation of the voice serve as signals to be read for meaning and to relay meaning. Infants read and relay these signals and their caregivers do the same. The result is an interpersonal dialogue that sets the stage for more elaborate conversations once language begins.

IN DIALOGUE WITH OTHERS

Imagine a parent speaking to her 3-month-old baby. The baby fixes her gaze on her parent, knits her brow, and drops her jaw slightly. She experiences the rhythm and pitch of the parent's melodic speech and the movements of her parent's head, eyebrows, and mouth. She emits a smile of recognition, then an animated coo. From her parent, she hears a matching utterance, followed by a high gliding phrase, repeated, and then a graceful beat of silence, to which she responds with a series of coos, smiles, and gestures of hands and body (Fernald, 1992). The vitality of the exchange lowers for a moment, as the baby turns her head slightly and shifts her gaze, pausing to recover from the excitement of this interaction. Like a delicate duet, marked by lilting and melodic pitch and timbre, baby and parent match rhythms and phrasing in an intimate conversational exchange (Fernald, 1992; Trevarthen & Malloch, 2002).

Infant-Directed Speech

Researchers describe the mode of speaking described in the preceding paragraph as *infant-directed speech.* Infant-directed speech is noticeably different from adult-directed speech. Infant-directed speech is characterized by an exaggerated rise and fall of vocal contours; a measured, rhythmic pattern; a slower delivery, with exaggerated vowel and consonant sounds; and a higher frequency average pitch. Infants are especially attentive to infant-directed speech. When given the chance to hear a recording of either infant-directed speech or adult-directed speech, infants as young as 4 weeks of age show a preference for infant-directed speech (Fernald, 1985).

The rising contours, the slower delivery, and the exaggerated sounds of infant-directed speech have the power to elicit and maintain infant attention, no matter the language (Fernald, 1992), but most significantly, infant-directed speech helps infants learn language. The characteristics of infant-directed speech support infants in hearing and distinguishing the distinct sounds and contours of speech, helping them detect, distinguish, and organize distinct speech sounds and contours into units that eventually acquire meaning as words and phrases.

When compared with adult-directed speech, infant-directed speech results in more brain activation in infants (Golinkoff, Can, Soderstrom, & Hirsh-Pasek, 2015). Laboratory studies with infants show that the more infant-directed speech a baby hears within everyday social encounters, the greater the ability to distinguish contrasting speech sounds (Liu, Kuhl, & Tsao, 2003). A similar pattern occurs with word recognition (Thiessen & Saffran, 2003). The more infant-directed speech a baby hears in the first 2 years, the larger the vocabulary will be at age 3 (Ramirez-Esparza, Garcia-Sierra, & Kuhl, 2017).

Protoconversations

Babies' first vocalizations appear early, within the first months after birth. Often described as cooing, they consist primarily of vowel sounds. Soon after, babies begin to utter strings of consonant and vowel sounds, called babbling. As early as 6–8 weeks of age, babies begin to babble in rhythmic patterns that have the flavor of typical conversations. Still without words, these babbles delight and invite a reply from attentive caregivers. Referred to as *protoconversations* (Bateson, 1979), these exchanges follow a pattern of attuned, alternating vocalizations between infant and caregiver, irrespective of the fact that the baby's vocalizations are not yet words.

Infants actively recruit partners for their protoconversations. When infants initiate a conversation through their own utterances, the conversation tends to be longer in duration, with shorter response intervals, as compared with conversations initiated by their caregivers (Jaffe et al., 2001). Babies hone their skill as conversationalists in protoconversations, precisely coordinating and synchronizing what they see in the face and body of the conversation partner with what they hear in the partner's voice, noting movements of lips, tongue, head, eyes, hands, and fingers. As a baby looks at a human face, the baby extracts information about the communicative power of expression, and this information shapes brain structures used to process social and linguistic information.

Anticipating Language Patterns

Babies' protoconversations tend to last from 20 to 40 seconds, a cycle that corresponds to the rhythmic cycles of heartbeat and respiration (Trevarthen, 1999). This attunement and rhythmic sensitivity guides infants in tracking the timing and rhythm of conversations and verbal exchanges. Babies are especially attentive to the rhythmic patterns of nursery rhymes. Nursery rhymes, like protoconversations, tend to last about 20–40 seconds, again corresponding with the rhythms of heartbeat and respiration. Nursery rhymes also tend to have a predictable pattern. Composed in stanzas, which are groups of phrases, each stanza has four short phrases, and each phrase lasts about 4 seconds. Each stanza, therefore, lasts about 15–20 seconds, followed by a pause. A pattern of rhyming vowels at the end of the second and fourth phrases, a variation in the beat of the last two phrases, and a lilting rhythm add excitement and vitality to the recitation of the rhyme (Trevarthen, 1999).

Babies as young as 4 months learn these patterns and can be seen eagerly listening and anticipating a particular point in a familiar nursery rhyme and chiming in with a vocalization or an animated hand gesture. This impressive ability has its roots in two language processing areas of the brain. One area, called Wernicke's, is activated when listening to and comprehending speech. The other, called Broca's, is activated when producing speech. A large bundle of nerve fibers connects these two areas and forms long before babies begin to speak. A young baby attending to the spoken voice will experience electrical activity in Wernicke's area (the listening area), and immediately afterward, will experience a flurry of electrical activity in Broca's area (the speaking or social interacting area). This pattern of activation occurs well before babies are able to speak, readying them to anticipate, and eventually to talk back, in verbal exchanges (Kuhl & Rivera-Gaxiola, 2008).

Taking Statistics on Language

To determine what language sounds babies can detect, scientists use electromagnetic equipment that monitors changes in electrical signals in the baby's brain while the baby listens to distinct speech sounds. A distinct speech sound is referred to as a *phoneme.* In laboratory studies, babies are outfitted with a special cap fixed with electrode sensors that record the electrical activity across brain regions. When they hear a specific phoneme repeated over and over, for example, the phoneme /bah/, and then hear a similar but different phoneme, like /pah/, a record of the pattern of electrical firing in the brain shows whether the baby detects the contrast in the language sounds.

Detecting Native Language Sounds. By monitoring brain wave patterns in babies as they listen to language, researchers have discovered that young babies, prior to about 6 months of age, can detect every sound used in every language throughout the world. This is quite amazing, in light of the fact that across all the languages of the world, there are about 600 consonants and 200 vowels (Ladefoged, 2001). After 6 months, however, something changes. When tested at 12 months of age, babies can detect only the sounds used in the languages spoken regularly with them. They can no longer distinguish the sounds that occur in other languages.

To explain how this change comes about, researchers track what goes on in the brain of a baby as the baby listens to conversation. Babies pay close attention to speech and track subtle shifts in language sounds. Within the neural circuits of the brain, babies precisely encode the sounds they hear used in speech, the frequency with which these sounds occur, and the order and patterns of speech sounds, including inflections and cadence. Researcher Patricia Kuhl refers to babies as computational geniuses (Kuhl, 2011; Kuhl & Rivera-Gaxiola, 2008), drawing on research that shows that young children rely on a form of computational learning in that they "take statistics" on the sounds and sound patterns they hear in language. The language spoken to babies determines the language patterns babies encode within their brains.

Babies who hear a string of phrases spoken in English, for example, will encode lots of /r/ and /l/ sounds, while babies who hear a string of phrases spoken in Japanese will encode very few instances of /r/ and /l/ sounds (Gopnik, Meltzoff, & Kuhl, 1999), as these are not common in Japanese. Over time, sound categories form in the brain, based on the frequency with which distinct sounds are heard. Infants learning Japanese, for example, will form different sound categories than infants learning English. An infant learning Japanese groups the sound units *r* and *l* into a single sound category, known as the Japanese *r.* In contrast, infants learning English keep separate these two sound units, in order to make words like *red* and *led.*

By 10 months of age, simply by hearing speech in social contexts, infants have begun to identify the distinct set of phonemes used in their native language. Although they cannot yet speak words, 10-month-old babies have begun to form language categories in the brain that reflect the language to which they are exposed in conversation. These patterns are so strong that babies in the first year will babble in sounds of their mother tongue; for example, a French baby babbles with the sounds and intonations of French, while a baby born into an English-speaking home babbles in English (de Boysson-Bardies, 2001). In similar fashion, babies under 1 year of age who are deaf, and those who are not deaf but are raised by caregivers who communicate by sign language, will "sign babble" around 6 months of age (Petitto, Holowka, Sergio, Levy, & Ostry, 2004).

Recognizing Words in Speech. Infants apply their knowledge of sound patterns to eventually isolate words from the continuous flow of conversation and give words meaning. How they do this is quite remarkable. Infants are aided in their language detection by infant-directed speech, characterized by higher and more variable pitch, shorter utterances, and exaggerated vowels. The frequency with which they hear certain sounds and sound patterns and the order in which sounds occur also helps them isolate sound units from a continuous stream of speech. Studies show that by 8 months of age, infants are using various strategies to identify potential words in speech (Kuhl & Rivera-Gaxiola, 2008). They notice which syllables tend to show up adjacent to each other. For example, babies may have heard a phrase like "pretty baby" quite frequently by 8 months of age, so the fact that they have frequently heard together the syllables "pre" and "tty" and the syllables "ba" and "by" allows them to treat such adjacent syllables as having a higher probability of occurring together. In contrast, it would be unlikely for a baby to hear the syllable "tty" followed by "ba," so they disregard "tty-ba" as a sound unit (Harris, Golinkoff, & Hirsh-Pasek, 2011). Over time, babies encode which sounds are used together frequently in the native language, allowing them to use this "transitional probability" as a reliable cue in isolating significant units of sound (Kuhl & Rivera-Gaxiola, 2008, p. 520). Within daily conversation, infants experience, compute frequency of, and isolate literally thousands of words from the continuous stream of speech, building a repertoire of sound units that begin to take on meaning.

Babies are also sensitive to stress patterns in language and use these patterns as a cue to pull out distinct words (Harris et al., 2011; Kuhl & Rivera-Gaxiola, 2008). The English language has many words that have a strong-weak stress pattern, like "BAby," whereas the French language has a frequent weak-strong stress pattern, as in "baGUETTE." Babies listen for this stress pattern and use it as a cue to figure out which syllables are likely to go together and which are not, thereby helping them identify words in the flow of language.

Frequency of word use also facilitates a word popping out as babies listen to a stream of conversation. One word heard frequently, for example, is the infant's name. Infants begin to recognize their spoken name at around 4–5 months of age. A familiar word, like the baby's name, serves as an anchor that helps novel words used with it to pop out in the language stream (Harris et al., 2011). For example, when baby Tommy hears the phrase, "Here is Tommy's sock," it is Tommy knowing his name that helps him isolate and begin to figure out the meaning of the word *sock*.

A CLOSER LOOK

Detecting Language Sounds Predicts Success in Reading

Infants 11 months old were tested on their ability to discriminate between two vowel sounds used in their native language. Some tested high in their ability to do so, and some tested low. In follow-up studies when these children were 5 years of age, they were tested for how well they did on a measure called phonological awareness, detecting the distinct sounds in oral language, which is a critical skill in learning to read. The children who, as 11-month-old infants, had done better in discriminating the difference between two vowel sounds in their native language, when tested at 5 years of age on preliteracy skills, showed significantly higher expressive and receptive language skills and significantly higher scores on phonological awareness (Kuhl, 2011). This finding suggests that experience in hearing and detecting sounds during the first months of life builds a foundation for acquiring later language skills.

Learning Language: The Social Context

To develop language, babies rely on people to be their conversation partners, generously supplying them with meaningful speech. Infants' language learning is powered by a shared social relationship between infants and caregivers (Golinkoff et al., 2015; Kuhl, 2007). Studies demonstrate that simply looking at a screen with speech sounds or listening to a recording of speech sounds does not help the baby learn language. Researchers exposed groups of 9-month-old babies from English-speaking families to a new language, in two distinct contexts (Kuhl, Tsao, & Liu, 2003). In the first context, a group of babies heard a native Mandarin speaker read stories during 12 weekly one-on-one sessions. In the second context, a group of babies was exposed to the same amount and intensity of Mandarin as the first group, but the language was delivered by way of a recording of someone reading the stories in Mandarin. A third control group was not exposed to Mandarin storytelling in any context.

At the end of 12 weeks, researchers tested each group of babies in a listening experiment. The babies heard recordings of recurring Mandarin sounds, sounds not used in English. The babies who heard someone in person read stories in Mandarin were able to detect these Mandarin sounds. The babies who watched a screen as someone read Mandarin language stories showed no evidence that they could hear or detect the Mandarin sounds. The same held true for babies not exposed to Mandarin storytelling. Researchers conclude that a key ingredient for learning to speak is social interaction and the presence of a responsive conversation partner. For infants to learn language, they need recurring social exchanges. Social isolation, without exposure to social contact and conversation, is devastating emotionally but also devastating linguistically.

Learning Multiple Languages

When it comes to learning multiple languages, babies have an advantage over adults. As noted earlier, babies are born with the capacity to detect all the language sounds used throughout the world, and up until about 6 months of age, are able to detect small differences between these language sounds. Babies exposed to multiple languages in social interaction on a regular basis will efficiently and easily organize the sound patterns of each language (Kuhl, 2000) and in, time, speak each language fluently.

A CLOSER LOOK

The Advantage of Being Bilingual

Researchers (Ferjan Ramírez et al., 2017) recruited a group of 11-month-old babies. Some were monolingual and some bilingual. Each baby, seated in a high chair, watched a researcher put a toy in the front door of a box, which the researcher then handed to the baby. Most babies opened the front door of the box and grabbed the toy. This sequence was repeated many times with different toys. Then, while the baby watched, the researcher closed the front door, lifted the side door, put the toy in the box through the side door, and then handed the box to the baby. Monolingual and bilingual babies differed in what they did next. The bilingual babies were quick to figure out that they needed to switch doors to retrieve the toy, whereas the monolingual babies tended to persist in trying to retrieve the toy through the front door. Researchers infer from these results that bilingualism may facilitate the invention of new solutions, an advantage when it comes to solving problems.

Infancy and early childhood mark a critical period for language learning. This window of opportunity starts to narrow as infants approach their second birthday. Over the course of the first 7 years, it continues to narrow, and by puberty, a child's ability to learn language has dropped significantly. By adulthood, learning a second language is more challenging, because well-developed neural networks are already set in place, dedicated to analyzing those language sounds heard early in life (Meltzoff, Kuhl, Movellan, & Sejnowski, 2009).

Of interest to researchers is how mastery of more than one language during the early years appears to maintain flexibility within the brain. Babies regularly exposed to two languages show significantly stronger activation in two brain areas known to be involved in executive functioning (Ferjan Ramírez, Ramírez, Clarke, Taulu, & Kuhl, 2017). Executive functioning involves processes like switching attention, flexible thinking, and updating information in working memory. Studies suggest that bilingualism may make it easier for a child to invent a new solution when faced with a problem, a sign of cognitive flexibility.

THE ROOTS OF READING BEGIN IN INFANCY

By the end of their first year, most infants have begun to speak their first words, but the age for doing so can vary tremendously. Babies begin to coo, with soft vowel sounds, between 2 and 5 months of age; to babble, with a connected series of consonant–vowel sounds, somewhere around 5 months of age; and to speak words somewhere near the first birthday. Midway through the second year, there is a rapid increase in the rate at which infants learn new words. By 2 years of age, most babies use two-word phrases, and by 3 years of age, they have progressed steadily to use short sentences. Vocabulary size at age 2 is an important marker, as it predicts how well children will do when entering school 3 years later.

Of concern is that a family's socioeconomic status correlates negatively with vocabulary size at age 2 and age 3, suggesting a social inequity that can impact success in school (Fernald, Marchman, & Weisleder, 2013). Caregivers who are economically and socially stressed or socially isolated may have few social supports, as compared to those who do not face these challenges. As a result, they may talk, read, and engage less frequently with their infants. Their infants may

A CLOSER LOOK

Toddlers' Vocabulary Size Links to Kindergarten Success and Family Income

Researchers found that children with larger oral vocabularies at age 2, when examined 3 years later, were better prepared to take on the academic challenges of kindergarten and beyond, with better reading and math achievement (Morgan, Farkas, Hillemeier, Scheffner Hammer, & Maczuga, 2015). Within the group of children studied, those from higher-income households were more likely to have larger vocabularies than children from lower-income households.

This is consistent with the findings of a landmark study by researchers Hart and Risley (1995), who recruited families with infants from across the socioeconomic spectrum and conducted monthly observations in their homes for 3 years. The researchers recorded every aspect of how the parents talked to their young children. They tracked the size and growth rate of the children's vocabulary. They found that children whose parents talked to them more and responded to them more frequently had larger, faster-growing vocabularies. By 3 years of age, the difference was significant. The children who heard more speech had a vocabulary of 700–900 words, as compared with 300–500 words for those who heard less speech. This difference increased as children aged. The family's socioeconomic status was significant, in that on average, by the time the studied children reached 4 years of age, those living in poverty had heard 30 million fewer words than those not living in poverty.

experience less conversation, hear fewer words, and develop smaller vocabularies.

Building Vocabulary

Vocabulary development begins long before infants begin to speak their first words. The ability to interpret sound patterns as meaningful words and ideas shows up at 6 months of age. When shown simultaneous videos of their mother's face on one screen and their father's face on another screen, 6-month-olds asked to "Find Mommy" looked significantly longer at the screen with a video of the mother, and, when asked to "Find Daddy," at the screen with the father (Tincoff & Jusczyk, 1999). In the latter half of their first year, infants are detecting words in the flow of conversation and are beginning to associate them with meaning.

Language Processing Time. How quickly children process spoken language is a key factor in building vocabulary (Fernald et al., 2013). Researchers are able to measure how quickly infants process sounds by seating them in front of two screens, each projecting a different image, such as a dog and a ball. Simultaneously, infants hear an audio prompt, such as, "Where's the dog? Do you see the dog?" Cameras record the moment when toddlers shift their gaze to the matching image. This allows researchers to calculate the time it takes the infant to process language sounds and to interpret them as words.

A concerning finding from these experiments is a significantly longer processing time for infants raised in households with lower incomes, with 18-month-old infants from higher-income families identifying the correct object in about 750 milliseconds, and infants the same age from lower-income families taking 200 milliseconds longer. To investigate further, researchers outfitted the infants in the study with small audio recorders worn in the home to capture the language they experienced throughout the day. The analysis of these recordings showed wide variability in the amount of speech directed at the infant per hour. The researchers compared the number of words the child heard per hour with the child's response time when asked to find a picture matched to a spoken word. The children who heard more speech directed to them had significantly faster response times than those who heard less speech directed to them.

Talking with Babies. Infants build vocabulary by learning words they hear frequently. Therefore, conversing with infants during everyday care and interactions is critical. Efforts to increase the amount of speech families direct to their children can offset some of the risks faced by families experiencing the stress of poverty and demanding work schedules that limit parents' time and energy. When parents have less time to interact with their infants, they may talk less to them, may use less infant-directed speech, and may spend less time reading to them. Encouraging parents, even in limited circumstances, to talk with their infants, to sing to them, and to engage with them during their everyday routines and interactions can reduce the potentially disastrous effects of poverty on children's language learning.

To understand how exposure to infant-directed speech predicts the ease with which a child learns to read, consider this phrase: "*Look at that apple on the table. It came from the garden.*" As soon as the listening child hears and recognizes a familiar word in the flow of words, the child can move quickly to an unfamiliar word in the stream. If the child is slow to recognize the word *apple,* for example, he gets stuck, not moving on to new vocabulary, such as the words *table* and *garden.* A child who has been exposed to ample infant-directed speech has a large store of familiar words at his disposal, within the language centers of his brain. This gives him the ability to recognize familiar words quickly and to move on more quickly to process and learn new vocabulary.

Language Relevance and Novelty. Vocabulary flourishes when those caring for infants watch for what sparks infants' interest and build on those interests in conversations. For example, consider what happens when, in response to an infant's pointed finger, an adult responds with a one-word answer, "dog," and says nothing more. In contrast, consider what happens when an infant hears, in response to his pointing, "That's a dog and he has long, soft hair you can touch." In the latter, more expansive response, the infant hears a higher density of novel and more complex words, relative to the total words heard (Harris et al., 2011). Also, the language the infant hears relates to the concerns and interests of the infant.

Adults who see infants attending to an object typically talk about the object. This facilitates infants' vocabulary development. Studies show that the children of parents who talk about what the child is looking at have more advanced vocabularies (Akhtar, Dunham, & Dunham, 1991; Tomasello & Farrar, 1986), whereas the children of parents who try to redirect the child's attention and label objects not of interest learn fewer words (Harris et al., 2011). When infant–adult conversations are interactive, responsive, and meaningful, infants build richer vocabularies and consequently are better prepared in a few years to take on the challenge of becoming a reader and a writer.

A CLOSER LOOK

Infant Gesturing Predicts Later Vocabulary Size

Vocabulary size may be rooted in the nonverbal gestural interactions that occur between baby and caregiver. The frequency with which infants use communicative gestures at 14 months of age predicts their vocabulary size at 54 months of age (Rowe & Goldin-Meadow, 2009). As caregivers pick up on infants' communicative gestures and talk with them about what the infants appear to be referencing, they facilitate exposure to novel vocabulary and more complex grammatical patterns, thereby helping babies build language.

LANGUAGE MILESTONES AND CAUSE FOR CONCERN

A baby's "first word," an utterance meant to stand for an object or event, occurs on average around the first birthday. Because infants develop their ability to comprehend words and speech long before they begin to speak, to accurately gauge infants' progress in language development, it is important to consider how much language infants comprehend—described as *receptive language*—as well as how much language they speak—referred to as *expressive language.* A typical 18-month-old might speak 50–100 words but understand many more.

As infants reach their second birthday, the number of words they speak varies from as few as 50 to upwards of 500 (Fenson et al., 1994). Language specialists suggest signs to watch for to identify concerns related to language development. These signs are listed in Figure 7.6 and can help parents and professionals gauge whether a child is on track or in need of support with respect to language development. Some language delays are the result of a hearing deficit, and others may be due to a speech or language disorder. A *language disorder* refers to difficulty understanding what others say through receptive language or trouble sharing their thoughts through expressive language. A *speech disorder* refers to children who have trouble producing speech sounds correctly or who hesitate or stutter when talking. The term *apraxia* refers to a specific

FIGURE 7.6. Cause for Concern in a Child's Language Development

Language specialists suggest the following as signs to watch for in the language development of children. Potentially, through assessment and intervention, language development can get back on track.

- At 1 year, the child does not babble and does not engage in protoconversations (i.e., mock conversations), coupled with not understanding or responding when spoken to.
- At 18 months, the child does not yet say at least one word.
- At 2 years, the child says only a few words and communicates primarily through grunting and pointing, with the additional possibility of showing a loss of prior language skills.
- By 2.5 years, the child does not put words together.

speech disorder that makes it difficult to put sounds and syllables together in the correct order to form words.

Several trends have been identified in the research on language development. Babies born prematurely may appear to talk later, but when the timing is adjusted for the anticipated due date, rather than the birth date, this lag disappears. Frequent ear infections during the first year can interfere with the ability to hear sounds, a fact that can account for a delay in speech. For some infants who are late in talking, the delay is simply a result of a focus on other emerging and energy-consuming skills, such as walking.

When concerns arise, medical specialists will refer a child to a speech–language professional, who uses special spoken tests to evaluate the child. There are many activities that can be recommended to help children with speech or language delays get back on track.

SHARING STORIES

Long before speaking their first word, babies participate in making and sharing stories with others. In animated interactions with attentive, responsive partners, babies participate in a reciprocal chain of gestures, movements, and expressions that evoke a shared story, a narrative. In a sympathetic exchange of meaning, adults will often put into words what they see expressed nonverbally by young infants, saying, for example, "Oh! And now you have something else to tell me. Keep talking! I am listening!" Infants listen with rapt attention, as their gestures, feelings, and intentions are represented in words.

It is within this context—the creation of a shared narrative or story—that expressive language begins and infants' first speech emerges. Oral narrative, the telling of stories, is one of the most powerful forms of human communication (Bruner, 2002), a representation of experience. To represent, that is, to *re-present,* is to participate in an active, dynamic transmittal of ideas and purposes through actions, gestures, and expressions. In oral narratives, the story is recounted through both words and actions, using inflections and cadences of voice along with expressive gestures and movements. Infants easily join in. Narratives are framed by a beginning, middle, and end. Researchers (Gratier & Trevarthen, 2013) point out that infants' early communications with adults fit this structural frame and follow the same energetic trajectory of successful storytelling, with an orientation, a precipitous event, a restoration, and an end. These shared narratives begin soon after birth and develop throughout infancy, described by Gratier and Trevarthen (2013) as follows:

> By the second month after birth, infants respond with eloquent vocal sounds and expressions of interest and joy, and it is clear that they themselves are motivated to make a contribution. Adults in turn start to listen attentively to what young infants have to say, taking them seriously. They formulate questions to which they expect answers, they tell them about the people and events that surround them. . . . Parents' speech is compelling for infants because it is organized in narrative time and . . . infants are called to participate, as they "wish to do," in the mutual "telling" of the story of their special connectedness to each other in a common meaning filled world. (pp. 129–130)

Engaged exchanges between infant and caregiver, marked by a "communicative musicality" (Gratier & Trevarthen, 2013, p. 123), can be compared to a performance by a group of jazz musicians, whose wordless composition does not tell about events but still moves the listener and conveys meaning through an improvisational interplay. Infants communicate in much the same way, in an improvisational composition of communicative gestures, expressions, movements, and eventually, words.

CHAPTER 8

How Babies Move

An infant's own movements, the development of these movements and every detail of this development are a constant source of joy to him.
—Emmi Pikler (1994, p. 12)

HOW BABIES SUCCEED in just a few years to master a vast array of motor skills—with fluency, balance, grace, and precision—is truly amazing. In quest of moving from place to place and manipulating with dexterity, they follow meandering, imprecise, and often unpredictable paths, with detours and reversals, and stumbles and falls. They pause midstream, veer off course, and vary speeds, charting a spontaneous path through their play space in a twisting, curling, winding, back-and-forth path of fits and starts (Adolph et al., 2012). They stop and stoop abruptly to examine nearby objects, turn to watch passersby, and load their arms with cargo that suddenly shifts their center of gravity, making balance more precarious. They average 43 bouts of carrying per hour (Karasik, Adolph, Tamis-LeMonda, & Zuckerman, 2012). In 1 hour, the average toddler takes 2,368 steps, travels the length of 7.7 football fields, and falls 17 times. This adds up, within 6 hours of playtime, to an average of 14,000 steps daily, 100 falls, and travel that spans 46 football fields. By the first birthday, they spend more than half of each hour of play examining objects with eyes and hands (Karasik, Tamis-LeMonda, & Adolph, 2011), and by 2 months of age, they have executed more than 2.5 million eye movements (Johnson, Amso, & Slemmer, 2003).

In this period of expansive motor development, patterns emerge in both fine and large motor skills. Muscles develop and strengthen in a top-down order, from head to toe. Development also proceeds in a proximal (close in) to distal (outward) direction, with shoulders developing before arms, arms before hands, and hands before fingers. Within the first year, a basic set of motor functions develops. This includes eye–head control, manual skills, and locomotion. As efficiencies improve, each earlier action system serves as a foundation for the action systems that follow. Key to the development of all action systems is postural control, maintaining fluidity and balance, in order to look steadily, to reach accurately, and to sit, stand, and walk confidently.

More motor achievements happen during infancy than during the rest of the lifespan (Adolph & Berger, 2015). This chapter focuses on this phenomenon, with a close look at how motor action develops prenatally and throughout infancy. Rounding out the chapter is a discussion of common misconceptions about motor development, the influence of childrearing and experience on movement patterns, and differences that emerge across cultural contexts.

FETAL MOVEMENT

Patterns of movement are first detected in utero. The fetus is equipped to experience a rich world of stimulation, and the womb abounds with stimulation. The sensory systems of the fetus are in place and working well prior to birth. A fetus hears, feels, tastes, and sees during the last 2 months of gestation. The sounds are many—the mother's voice, heartbeat, breathing, and digestion, as well as the sounds of speech and music outside the mother's body yet audible inside the uterus (Gerhardt, Pierson, & Abrams, 1996).

In this rich sensory environment, fetuses begin to move once they have muscles to activate the body parts and primitive neural circuits to activate the muscles. Spontaneous arches and curls appear about 5–6 weeks following conception (Luchinger, Hadders-Algra, Colette, & de Vries, 2008). A few weeks later, isolated movements of the extremities are seen, as fetuses startle and writhe in slow movements of arms, legs, neck, and trunk. Fetuses use fingers and hands to explore the uterine wall, the umbilical cord, the face, and other parts of the body. With a strong kick of the legs, a fetus can somersault through the amniotic fluid. Fetuses turn the head to the side and nod the head up and down, open and close the jaw, and show breathing movements (de Vries, Visser, & Prechtl, 1985). They can be seen yawning, sucking thumb or fingers, and swallowing amniotic fluid (de Vries, Visser, & Prechtl, 1982). By 18 weeks, face muscles come into play, and fetuses wrinkle the forehead, move lips and tongue, and raise eyebrows (Nilsson & Hamberger, 1990). By the end of gestation, all the muscles that make facial expressions are fully formed (Adolph & Berger, 2015). Once the eyelids open, around 23 weeks gestation, fetuses open and close the eyes (Moore & Persaud, 1993).

Fetal movements result from spontaneous neural activity and patterned muscle activity, and help shape the central nervous system (Hepper, 2003). Movement of all fetal body parts facilitates building bones, joints, muscles, and skin. The lungs develop through the breathing of amniotic fluid. Fetal movements also foreshadow those that will be seen in the newborn. For example, fetuses open the mouth in anticipation of, not in reaction to, their hand arriving at the mouth, perceiving on some level that the hand is approaching the mouth rather than another part of the face (Adolph & Robinson, 2013). The fetal movements of swallowing amniotic fluid may serve to regulate water balance, in addition to stimulating neural circuits. Other movements, such as the leg thrust, are key to navigating the fetus into a head-down position in readiness for birth. Ironically, just as mothers tend to first sense movement in the womb, often called "quickening," the fetal movements of arms, hands, and limbs begin to decline (de Vries & Hopkins, 2005), a function of the growth of the fetus making the uterine space more confining.

NEWBORN MOVEMENTS

Newborns are busy moving. Spontaneous movements may occur in isolation (e.g., a single leg kick) or in rhythmic bouts (such as repetitive flexing and extending of the legs). Infants are in frequent motion, a few hundred movements per hour, with some movements coordinated across the two sides of the body. Simultaneous kicks with both legs are more frequent than step-like alternation of leg movements or single-leg kicks.

Infants' movements may seem without purpose, yet researchers point out that aside from facilitating the working of the infants' developing nervous and muscular systems, infants harness these spontaneous movement patterns for intentional action. An often-referenced example comes from prominent child development researcher and theorist Jean Piaget. He described how infants just a few months old, lying on their back and with a tether connecting one leg to an overhead mobile, would soon notice how their spontaneous movements caused the mobile to sway into action (Piaget, 1952). With repeated movements, infants figure out which limb causes the action, and rather than move their whole bodies to see the mobile jiggle, they move just the tethered leg.

Infants' spontaneous movements provide practice, therefore, for many intentional actions that accomplish specific goals, such as grasping, manipulating parts, and using objects as tools (in the Piaget example, using the leg as a tool). Spontaneous movements, when harnessed for intentional actions, also support the development of movement patterns, including lateral movement, differentiating and moving one side of the body in isolation from the other.

Newborns experience the pull of gravity for the first time, no longer suspended within the fluids of the womb. They yield to the force of gravity as they lie relaxed against the chest of a parent. Something as simple as lifting the head puts new demands on their muscles. Newborns lack the muscle strength to hold the head up, but with experience their neck muscles adapt and strengthen, permitting them to push against gravity.

A newborn lying stomach down and resting on the parent's chest can rotate the head from side to side, but cannot lift the head for more than a brief moment (Bly, 1994). After 9 months in the womb, with the muscles of the chest and abdomen flexed inward in a "C" shape, these muscles begin to extend. This takes time. When placed on the parent's chest, the infant can begin to extend these muscles with support. This time spent tummy on tummy gives the newborn a supple, secure surface on which to extend abdomen muscles and contract back muscles, in preparation for pushing up (Figure 8.1). A tummy-down carrying position does this as well.

With such short bursts of extending and contracting muscles while lying prone, infants 2–3 weeks of age begin to lift the chin momentarily from the surface on which they lie prone, belly down, and by 5–10 weeks,

FIGURE 8.1. Extending and Contracting Muscles, Tummy on Tummy

Photograph by Justin Takeoka

they can lift their head and chest completely. By 3 months, they can hold the head steady while lying on a caregiver's chest (Figure 8.1), when held upright on a caregiver's lap, and when lying prone, pushing up with their arms (Bly, 1994), as shown in Figure 8.2. Motor control of the head gives infants a greater degree of control over what they can bring into view, as they are no longer captive to looking at only those objects that fall within their line of sight (Adolph & Joh, 2011).

FIGURE 8.2. Pushing up with Arms and Torso

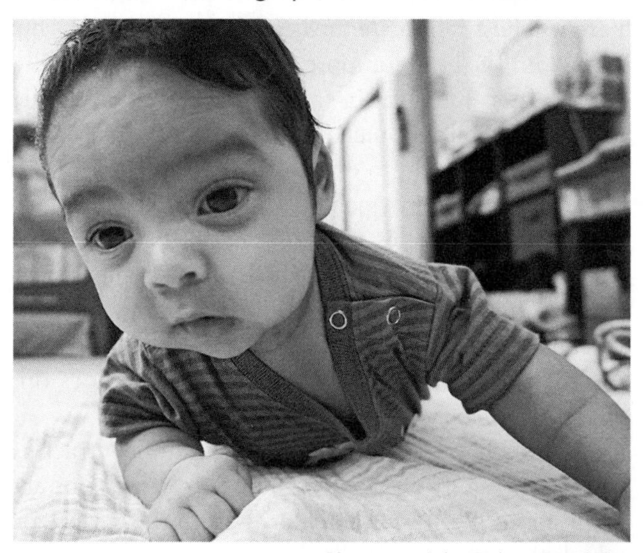

Photograph by Robert M. Chiles

REACHING AND GRASPING

In their early weeks and months, infants spontaneously flap arms, bang arms and hands against surfaces, bend and straighten elbows, rotate hands in circles, and wave fingers, in what might look to the casual observer like random motions. However, these movements coordinate the muscles of the shoulder and elbow to enable *pre-reaching.* Pre-reaching is the term scientists use to describe how infants, as young as 5–9 days old, extend the arm, with open hand, toward an object without making contact (Figure 8.3).

Goal-directed reaching first appears at around 4 months in infants lying on their backs, at around 5 months in infants lying prone and propped on one arm (Figure 8.4), and at around 6–8 months in infants sitting with legs outstretched in a "V" (Bly, 1994; Rochat, 1992). Indeed, if supported around the torso, infants can reach for desired objects at an earlier age, between 12 and 18 weeks, but these early reaches usually result in contact with the object, rather than capturing the object in the hand (Adolph & Joh, 2011).

Infants who have figured out how to get themselves into a seated position on their own can sit with confidence and balance and reach and grasp desired objects with ease. They can lean forward with a reach and still maintain balance, they can use right and left hands interchangeably, and they can reach, grasp, and retrieve objects that lie further away from their center of gravity (Rochat & Goubet, 1995).

FIGURE 8.3. Pre-Reaching

Photograph by Robert M. Chiles

FIGURE 8.4. Goal-Directed Reaching

Photograph by Robert M. Chiles

Successfully grasping and holding onto an object requires finger dexterity. Figure 8.5 charts the course of prehension, infants' ability to grasp objects with increasing precision. Initially, the infant's grasp is a whole-hand grasp, involving the fingers together in opposition to the palm of the hand (see Figure 8.6). This is called the palmar grasp. Once the muscles of the fingers strengthen, they begin to work together in opposition to the thumb, in what is called the partial pincer grasp, which gives way, with experience, to the neat pincer, with the index finger in opposition to the thumb.

FIGURE 8.6. Palmar Grasp Transforms with Practice into Neat Pincer Grasp

Initially, infants finger their own hands in play, in preparation for beginning to bat at objects using a whole arm movement, at around 4 months of age. Infants' repeated efforts at goal-directed reaching give them experience in anticipating the size, shape, and density of the target object. By 5 months of age, infants begin to change their grip to match the size and shape of target objects (Newell, Scully, McDonald & Baillargeon, 1989). By 7.5 months, they anticipate the size

FIGURE 8.5. Stages of Prehension

Stage	Hand Position	Average Age (months)	Range (months)
Bats at object	Arm and whole hand, fingers together	5.6	4–8
Palmar grasp	Fingers together in opposition to palm	6.8	5–9
Partial pincer	Fingers together in opposition to thumb	7.4	6–10
Neat pincer	Index finger in opposition to thumb	8.9	7–12

and shape of an object and "preform" (Adolph & Joh, 2011, p. 72) the orientation of the hand to align with the orientation of the target (Witherington, 2005). By 9 months, the grasp has reached a point of refinement such that infants will open the hand in anticipation of an object's size and shape, and as the hand gets closer to the target, will start closing it in anticipation of matching the object's size and shape (von Hofsten & Ronnqvist, 1988). By 9–10 months, infants' grasp is so precise that they can pick up a small object between index finger and thumb. By their first birthday, their accuracy in reaching and grasping has developed to the point that they can catch a moving object (von Hof, van der Kamp, Caljouw, & Savelsbergh, 2005).

ROLLING AND SITTING

Babies experiment with their body position and orientation long before they are able to move from place to place on their own. They pivot in circles on their stomachs, they move arms and legs in alternate patterns as if swimming in place, and they rock back and forth on hands and knees. These movements are a prelude to rolling over and sitting up, actions that expand infants' access to the surrounding world.

Rolling Over

When lying supine on a flat surface, infants not yet rolling over will reach out in the direction of objects, stretching the entire body. This effort may move them onto their side, and with a small pivot of the pelvis, they may stay on their side. By tensing their full body, they can maintain this side posture, before relaxing to return to either stomach or back. With repeated experience rotating from back to side, their balance improves and they can stay on their side for long periods, absorbed in seeing their surroundings from a whole new perspective.

Infants first turn from back to side as early as 2 months of age and as late as 7 months of age, with 4.4 months the average age of onset (Bayley, 1969). Not until some 8 weeks later, on average, do most infants rotate completely from back to stomach, with the average age for this move being 6.4 months, within a range that spans 4–10 months of age (Figure 8.7). Once babies accomplish rotating from back to stomach, they often choose to spend increasing amounts of time lying on their stomachs, a position from which they can readily extend the muscles of the torso and stretch and reach toward objects (Figure 8.8).

FIGURE 8.7. Development of Large Movement

Motor Skill	Average Age (months)	Range (months)
Rotating on own from back to side	4.4	2–7
Rotating on own from back to stomach	6.4	4–10
Moving forward by crawling (on abdomen), creeping (on hands and knees or hands and feet), or hitching (on buttocks)	7.1	5–11
Raising self to sitting position	8.3	6–11
Pulling to standing using rail or furniture	8.6	6–12
Moving intentionally from standing by furniture to sitting, without falling	9.6	7–14
Cruising, walking with support	9.6	7–12
Walking without support	11.7	9–17

Source: Bayley (1969)

FIGURE 8.8. Rolling Over Takes Practice and Time

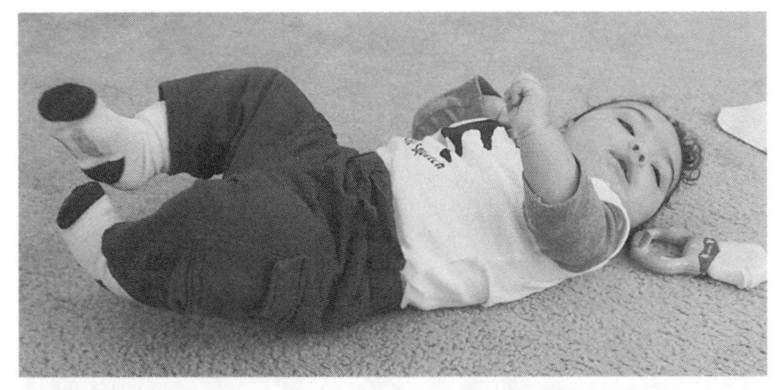

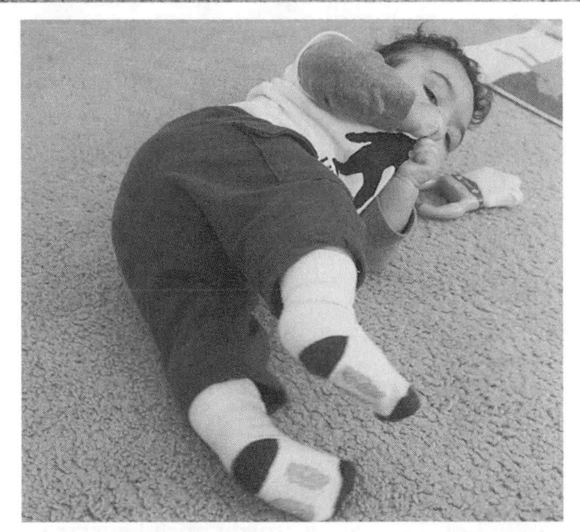

Photographs by Robert M. Chiles

Sitting Up

Rotating from back to stomach is a prelude to getting into a seated position and eventually to standing. Infants often rotate onto their side and then prop themselves in a half-seated posture. In time, they get into a fully seated posture. They might also move directly into standing by beginning on hands and knees and shifting the weight onto one foot and then the other, before pulling to standing against a solid surface.

The course of infants' learning to get into a sitting posture independently illustrates the top-down directional trend of infants' motor development. For postural support, infants must first gain control over the segments of their spine, from head to hips. If placed in a sitting position before the neck and back muscles are strong, infants may be able to stay upright with support, but without support their heads loll, their backs crumple, and they topple chest to knees (Adolph & Berger, 2015). Once muscle systems of the neck, shoulders, back, and sides have strengthened and organized, babies will pull themselves into a seated posture, with no strain on the spine.

With this in mind, pediatrician Emmi Pikler (1988) and infant specialist Magda Gerber (2002) argue for giving babies freedom to move and to get into sitting or standing positions on their own. They discourage propping babies in a sitting position, even with support. Indeed, babies who get into a seated position on their own quickly adjust their balance and learn to sit with confidence and ease, relaxed yet still moving freely. Getting into a seated position independently occurs within the range of 6–11 months, and on average at 8.3 months (Bayley, 1969).

Once babies learn how to get into and out of a seated posture, they explore variations of sitting, including kneeling and sitting on their heels. Eventually, infants acquire sufficient trunk and hip control to turn and reach while sitting. Between 7 and 9 months, they learn to push themselves backward from hands and knees into a sitting position and to move smoothly from sitting to kneeling or crawling, without a belly flop in between (Adolph & Berger, 2015).

LOCOMOTION

Locomotion, being able to move oneself from place to place, leads to one of the most heralded moments in infancy, walking. Many parents see walking as the point of transition from infancy to toddlerhood. Infant care is often described across three developmental phases—young infants, mobile infants, and older infants (Mangione, Lally, & Signer, 1990), with the ability to locomote marking the point of transition from one phase to the next.

Crawling and Creeping

"Mobility does not wait for walking" (Adolph & Robinson, 2013, p. 407). Infants demonstrate *many* variations of locomotion prior to the advent of walking. A baby might shuffle along the floor while seated, hitching one leg to propel forward, or might roll like a log from place to place, or propel forward on the back by moving arms and legs like a crab (Adolph & Joh, 2011). About half of infants who eventually crawl start out by crawling on their bellies, with the abdomen resting on the floor at some point during each crawling cycle, using arms to propel forward. Some drag their abdomens along the floor in what many call a "combat crawl." Others adopt an "inchworm" style, alternately pushing the chest up off the floor and then flopping down to propel themselves forward, or a "swim" style, using all four limbs simultaneously. Some infants skip the belly crawl phase entirely and move directly to crawling on hands and knees, or on hands and feet.

It is tempting to think that becoming mobile is simply an orderly sequence of one predictable action followed by the next. However, with respect to modes of locomotion, every infant develops a unique trajectory of moving from place to place. Some variation of a pre-walking mode for moving from place to place emerges around 7–8 months of age on average, with an expected range of onset between 5 and 11 months (Adolph & Joh, 2011; Bayley, 1969). The onset age is as variable as the mode of movement. The more experience babies have with their chosen mode of moving from place to place, the faster they move and the larger their movement patterns. Similarly, experience in actions leading up to these pre-walking skills, such as pivoting and rocking on hands and knees, facilitates improvement. Whatever the preferred mode, crawling opens access to a whole new world of objects and places.

Standing and Cruising

As arms and legs strengthen, infants begin to pull to a standing position by gripping the edge of a table or a low rung or knob. As they tire, they drop down. On average, babies pull to standing at around 8.3 months of age, and within a range of 6–12 months (Bayley, 1969). Pulling to standing tends to coincide with getting into a seated position independently. Often infants approach the task from a kneeling position, hold onto a sturdy edge to pull themselves up, and use arms and torso muscles to remain upright and steady (Figure 8.9). Babies who have just figured out how to pull to standing may, after a moment or two, begin to fuss before toppling to the floor. The average age for intentionally dropping from standing to sitting is 9.6 months, as compared to 8.3 months for pulling up, reflecting about a 5-week period (Bayley, 1969) during which leg muscles strengthen.

FIGURE 8.9. Pulling to Standing

As infants build sufficient leg strength, they can hold part of their weight on one leg while stepping from side to side. By holding onto a sturdy raised surface (e.g., a table edge), they begin to step sideways while upright and supported, a form of locomotion called *cruising*. Cruising occurs simultaneously with being able to walk forward with the support of a caregiver's hands. Infants who have begun to cruise to move around vacillate between crawling and cruising to get from place to place. Closely spaced, low, sturdy supports, such as a row of sturdy cardboard boxes, stacked cushions, or rungs, provide mobile infants with ways to rise to new heights and to gain access to a new level of objects to explore.

Walking

Walking independently with ease and confidence takes time. The average age for walking without support is

11.7 months, within a range of 9–17 months (Bayley, 1969). Babies take their first unsupported steps forward with legs and arms spread wide for balance and toes angled out. Their step width is often larger than their step length. They move slowly, with arms raised and flexed at the elbow. It takes several years of practice for their gait to become the smooth, swaying gait used throughout life (Smitsman & Corbetta, 2010), but in the first 4–6 months of independent walking, they make rapid improvements, toes directed forward, steps getting longer, feet moving closer together, and arms and legs relaxing and swinging reciprocally (Adolph & Robinson, 2013).

FREEDOM TO MOVE

Considering the wide range of movements that babies master in the first year, it is worth reflecting on the ways in which their caregivers make decisions that impact whether and how much opportunity infants have to move freely. Commercially marketed devices for carrying, bouncing, rocking, sleeping, sitting, supporting, and feeding babies abound. Each confines infants in some way and, most likely, restricts their movement in ways that may interfere with their biological expectation for moving in increasingly more complex ways. Indeed, it makes sense to buckle infants into car seats when they are being transported in automobiles; however, there is little to recommend most other types of infant seats, including those marketed to promote sleep, exercise, upright posture, or play. Most such devices inherently restrict infants' freedom to move during a period of development when such movement is critical.

Far from being a smooth trajectory, infant motor development is most accurately described as two steps forward and one step back (Adolph & Berger, 2006) or, in another sense, as "a series of overlapping waves" (Adolph & Robinson, 2015, p. 126). For example, to work on a motor skill that is just emerging, like walking, infants have to relinquish their accuracy, efficiency, and stability with a posture they have mastered, like crawling. Following weeks of steady practice with crawling, infants improve to a point where it is virtually effortless. Around the same time, they master pulling up to standing and start the difficult task of figuring out how to walk. Determined to master walking, they make many unsteady attempts to walk unsupported, some successful and some not. Improvement is slow, so when new walkers tire or when they absolutely need to get somewhere fast, they revert to crawling. Existing motor strategies recede, while new strategies rise, and there is an ebb and flow between the two. From these overlapping waves emerges an enriched repertoire of movements.

Experience matters when it comes to infants' moving with balance and ease. The more they activate a motor pathway, the likelier it is to be stabilized as a component of the motor system. Once a move is mastered, it requires less energy as the infant moves gracefully and effortlessly.

As infants move, their eyes gather information that helps them gauge the direction and speed of movement, building a sense of "self in motion" (Adolph & Joh, 2011, p. 75). Experience brings behavioral flexibility, meaning infants avoid steep inclines or drop-offs and adapt their body sway in relation to their base of support. Experience with motor skills also increases opportunities to discover new means for achieving end goals, such as climbing onto surfaces to reach a desired object or moving furnishings to create a desired path.

MOVEMENT: THE SOCIAL AND CULTURAL CONTEXT

Infants develop motor skills within a social and cultural context. Infants' first walking steps often come at the urging of caregivers' wide-open arms and expectant expressions. Social interaction influences and in many ways shapes the course of infant motor development. Those who care for infants determine where infants find themselves, what positions they are in, when, and for how long. How they are carried or held, what parts of the surrounding environment they have access to, what clothing they wear, and what nourishment they receive—these are all decisions made by caregivers that impact infants' experiences.

Beyond Universals

It is easy to assume that events like learning to sit, stand, reach, grasp, and walk are universal, that is, that they emerge within the same age range in *all* infants, irrespective of where infants are born or what caregiving they experience. Historically, researchers have assumed that there is an invariant sequence of motor development during infancy (Adolph, Karasik, & Tamis-LeMonda, 2010), and they have charted the average age and the average range of onset for this sequence of motor stages. The Bayley Scales of Infant Development (2006) is a widely used assessment that rates infants' progress along a sequence of stages. When this tool was created, it was assumed by researchers that motor development was biologically based and free of cultural influence. This assumption influenced the Bayley scoring system, which was based on three consecutive failures in the sequence of motor skills, despite the possibility that an infant might succeed on a later skill yet fail on a skill earlier in the sequence.

A growing body of research with children from regions around the world demonstrates the fallacy of assuming that motor development proceeds in an invariant sequence. Crawling provides a good example of this. Crawling is described in the Bayley scales (2006) as a major milestone that comes before walking. In some areas of the world, otherwise healthy infants who show normal development may never crawl and may proceed directly to walking, or they may crawl, but at a later age (Adolph et al., 2010).

Influence of Caregiving Practices

Caregiving practices profoundly influence what motor skills are acquired, the age of onset of motor skills, the sequence in which children acquire motor skills, and with what degree of proficiency they perform these activities. Where infants spend their time matters when it comes to building motor skills. In many parts of the world, babies spend a considerable amount of time in infant seats or strollers. In other areas, it is commonplace for babies to be wrapped and worn close to the mother's body as she works (Adolph & Robinson, 2015).

Formal training with motor skills also influences what, when, and how motor skills are acquired. In Jamaica, for example, it is not uncommon for caregivers to formally exercise infants in sitting and walking (Hopkins & Westra, 1988). Infants who receive such formal training exhibit better head control at 1 month of age, and they sit and walk at earlier ages compared with other infants not receiving this exercise. In many cultures in Africa, the Caribbean, and India, highly ritualized massage, stretching, and suspension accompany infants' baths, with limbs passively limbered and extended; skin rubbed with oil; bodies suspended, shaken, and tossed; arms and legs methodically crossed in a series of exercises; and body parts molded and tapped (Adolph et al., 2010). Such formal rituals and exercises stimulate development of particular skills, such as being held upright and supported around the waist to facilitate sitting, or being held up and supported in a standing position and bounced vigorously to facilitate walking. The frequency of such formal exercise predicts the ages at which infants sit or walk. The effects are limited to the exercised skill, be it sitting or walking, for example, with no effect on crawling. Indeed, with the appropriate environmental supports and social encouragements, infants can be trained to perform an amazing array of activities.

More common, across many cultures, is informal training, which happens simply by virtue of how infants are held, carried, bathed, dressed, fed, or positioned for sleep, with consequences for the development of motor skills such as reaching, sitting, crawling, and walking. For example, infants may spend the majority of the day lying down or may spend most of the day in sitting or standing positions. They may ride in a sling on the hip or back of an active caregiver and experience a high degree of visual, vestibular, and proprioceptive stimulation while being carried. These infants must continually adjust their posture to the caregiver's movements.

Just as concerted exercise impacts the onset of targeted motor skills, restricted practice delays their onset. Since the 1930s, researchers have recorded tragic delays in motor development for infants who were raised under impoverished conditions and deprived of opportunities to move freely, to engage in social contact, or to play with toys.

Cross-cultural research on infants' motor development challenges common assumptions about what skills infants should develop and when. It prompts reflection as to whether young infants are inherently fragile, or not; or whether one position is more natural than another, for example, lying horizontally on belly or back, or being held and carried upright. It also builds understanding about the wide age range for the onset of typical motor skills and the tremendous variability across cultures as to how and when these skills emerge.

Movement patterns, influenced by external and internal experiences, are exquisitely entwined with how we feel and how we think. Infants navigate an idiosyncratic path as they chart their course of motor development. If there is a single truth that emerges from research on infant motor development, it is that infants, prepared by their biology to master an extensive array of motor skills, do so in ways that are variable (Adolph et al., 2010) and highly dependent on the experiences they receive in care.

CHAPTER 9

How Babies Learn About People

It is a joy to be hidden but disaster not to be found.
—D. W. Winnicott (1965, p. 187)

The greatest thing we can do is to help someone know that they are loved and capable of loving. —Fred Rogers (2002)

THERE IS an affectionate companionship in infants' play. Infants actively look for friends in adventure, discovery, and invention. As noted in Chapter 7, in doing so, infants join caregivers in creating and sharing roles and meanings (Bruner, 2002; Trevarthen, 2005, 2015), enjoying the vitality of the shared experience in an affectionate exchange of signs and expressions. The most salient shared narratives occur within playful, everyday encounters with others, primarily those who provide their care.

Through play, infants learn about people, objects, and events. This chapter introduces the role of play within mammalian development and explores how infants play to engage with and learn about people—the social world. The discussion of the role of play in infants' lives continues in Chapter 10, which explores how infants' play facilitates their learning about objects—the physical world. Chapter 11 widens the lens to examine how infants play as a way to learn the roles, rituals, and expectations of the family, community, and culture—the sociocultural world of traditions, values, and beliefs.

THE BIOLOGICAL URGE TO PLAY

Infants are biologically prepared to play as a way to learn about their surroundings, and in many ways, to assure connection to others and a sense of belonging to a social group, both of which are key to ensuring survival. Babies are born seeking others who will love and care for them unconditionally and play with them joyfully (Trevarthen, 2005). As with all mammals, human babies biologically expect to be met by others who will nourish them, keep them warm and protected, and enjoy their companionship in play (Panksepp, 2013). Kittens play, baby monkeys play, puppies play, newborn mice play, and young human infants play. This common factor provides scientists a way to study the biological tie that connects social play to health, well-being, and optimal development. By investigating the emotional context of play in animals and the impact of play on the developing brain and nervous system, including epigenetic factors, scientists gain insight into the essential bond of social connection that is revealed in human play.

Studies that focus on animals' play and on the corresponding emotions that emerge during their play show that playful behavior is rooted in ancient structures that lie deep within the brain (Panksepp, 2013). These ancient brain structures form prenatally, function well at birth, and give rise to the urge to play, which is evident even in newborns. Whether in humans, rats, or chickens, these ancient brain structures look and function essentially the same. This is due to the fact that we share many of the same genes that store a wealth of information needed for growth and development. Some genes encode information that ensures that newborns, still largely dependent on others for survival, can connect with and solicit what they need from those who will ensure their care.

For human infants, social connection with caregivers is essential for survival. This social connection, when experienced by the baby, is processed through the epigenome, described in Chapter 2. The epigenome extracts information stored in specific genes and renders it useful for development. Caring social experiences with others *must* occur for the action encoded in these genes to be expressed (Panksepp, 2013). If caring social experiences do *not* occur, the action encoded in these genes is *not* expressed. As a result, babies' innate biological capacity to actively solicit such care from caregivers is disrupted. With social connection, there is a reciprocal experience of "I see you and you see me; I feel you and you feel me; and I trust in you and you trust in me," which fosters ongoing development. Without social connection, optimal biological development is put at risk.

In the emotion-rich interactive play of baby rats and baby chicks, neuroscientists have identified three neural systems that are activated with social connection (Davis & Panksepp, 2018). These three neural systems are active and undergoing rapid development in human infants. Each neural system triggers a distinct emotion. One system processes experiences of love, care, and affection, what Davis and Panksepp (2018) describe as the *CARE/Nurturance* system. This neural system enables bonds of love and care to form with others, for example, bonds of attachment, as described in Chapter 4. The CARE/Nurturance system works closely with the brain system that gives rise to the urge to play with others, described as the *PLAY/Joy* system. These two systems, CARE/Nurturance and PLAY/Joy, are interconnected, and they both have ties to a third system, described as the *PANIC/Sadness* system. The PANIC/Sadness system generates feelings of distress or panic upon separation from those on whom babies rely for companionship and care, a phenomenon described in Chapter 4.

These three interconnected brain systems influence each other. The PANIC/Sadness system is activated when there is a disruption in the CARE/Nurturance system. Activation of the PANIC/Sadness system and disruption of the CARE/Nurturance system interrupt smooth functioning of the PLAY/Joy system. Together, these three brain systems facilitate friendships, activate concern and empathy for others, and provide infants with a means to learn about people, a key function of social play. Affectionate care gives rise to play with those who provide care. Social play facilitates reflection, inhibition, and empathy toward others. When play or care is disrupted, infants feel distress, grief, sadness, or panic, and, in most instances, they cry, an appeal for care. In play with others, infants learn about people, and this in turn opens the door to learning about the surrounding world.

YOUNG INFANTS' SOCIAL PLAY

As explored in Chapter 7, infants are highly aware of others and actively communicate with others. Using their social engagement system (described in Chapter 4), they connect intentionally and emotionally with others and build bonds of attachment and friendships through affectionate play (Reddy, 2008). Initially, their social play involves person-to-person play. Within a few months, their social play incorporates objects, becoming person-person-object play.

Interactive Games with People

As psychologist Jeree Pawl explains, "Infants are born looking for us" (2006, p. 1). Newborns expect, by virtue of their biology, to be met by gentle, happy, playful people. In most instances, the care infants experience complies with this expectation. The adults who care for babies respond intuitively in playful, happy, and gentle ways. Researchers Papousek and Papousek (1989) describe this as *intuitive parenting*. Neither baby nor caregiver has to learn such behavior. Irrespective of where in the world they live, parents intuitively talk to their infants in a playful, lyrical voice, called infant-directed speech (see Chapter 7).

Caregivers also intuitively and playfully sing or chant lullabies and nursery rhymes, which, as described in Chapter 7, have a rhythm and cadence synchronized to heart rate and breathing (Trevarthen, 1999; Trevarthen & Malloch, 2002). Trevarthen uses the term *sympathy* to describe these patterns. What he means is that caring adults appear to be biologically attuned to interact with young infants in an intimate, affectionate, playful, sympathetic manner. The Greek word from which the English word *sympathy* is derived means moving and feeling with. Social play between infant and caregiver is marked by moments of sympathetic engagement, in which infant and caregiver synchronously reflect shapes of movement and sound, communicating a vitality of interaction—a playful state of mind—described by Trevarthen (2004) as:

> We intuitively get into other person's minds by actively sensing the impulses to action in their brains that enable them to move the way they do. . . . The baby is already trying to find "common sense" with the other person by "reading their mind." (p. 14)

Drawing on deep-seated systems within their brains, young infants engage with companions in person-to-person games. These take the form of simple back-and-forth, coordinated, and coherent exchanges. Over the first months, these playful exchanges become more elaborate and generate shared vitality, ranging from exuberance and pleasure to sadness and dismay. Nursery rhymes are an example of exuberant, shared, person-to-person play. An infant will follow closely the recitation of a nursery rhyme. She will watch intently, listen, and actively respond with corresponding expressions, vocalizations, and movements (Figure 9.1).

Nursery rhymes and person-to-person infant games like peek-a-boo are found across cultures and capture infants' rapt attention. Over time, games become more elaborate, with the infant assuming a specific role and the adult another, in a predictable sequence of phrases, gestures, and movements.

Interactive Games with Objects

By around 3 months of age, infants' curiosity leads to an expanded view of the world that is supported by their developing sensory and motor systems. They begin to move in more vigorous and complex ways. As they begin to roll, crawl, pull to standing, and walk, they experience a new environment, physically and socially. They begin to follow the shift in gaze of another person who is looking at or acting on an object (Muir & Hains, 1999), piquing their curiosity to explore

A CLOSER LOOK

Infant in Sync with Song

Figure 9.1 captures person-to-person play between 11-week-old Riley and her grandmother. Riley gazes intently at her grandmother as she begins to sing the first phrase of a familiar song, *Hickory Dickory Dock* (Figure 9.1A). Riley sees and feels Grandmother's fingers walking rhythmically up her chest as she sings the second phrase, "The mouse ran up the clock." Riley begins to move her arms upward and purses her lips (Figure 9.1B). As if preparing to join in, Riley sticks out her tongue, and vocalizes "ah-ah" (Figure 9.1C). Grandmother and Riley exuberantly reach the climax with wide-open mouths as Grandmother sings, "The clock struck one, and down he run" (Figure 9.1D). As the last refrain drops, Grandma's fingers walk down Riley's chest, and Riley scrunches shoulders and kicks in anticipation of the familiar ending (Figure 9.1E), after which she relaxes, perhaps waiting to do it again (Figure 9.1F).

FIGURE 9.1. Eleven-Week-Old Riley in Sync with Song

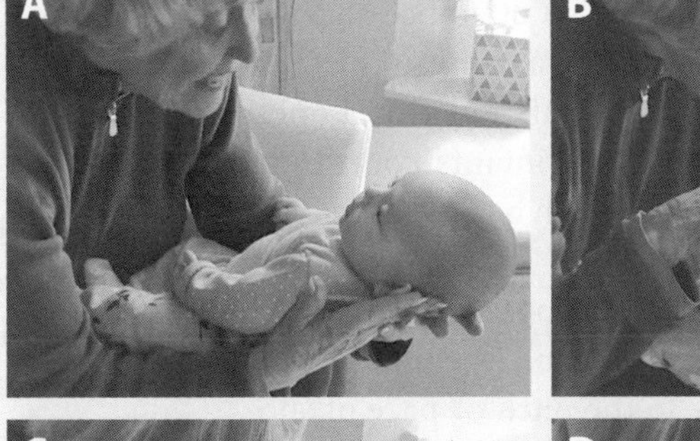

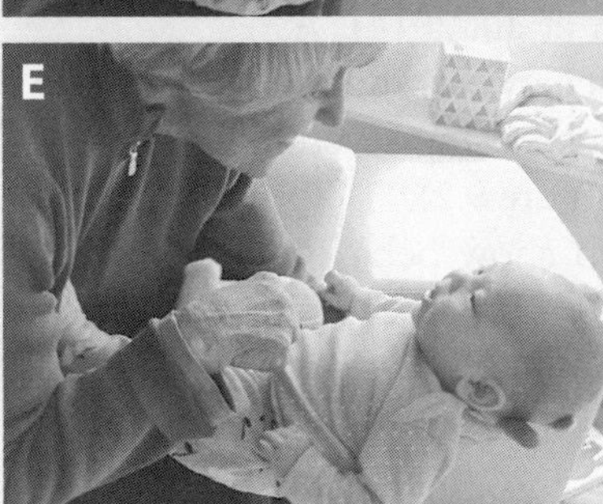

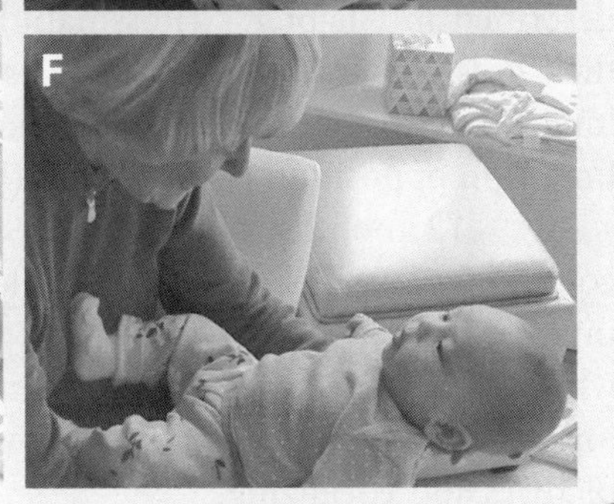

new things. Once they figure out how to control their hand muscles and reliably grasp objects, they begin to engage with others in games with objects. They offer and receive objects in a game of give and take, adding more complexity to person-to-person games and graduating to person-person-object games (Trevarthen & Hubley, 1978). Person-person-object games are simple and short, taking only a few seconds. For example, the baby might extend her arm with a toy for the other to take, and then reach with open hand in anticipation of it being returned.

Infants by 3 months of age enjoy shared reading of picture books. With a rise in the pitch of the caregiver's voice, the baby shifts his gaze from the book to the caregiver's face, and when the caregiver naturally pauses at the end of a phrase, the infant shifts his gaze to the caregiver again. Babies listen closely for changes in the reader's voice, as noted in Chapter 7, gathering statistics on the sounds and patterns of language. For example, the adult will intuitively place a relevant word at the peak of a phrase and will pause the flow of speech to create a desired effect. Infants being read to will look at the reader's face at the peak of an utterance and will also look at the reader's face during a pause at the close of an utterance (Rossmanith, Costall, Reichelt, Lopez, & Reddy, 2014). By 5–6 months, infants coordinate their attention fluidly back and forth between the caregiver's face and the book.

During a book reading, babies appear to feel within their bodies the structure, shape, and dynamics of the spoken words. In response to the pitch or pace of spoken lines, babies lift or reach with their arms, brighten their eyes, or widen the mouth in a smile, cues of engagement, as described in Chapter 4 (refer to Figure 4.2). These convey active participation with the narrative. At key points, the adult points at something on the page, or changes the pitch of the voice, or pauses, and the baby responds with a change in expression or gesture, using the repertoire of communication skills described in Chapter 7 (Rossmanith et al., 2014). As their grasp begins to develop, babies enjoy turning the hinged pages of sturdy cardboard books, using several fingers in opposition to the thumb (Figure 9.2).

By 9–12 months, infants begin to show behavior commonly associated with conventional book reading interactions, like sitting still and intently listening while looking at the pictures, turning the page, opening flaps to discover what lies below, and pointing to pictures and vocalizing.

FIGURE 9.2. Six-Month-Old Jackson Turns Pages of a Book

Photograph by Robert M. Chiles

A CLOSER LOOK

Participating in Shared Book Reading

Consider what cues this father relays to his baby to share the story in a book, and consider as well what signs the baby uses to actively participate in the story:

> Six-month-old Jackson sits on his father's lap. They are sharing a book about animals. On the left page is a photo of a swarm of bees. On the right page is a photo of a snake. "Here's a swarm of bees!" says the father, looking at the bees. As he curves his hand, touching his fingertips together, he says, "And the bees go, bzzzzzz, bzzzz." He watches Jackson, who, still looking at the page, reaches to touch the picture of the snake. Seeing this, his father moves his hand up and down in waves and says with declining tone of voice, "And the snake says, SSSSSSSsssssssssnake." Jackson looks up at his father's mouth and then at his eyes, begins to smile, and as he returns his gaze to the book, broadens his smile.

Person-to-person and person-person-object games stand in marked contrast to electronic infant toys programmed to play tunes or to simulate human actions. Electronic or digital toys initially excite a baby's interest, yet they lack the social context, that is, the creative, inventive, interpersonal interaction inherent in person-to-person or person-person-object games that take place within the social context. As described in Chapter 7 with respect to language acquisition, for infants, the social context is critical when it comes to making sense of people.

FIGURE 9.3. Six-Month-Old Jackson Laughs at His Trick

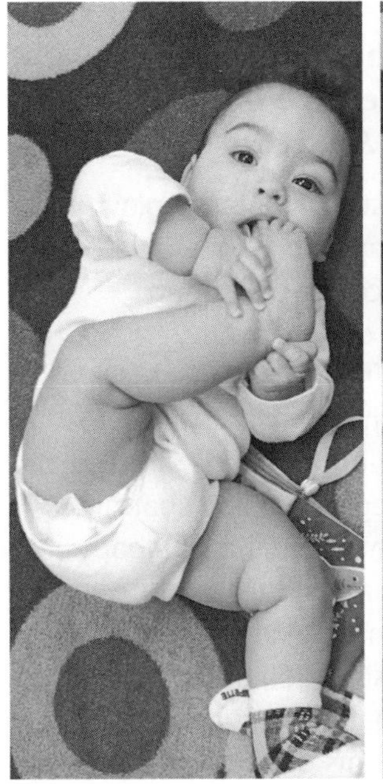

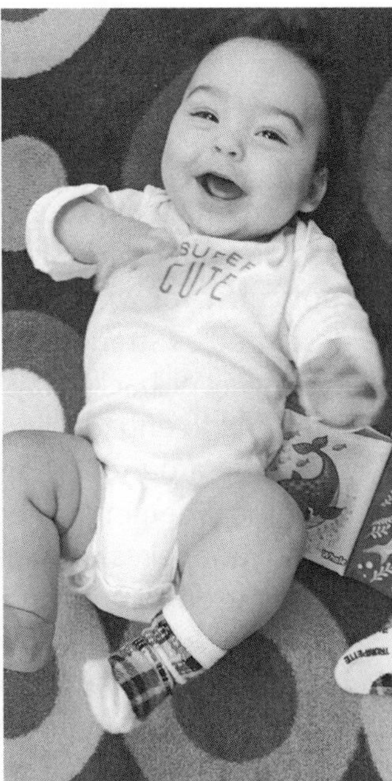

Photographs by Robert M. Chiles

Humor and Affection

Infants are aware of the funny side of everyday events in their lives and show smiles, laughter, and teasing even before they can speak. Researcher Vasudevi Reddy (2008) found that mothers of typically developing infants as young as 8 months of age report being able to distinguish genuine laughs from fake or artificial laughs and even describe an in-between kind of laughter in the category of forced or polite laughter. An infant's first laugh emerges from a smile, around 3 or 4 months of age (Darwin, 1877). These occur within face-to-face social engagements, in moments of "chatting" with other people.

Laughter in infants can be thought of as palpable joy. Shared laughter often accompanies an infant's delight in accomplishment, as illustrated in the photo sequence depicted in Figure 9.3, where 6-month-old Jackson laughs at his new trick, sticking his bare foot in his mouth. Not unlike adults who laugh at slapstick comedy, infants laugh in response to a variety of events, such as exaggerated, odd, or abrupt acts. Many studies of infants provide examples of babies laughing at visual and auditory slapstick, like funny noises, with rising pitch and abrupt ending, or people speaking in a squeaky voice or making funny faces. What delights infants is the suddenness of action and a degree of ambiguity in anticipating actions, as occurs in a game of peek-a-boo, chase, or tickling. As they age, infants begin to clown in a deliberate effort to make others laugh. By 8 months of age, infants might manipulate a favorite object in a way that causes others to laugh. For example, an infant might accidentally step on a rubber toy that emits a squeak, an accidental event, but then, seeing others laugh at this surprising event, might repeat the act deliberately, delighting in sharing his antic with others. Reddy (2008) describes such play as joking, in essence, playing with each other's thoughts, feelings, or actions, but doing so nonverbally.

As infants near the end of the first year, a form of "teasing" can be seen in their play—a playful, joyful form of teasing, rather than teasing that bullies or controls in the guise of humor. Infants tease by provoking or disrupting an action in an unexpected way. For example, in the midst of playful engagement, an infant might offer and then quickly withdraw an object, all the while watching the other person intently, or a smiling infant might pull away quickly, as the caregiver approaches to kiss her cheek (Reddy, 2008).

Teasing can also be seen in moments of playful noncompliance, as when an infant might reach out as if to touch something that the caregiver has forbidden the infant to touch, and, with eyes glued on the caregiver, do it again and again, reaching and withdrawing, with a playful laugh, even as the caregiver admonishes, "No." Teasing in this way can be seen at 9–10 months and becomes more frequent at 11–12 months (Reddy, 2008). Such teasing on the part of infants is done playfully and in a way that invigorates the play, resulting in a new way of relating in play and a new level of intimacy and companionship.

Teasing, joking, and sharing humor with others show up in the second half of the first year, signs that

A CLOSER LOOK

Missing the Joke: New Perspective on Stranger Anxiety

Trevarthen (2004) suggests that infants' playful teasing with familiar companions may be a root cause for what has commonly been described as stranger anxiety, when infants look away or back away from a stranger's attempts to engage. Such behavior often shows up around 7–12 months of age, around the time when infants begin to enjoy sharing humor and jokes with familiar adults. If a baby who is used to enjoying a playful, joking exchange with a companion attempts this same interaction with a stranger, the stranger may be puzzled by the baby's actions and respond in a way that seems out of sync to the baby. Confused by the stranger's odd response to his "joke," the baby disengages. Trevarthen describes this as "a kind of mockery that distresses the infant" (p. 16). Stranger anxiety, from this perspective, may be better explained as "an anxiety of seeming foolish with a person who can't comprehend" (p. 18).

babies are becoming aware of themselves as seen through the eyes of others. Reddy (2008) suggests that glimpses of this can be seen in babies as young as 2.5 months of age: for example, a baby, in the midst of a playful interaction with a caregiver, might draw her hands to her face, partially covering it, look away briefly, and then look back, with a smile of coyness or bashfulness.

Play with Peers

Infants show interest in interacting with peers as early as 10 months of age. When they meet for the first time in a toy-stocked playroom, infants play with the toys, as one would expect, but they also smile, vocalize, and imitate each other (Eckerman & Rheingold, 1974). To imitate, children must recognize the actions of the other as being the same as their own. A shake of a head in response to another's shake of the head is a simple act of imitation, and such simple acts evolve into simple, playful, spontaneous games.

In these spontaneous games, each infant has a role to play, with the infants repeating their roles, even alternating turns with one another. For example, two toddlers playfully walk in a line, one following the other. The leader spontaneously draws both arms back, and the one behind does the same. Upon reaching the wall, they turn around, and the follower becomes the leader, thrusts arms back, and is imitated, in turn, by the follower. Through imitation, toddlers experience shared behavior and, most likely, shared feelings, nurturing the roots of empathy and building strategies that are key to forming and maintaining friendships.

OLDER INFANTS' SOCIAL PLAY

In the second year of infancy, pretend play blossoms. In studies of infants' pretend play (Haight & Miller, 1993), infants 12–14 months of age engage in 0.06 minutes per hour of pretend play. By 24 months of age, this figure rises steeply to 3.3 minutes, and by 48 months, to 12.4 minutes. During infancy, pretend play centers largely on infants performing pretend actions themselves, such as pretending to talk on the phone, bathe a baby doll (Figure 9.4), or sleep on a blanket placed on the floor. In time, they incorporate other children or

FIGURE 9.4. Early Pretend Play with Objects

Photograph by Jillian Rich

adults into their pretend play, for example, a toddler pretending to feed another toddler with a bowl and spoon or talking to an adult on a pretend phone. As infants enter their second year, imitation and pretend play draw together pairs or groups of toddlers, and friendships develop.

Games of Imitation and Pretense

Between 16 and 32 months, toddlers spend increasingly more time in imitative games with others. Some games are simply short episodes of imitation, with one toddler performing an action, such as splashing in a puddle, and another toddler spontaneously repeating it (Figure 9.5). Others sometimes join, until a group of toddlers is repeating the same action to reproduce the same effect. Some games involve one infant starting an action and another infant completing it: for example, one infant bites down on the edge of a plastic plate while another infant watches, then, in turn, the watching infant removes the plastic plate from the first infant's mouth. A third type of game is more reciprocal, an example being one toddler throwing a ball and a second toddler retrieving it, followed by a reversal of the roles (Goldman & Ross, 1978; Ross, 1982). Of note, researchers have discovered that toddlers will tend to imitate their peers more readily than they will imitate adults (Ross, Vickar, & Perlman, 2010). Imitative games emerge spontaneously among toddlers, with no involvement from adults, clear evidence that toddlers are motivated to engage with peers.

In social play, infants cultivate self-regulation, cooperation, and understanding of expected behavior. Older infants enjoy replaying, through pretend play, the everyday routines, rituals, roles, and rules that they

A CLOSER LOOK

The Goal of the Game Is Being Together

The goal of toddler-peer games is to play together, a fact made clear in a study in which toddlers aged 15–24 months were successfully taught a set of complementary games with toys that they could play with peers (Ross, 1982). They were then brought together with peers, with the game toys present. The children rarely played the games they were taught. Instead, they invented new games and played together. For example, they rolled a ball between them, put a block on and off a child's chest, played peek-a-boo behind a mirror, or put blocks into a pail. The uniqueness and variety of the games invented highlights toddlers' sensitivity to others' goals and motivations.

FIGURE 9.5. Imitating the Actions of the Other: Splashing in a Puddle in Interactive Play

FIGURE 9.6. Pretend Play with Realistic Objects

Photograph by Jillian Rich

experience. In pretend play, infants use actions or objects to represent an experience or event. In the early stage of pretend play, infants use the real object in the game of pretense, for example, pretending to cook with realistic toy pots and spoons (Figure 9.6). Later pretend play shows less reliance on realistic objects and more creativity in adapting generic objects to substitute for the real object, such as using a wooden block for a phone or a cardboard box for a doll's bed (Figure 9.7).

FIGURE 9.7. Pretend Play with Generic Objects

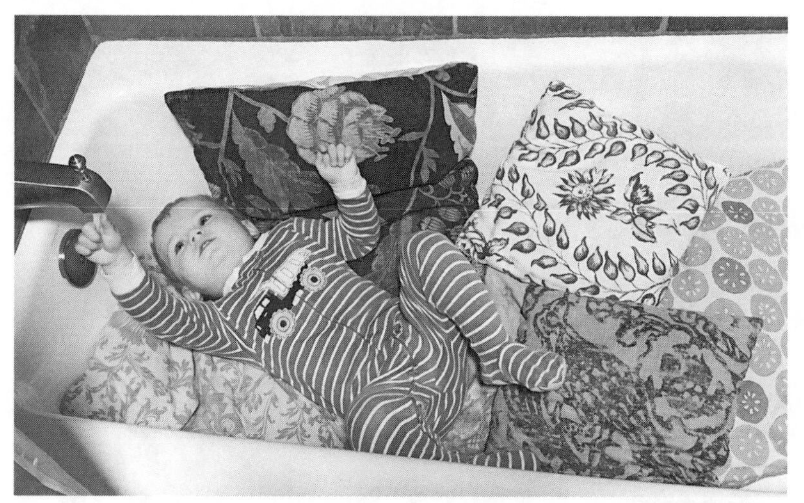

Photograph by Sean Madigan

Rough-and-Tumble Play

Not unlike older children, toddlers enjoy "rough-and-tumble" play. A key part of rough-and-tumble play is a signaling system (Bruner, 1972). Some signals are invitations to play. Other signals denote a role, like a scary face. And still other signals change the meaning of actions, such that the actions are not interpreted too seriously. For example, sensitivity to social signals allows one partner to make a scary face yet know that the play partner will not feel fear. In rough-and-tumble play, play partners may pretend to hit, push, and chase each other, but only as long as both partners are enjoying themselves and are keeping the aggression in check. Aggressive behavior during rough-and-tumble play is interpreted by a playmate as a playful encounter, not a threat. Once the play ceases to be fun, the play breaks down.

As such, rough-and-tumble play helps young children learn to modulate their behavior with respect to others. Children are sensitive to the motivations and feelings of their play partners, and they adapt their own motivations and feelings in response (Gray, 2013).

SOCIAL RESPONSIVENESS: WHEN CONCERNS ARISE

A lack of social responsiveness, often accompanied by a delay in speech and restricted or repetitive behavior, may suggest that a child is at risk for developing autism (Rogers, Dawson, & Vismara, 2012). For example, an infant may show reduced social-communicative behavior by failing to orient to social stimuli, or to respond to one's name, or to make eye contact, or to show positive affect, or to use communicative gestures. Each of these symptoms has the effect of interrupting typical patterns of play and interaction between caregiver and infant, with the added consequence of making it hard for infants to regulate emotional states. When such combinations of symptoms are detected and treated early in development, through what is described as *early intervention,* the outcome is very promising.

Some of the most effective interventions make use of play and interpersonal relationships, and focus on enhancing the caregiver's ability to respond to infant cues (Greenspan & Wieder, 2006; Rogers, Dawson, et al., 2012). Effective treatment is aimed at helping caregivers increase sensitivity to infants' cues, which can be very hard to read in infants who struggle with reciprocal interactions and self-regulation.

During a therapeutic intervention with a toddler diagnosed with autism, therapist and parent observe as the toddler plays, watching to see what captures the child's interest. The therapist or parent looks for a point of entry to engage with the toddler's play, doing so with respect for the child's play and with sufficient animation to excite the toddler's participation. They might offer an idea to the play, watching to assess the child's response and basing what they do next on what they see or hear in the child's response. In this way, the play becomes gradually more interactive and reciprocal, a communicative dance that the toddler and caregiver engage in together, gradually at first, but with increasing opportunities for the child to experience a social-communicative exchange that emerges from spontaneous play and interaction.

Research suggests that, with early intervention, symptoms of autism can be greatly reduced, and perhaps even reversed, in some infants and toddlers (Green et al., 2017; Rogers, Estes, et al., 2012). Studies are under way to identify infants at risk of autism as early as 6–12 months of age, when the brain is undergoing major development and before core autism symptoms emerge (Rogers et al., 2014). Such intervention gives the child regular experiences with positive social connection and communication—experiences that influence the development of social and language brain circuitry and put expected development back on track.

According to researchers, the emergence of core autism symptoms may be a complex interaction between genes and the social environment. If so, therapeutic intervention that impacts social connections with others may have a potent effect on how genes are expressed, that is, whether symptoms emerge or not. Social interactions have reward value, and if there is dysfunction or a delay in the development of neural circuits that process the reward value of social contact, a child may resist social contact. By intervening to repair this dysfunction or delay early in infancy, before the full onset of core symptoms, it may be possible to reverse this trend and return social connection and companionship to the child.

Infants and toddlers have a biological expectation to be in companionship with others and to engage in social play. Coming to know a few close others builds a strong foundation for coming to know a more extended social group, making way for friendships among peers and giving infants and toddlers entrée to the social world.

CHAPTER 10

How Babies Learn About Objects

The intention on the part of children to produce questions and search for answers is the genesis of creativity. —Carlina Rinaldi (2006, p. 22)

AT BIRTH, infants behold the object world for the first time. They see, smell, hear, taste, and touch objects, just as they do people. However, they experience objects in a different way than they experience people. People read their cues and respond to these cues, be it a look, a reach, or a cry. Objects do not. How babies perceive objects and make sense of them is the subject of this chapter. It describes some of what is known about how infants gather information about objects, how they act on objects and explore them, and how they use them to accomplish tasks and to build concepts that prepare them to be mathematicians, engineers, scientists, and artists.

WHAT INFANTS KNOW ABOUT OBJECTS

It may seem surprising, but at a very young age infants show proclivity to notice categories, number, causal relations, and core ideas about how things fill, fit in, and move in space (Rochat, 2001). In clever experiments, scientists have been able to tap what newborns and young infants are aware of with respect to the world of objects and events. Long before infants can reach to grasp and manipulate objects in play, they gaze intently at objects and events and appear to be gathering key pieces of information and relating one thing to another, building concepts and ideas.

Although infants' visual system is not fully mature until the latter part of the first year, and their muscle systems are still immature in the first months, infants are able to perceive and track objects with their eyes. They can distinguish basic physical features like depth, pattern, contrast, movement, and shape, even when these features vary in subtle ways (Rochat, 2001). These findings lead scientists to conclude that infants are born paying close attention to physical objects, and that they are figuring out what objects are like and what they can be expected to do.

Infants pay close attention, but they are more than spectators. They respond to what they see using core principles of physical knowledge, like number, causality, and categorization. For example, young infants, who have not yet learned to reach and grasp, appear to know that objects occupy space, that objects cannot be in two places at the same time, and that objects exist continuously in space if moving along a visible trajectory (Rochat, 2001).

Spatial Relations: Out of Sight, Not Out of Mind

For decades, scientists have explored the question "In the mind of the infant, do objects continue to exist when they move out of sight?" Jean Piaget (1952) theorized that for young infants, out of sight meant out of mind. Piaget argued that not until near the end of the first year are infants aware that an object continues to exist when it moves out of sight. He called this *object permanence.* In his classic experiment, he hid an object from view while the young infant was watching. Infants younger than about 8.5 months of age ceased looking for the object once it had gone out of sight. Piaget argued that this was proof that infants do not develop a concept of objects until late in their first year.

To test this theory, researchers use an experiment that is based on the fact that people look significantly longer at events that violate what they expect to see. In one version of this experiment (Baillargeon, Spelke, & Wasserman, 1985), 5-month-old infants view a scene in which a visible screen rotates through a space that the infant has seen occupied by a solid object. According to the laws of physics, when the screen hits the solid object, it should cease rotating. The question is, "Will infants know this?"

The experiment begins with the infant watching a screen rotate 180 degrees backward to lie flat on a table surface. Over and over, the infant watches as the researcher rotates the screen through the 180-degree trajectory. Then the infant is shown the same rotating screen again, but this time the infant also sees a solid object sitting behind the screen, in the path of the rotating screen. As would be expected by the laws of physics, the infant sees the screen stop moving when it hits the solid object. However, in the next trial, out of the infant's view, the researcher removes the object from behind the screen. The infant sees the screen rotate all the way back. The infants in this study, some as young as 3.5 months of age, look longer at this improbable event. Their surprise in seeing the screen pass the point where it should have stopped is interpreted to mean that they expect that the solid object still exists, even though it is out of sight. Contrary to what was once thought, from infants' perspective, out of sight is *not* out of mind.

A CLOSER LOOK

Response to a Surprising Event

Reflect on what you might do if you were watching a magician perform a magic trick that leaves you thinking, "That was impossible!" If given a chance to watch the magician repeat the trick, what would you do? Most likely, you would watch intently throughout the whole trick, trying to figure out what was going on. Babies do the same thing. They look at something intently if it seems surprising or unexpected. Knowing this, scientists have devised clever experiments to begin to get a glimpse of what might be going on in the mind of the infant. If an infant stares longer at one event than at another, scientists interpret this to mean that the infant is able to distinguish between one event and the other, with one event expected and the other event unexpected. It is this pattern of behavior that researchers use to measure what infants appear to know about objects and how they behave.

Causality and Spatial Relations

Movement is significant for the newborn (Nugent et al., 2007). Newborns attend more to objects that move than to static objects. They use this information about how objects move to make predictions about how objects move in space and fill space. In an experiment, 4-month-olds watch as an upright Y-shaped object drops behind a screen onto a stage (Rochat, 2001). The infant sees this repeatedly. Then the screen is lowered, and the infant sees one of two scenes. One is a probable scene, and the other is not. In the probable scene, the infant sees the object oriented upright, that is, the way you would expect it to land as it dropped behind the screen, assuming the law of gravity. In the improbable scene, the object is upside down, the reverse of what you would expect to see, assuming the law of gravity. In the improbable scene, out of view of the infant, a researcher inverted the object prior to raising the screen. The infants look longer at the improbable scene, one that defies what they expect to see. At a very young age, infants not only track how things move in space but they also make predictions about how they should behave.

In the first few months, as infants watch objects in motion, they detect what it is that sets the object in motion. In the prior experiment, gravity set the object in motion. In other situations, one object collides with another. Researchers test infants' understanding of the latter in an experiment in which infants are familiarized with a scene in which a red ball moves linearly behind a screen followed by a white ball emerging from the other side of the screen. Would the infants see the movement of the white ball as being caused by the red ball colliding with the white ball, even though they had not witnessed such a collision? After the infant has been familiarized with the original scene, researchers remove the screen and the infant views two different events. In the first event, the red ball moves close to the stationary white ball but does not touch it. The red ball stops and then, following a short delay, the white ball begins to move. In the second event, the red ball moves and hits the white ball, which then starts to move. Infants as young as 2 months old look longer at the first event than they do at the second event, the difference being that the first is a non-causal event and the second is a causal event (Rochat, 2001). Infants expect a predictable cause-and-effect relationship with respect to how these balls move. At a very young age, infants are aware of how things fit in and move in space and show an awareness of the concept of causality, how one thing causes another.

Number

To find out whether infants have any knowledge about number, scientists use an experimental design called *habituation,* in which they observe what infants attend to and then record the elapsed time before the infants tire and look away. Once the infants look away, researchers exchange the familiar object or event with a novel one that has a feature distinguishing it from the first. They watch to see if the infants attend to this "new and different" object or event. If they do, researchers interpret this as evidence that infants can detect the distinguishing feature.

Using habituation, researchers have found evidence that newborns can discriminate small number sets (Antell & Keating, 1983). When placed in front of a screen showing a set of two black dots, newborns attend to the two dots and then tire and look away, but they resume looking when the screen shifts to show three black dots. When shown four dots versus six dots, the newborns appear to detect no difference. Researchers interpret this to mean that newborns are sensitive to the magnitude of small sets of number. They refer to this sensitivity to number as *numerosity.* By 6 months of age, infants are able to distinguish between four dots and six (Xu & Spelke, 2000), showing improved numerosity.

In experiments to detect whether infants could detect differences in sets of larger numbers—5 versus 10—McCrink and Wynn (2004) showed 9-month-old babies a series of short clips. The first depicted 5 rectangular objects that moved behind a screen and out of view. This was followed by a clip of 5 more objects that moved behind the screen and out of view. After this sequence, the screen was lowered, and the babies saw the 10 objects. The researchers showed the babies the clips a second time, but when the screen was lowered in this second series, the babies saw 5 objects. The babies looked at this result longer, showing surprise and concern at the outcome—a screen with 5 objects as opposed to 10.

Such research provides evidence that infants possess a rudimentary concept of number long before the onset

A CLOSER LOOK

Detecting Number Has Survival Value

The ability to perceive an array of objects and to quantify them is not unique to humans. Indeed, other mammals and birds discriminate among objects based on some degree of quantification. Rochat (2001) recounts the story of a farmer trying to rid his fields of a troublesome crow. The crow's nest was in a tower, but each time the farmer entered the tower to find the crow, the crow flew away and returned only after the farmer exited the tower. The farmer attempted to trick the crow by having two men enter, one remain inside, and the other exit. However, the crow returned only after both men exited. The farmer repeated the experiment with three and then four men, yet the result was the same. Only when five men entered, and four exited, did the crow lose track and return to the tower. For smaller numbers, the crow could quantify, but not for larger numbers.

To notice and track small sets of objects, sounds, or actions, infants appear to be relying on ancient brain structures, ones shared with other animals. These structures enable creatures in the wild to quickly discriminate small amounts from large amounts, an advantage when it comes to foraging for food or detecting danger from approaching groups. Studies with animals suggest that specialized neurons in the brain are used to keep track of approximate quantities greater than three, that is, the more objects presented, the more neurons fire (Roitman, Brannon, & Platt, 2007). In parallel fashion, when a baby looks at a large array of objects, specialized neurons show a high degree of electrical activity, giving a neural representation of a large array of objects rather than a small array.

of verbal counting. Researchers have tracked changes in the activity in babies' brains as they attend to small sets of objects that differ in number. The electrical pattern in the brain changes in response to each incremental change in the number of objects being viewed by the baby (Izard, Dehaene-Lambertz, & Dehaene, 2008). Researchers note that the location of this electrical activity in the brain is the same brain region that lights up when adults do mathematics, suggesting that infants' awareness of numerosity may form the basis for more complex mathematics (Xu & Garcia, 2008).

Infants' ability to detect differences between small sets of objects appear to prepare them to begin to approximate number, that is, to make predictions about larger sets. For example, babies who have not yet reached their first birthday will look longer at a scene, as if surprised and concerned with the outcome, when they see the researcher pull a sample of mostly white balls from a clear plastic box that they have seen to contain mostly red balls (Xu & Garcia, 2008). This remarkable ability has led some scientists to describe infants as "taking statistics" on what they notice and then referencing this knowledge as they predict likely events (Gopnik, 2009; Gopnik, Meltzoff, & Kuhl, 1999; Saffran, Aslin, & Newport, 1996).

With small collections of objects, infants appear to be keeping precise track of number, suggesting that they may be prepared to notice when one object is added to another and when one object is taken away, essentially, the roots of addition and subtraction. Using a habituation research design, Wynn (1992) showed that babies as young as 5 months old can notice and track when an object has been added and when an object has been taken away.

How babies perform such mathematical feats at such a young age is a fascinating area of research, one that still holds many unanswered questions. Recent studies suggest that babies may have two distinct systems in the brain that support this knowledge of number (Hyde & Spelke, 2011), one that prepares infants to precisely track very small sets of objects and another that prepares them to compare large sets in an approximate way.

By their toddler years, infants map language to their understanding of relationships of quantity and number, with phrases like "all gone" and "more." They begin to count aloud, having memorized a short number sequence, but initially their counting is inaccurate. Not until post-infancy do they begin to map the appropriate number word to the perceived collection of objects.

A CLOSER LOOK

Five-Month-Olds Add and Subtract

Researcher Karen Wynn (1992) conducted a study in which she showed 5-month-old infants a doll, then covered the doll with a screen so that the infant could no longer see the doll. The infant watched as the researcher placed another doll behind the screen. This created a 1 + 1 situation—one doll and then another doll. A second group of infants saw a different scene—two dolls, followed by a screen that covered them from view. These infants watched as one doll was removed from behind the screen. This created a 2 – 1 situation—two dolls minus one doll. In both situations, before the screen was removed, the researchers either added or removed a doll, out of view of the watchful infant. Could infants this age detect "probable" from "improbable"? The infants watched as the screen was removed, showing either one doll or two dolls. Infants tended to look longer at the incorrect (surprising and improbable) event than they did at the correct (predictable and unsurprising) outcome.

By around 36 months of age, they quickly and accurately recognize the quantity in a small set of two or three objects without counting, a skill called *subitizing* (Clements, 2004).

Categorizing and Classifying

Aside from number, young infants perceive and group objects that look alike, sound alike, or share similar attributes. This is a rudimentary from of categorization. Researchers have shown that 3-month-olds discriminate between basic categories of animals, such as horses and cats (Eimas & Quinn, 1994). For example, infants are shown photos of different kinds of horses until they begin to habituate and look away. They are then shown either a novel horse or a cat. Infants regain visual attention to a cat, but not to a novel horse. This suggests that infants perceive the physical features of the cat as being categorically distinct. As illustrated in Figure 10.1, infants in their second and third year can draw on their understanding of number and classifica-

FIGURE 10.1. Toddler Uses Number, Classification, and Spatial Relations in Play

tion to group objects in categories and to identify how they are the same or different in fairly complex ways.

Infants also appear to categorize how objects move. Psychologists attach lights to the joints of people and then film them in the dark. To the adult eye, if the person is stationery, the lights appear as a random array of lights. However, when the person moves, the moving lights in the darkness are immediately perceived as someone walking or performing other meaningful actions, that is, as a dynamic, meaningful whole and not a random array of moving lights. When this experiment is done with infants 3 and 5 months of age, the result is the same as with adults. The infants habituate to a light display of a moving person, but return their gaze to the lights when the light display changes to that of an unfamiliar creature, such as a spider (Rochat, 2001).

Infants categorize objects and people but, as explored in Chapter 7, they also categorize language sounds, as they knit together the code of spoken language. They do not yet fully understand the language code, nor do they understand how one object relates functionally to another, but this ability to detect attributes that are the same, similar, or distinct is worthy of respect when it comes to appreciating what infants know and how they know it.

HOW INFANTS BUILD CONCEPTS IN PLAY

Infants use their ability to detect number, to notice causality, to track spatial relations, and to categorize as a means of building their understanding of the object world and in so doing, building concepts that are foundational to mathematics and science. They observe systematically, as spectators, but they also manipulate and transform objects in order to figure them out (Rochat, 2001). For infants, once they master prehension (see Chapter 8), an object in the hand becomes an object under study.

As they mouth, peer at, finger, turn, and squeeze objects, infants investigate inherent physical properties. For example, they discover that a ball is round, blue, and soft by observing systematically and by actively manipulating, that is, shaking, dangling, dropping, banging, and throwing. Through these actions, they build understanding of size, shape, color, smell, taste, and sound; and they organize and categorize these physical properties within the neural circuitry of their brains.

Infants also explore how objects relate to each other—how some are the same and some different; or how they move together; or how one changes another; or how one fits inside another or on top of another; or how together they make "two" or make up a set. These are examples of relational knowledge, sometimes referred to as *logicomathematical knowledge*. Logicomathematical knowledge—what we know about relationships among objects—is distinct from *physical knowledge*—what we know about the features that reside within the object itself (Kamii, 2014).

As infants explore objects in play, they inspect what objects are like, gathering information about the physical properties, and they experiment with how one object relates to another, that is, how an object reacts when they act on it. In object play, infants build increasingly more complex concepts of *categorization,* or *classification,* as they detect similarities and differences in physical features and detect patterns in how objects react or relate.

As infants play with objects, they also increase their understanding of the concept of *causality.* For example, shaking a rattle causes a delightful sound and builds a causal relationship—a shake creates a sound. As they play, they build the concept of *spatial relations,* that is, how objects fill, fit in, and move in space; and how they connect, balance, fit in containers, or nest together. They experiment with how objects fall or move with speed, force, and direction.

In play with objects, infants expand on their concept of *number* and explore filling and emptying containers, early experiences in addition and subtraction. Infants also build on their proclivity to hold a mental image of objects once they move out of sight. This is the concept of *representation.* Infants build on their ability to represent when they begin to engage in symbolic or pretend

FIGURE 10.2. Recognizing That an Image Represents a Familiar Object

play, using one object or action to represent another or to recognize a familiar object from a photo or illustration of the object in a sturdy book (Figure 10.2).

As these concepts blossom and grow during infancy, a foundation for mathematics, reading, writing, art, and science develops. The pages that follow provide examples of play materials that support infants in building these concepts across sequential phases of infancy. The first phase, referred to as *young infants,* includes infants from birth to approximately 8 months of age. The second phase, referred to as *mobile infants,* includes infants from about 8 to 18 months of age, and the third phase, referred to as *older infants,* includes infants from about 18 to 36 months of age.

Infants enjoy exploring a wide range of objects—a range that far exceeds those identified and sold as toys. Infants delight in everyday, ordinary objects, like sturdy boxes, bowls, swatches of fabric, tubes, cups, containers, or lids (Maguire-Fong, 2015). When selected with care, these ordinary objects offer infants safe, nontoxic opportunities to learn about the surrounding world. A wide assortment of common household objects can be readily repurposed in service to infants' playful exploration (Figure 10.3).

Infants also relish exploring natural materials, that is, things from the world of nature (Figure 10.4). Natural materials—a smooth, wide tree round; a bumpy dried gourd; a fabric bag filled with herbs; or a basket

FIGURE 10.3. Ordinary Objects for Infant Play

FIGURE 10.4. Natural Materials Offer Infant Play Possibilities

of sturdy vegetables, fresh from the garden—broaden infants' sensory exposure to the sights and smells of nature.

A rich assortment of ordinary objects can be found in kitchen cupboards: for example, storage containers, pots with lids, measuring cups, and short-handled wide-based brushes. Some ordinary objects can be easily assembled as collections, such as a bin full of metal jar lids or a basket of conical plastic cups. When infants can access a collection of ordinary objects of the same type, they can explore the materials in a wide variety of ways. For example, conical cups can be stacked, nested, lined up, or used as containers to hold things. Such collections of ordinary objects can be transformed, arranged, and used to show number, to categorize, to demonstrate causality, to explore spatial relations, and to represent.

Play materials, when accessible to infants, must be safe to use, with no risk of choking or toxic exposure. Any object left in reach of infants who still mouth toys should be absolutely safe and hazard-free. Most infants stop exploring objects with the mouth sometime around the second birthday; however, infants vary greatly in this regard, so a good rule of thumb with infants under 2 years of age is to avoid objects that fit, *along any one dimension,* inside a cardboard tube the size of that used for paper towels or toilet tissue. What to avoid, therefore, would include objects that are sufficiently narrow to fit inside the tube, yet still long enough to protrude from the top of the tube, like a spoon or a pencil. Figure 10.5 provides a sampling of the types of objects to avoid due to small size.

FIGURE 10.5. Objects Small Enough to Present Choking Hazard

Young Infants' Object Play

Infants in the first 3 months, although limited in their ability to grasp objects independently, readily gaze at and begin to extend an arm toward objects that are in their line of sight. They do so with ease while lying on their back. They can turn the head to the side and eventually, turn the torso as well, reaching with the whole body in the direction of a toy that captures their attention. Toys that have height or that rise from the floor surface at a slight angle are within very young infants' line of sight (Figure 10.6). Initially, they simply gaze and then reach, without yet batting at the object. Objects with a bit of height, rather than those that rest flat against the surface of the floor, support this first phase of infant play.

Around 4 months of age, babies begin to bat at objects in an attempt to grasp them. Toys that will not roll or move away when touched, and toys with features that can be easily grasped, work best for these babies. This means avoiding round objects with a smooth surface, like plastic balls. Features that accommodate a baby's developing grasp include handholds, like the leg of a stuffed animal, a handle on a rattle, flaps stitched to the side of a cloth basket, or holes in a flat surface. Object weight is an important feature, as well, because young babies still have limited control of the muscles of the arm. Objects that are resilient to the touch work well, like a tightly woven cotton tea towel that can be propped into a small peak, as shown in Figure 10.6 (Gerber, 2002). Such objects are easily seen by babies lying on the back and have features that support a successful grasp.

FIGURE 10.6. First Toys: Lightweight, Supple Rather Than Rigid, Resilient to the Touch, Easily Seen by an Infant Lying on the Back

FIGURE 10.7. Toys with Features That Invite the Palmar Grasp and Are Easily Held in One Hand

From 4 months on, infants refine their ability to grasp objects. Toys that work for infants using the palmar grasp (see Chapter 8) include objects that are resilient to the touch and that can be easily held in one hand. Figure 10.7 provides examples of such toys, all of which are lightweight and easy to grasp.

After a month or so of practice with the palmar grasp, infants master the more refined partial pincer grasp (see Chapter 8), with several fingers working together in opposition to the thumb. Toy features that work well for infants using the partial pincer grasp are objects with edges easily grasped using fingers and thumb (Figure 10.8). A small basket or box, with edges that invite the fingers and thumb to work together, is an inviting toy, sufficiently lightweight and easy to wave, bang, drop, or fling. Cloth or woven baskets, jar lids, hoops, and metal bracelets are examples of ordinary objects that have edges and handles that invite the partial pincer grasp.

With practice, infants eventually master the neat pincer grasp, when the index finger is separated from the other fingers and works together with the thumb to pick up small items with precision. With a neat pincer grasp, infants can pinch, poke, and investigate small openings and crevices in objects. Therefore, features to look for in selecting toys for this phase include objects with holes, openings, edges, and short handles, all of which invite infants to use the neat pincer grasp, using index finger in opposition to the thumb (see Figure 10.8).

Young Infants and Classification. Infants grow in their ability to classify as they group, sort, categorize, and connect based on their experiences noticing and distinguishing attributes of objects and people. When infants find objects in the play space that have like features that "go together," they build the concept of classification. Objects that are identical prompt infants to

FIGURES 10.8. Toys with Holes, Handles, Edges, Protrusions, or Indentations That Invite the Pincer Grasp

discover common features. When infants explore objects that are similar but distinct in one or more features, they discover differences and similarities. Collections of toys that are similar but slightly different present infants with the challenge of figuring out what features are the same and what features are different (Figure 10.7). Over time, infants begin to categorize physical properties of objects, selecting some objects that share a common feature while bypassing those that do not. A collection of blocks, each the same color and texture, but each a different shape—cubes, spheres, triangles, and rectangles—presents such a challenge, as does a stack of clear round plastic plates next to a stack of opaque round plastic plates, or a basket of swatches of flannel cloth, with each swatch the same color but in a different print design.

FIGURE 10.9. Young Infant Toys That Support Classification and Investigation of Spatial Relations

A CLOSER LOOK

Select Young Infant Toys with Classification in Mind, and Observe the Play

- For an infant not yet rolling over, place three or four play objects within reach while the infant is lying on her back, close enough that she can reach them, but not so close that she encounters them simply by waving her arms.
- Offer two similar but distinct objects, such as metal cups or malleable plastic soap dishes, each a slightly different design, and each easily rotated, mouthed, or fingered (Figure 10.9).
- To facilitate infants' developing grasp, offer play objects that are easily grasped without risk of being pushed away, such as two sturdy cloth napkins, propped into a peak, each a different color or design.
- Provide two identical objects that offer some kind of handhold, such as flaps, handles, or holes (each a feature that facilitates the emerging grasp), and follow with a third object similar but distinct in some feature, like color or pattern.
- Look for play objects that have differing features that can be detected when mouthed, fingered, or looked at, like ribbed canning jar rings, smooth metal bracelets, and a stuffed fabric ring.
- Provide objects that babies can grasp and fully inspect from all angles, some features identical and some similar but distinct, avoiding toys fastened to a structure.

Young infants explore using all the senses, so attention to play materials that enlist all the senses in exploring objects adds to the play possibilities. For example, a collection of washable cloth bags with nontoxic dried herbs puts into an infant's hands the scents of nature. A basket of materials that respond to pressure, such as loofah sponges or short swatches of stretchy fabric, gives infants a proprioceptive experience, as they experience what happens when they apply pressure to an object. A low platform or large floor pillows to crawl onto and over offers opportunity for infants to use their kinesthetic sense to keep themselves in balance as they move over and onto a raised surface.

Young Infants and Causality. Like small scientists, young infants show evidence of acting on an object with their hands and fingers in order to cause some-

A CLOSER LOOK

Select Young Infant Toys with Causality in Mind, and Observe the Play

- Offer easily grasped objects that change appearance when turned over, like a metal cup, a box, or a bowl.
- Provide objects that offer a range of reactions when banged, such as a cloth doll, a metal saucer, and a wooden block.
- Create a selection of rattles, using clear plastic containers with lids, each holding an object that makes a distinct sound when the container is shaken, like fabric swatches, ping pong balls, and wooden rounds cut from a tree branch.

thing interesting to happen. The question "What can I make this do?" seems to be at the heart of such play and gives rise to the concept of causality. Initially the actions infants perform on objects are simple, for example, examining how an object changes as they rotate it in their hands. Toward the end of the 4- to 8-month period, infants increasingly explore objects by banging them, a more complex skill.

Play objects that offer interesting reactions when turned, shaken, or banged support infants in developing the concept of causality (Figure 10.10). The most widely recognized toy in this regard is the commercial rattle, but many everyday objects hold this potential, as well, such as boxes and jars. A feature to consider, when selecting toys that support infants in building the concept of causality, is that the infant should be able to easily see the source of the sound in order to build a connection of causality (Kálló & Balog, 2005). This would be the case with a clear plastic container holding some plastic balls, for example. It would also be true with a simple cardboard box with a lid, as the infant can go in search of the object making the sound by taking off the lid to the box to look inside. When coupled with a collection of safe objects that make distinct sounds, simple containers can produce rich rewards in building the concept of causality.

Young Infants and Spatial Relations. Young infants delight in exploring how objects fill, fit in, and move in space. They repeat simple actions, like dropping toys into a container, dumping them out, and dropping them in again. This gives them a sense of how containers work as tools for holding things. Young infants also explore how things move in space as they drop, shake, fling, flip, twist, push, and pull objects in hand. The transparent object in Figure 10.10 offers opportunity

FIGURE 10.10. Young Infant Toys That Support Exploration of Causality and Spatial Relations

A CLOSER LOOK

Select Young Infant Toys with Spatial Relations in Mind, and Observe the Play

- Offer collections of objects that have curved sides and that have angular sides, for example balls alongside square metal tins, to give experience with line, shape, and the impact of each on how objects move in space.
- Fill a low, wide container with an interesting collection of safe play objects that infants can use to fill and empty the container.
- Provide nesting objects, like boxes or bowls that vary in size and nest, one inside the other.
- For infants who are not yet rolling over, place play objects to the side, and slightly beyond reach of their hands or feet, to facilitate the infants' exploring how to maneuver their bodies to connect with the objects.

for infants to notice how objects move inside a container, as they rotate the container.

Young Infants and Number. By 6 months of age, infants have constructed a simple concept of number, in that they are able to notice differences in small numbers of objects (like "some") and large, approximate quantities (like "lots of"). As infants experience and experiment with objects in hand, they literally "make number," for example, "one" in this hand and "one" in that hand. An ample collection of objects of the same type, such as a dishpan filled with jar lids of various colors or a basket of smooth rocks, all of safe size, provides infants with experiences with one, then another, then another, making one, then two, then three (Figure 10.11).

FIGURE 10.11. Young Infant Makes Number in Play with Objects

A CLOSER LOOK

Select Young Infant Toys with Number in Mind, and Observe the Play

- Provide experiences with one object and then two, by offering a small collection of pairs of objects, easily grasped, picked up, and manipulated freely in one hand.
- Offer collections of identical objects that can be easily grasped and held in one hand and held next to one another, giving opportunities to make one, two, and "a lot."

Mobile Infants' Object Play

Mobile infants, ranging from about 8 to 18 months old, include those crawling, pulling to standing, cruising from place to place while holding on, and beginning to walk. Their mobility provides new opportunities to experience play materials and deepen the emerging concepts of classification, causality, spatial relations, and number. Infants in this period also begin to engage in simple episodes of pretend play, building the concept of symbolic representation.

Mobile Infants and Classification. As they play, infants 8–18 months often go in search of a specific type of object, for example, a blanket to cover a doll, or balls to fill a basket. As they do so, they are spontaneously sorting and classifying by shape, size, color, or function (Figure 10.12). Their passion for filling and emptying containers generates much practice in sorting and classifying.

By their second year, infants begin to collect with intention (Kálló & Balog, 2005). Initially, they might add any object to their collection. In time, they get more particular and go in search of a specific kind of object. Collections of objects that are identical or similar in shape, function, color, or size can inspire a mobile infant to seek out objects that have a specific feature. For example, a young toddler might search for blue vehicles or cardboard tubes. Simple objects—like baskets, boxes, cups, blocks, balls, stuffed toys, figures of people, plastic animals, jar lids, and cloth blankets—lend themselves well to making collections. A yellow basket and a green basket next to a stack of yellow fabric swatches and

FIGURE 10.12. Mobile Infant Builds Classification in Play

A CLOSER LOOK

Select Mobile Infant Toys with Classification in Mind, and Observe the Play

- Offer a variety of containers for filling and emptying, some with handles, some without, some big, some small, some clear, some opaque.
- Match a variety of colored baskets with corresponding swatches of colored fabric.
- Assemble a collection of small dolls alongside a collection of small boxes, sized to correspond to the dolls.
- Offer a dishpan filled with jar or cylinder lids, some plastic, some metal, and in a variety of colors.
- Look for ordinary objects, safe and nontoxic, with distinctive features, some the same, some different.
- Fill a low, wide basket with smooth wooden blocks, two of each shape: for example, cubes, cylinders, and cones.

green fabric swatches might inspire an infant to select one color rather than another to fill the baskets.

Containers are an essential type of toy for mobile infants, as they facilitate the act of collecting. Mobile infants enjoy carrying around containers with their collected items. At first, they collect whichever objects fit in the hand and happen to be in reach. They add one item after the other to an armful of objects or to a basket, and just as readily they drop or dump them out, one by one or all in one fell swoop.

Mobile Infants and Causality. Mobile infants begin to connect objects in terms of action. They delight in how their actions on an object result in a change or a movement in the object. They build the concept of causality as they discover what happens when they set objects upright and then knock them down or when they push a small car and watch it move through space. Objects that offer interesting options for pushing, squeezing, banging, swinging, shaking, fingering, twisting, and throwing delight the mobile infant. Mobile infants approach cause-and-effect toys with the idea, "If I do this, I wonder what will happen." Simple and safe dials, knobs, latches, hinges, and rattles provide experiences with cause and effect, as do simple sound makers and musical instruments. Wooden, metal, or plastic bells, shakers, chimes, xylophones, or cooking utensils offer cause-and-effect discoveries (Figure 10.13). Some objects, like metal lids, make one

FIGURE 10.13. Objects That Support Mobile Infants in Building the Concept of Causality

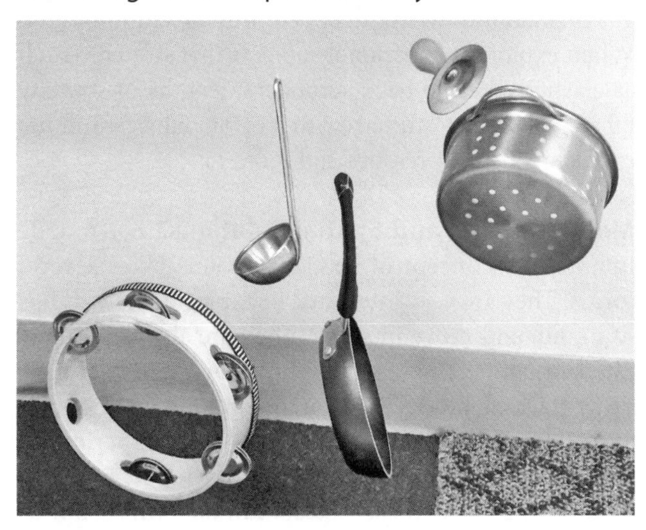

A CLOSER LOOK

Select Mobile Infant Toys with Causality in Mind, and Observe the Play

- Offer play objects that can be shoved about or positioned upright and knocked over, like a tall cylinder or box, or a plastic bowling pin.
- Provide sturdy tubes of various lengths that can be positioned upright and toppled with a push or rolled from place to place.
- Assemble a collection of bowls, cups, or baskets that have various effects when upright or upside down. For example, an upright, curved basket will wobble when the edge is pushed down, but when turned upside down, can be pushed to slide along the floor.
- Offer safe objects with features that twist or turn, such as knobs, dials, and large plastic washers and nuts.
- Offer sound-making toys that allow the infant to see the parts making the sound.

sound when dropped into a tin container, another sound when dropped into a dried gourd, and yet another sound when dropped into a cloth basket. When exploring expandable objects that stretch—such as elasticized cloth back scrubbers, lengths of stretchy fabric, or socks stuffed with cotton fabric—infants experiment with pressure and force.

Mobile Infants and Spatial Relations. For mobile infants, the concept of spatial relations takes several forms. They are very interested in exploring how things fit in, fill, and move in space. They are also very interested in connecting and building, for example, lining up or stacking blocks. It is not uncommon for an infant at the beginning of the 8- to 18-month period to repeatedly pick up an object and then drop it, an investigation into how these objects fall and what sounds they make upon impact.

As crawling improves, infants delight in flinging an object away from them and crawling after it to retrieve it. Such play, which is centered on making things move through space, offers initial experiences with gravity, weight, and velocity. Toward the end of this period, infants' investigation of spatial relations grows more complex, as they explore ways to move objects in space without picking them up (Kálló & Balog, 2005). Balls, small vehicles, and tall plastic bowling pins or bottles invite infants to push them away and retrieve them, or knock them over and try to reposition them upright. Gravity becomes apparent in such simple play—tall, thin objects tip over more readily than short, squat ones. Some objects stay put when knocked over, while others roll away.

FIGURE 10.14. Play Materials That Support Exploration of Spatial Relations in Mobile Infants

A CLOSER LOOK

Select Mobile Infant Toys with Spatial Relations in Mind, and Observe the Play

- Offer large, lightweight objects, such as plastic dishpans or woven baskets that mobile infants can easily lift and rotate overhead.
- Assemble a collection of play vehicles amid a collection of small, sturdy cardboard boxes.
- Offer a wide variety of containers, bags, boxes, and bins for collecting and carrying.
- Create low, wide surfaces for lining up objects and stacking, alongside a basket of stackable objects, like boxes or plates.
- Offer a variety of objects that nest, one inside the other, like bowls, boxes, and cups.
- Provide some objects with angled edges and flat sides, alongside some with curved edges and no flat surfaces, to prompt infants to notice features that facilitate stacking and rolling.

At around 1 year of age, infants add to their desire to collect and pursue a desire to connect. They collect similar objects in arms or in containers and then deposit them in one space and begin to place one object next to another object of similar kind. As they physically connect one object to another, they build something bigger from something smaller (Kálló & Balog, 2005). Sometimes they connect objects by resting one object on top of another, or setting one next to another or inside another (Figure 10.14), for example, three plastic cones stuck together. Midway through the second year, infants stack and line up flat-sided objects on the floor or on low raised surfaces, building length, line, height, and pattern.

Mobile Infants and Number. Mobile infants are busy building a sense of quantity, figuring out that there are different amounts of things. They begin by holding a block in each hand and banging the two together or by putting on one metal bracelet and then another, experiencing two. They explore the concept of *more, little,* and *big* as they struggle to hold onto two items while grabbing a third.

As they fill containers and dump them, they construct concepts of *more, all, some,* and *none.* Filling and emptying containers can be messy play, but it is rich in opportunity to learn about shape, size, number, quantity, and estimating, all foundational math skills. For example, mobile infants might go in search of *all* of a certain kind of object, or they might repeatedly fill and empty a container, and in doing so, they figure out how much is just enough and how much is too much, or which ones are too big and which ones are too small, first steps in learning how to estimate. Toward the end of this period, infants go in search of all there are of a particular type of object (Kálló & Balog, 2005). Ample quantities of objects with the same or similar features, along with sufficiently large containers, facilitate mobile infants' attempts to carry *all* and not just *some.*

A CLOSER LOOK

Select Mobile Infant Toys with Number in Mind, and Observe the Play

- Provide duplicates of objects to create occasions to hold and make two (Figure 10.15).
- Near a ramp or set of stairs, place a collection of foam blocks and a basket of balls, for mobile infants who wish to challenge their ability to walk up and down while grasping one object, then add another, and possibly a third.
- Offer a variety of containers, varying in size, and an array of different collections of objects to gather a few, some, or many.

FIGURE 10.15. Toys That Support Investigation of Number in Mobile Infants

Mobile Infants and Representation. Symbolic, or representational play, commonly called pretend play, shows up during the mobile infant period. The concept of representation is essentially the ability to represent one object by using another. At first, mobile infants use a toy or other object in ways similar to a real object, for example, talking on a toy phone. Once they start to walk, infants begin to act out familiar rituals in play. Toward the end of this period, they are able to hold in mind past experiences in order to play them out later in simple symbolic or pretend play. An infant might gently draw a blanket over a doll's body and pat the doll on the tummy or pretend to feed the doll with a cup.

Familiar items from infants' surroundings (e.g., plastic dishes, hats, bags, and dolls) support mobile infants' pretend play. Midway through the second year, infants begin to enjoy simple dress-up clothes and safe accessories that they can easily pull over their heads.

A CLOSER LOOK

Select Mobile Infant Toys with Representation in Mind, and Observe the Play

- Provide an assortment of baby blankets and dolls, along with other props an infant might recognize as being used in daily care.
- Offer ordinary objects to support pretend play, such as cooking pots and lids, pitchers, and cups, or short-handled brooms, dish scrubbers, or shaving brushes.
- Supply an assortment of clothing that mobile infants can easily put on and take off, without help: for example, capes with Velcro fasteners, skirts and pants with elasticized waist, or vests.

Older Infants' Object Play

Older infants, from 18 to 36 months, are confident in locomoting from place to place, whether walking, running, or climbing. This ability to move into a wider realm expands their access to objects and invites new opportunities to classify similarities and differences and to explore causal, spatial, and numerical possibilities. Infants in this period also begin to engage in simple episodes of pretend play, building the concept of symbolic representation.

Older Infants and Classification. Older infants are fairly adept at distinguishing the features of objects. They can sort objects into two groups based on a single attribute, such as all the blue cars in one basket and all the plastic lion cubs in another. Their interest in collecting objects takes on a new focus, as they frequently collect objects for their value as "treasures" (Kálló & Balog, 2005), selecting one object from among others and giving it special value—holding it in hand, depositing it in a pocket, or entrusting it to the hands and the protection of the caregiver. From an outing, they return with treasures from nature, picked from the ground or a low branch. Garments with pockets, as well as a variety of containers, boxes, carts, and wagons support their interest in carrying these treasured items. Props to accompany their collecting—such as raincoats, boots, umbrellas, hats, shoulder bags, magnifying glasses, and collection jars—prompt older infants to go in search of items like leaves, pine cones, seed pods, and flowers.

Older infants enjoy the challenge of making simple patterns with objects they collect. As they select items based on a particular physical property and connect them together, they make pattern relationships (see Figure 10.1). Collections of cloth blankets—some the same and some different—made from different shades and patterns of cloth invite toddlers to use and arrange them based on properties of color or design. A small red woven basket might be offered with six pieces of cloth, each a different shade of red, exposing toddlers to a full range of tints within the color red. Cloth placemats with matching coasters, or a set of plastic dishes in which each place setting is a different color, offer opportunities to classify, sort, and pattern. Simple building blocks invite older infants to distinguish among the features of different blocks and to make patterns, as they line up the blocks along with collections of plastic animals, vehicles, and figures of people.

Older Infants and Causality. Older infants enjoy the challenge of complex cause-and-effect toys, such as

A CLOSER LOOK

Select Older Infant Toys with Classification in Mind, and Observe the Play

- Provide sets of play items (such as toy trucks), varying in size yet similar in all other features and all the same color, alongside plastic figures of people that vary by height, providing the opportunity to classify and to sequence along the dimension of size (see Figure 10.1).
- Offer a cardboard picture book with photos of a particular type of animal, alongside a collection of stuffed animals, some of which are the animals depicted in the picture book.
- Select two low, wide baskets, each a different color, and fill each with a variety of safe objects or swatches of fabric the same color as the basket.

A CLOSER LOOK

Select Older Infant Toys with Causality in Mind, and Observe the Play

- Offer older infants safe opportunities to experiment with marking and writing tools, for example, a pencil secured by strong string to a table leg.
- Offer materials that reflect or transmit color and light, such as translucent cups, each a different color, alongside a collection of metal bowls that will reflect the color of objects placed inside (Figure 10.16).
- Near an exterior window where sunlight enters, offer a collection of safe, reflective metal objects, as well as objects that project interesting shadows, like small colanders or metal cooking racks.

FIGURE 10.16. Objects Older Infants Can Use to Explore Causality: Reflection and Light

simple action tools that have knobs that twist to make a sound or to make an object move; levers that slide to open or to make a sound; latches that open and close; nuts and bolts that screw together; and lids that fit on containers of various sizes and shapes. Musical instruments like simple flutes, drums, xylophones, pianos, chimes, and bells invite cause-and-effect exploration and enhance the play with delightful sounds when shaken, tapped, plucked, or blown. Windsocks, chimes, scarves, or sun-reflectors added to an outdoor fence invite older infants to explore the cause-and-effect relationships of the wind and the sun. A basket of plastic mirrors, old CDs, or Plexiglas translucent colored panels placed in a sunny area of the yard or near a window invites toddlers to explore how their actions impact light and shadow.

Older infants show evidence of being able to predict the outcome of an action, such as water trickling from a hose when the tap is opened. They begin to share ideas about what is about to happen or to reflect on the action that caused a particular reaction, as in "The sun is out. No more rain!" They enjoy the cause-and-effect actions of simple tools used in daily routines, like ringing a bell to signal the start of a meal or pushing the lever on a soap dispenser, and they delight in both hearing and telling the story of what occurs, as in, "You pushed hard, and the soap came out!"

Older Infants and Spatial Relations. Older infants can predict the size of objects that will fit into a container. They enjoy exploring how to balance a variety of objects, one on the other, or on top of raised surfaces. They recognize that round objects roll off and that flat, angled objects stay put. Play spaces with a variety of raised surfaces, such as low shelves, overturned bins, baskets, boxes, or pillows, give older infants a variety of challenging places on which to balance and build. As they build, older infants confront problems about weight relations and gravity (Kálló & Balog, 2005): "What happens when I place the block or the ball on the edge of the box? What happens when I put it in the center of the box?" or "What does it take to make this cup stay up on the thin gate?" or "What happens when I remove the box from below the plastic block?"

Older infants nest one object inside another to build tall structures. They figure out how to connect a series of conical cups, baskets, bins, sand pails, or recycled containers to make tall towers or long staffs. They play with color and invent patterns as they nest, stack, or line up objects, placing a particular color in a certain spot, at the bottom, the top, or in the middle. As they nest objects, one inside the other, they discover that one object shaped the same as another smaller object can contain the smaller object, building the concept of volume. With repeated practice, they learn to tell, simply by looking at objects, which ones will stack, nest, or connect, and which ones will not (see Figure 10.17).

FIGURE 10.17. Toys to Support Older Infants' Concepts of Spatial Relations and Number.

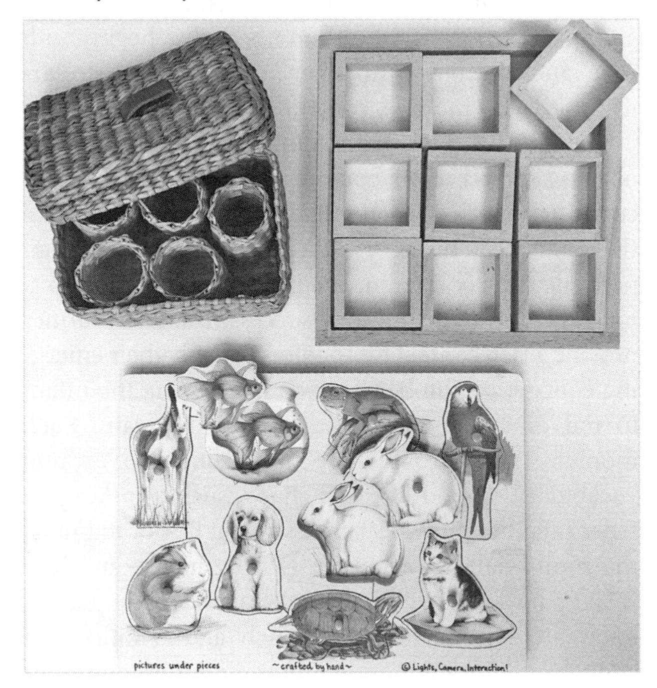

A CLOSER LOOK

Select Older Infant Toys with Spatial Relations in Mind, and Observe the Play

- Provide an array of stackable objects for balancing and building.
- Offer play props, such as wooden trees or figures, alongside building blocks, for arranging simple scenes.
- Provide collections of sturdy, safe objects from nature as well as repurposed ordinary objects to use as props in simple scenes.
- Offer one-piece puzzles and other sturdy frames that can be filled in or filled up (see Figure 10.17).
- Add objects that connect together with simple knobs, bristles, or Velcro, as well as conical cups for nesting and connecting.

A CLOSER LOOK

Select Older Infant Toys with Number in Mind, and Observe the Play

- Prepare a collection of baskets, one with three stuffed animals, another with three plastic figures, and a third with three small vehicles, to provide the possibility to select one, and then a second, and then a third, an experience in addition.
- Offer big collections of safe, recycled objects and natural materials, and extend invitations to use "all" or "some."
- Invite older infants to go in search of pairs of shoes, socks, or gloves, and then help them count "one" and then "two" as they don each item.
- Provide a collection of interlocking blocks or tracks to give infants the opportunity to add one to the other to make something long (see Figure 10.18).

Older Infants and Number. Older infants experience a language spurt that coincides with a developing sense of number. They begin to use relational words that indicate emerging understanding of quantity, such as "more" and "all through." They love to accompany others in counting. For older infants, counting is an enjoyable chant, a series of numbers that begins with "one" and continues with other numbers, not necessarily in order, as in, "one, two, three, six, ten."

Older infants begin to count small collections of objects. At first, their counting is an imitation of the counting they have seen others do. They may point to the same item twice or say a number word without pointing to an object, but continue on with their counting, quite satisfied with their success. The care routines provide a rich context for toddlers to apply their emerging concept of number, for example, asking the infant to put on two boots for a walk in the rain. Such moments also provide the opportunity to expand vocabulary around line and shape, such as asking an older infant to push a cart in a straight line or to put all the round balls in a bucket. During meals, an older infant enjoys an invitation to take one scoop of peas or to be careful not to pour "too much" and to notice "not enough."

As they near the end of their third year, older infants show evidence that they are understanding cardinality, which means that the last number word when counting represents the total number of objects. For example, an older infant exclaims, "One, two, three! Three candles!" Or a 3-year-old, when asked how many crackers are left on the plate, will look at the plate and, without counting, quickly respond, "Two!" As explained earlier, by their third birthday, older infants demonstrate the ability to quickly and accurately recognize the quantity in a small set of objects without counting, a mathematical skill called *subitizing* (Clements, 2004).

Older Infants and Representation. In the second year, infants' pretend play becomes more complex. They use objects as symbols to represent other objects, for example, using a block of wood to represent a telephone, or using a section of plastic tubing to put pretend gas into a tricycle. By 3 years of age, they are fairly adept at creating their own play scripts as they engage in make-believe play. Their play reveals their

FIGURE 10.18. An Older Infant Builds Concepts of Spatial Relations and Number in Play

Photograph by Carol Grivette

A CLOSER LOOK

Select Older Infant Toys with Representation in Mind, and Observe the Play

- Offer baskets of cotton scarves, purses, back-packs, and other garments and accessories in common use.
- Offer simple, safe tools that older infants see used by those around them, such as metal whisks, shaving brushes, or dish scrubbers.
- Select play materials that correspond to recent experiences: for example, a pretend measuring tape, shovels, and dump trucks if near a construction project.

ability to recall and represent prior experiences in simple pretend narratives (Figure 10.19). An older infant will place utensils on a small box as if it were a table and serve food to stuffed dolls, using a bucket as a cooking pot.

PLAY SPACE AS CONTEXT FOR LEARNING

Infants rely on those who care for them to provide play materials that support invention, transformation, and

FIGURE 10.19. An Older Infant Represents in Play His Earlier Experience Feeding a Giraffe at the Zoo

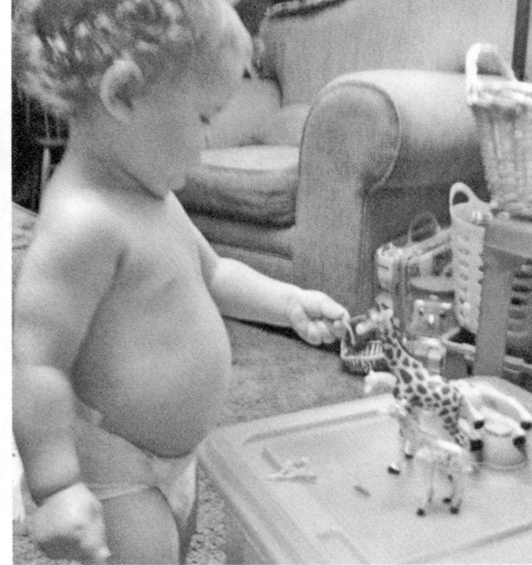

Photographs by Carol Grivette

representation. Just as scientists research the unknown, infants investigate the world they encounter, building more complex understanding. In many ways, infants' play space is like their laboratory for learning. Those who care for infants support them in their experiments in play, supplying the materials for discovery, observing what captures their interest and what materials are being used, and taking note of what more might be offered to deepen the play, to extend the investigation, and to add complexity to the learning. From the perspective of infants, simple moments of play with ordinary objects are much more than ordinary. They are extraordinary opportunities to experience the wonder of learning.

PART IV

Widening the Lens

HOW INFANTS DEVELOP and how they learn depends on many factors present in their surrounding family and community. A family's culture impacts in many ways what infants learn and how they expect the world to be. Chapter 11 looks at infants' biological expectation to belong to a caring social group, explores how they build friendships with others, and describes how infants learn the expected values and behavior of the culture in which they are raised. Chapter 12 examines what happens when infants experience adversity or trauma and how supportive intervention can begin to heal the impact of such experiences. Chapter 13 returns to the question posed in the title of this book, "What do babies ask of us?" This final chapter looks at policies that align with infants' biological expectations, support their optimal development, and treat babies and their families with dignity and respect.

CHAPTER 11

Belonging

Infants' efforts appear similar to those appropriate for anyone learning in an unfamiliar cultural setting: stay near trusted guides, watch their activities and get involved when possible, and attend to any instruction the guides provide. —Barbara Rogoff (2003, p. 69)

FOR NEWBORN INFANTS, it is as if they walk onto the stage of a theatrical production, knowing nothing about what the production is about, what their role is, or what their lines are (Bruner, 1990). The script that will become the story of their lives is as yet largely unwritten. Newborns readily take their role in the production. They are primed by their biology to expect to be met by affectionate caregivers who will show them the way and invite them to be active participants.

From the first breath, a baby becomes a part of the surrounding community and joins with others in creating the script that will become the baby's life story. This chapter begins with a discussion of how cultural context influences *what* infants learn, followed by an examination of how infants form ideas, expectations, and beliefs prevalent in the culture, derived from experiences they have with others. With this foundation, the chapter concludes with a discussion of the role played by caregivers in support of helping older infants live within the expectations of their family and community, in essence, the "house rules," and guiding them through the joys and tribulations of making and keeping friends, topics often referred to as guidance and discipline.

LEARNING BY PITCHING IN

Scientists who study child development across cultures (LeVine et al., 1994) point out that what babies learn is not universal, that is, not an identical package of skills, concepts, values, and beliefs. What babies learn is a function of where they are born, when, and to whom. Expectations, beliefs, skills, and concepts deemed valuable vary considerably from one family to the next, from one community to the next, and from one point in time to another.

Although humans develop along a predictable trajectory, the skills and concepts a child learns are influenced greatly by the routine ways of doing things in the culture and community that surround the child. Across cultures, and across time, there is tremendous variation in how people carry out everyday routines that organize daily life. Developmental psychologist and researcher Barbara Rogoff (2003) describes human development as a cultural process. She explains that infants and young children learn the ways of their culture and develop their thoughts and attitudes by "pitching in." Rogoff refers to the work of pioneering early childhood educator Caroline Pratt (1948) to illustrate this point, drawing on Pratt's description of what she was expected to learn and how she was expected to learn it as a child in the 1800s:

> When I grew up in Fayetteville, New York, school was not very important to children who could roam the real world freely for their learning. . . . I drove the wagon in haying time. . . . At ten, my great-aunt used to say, I could turn a team of horses and a wagon in less space than a grown man needed to do it.
>
> No one had to tell us where milk came from, or how butter was made. We helped to harvest wheat, saw it ground into flour in the mill on our own stream; I baked bread for the family at thirteen. (Pratt, 1948, pp. xxi–xxii)

As Pratt's description illustrates, in the 1800s, many children in the United States participated alongside adults in the work of the family farm. Consequently, many children growing up on farms did not attend school. In cities, too, many children did not attend school. Instead, they spent their days working in factories or in service positions. A century later, the context had changed and children in the United States no longer spent their days laboring in fields and factories. With passage of national legislation, child labor was outlawed, and school became compulsory for all children. As a consequence of such policies, school attendance for children in many countries is considered a natural part of childhood, whereas the presence of children in the workforce is not. The experience of being a child and the experience of raising a child vary with respect to prevailing beliefs valued within the cultural context, and the cultural context changes over time.

Cultural context influences both *what* children learn and *how* they learn it. The work of anthropologist Barry Hewlett illustrates this point. Hewlett (1991) describes how families socialize infants within the Aka Pygmy community in the Central African Republic:

> The training for autonomy begins in infancy. Infants are allowed to crawl or walk to wherever they want in camp and allowed to use knives, machetes, digging sticks, and clay pots around camp. Only if an infant begins to crawl into a fire or hits another child do parents or others interfere with the infant's activity. . . . By three or four years of age children can cook themselves a meal on the fire, and by ten years of age Aka children know enough subsistence skills to live in the forest alone if need be. (p. 34)

This description may be surprising and even alarming for many; however, Rogoff (2003) poses this question: "So, at what age do children develop responsibility for others or sufficient skill and judgment to handle dangerous implements?" Her response is, "It depends" (p. 6). She points out that if you pose this question solely within your own cultural context and sphere of experiences, the answer might be, "Certainly not as a young child!" However, when posed within the Aka hunting and gathering community, the answer may be quite different. Hewlett (1991) describes how both Aka women and men hunt and forage for food, and children accompany their parents as they do so, getting much exposure to knives and the rituals of preparing food. Aka fathers hold or are within arms' reach of their infants on average 47% of the time, almost as much as Aka mothers—an intense web of social supports, with children always within the protective reach of an adult.

Ideas about what infants and young children should know and how they should play and learn vary widely, in service to raising successful members of the culture. Rogoff (2003) cautions against passing judgment on childrearing practices without a good understanding of the cultural context, as she explains in the following:

> Variations in expectations for children make sense once we take into account different circumstances and traditions. They make sense in the context of differences in what is involved in preparing "a meal" or "tending" a baby, what sources of support and danger are common, who else is nearby, what the roles of local adults are and how they live, what institutions people use to organize their lives, and what goals the community has for development to mature functioning in those institutions and cultural practices. (p. 6)

Babies delight in the experience of the wider world. While very young and either carried in slings or lying nearby, they watch a meal being prepared, or they watch an object being moved from one spot to another. They attend closely and listen in on the discourse that accompanies these encounters. They get a close-up view, or an opportunity to touch and handle, if an object in use is placed within reach. There is an exchange of looks, facial expressions, vocalizations, or gestures. For babies, these are moments of fascination and delight, opportunities to listen in on and to participate in everyday activities.

Irrespective of age, one way people learn is by "listening-in" (Rogoff, 2003) on ongoing activities. Infants and young children are intently curious about the actions, events, people, and emotional context of their surroundings, and they find ways to listen in, a form of participation. They join in by imitating what they see and hear others do, experimenting with the conventions and behavior they witness. Eventually this transforms into a shared endeavor. Figure 11.1 illustrates this with respect to hanging clothes on a clothesline. The toddler watches someone pull damp clothes from a basket, and then the toddler pitches in by doing this herself, a shared social encounter.

Infants see what others do, they imitate this in their own way, and they accommodate their own actions to the actions of others. In so doing, they become familiar with the shared rituals, practices, and stories that define their community. These moments, led by infants' curiosity and experimentation, are not designed to teach

FIGURE 11.1. Pitching-in: A Shared Social Encounter

Used with Permission from the Program for Infant/Toddler Care at WestEd. Copyright © 2018 WestEd

skills and concepts, yet they make up a key element of what infants and young children learn and how they learn it. Infants and toddlers seek friendships with people of all ages and are intent on participating in what others know and do. It is this that motivates their entry into the culture and the community.

DETECTING GOALS AND INTENTIONS

Infants are primed by their biology to be acutely sensitive to sights, sounds, smells, sensations, and rhythms of movement and sound. Their sensory systems process a vast array of information about the physical world and the social world, organizing it within developing brain systems. By the end of the first year, they show marked advances in their awareness of themselves in relation to others and their awareness of the behavior of others. Between 9 and 12 months of age, the focus of their attention turns from an awareness of what people *do* to an awareness and an interpretation of what people *think* (Rochat, 2001). This higher-level thinking can be seen in the emergence of three notable skills during this period of infancy—joint attention, pointing, and social referencing.

Joint Attention and Pointing

From birth infants are capable of gazing at people and, when ready, gazing away, or disengaging the gaze (see Chapter 7). To this early mode of communication, infants add another strategy for communicating with people, called *joint attention*. This occurs halfway through the first year. *Joint attention* (Bruner, 1975) refers to a preverbal behavior in which infants shift their gaze to look at the object a companion is looking at (Figure 11.2). Joint attention marks the onset of communicative behavior that allows one person to reference another. In joint attention, infants signal that they have figured out that a companion's gaze, even when the gaze is not focused on them, is the source of important information. By following the companion's gaze to look at the object of interest, they reference the mind of the other.

Joint attention is, in essence, infants' first experience in sharing. If one could imagine words put to the baby's experience, they might be, "What you gaze at, I behold as well." In time, infants spontaneously initiate a bid for another person to attend to that to which the infant

FIGURE 11.2. Joint Attention

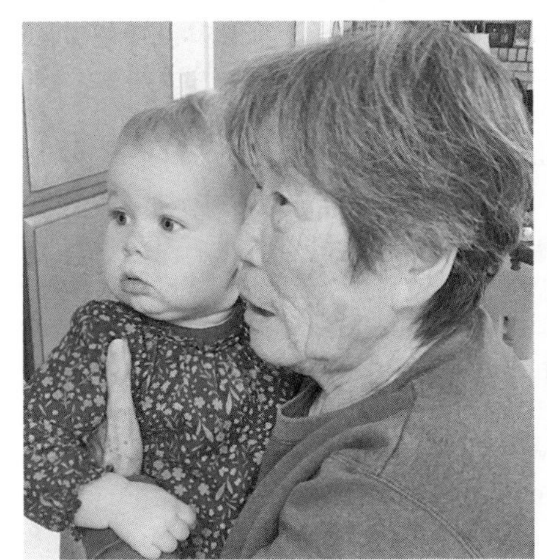

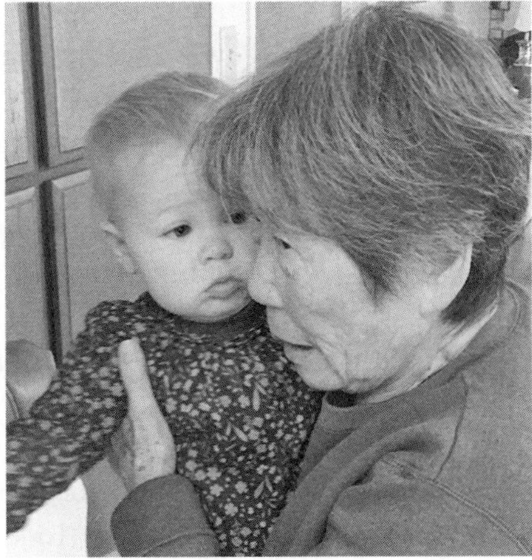

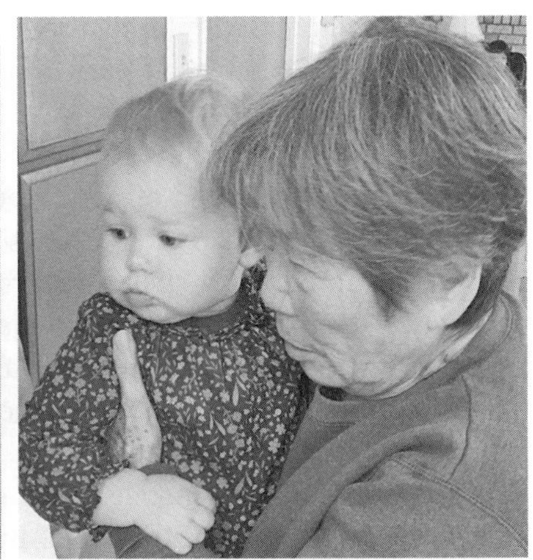

Photographs by Jillian Rich

attends. With joint attention, infants and others join in a triangle of attention, made up of infant, companion, and object.

To direct the attention of another person, infants shift their gaze, but they also begin to point, as a way to share interest with another person. As they point, infants realize that this simple gesture will cause someone else to pay attention to the same thing that captures their attention. They also figure out, quite soon, that pointing serves as an effective way to make a nonverbal request. By deliberately pointing at a desired object and making eye contact with a companion, infants convey a silent request, expecting that the companion will provide them with the object of desire. Through the gesture of pointing, the mind of the infant connects to the mind of another person, a nonverbal dialogue.

Joint attention plays a role in language acquisition and learning, with studies showing that the frequency with which infants engage in joint attention is related to their language acquisition (Mundy et al., 2007). For example, in everyday conversations, a parent refers to a new object, and the infant, in making sense of what the parent refers to, uses joint attention and the direction of gaze of the parent to attend to the correct object and gather a clue as to what the novel word means. A child's use of joint attention is related to measures of IQ, self-regulation, and social competence (Mundy et al., 2007). The emergence of joint attention in the months leading up to the first birthday marks a pivotal point in social engagement and learning.

A CLOSER LOOK

What You Like Influences What I Like

Midway through the second year, toddlers are capable of referencing multiple cues from a person's gaze and emotions to interpret the person's motivation. Researchers observed 15-month-old infants, seated on the parent's lap, as they watched an experimenter demonstrate how to use a noise-making toy. A second person entered the room, sat in a nearby chair, and as the experimenter repeated the demonstration, the new person complained in an angry voice, a simulated argument. After witnessing this, the children were given a chance to play with the toy. For some, the angered person left the room. These children eagerly grabbed the toy and played with it as they had seen demonstrated. For others, the angered person remained and maintained a neutral expression. These children hesitated before touching the toy, and when they finally did, were less likely to use it to make sounds as they had seen demonstrated.

Social Referencing

Joint attention, during the latter half of a baby's first year, coincides with a baby's learning to crawl and to walk. This is noteworthy in that joint attention, while expanding what a baby can learn about the surrounding world, also keeps the baby visually linked to the caregiver, at a time when the baby experiences the thrills and uncertainties of a newfound freedom to move away from the caregiver (Tomasello, 2009). What follows is another new skill, *social referencing. Social referencing* refers to how infants, in the months leading up to the first birthday, begin to look to the reactions of others to know what to do when encountering novel objects and events.

As infants become mobile, their encounters with novel objects and events increase. By looking to the face of the caregiver, infants seek emotional signals to interpret how to respond to new or ambiguous situations. They do so most frequently with those to whom they show bonds of attachment. Often, the novel encounter elicits strong feelings, and infants reference the caregiver's facial expression, vocalization, or behavior for advice. For example, if a stranger walks into the room, an infant will look to the caregiver, or if another child reaches to grab a toy the infant is using, the infant will look in the direction of the caregiver for cues to gauge an appropriate response.

Referencing the emotions of others in order to guide their own actions begins to show up midway through the first year of infancy. Studies show that infants 5–6 months of age are more likely to approach and touch a novel toy that a caregiver has appeared to like, through positive emotional cues, and less likely to approach a novel toy that a caregiver has appeared to dislike. Infants this age will also gaze more intently at an event during which they have seen their parent smile, laugh, or appear to enjoy what is happening (Mireault & Crockenberg, 2016).

Of concern is what happens when caregivers of infants suffer from depression and thereby offer infants only a limited range of emotional responses to reference. An infant who references a depressed caregiver for affective cues will find little in terms of cues, most likely a look of disengagement. In a classic experiment called Still Face (see Chapter 4), mothers are asked to adopt a still face in the midst of animated face-to-face play with their infant (Tronick, 1989). The still face, in essence, replicates what occurs when a parent suffers from depression. In response to the parent's still face, infants stop smiling and show signs of anxiety and despair.

As they approach their first birthday, infants show evidence of being aware of others having plans, goals, and intentions (Agnetta & Rochat, 2004). For example, 1-year-olds are able to distinguish between an adult who teases them by purposefully withholding a desired toy and an adult who appears to be *unable* to give it to them (Behne, Carpenter, Call, & Tomasello, 2005). As they enter their second year, infants also show evidence (Gergely, Bekkering, & Kiraly, 2002) of noticing and interpreting what others intend, desire, or feel, in addition to having their own intentions, desires, and feelings, which they communicate clearly to others. This capacity—to be intently aware of and responding to their own intentions, desires, and feelings, as well as those of others—prepares toddlers to experience the joys and challenges of sharing possessions with others.

SHARING

The act of sharing begins in infancy. A newborn shares an awareness of the face or the touch of another and reciprocates a look or a touch with a look or a move of her own. A more conventional view of sharing can be seen when an 8-month-old nibbles on a cracker and then reaches, cracker in hand, to offer the cracker to his caregiver. By 18 months of age, infants share with parents, peers, and even strangers (Rheingold, Hay, & West, 1976) as a way to maintain contact. For example, a toddler will offer one of his own toys to a companion toddler, in what appears to be a means of getting the attention of a potential playmate.

Although research shows that toddlers are more likely to share toys than to take toys away from playmates, conflicts are not infrequent in toddler play. Although such moments are difficult for child and caregiver alike, peer conflicts play an important and positive role in a child's development. As toddlers play together, they are faced with coordinating multiple points of view—their attention to each other, their understanding of each others' intentions, and their desire to secure or maintain possession of playthings. Sometimes this goes smoothly, and sometimes it goes awry and a conflict ensues.

A conflict between toddlers is best viewed as simply a breakdown in toddlers' coordination of their attention, intention, or desires with those of others. Toddlers, like adults, grapple with the messiness of social discord as they try to get things back on track. Most conflicts between toddlers do not involve the use of physical force or hostile aggression (Ross et al., 2010), but instead are characterized by an attitude of opposition. For example, a toddler might signal another toddler that she wants control of a toy that the other toddler has. In a back-and-forth relay of primarily nonverbal signals, each reads and responds to the other's behavior and intentions, yet without aggressive use of force.

Researchers Hay and Ross (1982) observed pairs of 21-month-olds in play and saw that nearly all the toddlers, at some point, engaged in conflict. The conflicts occupied only about 6% of the play period, however, and the episodes of conflict tended to be brief. Most of the conflicts, 88%, involved toys, yet over half of the moves identified within the conflict involved some form of communication that indicated, through words or gesture, their interest in the toy held by the other. In most instances, the conflict began with communica-

A CLOSER LOOK

Toddlers Are Good at Sharing

To determine how often toddlers share, researchers tracked the play of pairs of toddler friends and recorded whenever a toddler either took toys away from a peer or offered, handed, or added objects to an array of toys being used by a peer (Hay, Castle, Davies, Demetriou, & Stimson, 1999). They discovered that toddlers shared toys with others significantly more than they took toys away from others. They shared most often when there were plenty of toys available and identical versions of toys.

tion and ended when one toddler wrested the toy from the hands of the other. The tugging and resisting was most successful in ending the dispute when it was accompanied by gestures and vocalizations. For example, an attacker might exclaim, "My truck!" while tugging on a toy, and a defender might protest, "No!" or "Don't!" Typically, both laid claim to entitlement, proclaiming, "Mine!"

Conflicts occurred even when there were duplicates of the toy in dispute, suggesting that the conflict was less about the toy and more about the social interaction. Further evidence came from the fact that the victors in these conflicts often showed little interest in the spoils of their victory, the disputed toy, and instead, turned their attention to a different object of interest.

Even though most toddler conflicts involve disputes over toys, they center more on learning about people than learning about the right of possession. Investment in possession of an object changes dramatically over the course of infancy. In a laboratory study of 6-month-old unacquainted infants, the infants touched toys that others were playing with, but they showed little sign of struggling over possession of a toy (Hay, Nash, & Pedersen, 1983). By the end of the first year, however, infants began to cry and struggle when others tried to take a toy from their possession. By 18 months of age, toddlers actively defended their possessions when other toddlers attempted to reach or gesture toward these objects. They read and interpreted the behavior of the aggressor and protested or withdrew the object in advance of the aggressor's move (Hay, Castle, & Davies, 2000).

CARING

Social conflicts involve strong feelings. The ability to notice and respond to the feelings or intentions of others transforms over the course of infancy. Young infants, upon seeing someone in distress, will recognize the distress but will respond primarily by becoming distressed themselves. This changes around the middle of the second year, when they begin to take action to alleviate the other person's distress. An older toddler might offer comfort and help to a distressed friend, including sharing a toy as a means of helping the friend cope with the distress (Zahn-Waxler, Radke-Yarrow, Wagner, & Chapman, 1992). Occasionally, the action the observing toddler takes may also display itself in negative behavior toward a distressed friend (Demetriou & Hay, 2004).

A fascinating series of studies shows just how early infants appear to be aware of actions that help as compared with actions that hurt. Infants as young as 3 months (Hamlin, Wynn, & Bloom, 2010) were positioned in front of an animated scene in which simple wooden shapes fitted with plastic eyes depicted characters performing either a helping action or a hindering action. The infants saw a round shape repeatedly try and fail to move up a hill. Then they saw a triangle shape enter at the bottom of the hill and push the round shape up the hill. The infants saw the scene a second time, but this time, as the round shape struggled to move up the hill, a square shape entered at the top of the hill and pushed the round shape back down. An experimenter entered the room and presented the babies with a tray on which rested the square shape and the triangle shape. The babies overwhelmingly reached for the triangle shape, the helper object.

A similar series of experiments recruited a cohort of 5- to 12-month-old infants and another cohort of 19- to 23-month-old infants (Hamlin & Wynn, 2012; Hamlin, Wynn, Bloom, & Mahajan, 2011). The infants were positioned so they could watch the action on a puppet stage. One scene opened with a puppet struggling to open a box. A second puppet approached and helped open the box. Then the scene changed. As before, the infants saw the first puppet struggle to open the box, but this time a different puppet approached and, just as the box was about to be opened, plopped down hard on the box, snapping it closed.

A second set of experiments used a different scene. One puppet agreeably played catch, back-and-forth, with a second puppet. Then a third puppet entered the stage, and when thrown the ball, the third puppet grabbed it and ran away. Later, when given a chance to pick from a tray of puppets, the observing infants, both young and old, responded in the same way across all the experiments. After observing puppets either help or hinder, the infants favored the helping puppet.

How this plays out in scenes with people, rather than puppets, is a question explored by another team of researchers who placed 18-month-old infants in situations in which an adult was having trouble achieving a goal (Warneken & Tomasello, 2006). In one task, the 18-month-olds watched as an experimenter used clothespins to hang towels on a clothesline. The experimenter accidentally dropped a clothespin on the floor and unsuccessfully reached for it. The infants, seeing the distressed adult, walked to the dropped clothespin, picked it up, and handed it to the experimenter. In a

FIGURE 11.3. Helping a Friend

Photograph by Carol Grivette

second experiment, an adult tried to put an armload of stacked magazines into a cabinet, but with hands full, could not open the doors. The 18-month-olds saw this, walked to the cabinet, and opened the door.

These experiments were repeated with 14-month-olds, with similar yet noticeably distinct results. The younger infants helped only on the less cognitively demanding task, helping reach for a dropped object (Warneken & Tomasello, 2007). These studies demonstrate a gradual shift in how infants help others. Sometime after the first birthday, children begin to spontaneously help others, and over the course of the second year, they become more flexible in their ability to intervene to help others in need.

Further studies show that concrete rewards appear to have a negative effect on children's future helping. Researchers offered 18-month-olds a toy as a reward for helping. Children who received a material reward for helping during an initial situation were subsequently less likely to engage in further helping, as compared with children who had not received such an award (Warneken, Hare, Melis, Hanus, & Tomasello, 2007; Warneken & Tomasello, 2008). The origins of altruistic behavior, that is, helping others, appear to begin in infancy, as young infants offer spontaneous, unrewarded help to others in need (Figure 11.3).

LIVING WITHIN THE HOUSE RULES

Infants' desire to help others is a primary factor when it comes to resolving conflicts between playmates. When caregivers try to see a conflict through the eyes of infants, they find ways to support infants in successfully negotiating a resolution. Infant specialist Magda Gerber, in discussing how to handle infant and toddler misbehavior, used the term "house rules" to describe the limits of acceptable behavior in a particular context (Lally, 2011). For example, when two or more infants or toddlers play together, a common rule of fair play is, "A toy is yours to play with until you are ready to give it up." From this perspective, grabbing a toy away from someone who is still using the toy is not acceptable, that is, against the house rules. From the child's point of view, grabbing the toy accomplishes her desired goal—getting the toy—but from the perspective of the house rules, her action falls outside the limits of acceptable behavior.

Children are not born knowing the expected rules of behavior. They rely on adults to clearly describe to them the limits of what the family, culture, and community consider to be acceptable behavior—that which they *may* do and that which they may *not* do. Jean Piaget, a renowned theorist of child development, categorized this type of knowledge as *social-conventional* knowledge (Kamii, 2014), referring to the conventions that people create over time and are conveyed from one person to another. A code of language, for example, is social-conventional knowledge, as are holidays, customs, and traditions. The rules of acceptable behavior within a society are also social-conventional knowledge. Social-conventional knowledge is distinct from physical, logical, or mathematical knowledge, which is knowledge that we build when we act on objects or engage in mental calculations, as described in Chapter 10. Infants rely on the adults who care for them to convey social-conventional knowledge, including language, traditions, custom, and societal rules.

Limits and Redirection

Infants' misbehavior is often a consequence of what, to the infant, was a good idea. For example, a young child who wants a toy that is in the hands of another child might reach for the toy and protest, with the hope of being handed the toy. The outstretched arm and protest might merit a glance from the other child, but the other child maintains a tight hold on the desired toy. To get the toy from the other child, the first child might then forcibly grab the toy away. The other child, distraught on losing the toy, might hit the aggressor to get the toy back. Each action, despite breaking the house rules, is a response to a "good" idea intended to get or to keep the desired toy.

In another example, an infant might be fearful as a stranger approaches, and the infant might hit or push

> **A CLOSER LOOK**
>
> **Limits and Redirection**
>
> Placing limits and employing redirection, as a guidance strategy, rescues the infant in the moment, giving clear direction as to what is and is not acceptable in meeting the desired goal, and it also serves as a reference for the future. For example:
>
> "You are angry because he won't give you the bucket. You may not hit him, because hitting him hurts. If you want the bucket, tell him, 'I want the bucket, too.' But you may not hit people."

the approaching person to put distance between them to alleviate the fear. Or an infant might be frustrated at not being able to make something work and throw the malfunctioning toy to the ground in anger. Each is an example of behavior that might be a "good" idea from the infant's perspective, but within the context of the house rules, is outside the limits of acceptable behavior.

Infants rely on their caregivers to inform them clearly and respectfully of the house rules. They acquire the rules of expected behavior through interactions and conversations with others. This means simply telling the infant what it is they may do and may not do, and why, when they find themselves in this situation. Infants expect and appreciate clear limits from those who provide their care. In fact, they thrive on this.

A clear limit is a statement of what the child may *not* do in a situation as well a statement of what the child may do. Sometimes, this is referred to as *redirection,* redirecting the child through a clear statement of what the child may do to accomplish the child's intent, desire, or goal.

To successfully redirect a child, an adult must listen closely to figure out what appears to be the child's intention, desire, or goal (Maguire-Fong, 2015). For example, a child frustrated in not getting a toy to work as she desires might throw the toy against the wall. The child's intent appears to be twofold, to get the toy working and to express anger and frustration. By acknowledging the child's goal and feeling, an adult conveys a clear signal to the child that the child's intent and strong feeling are seen and understood, "You are angry because it does not work and you want it to work. Please don't throw the toy, because that will break it. Bring it to me, and we will try to make it work."

Limited Choice

Clear limits and redirection work best in situations where the misbehavior has already occurred, and the adult is stepping in to assist. In other situations, the misbehavior is a child's refusal to comply with a responsible adult's needed request. As with limits and redirection, adults show respect for the child's thinking by acknowledging the child's idea and then offering a simple choice. For example, an adult might say, "I can see that you want to keep playing outside. But it is time to come inside now. You may either walk inside by yourself or you can hold my hand. Which do you want to do? You decide."

In this example, the caregiver offers a limited choice. A limited choice gives the child a degree of decision-making power, within clearly defined limits. The clearly defined limits assure that the required action is completed. A limited choice is a win–win for both child and adult, in that the child is the decision-maker, and either decision is acceptable to the adult. A limited choice has four components, conveyed in any order:

> **A CLOSER LOOK**
>
> **Limited Choice**
>
> Reflect on this interaction in which the caregiver Ashley is trying to get the toddler to do something specific. See if you can identify each of the four components noted in the description for a limited choice.
>
> Ashley struggles to get two-year-old Brian to leave his toys and get ready to walk to the mailbox. She says, "Brian, you are really loving playing with those blocks, but we need to take this letter to the mailbox. Do you want to walk with me or ride in the stroller? You decide."

- Acknowledge the child's feeling, intention, or goal.
- Clearly state to the child what you need him to do.
- Clearly state the reason why you need the child to accommodate your request.
- Offer the child two equally acceptable ways to accommodate the request.

Tempers, Tantrums, and Strong Feelings

Another dilemma arises when a child simply experiences strong feelings that trouble both child and caregiver. A child may cry uncontrollably, rage in a tantrum, or pull inward in silence. These are all normal feelings in response to anger, frustration, or sadness, yet the behavior is troublesome and often difficult to cope with.

A respectful response to a tantrum begins with assurance that the child is in a safe place physically. An assurance of emotional safety comes in the form of an acknowledgment of the child's anger, rage, or frustration, for example, naming the child's feelings, as in, "You're sad. You're missing your Daddy. He just left, and that makes you sad." The aim is not to judge the appropriateness of the feelings nor to resolve the problem. The aim is to help the child cope with and begin to understand what is happening.

WHEN CAREGIVERS acknowledge children's strong feelings, when they offer them clear limits and redirection, or when they propose a limited choice, they help children access their inherent motivation to engage with others in sympathetic exchange. In so doing, they enlist children's willingness to help others in need (Warneken & Tomasello, 2008), without expectation of reward. Because infants pay close attention from birth on to the interactions and conversations of others, caregivers can draw on infants' inherent sensitivity to others' feelings to access their sense of altruism during moments of conflict—and thus help them maintain and sustain their connection to family, friends, and community.

CHAPTER 12

How the Light Gets In

Coping with Adversity

There is kindness that dwells deep down in things; it presides everywhere. . . . The world can be harsh and negative, but if we remain generous and patient, kindness inevitably reveals itself.
—John O'Donohue (2008, p. 185)

WITH PSYCHOBIOLOGICAL descriptions of infant development throughout, this book has focused on ways to support optimal development. Because the majority of brain and nervous system growth takes place during the infant years, adverse events can render the developmental experience of some infants less than optimal, with profound and long-lasting impact. Despite exposure to adversity during gestation or the first 3 years, there are measures we can take to help infants and their families cope with and manage adversity, thereby protecting every infant's right to optimal development.

This chapter draws on a large body of research on the consequences of developmental disruptions on health outcomes, but most important, it focuses on ways that parents, and those supporting families with infants, can deal with these disruptions to ameliorate the impact of adversity on infants' development. By exploring the basis of health and well-being, with respect to how adverse experiences affect development, we can begin to repair and heal the effects of adversity. Just as poets, such as Leonard Cohen, saw light shining through the cracks, while the potter finds beauty in broken objects, this chapter points to strengths that can emerge from wounded places when given appropriate support.

BODY IS HOME FOR LIFE

In human life the body is central—the holder, the container, the translator, and the mediator of all experiences. Stress, trauma, or violence leaves an imprint on the body that is woven into neural, sensory, motor, and muscle systems. However, the body, by nature, holds a blueprint for maintaining health (Chitty, 2016). It is this blueprint that serves as the basis for restoring health and well-being.

The Embodied Self

From the beginning, infants are part of a family, their development occurring within a social context, as discussed in Chapter 11. To paraphrase Winnicott (1964), without the family, there is no infant (see Chapter 1). Whether considering prevention or repair from harm, for the infant the family is central. The health and well-being of infants are intertwined with the health and well-being of their families.

From conception through gestation, from the powerful experience of birth to the welcoming arms of loved ones, and on to joyful companionship and play—these are all experiences of the body, felt within the senses, skin, and heart. From cell to fluids, from neural networks to organ systems, development is the result of billions of complex, interconnected processes, including "genetic, epigenetic, and developmental" ones (Perry, 2014b, p. 21). From prenate to newborn, the body is created in the context of internal and external influences. Infants experience themselves through their bodies, and their emerging sense of "self" is inextricably tied to the body. One way to describe this is as an "embodied self."

Decades ago Winnicott (1964) observed differences in young children—those who were in contact with what he described as the "True Self" and those who were not. Winnicott believed that the "True Self is our embodied self-awareness, our ability to stay comfortably in the chaos of the subjective emotional present" (Fogel, 2009b, p. 103). From this understanding, Winnicott proposed that mothers facilitate a baby's sense of self by reflecting him back to himself. He maintained that the physical caring of the mother, what she communicates through her own body—her hands and the quality of her touch—lays the groundwork for how babies come to know themselves and how they see themselves. The baby begins to be able to use her body to be comfortable in emotional flux.

Interoception

As discussed in Chapter 4, neuroception is the capacity to read cues from outside the body. Embodied self-awareness is felt through a process called *interoception*, the "ability to feel one's own body, states and emotions" (Fogel, 2009b, p. 39). Interoception allows us "to feel and sense one's organs, skin, viscera and receive information about the internal condition of our body" (Mahler, 2017, p. 1). These sensations include cues related to survival—like hunger, thirst, pain, temperature, and respiration. Other sensations that prompt action may include itching, muscular tension, drowsiness, and elimination cues. Each sensation reflects a feeling state in the body, and each feeling state conveys information about what is happening within the embodied self. Such body-based information is critical to one's comfort and survival. Beyond physical cues, interoception is the ability to feel emotions and states (Fogel, 2009b).

As awareness of bodily sensations and emotional states develops, neural connections grow in the middle prefrontal cortex (refer to Chapter 2 and Figure 2.12). This brain region is linked to emerging self-awareness (Siegel, 2015). Internal and external sensory experiences wire the neural connections that form in this brain region and establish the connection to the body-self (Fogel, 2009b). Supporting babies as these body-self connections are growing is important.

Babies have not yet learned how to regulate their emotional states, "much less the changes in heart rate, hormone levels, and nervous-system activity that accompany emotions" (van der Kolk, 2014, p. 114). If an infant in a state of arousal seeks connection with a caregiver in order to calm, thereby relaxing his muscles and stabilizing his heart rate and breathing, he will return to a state of emotional balance. As described in Chapter 4, a parent can transfer to the infant a sense of safety, comfort, and mastery over strong and overwhelming emotions. This helps the baby begin to build a foundation for self-regulation, self-soothing, and self-nurture (van der Kolk, 2014), while simultaneously growing neural connections that are central to embodied self-awareness.

COMPANIONSHIP

When infants' emotional and biological expectations are met with loving, responsive, attuned care, healthy outcomes are likely. According to child psychiatrist Bruce Perry (2014a), when infants' expectations are disrupted, whether through intrauterine stress or substance exposure, neglect, chaos, or trauma, brain development is compromised. Most parents want the best for their children, but not all parents can define what best outcomes might look like. Proclamations about optimal development should not be seen as a measure against which parents are judged (by themselves or others). Instead, descriptions of optimal development can be used as a map that can lead to expansive views and delightful surprises along the path. Parents learn through trial and error, and most will experience missteps as well as successes. Here is one description of the foundations of optimal development that may serve as a guide (Brandt, 2014):

> Every child must be provided with five essential ingredients for optimal development in all domains, but especially mental health: 1) a safe, healthy, and low-stress pregnancy; 2) the opportunity and ability to "fall in love" and "be in love" with a safe and nurturing adult; 3) support in learning to self-regulate; 4) support in learning to mutually regulate; and 5) nurturing, contingent, and developmentally appropriate care. (p. 2)

Without these ingredients, children are at greater developmental, relational, and behavioral risk (Brandt, Perry, Seligman, & Tronick, 2014).

In the infant's early years, there are many opportunities to support optimal well-being, to prevent disruptions whenever possible, and to repair disturbances before they consolidate into unhealthy physical, social, or behavioral problems. For infants and toddlers, it must be done within the social contexts of care. It is this that comprises a field of intervention called infant–parent mental health, one in which parent as well as infant benefits from the social context of care that supports growth and development.

Regulatory Companions

Early in life, support from others is a biological necessity for survival. The newborn is not equipped with a fully functioning nervous system. It is only through ongoing parental co-regulating interactions that the infant's nervous system is wired for long-term health (Dana, 2018). Parents are regulatory companions when they help infants build a healthy regulation system (Lillas & Turnbull, 2009):

> The regulation system describes those brain mechanisms that are involved in bodily processes and the regulation of energy. The primary constructs presented within the regulatory system include states of arousal (such as sleep and alertness), stress responses (such as to challenge and threat) and stress recovery, and efficient and adaptive energy regulation. (p. 32)

The regulatory processes of the nervous system control arousal, what therapists Connie Lillas and Janiece Turnbull (2009) term "the fundamental ingredient of all behavior" (p. 51). Lillas and Turnbull describe arousal states along a continuum (illustrated in Continuum A), from low-energy (left side) to high-energy (right side) expression (p. 52).

Each distinct arousal state has a different energy cost (Lillas, 2014). A bout of intense crying or a burst of anger (flooding) drains energy reserves within the infant. Infants with well-regulated nervous systems are able to recover more easily from arousal states and therefore restore their energy reserves. An infant whose communication cries are understood and responded to will learn her own capacity, that is, "I am able to alert my caregiver," as well as the capacity of the other, that is, "She is reliable," without moving into a high-cost arousal state.

A responsive parent or companion facilitates efficient use of energy so infants can spend it on connection and learning. In contrast, infants who do not have an attuned response to their cries will have a different experience, which if repeated will likely delay the development of their capacity to smoothly regulate their states. The soothing presence of stable, nurturing caregivers is essential to healthy regulation, and healthy regulation is central to learning (Lillas & Turnbull, 2009).

The regulation system is responsible for utilizing and distributing energy, managing states of arousal, optimizing stress response capacity, and facilitating stress recovery. These capacities develop through supportive infant–parent interactions. As biological systems stabilize, they form the basis for emotional regulation. Caring, responsive companions act as coregulators (Als, 2007; Lillas & Turnbull, 2009; Schore, 2001). This interactive regulation is the foundation from which self-regulation emerges. The earliest form of this occurs during gestation, when mother and prenate are biologically connected (see Chapter 2). The mother's body maintains stability for the fetus by providing warmth and oxygenation and by facilitating nutrition and elimination. Co-regulation initially focuses on these baseline survival processes. In addition, as the pregnant mother encounters stress and her own regulatory processes respond, her system primes the stress response patterns in the developing prenate's regulation system.

Once born, maternal skin-to-skin care between baby and mother continues to support the newborn in regulating temperature, heart rate, and respiration, along with reducing newborn discomfort and distress (see Chapter 4). As parents get to know their newborns, they are better able to read their cues. As a result, they become more effective at soothing and calming an infant's emotional states.

This process can be satisfying for both parent and infant. A mutually satisfying exchange regulates not only the baby's nervous system but the parent's nervous system as well. Two biological systems in synchrony—co-regulating and experiencing a sense of well-being together—fosters deeper bonds between the two and provides the child with a sense of her authentic, embodied self. As parents allay fears and anxieties in the infant, they lay the foundation for other adults

Continuum A. Arousal States

Sleep → Drowsy → Hypoalert → Alert → Hyperalert → Flooded

to step in as trusted companions. In daily, attuned encounters with loved ones, an infant's capacity for self-regulation grows. An infant with a well-developed regulatory system demonstrates it in three areas—physiological, emotional, and attentional.

Physiological Regulation. Regulation of basic physiological rhythms, such as sleep/wake cycles and feeding, consume much of parents' and infants' energy in the first weeks following birth (see Chapters 5 and 6). This makes sense, considering the full range of physiological rhythms that babies must regulate—the capacity for deep sleep cycling, alert processing, adaptive stress responses, efficient stress recovery, and distinct states of arousal, with smooth transitions between them. As described in Chapter 6, in discussions of infant sleep, most typically developing infants take time to establish these primary biological rhythms and enjoy the benefit of parents serving as external regulators. While parents serve in this role, the image of a guide may be more appropriate than that of an enforcer.

Emotional Regulation. Emotional regulation impacts attentional regulation, which in turn is tied closely with physiological regulation. Babies who are persistently fussy or irritable, or who have difficulty with sleep or feeding, experience high levels of stress, as will their parents (see Chapter 4 and Chapter 6). High stress levels, especially if chronic, accumulate and result in wear and tear, disrupting other aspects of regulation. To effectively regulate their baby's emotions, parents must be aware of their own emotional regulation.

Adults are better regulatory companions when they pay attention to their own physical and emotional sensations. This concept is not unlike the advice delivered on a commercial airliner: "Put on your own oxygen mask before tending to your child's mask."

Attentional Regulation. As physiological rhythms stabilize and emotions are regulated through ongoing interactions with companions, infants have more energy to pay attention to their surroundings. Attentional regulation means one is able to orient, focus, and attend to surrounding people, objects, and events. Over time and with practice, this capacity is enhanced and allows for self-regulation while the infant is engaging socially and investigating in play. It is through attention in play and interactions that infants build understanding.

Responsive Care

Responsive care is key to helping infants build a well-functioning regulatory system. When parents' ability to regulate their own state is impaired, it may contribute to poor infant regulation. Parents whose interactions are disruptive or unpredictable will contribute to poor regulatory function in their infants. A poorly functioning system may impact a child's physical and psychological health dramatically. As Lillas and Turnbull

A CLOSER LOOK

What's in Your Tool-Kit?

Within the field of trauma and repair, a well-established practice is to identify resources one has available. What are resources? Resources can be people, animals, places, processes, practices, images, personal qualities, and activities that give you strength. A friend or loved one to talk to, or a beloved pet to walk with can help. Activities like tennis, dance, yoga, or playing a musical instrument can replenish one's resources. Religious or spiritual practices such as prayer or meditation serve as sources of strength and calm for some.

Taking stock of what's in place—in the way of supportive relationships, engaging activities, and calming practices—prepares one for healing. The best time to make such an assessment is early in the repair process. When trauma has been severe or prolonged, the first work should always be to "stock up" on resources, making sure they are adequate and varied. The idea is to have a stable foundation from which to work.

A resource should help keep you connected with yourself in the present moment (a key component for healing) and to find inner balance. Take time to identify whatever is in your personal tool kit that allows you to feel whole and to feel connected to your authentic self. These might include:

- People or animals
- Activities or practices
- Places

point out, "Poor stress recovery has been implicated in childhood and adult-onset conditions, such as diabetes, asthma, cardiovascular disease, autoimmune diseases, depression and anxiety" (2009, p. 119).

Throughout the day, in multiple ways, parents and professionals have many opportunities to enhance an infant's regulatory system, which will bolster the capacity for relational and individual well-being (Lillas & Turnbull, 2009). Parents, teachers, home visitors, and health professionals do this when they read and respond to cues and underlying needs of the infant or child in their care. Understanding and making use of the neural circuitry of social engagement is part of this process. Regulating one's own arousal states is another.

TRAUMATIC HARM

As discussed in Chapter 4, the three branches of the autonomic nervous system (ANS) maintain equilibrium in all the body systems and manage stress responses and recovery. When these three branches are working smoothly together, states of attention, relaxation, and engagement are balanced. According to Fogel (2009b), when the ANS is functional, "we can feel and express our emotions while at the same time being able to empathize with and relate to others" (pp. 147–148).

These neural pathways, by design, have the potential to activate and respond to stress in distinct ways. The parasympathetic nervous system response is immobilization (fright, shutdown), the sympathetic nervous system response is mobilization (fight–flight or tense–freeze [i.e., brakes "on"]), and the social engagement system response seeks others for safety and reassurance. In a healthy system, these pathways activate to protect the immediate needs of the individual and then cycle into recovery mode as conditions change.

In children or adults whose nervous system has been taxed through high levels of stressful events, the functioning of the ANS (maintenance, stress response, and stress recovery) may be impaired. Using the metaphor of cracks and light introduced at the beginning of the chapter, it is through the crack that the light gets in. Even when early experiences have nudged the ANS toward dysfunction, positive reparative experiences will nudge it back toward healthier function. Health is always present in the system; it is simply a matter of finding it beneath the maladaptation.

Safety or Threat

When threat or danger is imminent, interoception or embodied awareness shuts down and the more primitive parts of the brain become activated (Fogel, 2009b). Trauma, however, is an altogether higher order of stress, overwhelming the physiological and psychological body and mind. If the situation allows for proximity seeking, that is, engaging with others close by, one may find safety and relief, a safe haven. Within a safe haven, one is more capable of shifting into recovery mode. In a state of safety, one can draw on physical and emotional reserves to find stability again, allowing a return to attentional awareness and social interactions. Within a safe haven, infants and young children can again make meaningful use of their surroundings and the people in their world.

There are a variety of ways one might respond to a potential threat. At the first hint of danger, an alarm system in the brain is activated, triggering an alert state focusing on what may have triggered the alarm. Perhaps it was a loud sound. When this happens within a group of people, it is human nature to turn to others for social reference, "Did you hear that? Is it friend or foe?" If danger is imminent, the body releases high doses of stress hormones prompting intense activity, either fighting or fleeing. Both responses engage large muscle systems, so these are action-based states. If fight–flight is not an option, another response is to freeze yet remain vigilant. This is a tension-filled state, sometimes described as having a foot on the gas and the brake pedal at the same time. In the animal world, this freeze state can dissuade predators from following through with eating prey. This biological response is wired into humans, successfully adaptive across generations. Those who used a tense–freeze response survived to reproduce. Finally, there is another freeze/immobility response that can be life-threatening. Physiological systems slow down significantly and may stop temporarily (e.g., digestion). If this state is prolonged, it can endanger survival.

In circumstances when the novel stimulus is easily identified, the process might look like Continuum B. In threatening circumstances, when a sound indicates a real threat, it might look like one of the scenarios depicted in Continuum C.

A familiar childhood game, hide and seek, can be used to illustrate the recovery process. There are variations of this game, but the simplest is when one child is the seeker and the others run to hide. The seeker counts

Continuum B. An Easily Identified Novel Stimulus

Arousal/Alert → Orient (connect to another) → Rest and restore

A loud sound → "Did you hear that?" → "Yes, it was just a door shutting."
Return to normal state of attention/activity in play or work

Continuum C. A Sound That Indicates a Real Threat

Arousal/Alert → Fight/Flight

A loud sound/"What's that?!" → "Fight!" or "Run!"

OR

Arousal/Alert → Freeze/Hypervigilant

A loud sound/"Oh no . . ." → Don't move . . . very still, yet tense . . .

Continuum D. Hide and Seek

Arousal/Alert → Flight → Arousal/Alert → Flight → Rest and restore

"Seeker" covers her eyes → Others run and hide →
Listen for "ready or not " call → Run to safety → Rest happily

loudly with eyes covered, then calls out, "Ready or not, here I come!" The goal is to find playmates before they reach a designated home base. This is an exciting activity that involves running (flight for fun). Children are running *from* someone (to avoid being caught) and *to* something (safety). The stress recovery process might look like Continuum D.

Adversity

In 1998, Felitti and colleagues released the results from their groundbreaking Adverse Childhood Experiences (ACE) Study. This work was a collaborative effort between Kaiser Permanente and the Centers for Disease Control and Prevention. Designed to determine whether there was a relationship between adversity and the quality of physical and mental health over a lifetime, the study surveyed 17,000 adults, middle class, mostly white. They were asked questions related to exposure to a range of traumatic experiences in childhood. The researchers framed these adverse experiences within three categories: abuse (emotional, physical, and sexual abuse), neglect (emotional and physical), and household dysfunction (domestic violence, divorce or separation, mental illness, substance use, or an incarcerated member).

The findings were staggering: 63.9% of the adults had at least one adverse childhood event. There was a strong correlation between the number of traumatic or abusive events in childhood and poor mental and physical health outcomes. In the analysis of the data, it was clear that the behaviors previously seen to be simply "lifestyle choices" were more accurately recognized to be coping behaviors in response to adversity. When no obvious interventions are available, unresolved early adversity is often masked with substance use and can lead to poor mental and physical health outcomes.

In the decades that followed publication of the ACE results, research studies from multiple disciplines have corroborated the initial findings of the study. More than 440,000 people have been surveyed for exposure to adverse childhood experiences (ACEs), and the results have shown a consistent and alarming fact—childhood trauma is common, and those with a higher

FIGURE 12.1. Potential Health Outcomes Associated with Adverse Childhood Experiences

- Changes in the nervous system—specifically the amygdala, hippocampus, and prefrontal cortex—that may result in attention and cognitive deficits. In addition, there may be learning disabilities, memory problems, hyperactivity, anxiety, and delays in self-regulation.
- Changes in the immune system, which may result in more vulnerability to infection, higher risk of autoimmune disorders, and complications from chronic inflammation.
- Changes in the cardiovascular system, which may result in chronic inflammation. Inflammation is correlated with high blood pressure, arterial damage, and greater risk for heart disease, heart attack, and stroke.

Source: Center for Youth Wellness (2014).

number of these experiences are at greater risk for chronic illness. Untreated early trauma disrupts systems throughout the body. Figure 12.1 summarizes the range of illnesses and chronic conditions that can result from accumulation of ACEs.

The impact of ACEs on health outcomes cuts across socioeconomic and other demographic factors. As noted earlier, the original study found that approximately two-thirds of the population had undergone one or more ACEs. The results of subsequent studies are similar regardless of location, race, or income level. When two of three people surveyed have had one or more ACEs, this is cause for concern and highlights the critical need for broader public awareness of the impact of early life adversity on lifelong health and well-being.

Dissemination of findings from this research has benefit for all and is key to mitigating the incidence of adversity. With accumulated adverse childhood experiences affecting such a large segment of the population, there is a high likelihood that many parents, teachers, and health, legal, and justice professionals may be impacted, potentially affecting not only their own health but also the way they perceive and interact with others. Evidence shows that safe, stable, nurturing relationships are essential to preventing emotional, physical, and psychological trauma and adversity (Powell et al., 2013). Indeed, the benefits of healthy relationships in the home and at work may be even more critical for those with a history of ACEs (Schofield, Lee, & Merrick, 2013).

Adversity, when recognized and worked with, can benefit the individual and those with whom they interact through increasing empathy and compassion. Conversely, when early adversity is not recognized, not acknowledged or worked with, it may interfere with healthy parenting, teaching, and other professional roles.

As with other public health concerns, addressing the impact of early life adversity requires three levels of mitigation: primary (prevention and education), secondary (early detection and intervention), and tertiary (programs and services to manage well-being over time). Each level is best provided within a relationship-based model of support and care. Figure 12.2 illustrates the full spectrum of adverse conditions that impact lifelong health outcomes. It draws in a dimension of adversity that requires systemic change, that is, adversity as it exists within the community. Education aimed at individual families will not be effective if it is not accompanied by systemic change within the greater society. It will take a broad-based effort on the part of individuals, families, educators, organizations, and policy-makers to effect long-term change.

Impact of Trauma

The impact of traumatic or stressful events that occur in one's life depends a lot on how the individual responds to the events and on the person's social support network. Trauma happens to everyone, either directly or indirectly. When a traumatic event is experienced in one person's life, it ripples throughout the relational network. Trauma leaves an imprint on bodies, minds, and emotions, affecting, as psychiatrist and trauma expert Bessel van der Kolk (2014) states, "our capacity for joy and intimacy, and even our biology and immune systems" (p. 1). Trauma has been defined as something that overwhelms the physical and psychological capacity to cope in the moment and over time. Perry (2014a) defines trauma as "a psychologically distressing event that is outside the range of usual human experience, often involving a sense of intense fear, terror, and helplessness" (p. 15). Life is experienced differently after trauma, "with a different nervous system," and individuals' energy "becomes focused on suppressing inner chaos, at the expense of

FIGURE 12.2. Pair of ACEs

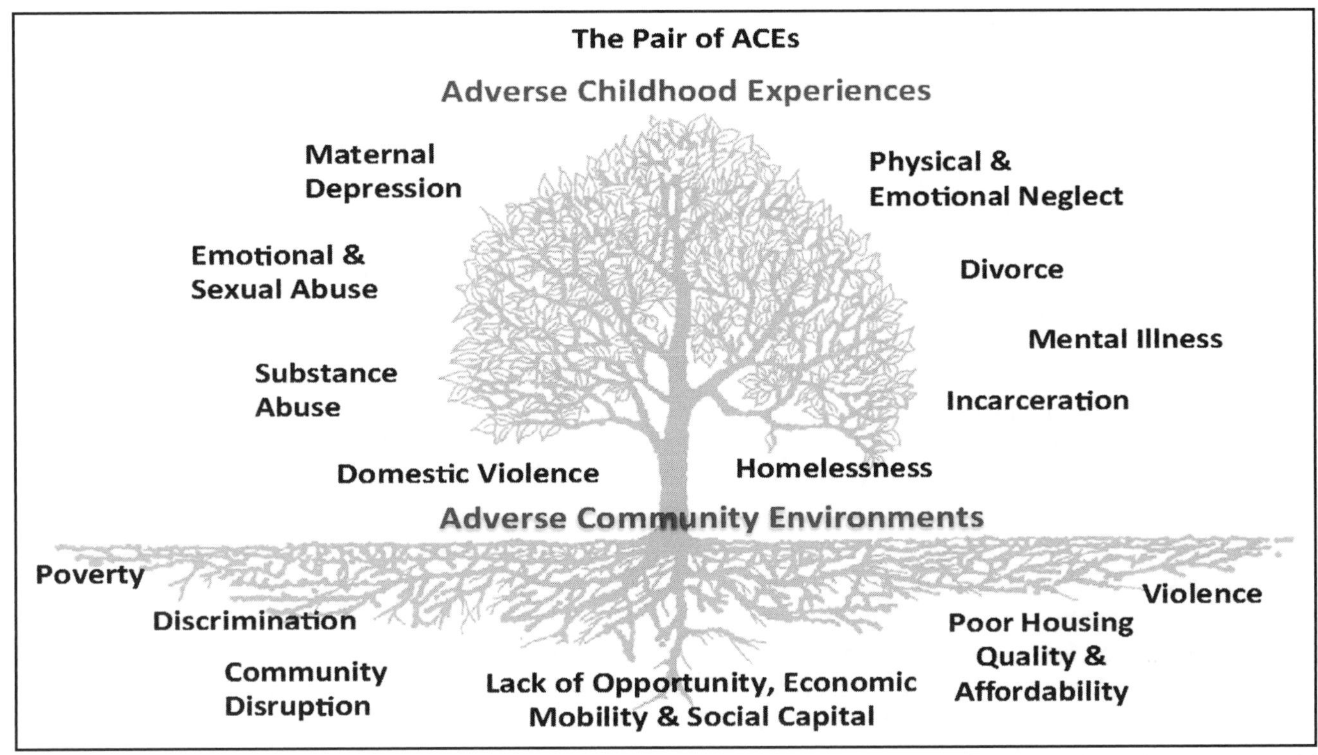

Source: A New Framework for Addressing Adverse Childhood and Community Experiences: The Building Community Resilience (BCR) Model (Ellis & Dietz, 2017). Used with permission.

spontaneous involvement in their life" (van der Kolk, 2014, p. 53).

Not all terrible events result in traumatic effects. Two individuals can experience the same event and have two completely different outcomes. Multiple factors contribute to how trauma is experienced by a child or an adult. These factors include epigenetic and environmental factors, family context, and prior history. Regardless of the trauma, the presence of aware, loving, attuned adults can make an overwhelming event easier to integrate. Integration, even of terrible events, can moderate the impact of the events and is important to the healing process that may come later. In fact, trauma occurs when one "becomes unable to integrate the resulting interoceptive experiences, emotions, and changes in body schema, and thoughts" (Fogel, 2009b, pp. 142–143).

Trauma can be the result of a single incident (falling out of a tree) or ongoing experience (neighborhood violence). Traumatic events can be personal and focused, in that they happen to a "me-self." Or they can be random and impersonal, as in extreme climate disasters. Relational traumas are those that happen within close personal relationships, as in neglect or emotional, physical, or sexual abuse. Such occurrences in personal relationships are more likely to be traumatic because they involve betrayal of trust. Developmental trauma occurs when these forms of betrayal are chronic. Even planned events such as a surgery or a painful medical procedure can be traumatic, in some cases. Even when an adult knows what is coming next (e.g., anesthesia followed by an incision), the event can overwhelm one's capacity to regulate and manage one's body and physical processes in routine, everyday ways.

Physical Expressions

It is important to understand that "trauma produces actual physiological changes, including a recalibration of the brain's alarm system, an increase in the system that filters relevant information from irrelevant" (van der Kolk, 2014, pp. 2–3). In addition, trauma puts people at risk for a whole array of social, psychological, and physical health problems (Perry, 2014a). As described earlier, the infant experiences the world through his body. Every part of the body is affected by trauma, described by van der Kolk (2014) as follows:

A CLOSER LOOK

Checking In with Sensations and Feelings

Reading, viewing media, or engaging in discussions about stressful, traumatic, or threatening events can be disturbing, even for those who did not experience significant childhood adversity, so as you read about such events, pay attention to these signals and feelings:

- Notice the position of your body. Become aware of contact points your body is making—your feet on the floor, your bottom on a chair, perhaps your back against a pillow. Simply notice.
- Take a slow scan of your surroundings. With a soft gaze, gently notice what is in front of you, what is on each side, what is beneath you, and what is above. Here you are, in the midst of this space. Make note of signals from other senses—sounds, smells, a cool breeze, or the warmth of the sun.
- Notice your breath. Without effort simply pay attention to breathing—inhale and exhale. If you like, you can follow your breath through three or four cycles. You might want to try a slow count of three (1-2-3) on each inhale, and a count of six (1-2-3-4-5-6) on each exhale.
- If you become aware of feelings or thoughts, simply notice them as they show up. Often feelings and thoughts will dissipate as you make note of them, especially as you return your attention to your breathing or physical sensations.
- If a troubling emotion comes up, simply identify it (e.g., sadness) and return attention to your breathing and awareness of physical sensations (e.g., feeling your back against a cushion).

Continue this conscious awareness as long as you wish, to reconnect with your emotional and sensory experience in the moment. This time is meant to be restorative. If it feels right, jot down your impressions after you are done.

> Breathing, eating, sleeping, pooping, and peeing are so fundamental that their significance is easily neglected when we're considering the complexities of mind and behavior. However, if your sleep is disturbed or your bowels don't work, or if you always feel hungry, or if being touched makes you want to scream (as is often the case with traumatized children and adults), the entire organism is thrown into disequilibrium. It is amazing how many psychological problems involve difficulties with sleep, appetite, touch, digestion, and arousal. Any effective treatment for trauma has to address these basic housekeeping functions of the body. (p. 56)

The nervous system can become locked into a pattern, either frozen or hypervigilant, and that process naturally involves multiple brain structures and neural networks. Traumatized people of all ages can get stuck in dysfunctional and chronic patterns (van der Kolk, 2014). Childhood trauma is distinct, however, because the child may be continuing to live within the relational context where the abuse or maltreatment happened.

Behavioral Expressions

The effect of trauma on behavior varies, depending on the developmental age when the trauma occurred. A 3-year-old with a first single-incident trauma may recover well or may suddenly begin behaving like a 1-year-old. Newborns and young infants are not able to explain what happened to them. Parents and caregivers may need to boost their own sensory awareness to detect and interpret the cues of infants or toddlers. Infants may express traumatic effects through biobehavioral changes, facial expressions, and changes in state regulation, for example. Children who have experienced abuse or neglect at the hands of caregivers "consistently demonstrate chronic and severe problems with emotion regulation, impulse control, attention and cognition, dissociation, interpersonal relationships, and self and relational schemas" (van der Kolk, 2014, p. 161).

In a wide review of studies, the National Child Traumatic Stress Network identified common patterns observed in those who experienced childhood trauma—a pervasive pattern of dysregulation, problems with attention and concentration, and difficulties getting along with themselves and others (van der Kolk, 2014). These children had problems with their emotions swinging from one end of the spectrum to the other, from tantrums to emotional flatness and

A CLOSER LOOK

Longitudinal Study of Risk and Adaptation

For more than 30 years, beginning in 1975, a team of researchers led by L. Alan Sroufe tracked first-time mothers and their children (Sroufe, Egeland, Carlson, & Collins, 2009). They used interviews and a variety of assessments, beginning in the third trimester of pregnancy. By age 6 each child and parent had been assessed 15 times. Several key findings of Sroufe's study were discussed by van der Kolk (2014).

How parents felt about their children and the quality of their interactions were essential to the children becoming healthy adults. Children who were regularly "pushed over the edge into overarousal and disorganization" (van der Kolk, 2014, p. 163) did not develop healthy regulatory patterns to cope with or manage distressing and disturbing emotions.

The difference between the healthy and the struggling children was very clear. Those who received consistent caregiving became well regulated. The children who experienced erratic caregiving were "chronically physiologically aroused" (van der Kolk, 2014, p. 163). These children were chronically anxious, causing them to focus their energies on various ineffective strategies to manage those states, which interfered with their play and exploration. They grew up nervous and unadventurous.

Sroufe also observed children bounce back from adversity. His study found that the strongest predictor of how well they met challenges was the degree to which they had a secure and loving presence in their lives. Sroufe commented, "resilience in adulthood could be predicted by how lovable mothers rated their kids at age two" (as cited in van der Kolk, 2014, p. 163).

detachment. When they got upset, they could "neither calm themselves down nor describe what they were feeling" (van der Kolk, 2014, p. 160). The amygdala—the smoke detector of the brain—has made these children hypersensitive to threat and/or perceived threat.

Children who have been traumatized, and who have not had adequate intervention or repair, expend a lot of energy managing difficult emotions, attempting to stay in control, and using strategies that might aid them in the moment, but which, in the long run, have little benefit and may engender more problems. Young children who have been neglected or abused may also be living with internal developmental gaps that are not seen, felt, or recognized. This can lead to misreading of cues, interpersonal missteps, mistrust, isolation, and behavioral problems. These may lead to more maladaptive behaviors, which in turn result in more rejection and conflict. Children may have increased fearfulness, more bouts of sadness, or sleep problems (including nightmares), and some will show signs of re-experiencing or re-creating a traumatic event (Perry, 2014a). If there is no intervention, these behaviors and emotional states will become traits (Perry et al., 1995). When problems persist—some clinicians suggest 3 months or longer—they should be addressed by a professional. Without intervention, such children are at increased risk for subsequent problems.

HEALING HAPPENS IN THE BODY

Parents and teachers can help an infant or young child who has experienced stress, maltreatment, or trauma. This support can take several forms. Seeking professional guidance and help is necessary in many instances. Professional help can be of tremendous value, yet in light of the fact that the hours spent with a trained professional pale when compared to the time spent with family, friends, and teachers, another very important avenue of support is essential. Finding ways to support parents, teachers, and others who spend their days with young children is key.

Tend and Befriend

There is much that caring companions of young children can do to support the underlying physical and mental health of each child, especially those who have experienced stress, maltreatment, or trauma. As discussed

> **A CLOSER LOOK**
>
> **Your Role in Tending and Befriending**
>
> The importance of a circle of caring, safe, stable, and nurturing adults is essential to all children's healthy development. Consider how your own interactions with infants and young children support them with healthy regulatory function. Consider your own reflective capacity as you interact with young children, and think about how this capacity enhances your ability to reflect back to a child his or her own embodied and authentic self. Consider how these elements, alone and in combination, support infants or young children to know themselves through reflective interactions, allowing them to feel secure, alive, and real in the present and in connection with another.

extensively in this and earlier chapters, infants are social beings and require relationships to survive and thrive. In daily routines, when a momentary rupture occurs, parents can repair and benefit their relationship with the infant (see Chapter 4). At no other time do young children have a greater need for the steady presence of a loving adult than they do during moments of distress, destabilization, and dysregulation. During times of struggle, those in deep relationship with children can provide a sense of holding and a sense of containment.

These supportive adults can also help the infant to digest or metabolize intense feelings. When adults understand the roots of troubling behavior, they can intervene in supportive ways to help young children heal. When they understand that challenging behavior is an automatic response within the nervous system, a response that was set in motion earlier in the child's life and, as such, may be beyond the child's conscious awareness, their responses can be compassionate and ultimately more effective in helping the child heal.

How parents and caregivers respond immediately after a highly stressful or traumatic event is important to the healing. They should maintain or return to routines that support biological rhythms, paying attention to regular meals, comfort care, and restorative sleep. There is much that parents and teachers can do in everyday interactions to support children to build a healthy and robust sense of self and a flexible and adaptive mind (Siegel, 2015).

Tapping into the Social Engagement System

Relationship is the center of all reparative experiences. In keeping with the "oxygen mask on the airplane" rule, adults must regulate their own reactivity, triggers, and inner stress responses. Monitoring in-the-moment interoceptive cues, bodily sensations, and arousal states takes practice, but doing so is essential if one is to tend and befriend oneself. Children need to have reliable companions, people who care and are willing to adapt to a child's changing needs. They need the presence of a caring adult who will help them manage their sometimes overwhelming feelings, states, and behaviors. Traumatized children need compassionate reflection of their experiences "because trauma almost invariably involved not being seen, not being mirrored, and not being taken into account. Treatment needs to reactivate the capacity to safely mirror, and be mirrored, by others" (van der Kolk, 2014, p. 59).

A child needs to feel safe and to be able to trust an adult to stick with them through the process of returning to health. However, some trauma requires more intentional and focused effort. Interventions for serious trauma should always involve professionals. Intervention is most effective when it is matched to the developmental needs of the infant, toddler, or child. An important dimension of treatment is educating and guiding the adults in a child's life to build on the professional's work with the child.

According to leading trauma experts Perry (2014a, 2014b) and van der Kolk (2014), treatment is most effective when the developmental period of the trauma is taken into account. As van der Kolk states, "we need to help bring back those brain structures that deserted them when they were overwhelmed by trauma back then" (p. 73). Therefore, it is important to have an understanding of which interventions work best with which brain structures. When a child is struggling with fear, as is often the case in trauma, interventions that activate key neural circuits in the brainstem may be more effective. Examples of such interventions include patterned, predictable, rhythmical, and repetitive bodily experiences. For a very young infant this might be rocking, singing, walking, or gently bouncing. The key is to remain in touch with the cues of the infant to determine what is working. The infant or child will let you know.

For toddlers, helpful interventions might include games involving patterned, predictable rhythms, like rolling a ball back and forth, or dancing and clapping in synchrony. Some children will benefit from respectful, nurturing massage or playful body tapping games, where a child taps on his own body in response to the adult's tapping patterns. Blowing bubbles can be soothing to the deeper autonomic regions of the brain, especially if the breath can be slowed down as part of the play. Drumming, swinging, and other forms of more vigorous body movements may also be beneficial.

Being in contact with a caring person who is monitoring how the child is responding to the rhythmical play is important. Note the use of the word *play.* For young children who have been subject to traumatic pain or loss, a gentle reintroduction to playful, joyful contact is the return path to awakening their social engagement system. As the capacity for handling joy and delight increases, a child will enjoy experimenting with adding a few more people to the play, to sing, drum, dance, and play together. This can heighten a sense of belonging and bring a surge of positive hormones of love and delight. The essence of repair is safe, attuned, mutual connection; rhythmic play; joy in one's own body; and pleasure in the companionship of others. It is important to recognize that some infants may need a slower buildup to re-engaging with play. Kindness, patience, and openness to the next opportunity will serve all.

Healthy infant–parent relationships are foundational for infants, families, and the greater society. All of the evidence from research and lived experience supports the notion that safe, supportive, and nurturing relationships are essential for optimal infant–parent development. When there is adversity that opens a crack in the body-self-being of either the infant or the parent, putting them at risk, it is important to see the crack as an opening through which the healing light of safe, supportive, nurturing relationships can enter.

A CLOSER LOOK

Using Rhythmic Breathing to Calm

Using the breath to calm an aroused nervous system is accessible even to very young children. Adults can show infants how to blow slowly through a straw or to slowly blow soap bubbles, which results in more control over their breathing. Both activities engage the social engagement nervous system: shaping the mouth, pursing the lips, and moving the breath in and out, slowing on the exhale. Adults can guide children, according to their developmental age, to breathe in and out in a rhythmic fashion. Another playful breath activity is to ask children to imagine they are holding and blowing on a dandelion flower or a pinwheel. Taking a deep breath in and slowly breathing out settles the child and brings a sense of calm.

A CLOSER LOOK

Helping Parents Cope with Stress

- Remind parents that some stress is normal, and parenting is stressful for everyone. How one responds makes the difference between adaptation and more stress.
- Families can plan "dates" to create art, play games, tell stories, or go to a park together.
- Reminders on the calendar can prompt parents to take time for themselves, even if only to focus on breathing for a few moments.
- Encourage parents to insert restorative activities into the week, such as quiet or playful time together at home or in nature.
- Taking time to think about the hopes and goals they have for their children can help parents focus on the big picture.
- Identifying and cultivating their own inner and outer resources or strengths can help parents better face daily challenges.
- Remind parents that if or when interactions with a child break down or are hurtful, they need to work to repair the harm. Point out to them that when they are nurturing and respectful of others, they are modeling this behavior for their children.
- Encourage parents to cultivate a circle of caring for their family and to ask for help when they need it.

CHAPTER 13

What Babies Ask of Us

Baby-Friendly Policies

One of the greatest dignities of humankind is that each successive generation is invested in the welfare of each new generation.

—Fred Rogers (2003, p. 155)

A CENTRAL QUESTION was posed in Chapter 1 and carried throughout this book, "What do babies ask of us?" This final chapter returns to this question, linking research findings described in this book to policies and practices that have the potential to vastly improve outcomes for infants and their families. A global initiative called 1,000 Days is attempting to raise awareness and take action on the fact that the first 1,000 days of human development are critical for the development of the infant and, consequently, for the economic success of society. Thurow (2016) describes this initiative as follows:

> If we want to shape the future, to truly improve the world, we have 1,000 days to do it, mother by mother, child by child. For what happens in those 1,000 days through pregnancy to the second birthday determines to a large extent the course of a child's life—his or her ability to grow, learn, work, succeed—and, by extension, the long-term health, stability, and prosperity of the society in which that child lives. (p. 7)

This initiative is built on research that identifies clearly that when children miss out on the resources they need in their earliest days, the result is an intergenerational cycle of disadvantage and inequality (Sullivan & Brumfield, 2016). This chapter addresses policies and practices that, if heeded and implemented, can reverse this negative cycle and ensure every infant's right to an optimal and equitable start in life.

PRE-CONCEPTION

Babies rely on caregivers to provide them with the resources needed to survive—food, warmth, protection, and social contact. This quest begins prior to conception, in the sperm and the eggs of the prospective parents, which carry the influence of epigenetic effects from prior generations. A multitude of factors, some described in Chapter 2, influence the status of what potentially can become a fertilized egg and a fertilizing sperm. The environmental conditions of parents and grandparents can potentially influence how genes are expressed in the generations that follow. For females, the developmental period when their genes are most sensitive to epigenetic change is when their eggs are forming prenatally, in the womb. For males, this sensitive period is late childhood, when they enter puberty.

As explored in Chapter 2, optimal human development across generations requires thoughtful attention to mental and physical health, not just during pregnancy and gestation, but during the years that come before and those that follow. Eliminating or reducing exposure to toxic environments and assuring access to nutritional food and health care are key factors in protecting reproductive well-being.

As young adults enter the reproductive years, every effort should be made to support their physical and emotional health and well-being and to make sure that they know how pre-conception health and behaviors can influence the development of a fetus. Educational opportunities for learning about prenatal development need to be accessible, relevant, and individualized as much as possible. This requires a broad campaign designed to reach those of various ages, levels of literacy, and cultural and linguistic contexts, inclusive of health-care providers and wrapped into health insurance coverage, regardless of socioeconomic status (Lally, 2013).

GESTATION AND PREGNANCY

Gestation is a time when the embryo and the fetus read signals in the surrounding environment of the womb, in preparation for expected life outside the womb. What these signals indicate, through epigenetics, depends on the environment to which the birthing parent is exposed, as well as the environment to which the maternal grandparent and great-grandparent were exposed, as described in Chapter 2. Epigenetic factors cross generations and determine when, where, and how genes are switched on or off during fetal development. With respect to the environment to which the mother is exposed, there are some factors that she can, in general, control, such as diet, exercise, and sleep. Other factors, such as exposure to pollutants in the air or water or the trauma that comes with natural disasters like floods, hurricanes, or earthquakes, may be exposures over which the mother has little control.

Reducing Risk

Although psychological and physical preparation for pregnancy is best, with education about pregnancy delivered prior to conception, such early preparation is rare. Young adults entering their childbearing years may not realize the harmful impact of substances, diseases, and behaviors on their own reproductive health, much less the potential effects once pregnant. First-time parents may not understand the importance of reducing stress or the impact high levels of stress may have on their newborn.

Many women may delay meeting with an obstetrician or a health-care provider until midway through their pregnancy. The delay is often simply due to an inability to pay for health-care and maternity services. By that time, however, much embryonic and fetal development has occurred (see Chapter 2). An additional concern is that many women wait until late in pregnancy to participate in childbirth education courses. As a result, they learn about prenatal development and maternal health after weeks of development have already occurred.

Health and Well-Being

Pregnant families benefit from a healthy and loving circle of support. Parenting is an unexpectedly demanding endeavor, even for those with adequate resources and supportive role models. Most new parents feel uncertain about their abilities. Some seek the advice of friends and family. Sometimes that advice comes unsolicited, which may or may not be welcomed and helpful. Concerns and worries that arise during pregnancy and in the days and months that follow are natural and very much a part of the process of becoming a parent. When parents have access to supportive prenatal care and to caring people with whom they can share feelings and concerns, burdensome fears and doubts become easier to bear. To quote Fred Rogers, "Feelings are mentionable, and whatever is mentionable can be more manageable" (1994, p. 97).

Access to Prenatal Care. Critical to maintaining regular and ongoing support during pregnancy is establishing a relationship with a health-care professional who engenders confidence in the pregnant mother and birthing family. With so much of a child's future dependent on what occurs during gestation, universal access to regular health check-ups, assessments, counseling, and support services should be a public good protected through systems of public health. However, many low-income, inner-city, rural, and teen mothers receive less prenatal care than mothers in other settings (Anderson, 1995). Between 8 and 14 prenatal care sessions are recommended, with the first beginning around 6–8 weeks following conception. Prenatal care includes assessment for risk factors, including counseling for cessation of smoking or misuse of alcohol. The cost of providing prenatal care generates savings in the long run, because identifying and responding to high-priority risks during prenatal care visits has the effect of reducing costly admissions to hospital and neonatal-intensive-care nurseries once babies are born.

Models of Care. During gestation, birth, and the neonatal period, there are multiple models for mother–baby care. In one model, an obstetrician or a family doctor is the lead health-care provider. In another, a midwife takes the lead. A third model, referred to as a midwife-led continuity of care model, involves shared responsibility between obstetrician and midwife, with a midwife the primary contact.

The role of midwife has a long tradition across time and across cultures. A midwife provides necessary support, care, and advice during pregnancy, labor, and the postpartum period. A midwife brings skilled, knowledgeable, and compassionate care to birthing mothers, newborns, and their families, described by Renfrew et al. (2014) as follows:

> Core characteristics include optimizing normal biological, psychological, social, and cultural processes of reproduction and early life; timely prevention, and management of complications; consultation with and referral to other services; respecting women's individual circumstances and views; and working in partnership with women to strengthen women's own capabilities to care for themselves and their families." (p. 1130)

In a report produced by the United Nations Population Fund, the International Confederation of Midwives, and the World Health Organization (2014), the value of the midwifery model of care was affirmed in findings from 73 low- and middle-income countries. The report concludes that midwives, when educated and regulated to international standards, have the competencies to deliver 87% of the services required by birthing mothers and babies. In a review of studies looking at midwife-led continuity of care models, researchers found that women in such care were less likely to have an epidural, an episiotomy, or an instrumental birth, and were more likely to have a vaginal birth (Sandall, Soltani, Gates, Shennan, & Devane, 2016). There were also fewer preterm births, a critical concern described in Chapter 2. The authors of this review conclude, "Midwife-led care confers benefits and shows no adverse outcomes" (p. 3). It is important to emphasize that in midwife-led continuity of care models, midwives consult, collaborate, and refer to specialists when an aspect of care falls outside their scope of practice (Goer & Romano, 2012).

HIGH-QUALITY, HIGH-VALUE MOTHER–BABY CARE

The field of Maternal and Child Health arose from the view that the health of mothers and children is influenced by social and economic factors. Maternal and Child Health programs developed as a way to mitigate the harmful effects of these factors. To that end, these programs focused their efforts on improving birth outcomes during the 9-month period of pregnancy and, to varying degrees, attempted to improve the social conditions of mothers.

Pregnancy and birth are a critical time to identify and mitigate existing or potential health risks in women and their children. Improving the well-being of mothers, infants, and children has long been identified as an important national and global public health goal, with the understanding that all women deserve access to high-quality care that is comprehensive, coordinated, cost-effective, and available within the communities where they live (Transforming Maternity Care Symposium Steering Committee, 2010).

Optimal Maternal Care

Providing optimal maternal care requires a comprehensive re-visioning of the maternity care system, and efforts to do so are being led by organizations such as the March of Dimes, the United Nations, and the National Partnership for Women and Families. Optimal maternity care is best integrated into a system of primary health care. As described by Goer and Romano (2012), an optimal system of care provides each woman "the most benefit with the least harm given her individual circumstances, risk factors, health status, and preferences" (p. 449)—in essence, the care that is "right" for each woman. The "right" care includes the basic needs that all women require, such as comfort, emotional support, and adequate information, but it also includes support for condition-specific needs, such as care that is sensitive to cultural values and expectations.

In recent years, well-researched and evidence-based protocols have emerged to provide detailed guidance in rendering care that supports optimal birth experiences. Prominent among them is the Mother-Friendly Childbirth Initiative (Improving Birth Coalition, 2018). This protocol is being adopted worldwide by hospitals and birthing centers. Mother-friendly hospitals and birthing centers must meet a list of specific criteria:

- Offering birthing women unrestricted access to the birth companions of their choice and access to professional midwifery care
- Providing birthing women with the freedom to walk and move about during labor and birth
- Keeping babies close to their mothers right after birth so that they can breastfeed as soon as they are ready

FIGURE 13.1. Normalcy of the Birthing Process

- Birth is a normal, natural, and healthy process.
- Women and babies have the inherent wisdom necessary for birth.
- Birth can safely take place in hospitals, birth centers, and homes.
- The midwifery model of care, which supports and protects the normal birth process, is the most appropriate for the majority of women during pregnancy and birth.
- Babies are aware, sensitive human beings at the time of birth, and should be acknowledged and treated as such.
- Breastfeeding provides the optimum nourishment for newborns and infants.

Source: Improving Birth Coalition (2018).

- Keeping healthy babies and their mothers together, rooming in day and night
- Training staff in how to support successful breastfeeding

The Improving Birth Coalition outlines a set of principles that "normalize" the birthing process. These are listed in Figure 13.1.

As research expands understanding of the physiological, social, and cultural context of birth, models of maternal and child care are undergoing transformation. The traditional model of maternity care has been described as a *medical-management model,* meaning it is based on the premise that pregnancy and birth are difficult and dangerous in all cases, and if left to progress without a range of interventions, will result in poor outcomes. On both a local level and a global level, the medical model is giving way to what is described as the *physiologic model,* which aligns more closely with human physiology (i.e., how the body works) and strives for optimal well-being of the mother and baby within the context of the family (Figure 13.2). Physiologic care consistently demonstrates better outcomes for mothers and babies (Goer & Romano, 2012).

Life-Course Perspective on Maternal Care

From a public health perspective, although providing optimal maternity care and normalizing birth are worthy goals, of concern is that there are persistent and as-yet-unexplained racial and ethnic disparities in birth outcomes. Researchers Lu and Halfon (2003) describe one disparity within the population of the United States as follows:

> An African American infant born today is still more than twice as likely to die within the 1st year of life as a White infant. A significant portion of this Black-White gap in infant mortality is attributable to the near twofold increase in low birth weight (LBW) and preterm births, and the near threefold increase in very low birth weight (VLBW) and very preterm births, among Black infants. (p. 13)

FIGURE 13.2. Two Models of Birth: Physiologic and Medical-Management

Physiologic Model	Medical-Management Model
Wellness oriented	Pathology or disease oriented
Trust orientation	Fear orientation
Birth is a natural and normal process	Birth is a crisis that must be managed for safety
Pregnancy and birth are experiences of health	Pregnancy and birth are hazardous times, and women need medical rescue
Supportive care	Interventive management
Woman is active agent	Doctor is active agent

This discrepancy may best be understood by factoring in the complex interplay of lifelong and cumulative biological, behavioral, psychological, and social factors, some of which can be protective of birthing mothers and newborns and some of which can put them at risk of adverse birth outcomes.

Birth outcomes are the expression of the mother's entire lifetime of experience, including early life experiences as well as accumulated life experiences. Access to good prenatal care is important; however, it may not be sufficient to avoid outcomes like prematurity or low birth weight, if the cumulative "wear and tear" to the mother's system has included a relatively high load of stress. The cumulative impact of such life-course experiences may make the mother more susceptible to complications and more vulnerable to infections (Lu & Halfon, 2003).

Early exposures and experiences during sensitive developmental periods (see Chapter 2) early in life may be a factor in birth outcomes, in that they "encode the functions of organs or systems that become manifest in health or disease later in life" (Lu & Halfon, 2003, p. 16). For example, researchers are exploring hypotheses linking fetal undernutrition during middle or late gestation to increased risk of certain diseases that show up in adulthood, such as those related to blood pressure regulation or metabolism of cholesterol. As another example, perinatal stress is associated with high stress reactivity that persists well into adulthood (Lu & Halfon, 2003).

The cumulative wear and tear of life-course experiences can add up over time and affect health and how the body functions. For example, chronically elevated levels of the stress hormone cortisol may lead to immune suppression, and over the life course may lead to increased risk for cardiovascular diseases, cancers, autoimmune disorders, and many other chronic adult diseases.

These two mechanisms together—early exposure and the cumulative life-course pathway of stressors—may, over a lifetime of events leading to pregnancy, affect a mother's reproductive health. For example, a mother who has been subjected to chronic and repeated stress may respond to stress during pregnancy with a higher output of stress hormones. These higher levels of stress hormones could then "dial up" gene expression in ways that lead to preterm labor (Lu & Halfon, 2003).

This perspective on maternal and child health takes into account the conditions under which a woman is born and grows up, as well as the conditions under which her pregnancies occur. Both influence her reproductive success. Life events during pregnancy matter, but equally important for reproductive success are the life events that come before. Because "healthy women beget healthy children" (Lu & Halfon, 2003, p. 25), the focus of maternal and child health cannot be solely on 9 months of prenatal care. Care must also focus on interventions that promote protective factors and lower the risk factors for women over their life course. This means access to quality health care not only during a woman's reproductive years but from her own birth onward (WHO, 2014a). It also means access to healthy, nutritious, affordable foods in the communities in which women and children live (Figure 13.3).

Breastfeeding Support

During pregnancy, a mother's health and nutrition impact the development of the fetus and the future well-being of the child, but benefits to infants' health and their immune systems continue to transfer from mother to child when infants are breastfed, as described in Chapter 5. Health organizations worldwide (American Academy of Pediatrics, 2012; WHO & UNICEF, 2014) recommend that babies be fed only breastmilk for the first 6 months. The United Nations Human Rights Office of the High Commissioner, in a joint statement of the Committees on the Right to Food, Right to Health, and Rights of the Child, and others, declared the following (2018):

> - Breastfeeding is a human rights issue for both the child and the mother.
> - Children have the right to life, survival, and development and to the highest attainable standard of health, of which breastfeeding must be considered an integral component, as well as safe and nutritious foods.
> - Women have the right to accurate, unbiased information needed to make an informed choice about breastfeeding. They also have the right to good quality health services. (¶ 1)

In the United States, by 3 months of age, only 44% of infants are exclusively breastfed, and by 6 months of age, this rate has dropped to 22% (Centers for Disease Control, 2016). Nearly 20% are never breastfed (Sullivan & Brumfield, 2016). Most women who initiate

FIGURE 13.3. Investing Saves Women and Newborns

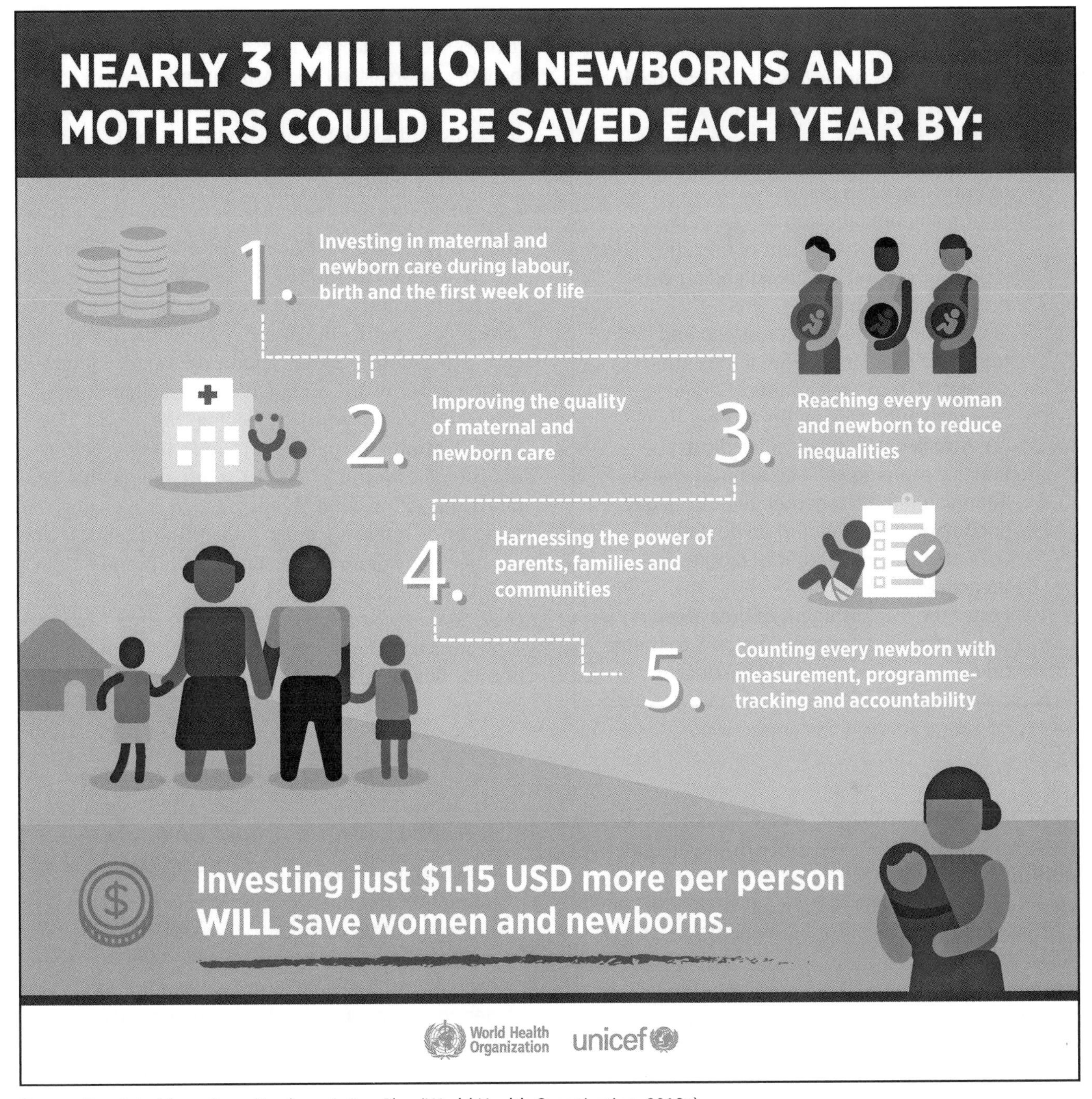

Source: Reprinted from *Every Newborn Action Plan* (World Health Organization, 2018a).

breastfeeding intend to do so for the recommended time, but they lack the supports they need to comply with this recommendation, including access to breastfeeding-friendly communities—both in the workplace and in health-care facilities—and paid parental leave from work. Especially important for increasing the success of breastfeeding is access to counselors, lactation consultants, and other health-care professionals trained in breastfeeding support. Women tend to turn to their family physicians for support, yet many doctors report having insufficient knowledge and limited clinical competence in supporting breastfeeding (United States Department of Health and Human Services, 2011). In many settings, there is no expectation that hospitals provide access to the services of a lactation specialist.

FIGURE 13.4. Ten Steps to Successful Breastfeeding in Hospitals and Birthing Centers

1. Have a written breastfeeding policy that is routinely communicated to staff and parents.
2. Train all health-care staff in skills necessary to implement this policy.
3. Inform all pregnant women about the benefits and management of breastfeeding.
4. Help mothers initiate breastfeeding within one hour of birth.
5. Show mothers how to breastfeed and how to maintain lactation, even if they are separated from their infants.
6. Give infants no food or drink other than breastmilk unless medically indicated.
7. Practice rooming in—allow mothers and infants to remain together 24 hours a day.
8. Encourage breastfeeding on demand.
9. Give no pacifiers or artificial nipples to breastfeeding infants.
10. Foster the establishment of breastfeeding support groups and refer mothers to them on discharge from the hospital or clinic.

Source: Ten Steps to Successful Breastfeeding (Baby-Friendly USA, 2018).

To remedy this situation, WHO and UNICEF, in 1991, launched The Baby-Friendly Hospitals Initiative, with the intent of protecting, promoting, and supporting breastfeeding (WHO & UNICEF, 2014). This initiative guided birthing facilitates with policies and procedures. Figure 13.4 provides a summary of what hospitals and birthing centers can do to support breastfeeding.

Another cause for concern with respect to breastfeeding support is the prevalence of marketing and promotion of formula to families with infants. Whether to breastfeed or to bottle feed using infant formula has long been considered a lifestyle choice. As evidence accrues as to the benefit of breastfeeding to infant and maternal health as well as to lifelong strength of the immune system, exclusive breastfeeding for the first 6 months becomes a public health issue, not a lifestyle issue (American Academy of Pediatrics, 2012; ACOG, 2017c; WHO & UNICEF, 2014).

Recommended practice is often slow to catch up with the research, however. Despite being *encouraged* to breastfeed by health-care providers, 85% of surveyed mothers report being told by these same health-care providers that formula feeding is a perfectly fine option. This reflects a deep-seated misunderstanding of the benefits to breastfeeding over formula feeding (Sullivan & Brumfield, 2016). The belief that formula feeding is "just as good as" breastfeeding is perpetuated by aggressive marketing and promotional campaigns of formula manufacturers. Birthing families receive unsolicited free samples of formula in the mail, attractively and conveniently packaged. Free samples of formula are frequently distributed to new mothers in maternity facilities and hospitals. Such marketing creates the impression that formula is recommended by health-care professionals as an appropriate and equivalent substitute for breast milk. On the basis that this practice is a deterrent to breastfeeding, the World Health Organization's *International Code of Marketing of Breastmilk Substitutes* (1988) states clearly that hospitals should prohibit the practice of dispensing free samples of infant formula to birthing families. This practice, though on the decline, is still prevalent (Nelson, Li, & Perrine, 2015; Sadacharan, Grossman, Sanchez, & Merewood, 2011).

Protecting infants' right to optimal health goes far beyond lifestyle decisions made by each family and is

A CLOSER LOOK

Marketing of Infant Formula

For companies invested in the production of infant formula, among them many of the large pharmaceutical companies, growth in the formula business declines as breastfeeding rates rise. Growth in the formula business is also dependent on a higher birth rate and more newly birthing women in the workforce. Infant formula is described in marketing campaigns as a "premium nutrition product" (Thurow, 2016, p. 136), and labels on infant formula samples suggest that immune system supports, present in breast milk, are added to the formula, despite the fact that such replication is still not possible (Gura, 2014). Aggressive marketing of infant formula is especially strong in emerging markets like Brazil and China, where the percentage of women in the workforce is on the rise (Thurow, 2016).

an issue of equity and economics, as well as an issue of public health. Low-income households are more likely to have mothers in the workforce. As a consequence of inadequate supports for breastfeeding, infants in these families are disproportionately affected by limited access to breastmilk. Because infants in their early months are vulnerable to illnesses like diarrhea and respiratory infections, two of the leading causes of infant death globally, infants whose low-income mothers are in the workforce are more vulnerable. Diarrhea and respiratory infections are much less prevalent in breastfed infants than in formula-fed infants (Victora et al., 2016).

When women are supported in breastfeeding as long as they wish, their infants are supported by the protective factors in breastmilk (Sullivan & Brumfield, 2016) and are less likely to succumb to disease. Breastfeeding also brings reduced incidence of sudden infant death syndrome, a leading cause of infant death in the United States (see Chapter 6). Mothers reap a benefit from breastfeeding, as well. Every year that a mother breastfeeds significantly lowers her risk of ovarian cancer, invasive breast cancer, and heart disease (Schwarz et al., 2009; Victora et al., 2016).

Access to health care, without economic concerns, is key to maternal and infant health. Access begins with high-quality care prior to conception and prenatal care during pregnancy. Healthier pregnancies lead to safer births, healthier babies, and lower health-care costs to society. Breastfeeding counseling, breast pumps, and other supplies, when included in health insurance coverage, help working mothers sustain breastfeeding over the first 6 months. In addition, health-care laws and regulations should allow for adequate break time and access to quiet spaces for nursing mothers to either breastfeed their babies, when in nearby care, or to pump their milk.

Postpartum Depression: Screening and Treatment

Newborns are prepared biologically to seek companions who will care for them. As described in Chapter 7, their innate capacity to communicate their needs through a gaze, an expression, a gesture, or a cry attracts the companionship of others. This biological programming is designed to ensure that infants have the nourishment, warmth, and protection they need to survive. Not infrequently, however, mothers of newborns experience a form of depression called *postpartum depression,* which can have negative consequences for the newborn. Infants of mothers with chronic depression that persists over the first 6 months (Field, 1998) show limited responsiveness to facial expressions, excessive sleep, and elevated levels of stress hormones. Mothers with postpartum depression experience feelings of extreme sadness, anxiety, and exhaustion—feelings that make it hard for them to complete, with focused attention, the everyday care of the newborn. The intense mood swings common in postpartum depression reflect a physiological change in the mother's body driven by the intense hormonal surges under way during the perinatal period and the weeks that follow. These changes, in some women, trigger chemical changes in the brain that, when coupled with disruptions of sleep, result in postpartum depression.

Screening for postpartum depression is important for all new mothers, because most do not recognize the problem as depression (Seidman, 1998). Many new mothers experience "baby blues," characterized by being tired and overwhelmed with the changes in lifestyle that come with the birth of a baby, feelings that are relatively mild and that last just a week or two. However, a screening for postpartum depression can identify the 10–15% of new mothers who are clinically depressed and can be used to initiate treatment. Diagnosis and treatment are critical, because 25% of cases of severe postpartum depression become chronic if left untreated (Forman, Videbech, Hedegaard, Dalby, & Secher, 2000).

Postpartum depression is very disruptive for the mother, the baby, and the entire family. For babies of depressed mothers, the companion they expect to meet is at times distant and inattentive, with little nurturance to give. This weakens the bond of attachment between baby and mother. Infants as young as 3 months of age detect depression in their mothers, triggering grief, panic, and despair in the infant (Weinberg & Tronick, 1998) and activating the stress-response system, a condition that if sustained is devastating for the baby (see Chapter 12). Identifying and treating postpartum depression, through medication or therapy, is key to assuring maternal and child health.

Infant and Early Childhood Mental Health

Access to appropriate health care includes opportunities to receive infant and early childhood mental health services, some of which are described in Chapter 12.

During infancy and early childhood, emotional disturbances can be prevented from taking root, with subsequent negative consequences to health and well-being (Zero to Three, 2017). When policy-makers invest in and support professional infant and early childhood mental health services, including a financing mechanism that covers the cost of therapeutic consultation for families and for those providing child care services, their investment reaps ample benefits with respect to long-term health and lower costs to society.

PAID FAMILY LEAVE

Ron Lally (2013), in *For Our Babies,* which describes a campaign to "end the invisible neglect of America's infants," explains that "U.S. families are putting their children in child care at much earlier ages than parents in other countries" (p. 53; see also For Our Babies, 2018). For many parents, economic circumstances may make it impossible for them to provide everyday care for their infants and to breastfeed for the first 6 months, despite their knowing the impact of bonding and breastfeeding on the development of the baby's brain and immune system. For these parents, the necessity of earning an income may mean leaving the baby to be cared for by others. The United States is the only industrialized country that has no national paid parental leave policy.

In all but a few industrialized countries, parents of infants are guaranteed time away from work with compensation, in order to bond with the baby and make breastfeeding possible. The United States is among the exceptions, one of the few countries where parents of newborns are often forced to choose between taking time off from work to care for their newborns and earning needed income to support the family. Only a fraction of U.S. families, typically workers in higher paid jobs, have access to paid family leave through their employers.

A quarter of U.S. parents with infants have one option, to return to work 2 weeks after giving birth, putting the health of the infant and the mother at risk (Sullivan & Brumfield, 2016). Lally (2013) points out that for many of the working poor in the United States, leaving their babies in the care of others in the first weeks of life is "an act almost mandated by the government" (p. 53), because many states have made returning to work as early as 3 months after the birth of a child a condition for the continued receipt of cash assistance.

When parents are free to stay at home to care for their newborns, babies benefit with respect to better health. With paid parental leave, babies are much more likely to receive regular pediatric checkups and sequenced immunizations in the first year. The result is reduced infant death and illness. With paid parental leave, mothers are much more likely to breastfeed exclusively for the first 6 months, which brings health benefits to baby and mother.

In addition to health benefits, there are substantial and well-documented labor market benefits (Ruhm, 2017) when parents are ensured up to 6–9 months of paid leave. The strongest evidence comes from research related to labor market gains for women. Participation of women in the workforce is a driving force in economic growth. Job-protected leave for new parents ensures continuity of employment and increases the likelihood of women remaining in the workforce after the leave period.

A comprehensive paid family and medical leave program covers all workers, be they a mother or a father, and includes those in small businesses and those self-employed. It ensures that an employee retains the right to resume full paid employment after taking leave and that the percentage of wages received during the leave is sufficiently generous. The duration of the leave must be a minimum of 6–9 months (Lally, 2013; Ruhm, 2017) in order to align with the infants' developmental trajectory and the recommendation of health organizations worldwide that babies be exclusively breastfed for 6 months.

Despite the fact that paid leave improves both economic and health outcomes, it is rare for such benefits to be included in employment packages. Less than half of U.S. mothers receive any paid time off to care for their newborns (Sullivan & Brumfield, 2016). While the federal Family and Medical Leave Act allows them to take up to 12 work weeks of leave for pregnancy or care of a newborn, it does not require paid time off from work, nor does it apply if they work in a small business with fewer than 50 employees. In 2014, only 14% of workers in the United States had employer-sponsored paid family leave coverage (Ruhm, 2017), and for workers in small businesses and for part-time workers, whose positions required less skill and had lower compensation, the rate was even lower. While some states have attempted to implement modified paid leave programs, the United States falls far behind other industrialized countries with respect to a job-protected paid leave for parents of newborns.

AFFORDABLE, QUALITY INFANT CARE

Who cares for babies matters—whether in the baby's home or in group care settings, and whether by family members or paid infant care professionals. The care babies receive impacts not only their physical and mental health and well-being but also how and what they learn. Infant care and education are inextricable (Maguire-Fong, 2015).

Birth to Age 8: Where Education Begins

Early childhood education spans the period between birth and 8 years of age (National Association for the Education of Young Children, 2009), with birth to age 3 the first phase along this continuum. There are many terms used to describe those who serve infants and families during this period of learning, among them *caregivers, care providers, teachers,* and *infant–family specialists,* but all serve as early childhood educators.

Contexts for Learning. Everyday experience is central to how infants and toddlers grow and how they learn about the world of objects, people, and events. For these learners, curriculum must take on a new look. As Lally (2009) explains, "The most critical curriculum components are no longer seen as lessons and lesson plans but rather the planning of settings and experiences that allow learning to take place" (p. 52). Such settings include play spaces where engaging materials are assembled for playful exploration. They include everyday experiences that define the rituals of the day, like mealtime, naptime, dressing, diapering, and toileting. Moments of sadness, of anger, or of delight in sharing story, song, or conversation with others are also important contexts for curriculum.

For infants and young children, who newly discover the surrounding world, "the play's the thing" (Jones & Reynolds, 2011) when it comes to how they learn (see Chapters 8, 9, and 10). For young children, moments of play and interaction with others are the essence of learning. The essence of teaching young children can be thought of as the thoughtful assembly of materials, the purposeful orchestration of daily routines as invitations to actively participate, and interactions and conversations that hold possibilities for investigation, exploration, and learning about people, objects, and events.

These three contexts for learning give new definition to the term *curriculum* when working with children birth to age 8. Curriculum, when seen through the eyes of infants and young children, is what happens when they encounter engaging contexts for play, are invited to be active participants making meaning within the daily routines like eating and dressing, and are respected for what they might learn during everyday interactions and communications around ideas and feelings, such as sadness and sharing (California Department of Education, 2012, 2016; Maguire-Fong, 2006, 2015). Each of these contexts, when created with intention and respect, builds on infants' biological expectation to research and figure out the world they encounter.

Preparation and Certification of Teachers. In response to a wide body of research drawn from multiple disciplines, the Institute of Medicine and the National Research Council, in affiliation with the National Academies of Sciences, Engineering, and Medicine (2015), issued recommendations designed to strengthen professional preparation standards for those providing the care and education of young children from birth to age 8. These recommendations include transitioning to a minimum requirement of a bachelor's degree, with specialized knowledge and competencies, for all lead teachers working with children from birth to age 8. To assure high-quality care for infants and toddlers, the recommendations describe competencies that reflect knowledge of how to structure infant–toddler learning environments and how to build on infants' interests to provoke cognitive growth. Such competencies are addressed in teacher preparation courses specific to the first 3 years. Incorporating such courses in early childhood education degrees and certification is key to meeting the goal of quality services for children from birth to age 8.

Rigor in teacher preparation should be matched to fair compensation. In their assessment of infant–toddler teacher competencies and compensation, Whitebook, Austin, and Amanta (2015) note:

> The bachelor's degree requirement for teachers working with infants and toddlers represents recognition of the complexity of facilitating the optimal development and learning for babies and toddlers. It also represents a significant shift in our expectations about the preparation and ongoing professional development of the infant and toddler workforce. (p. 2)

This significant shift refers to the fact that what is known from science, with respect to the critical learning that happens in the first 3 years, is not yet reflected in how we value and pay those who care for infants and toddlers. Higher levels of certification for educators working with infants and toddlers will require policies that ensure compensation, health benefits, and workplace supports that are on par with those of teachers working with children in kindergarten and beyond (Lally, 2013; Whitebook et al., 2015).

The True Cost of Care

Caring for infants and young children has long been considered "worthy work" (Whitebook, Howes, & Phillips, 1989), yet studies show that the vast majority of those taking on this work do not receive worthy, livable wages. This is largely because most parents cannot afford to pay the full cost of care, so this burden shifts to those dedicated to doing this worthy work without fair compensation (Whitebook, Phillips, & Howes, 2014). This leads to a situation where early childhood teachers experience economic insecurity coupled with reliance on public income support. According to Whitebook et al. (2014), who conducted an in-depth study of the compensation status of teachers working with infants and toddlers:

> Individuals who work with infants and toddlers face the harshest consequences of early childhood employment in the United States. . . . One quarter of center-based teachers and caregivers serving infants and toddlers earn, on average, only slightly more per hour than the current Federal minimum wage of $7.25. (p. 3)

The authors of this report point out that the current Federal minimum wage of $7.25 per hour is considered by economists (Cooper, 2015) to be inadequate to support a single adult without children.

The true cost of providing quality care for infants must factor in level of competence, preparation, and certification of those providing services during one of the most critical periods of learning. When relationships within infant care are strong and supportive, infants, their families, and those doing the care thrive. When these relationships are absent or neglectful, infants grow anxious, vigilant, and stressed, which over time compromises immune function, development, and learning (Badanes, Dmitrieva, & Watamura, 2012; Gunnar, Kryzer, Van Ryzin, & Phillips, 2010).

A report from the National Research Council (2000) reviews the research related to early childhood education and states the issue as follows:

> The time is long overdue for society to recognize the significance of out-of-home relationships for young children, to esteem those who care for them when their parents are not available, and to compensate them adequately as a means of supporting stability and quality in those relationships for all children, regardless of the family's income and irrespective of their developmental needs. (p. 7)

Irrational Financing Structure. As currently structured, compensation for educators serving children from birth to 8 years is tied to the age of children served rather than to the professional preparation and competence of those providing the service (Whitebook et al., 2015). Even when qualifications to do the work are equivalent, those working with infants and toddlers tend to be paid less than those working with slightly older children. The tensions around this irrational financing structure are a result of several factors. One is the higher costs associated with a smaller ratio of children to adults when caring for infants and toddlers. Another factor draws from the fact that, in countries like the United States, families bear the cost of care for children prior to kindergarten entry, with families of young children having limited access to public dollars. In this financing structure, public education tends to largely omit the early years of learning, despite the fact

A CLOSER LOOK

Three Pillars of Infant Care Policy: Quality, Cost, Affordability

Three intertwined factors weave through the discussion of who cares for infants (Maguire-Fong, 2015):

- ***Quality:*** Optimal care that supports optimal learning
- ***Compensation:*** Appropriate compensation tied to teacher qualifications
- ***Affordability:*** Reasonable cost for families

As with the pillars of a structure, these factors are the pillars that support infants, their families, and those who serve them. Consider the dynamic relationship among these factors. What will it take to achieve a fair solution for infants, for their families, and for the professionals who provide infant care?

that the early years are the most formative period of development, shaping the architecture of the brain, tuning the immune system for lifelong health, and building a foundation for all learning that follows.

Economic Insecurity. The consequence of low pay in early childhood education is that a significant proportion of early childhood teachers experience economic insecurity. In the United States, nearly half of child care workers, compared to 25% of the national workforce, reside in families enrolled in at least one of four public support programs designed to shore up a family's welfare (Whitebook et al., 2015). Since, as noted previously, the average hourly wage drops for those working with infants and toddlers, those working with infants and toddlers are even more likely to experience economic insecurity and reside in families receiving public support. Whitebook et al. (2015) conclude:

FIGURE 13.5. Three Pillars for Good Child Care Reform

Illustration by J. Ronald Lally, WestEd

> Economic insecurity fuels stress and depression among adults and affects their interactions with children, placing our most vulnerable infants and toddlers who live in poor families doubly at risk. Those employed to care for and educate our nation's babies should not be worrying about feeding and housing their own families. We can and should begin today to find a way to increase compensation for the infant toddler workforce. Increased compensation is the precondition for attracting and retaining an infant toddler workforce with the necessary knowledge and competencies to effectively facilitate young children's learning during their most critical phase of development. (p. 14)

As emphasized earlier, to assure high-quality care for infants and toddlers, those working with infants and toddlers in early childhood education should be prepared with coursework specific to infants and toddlers and hold certification that assures this area of competence. Rigorous preparation and certification should be tied to compensation, health benefits, and workplace supports that are on par with those of teachers working with children in kindergarten and beyond (Lally, 2013). As depicted in Figure 13.5, only by addressing paid parental leave, affordability and quality of child care, and infant–toddler teacher compensation can we reverse the pattern of teachers doing worthy work yet receiving unlivable wages (Whitebook et al., 2015). As described by early childhood pioneer and champion Betsy Hiteshew, "High quality child care makes a difference. The immediate changes and differences are subtle . . . [but] the changes are cumulative. . . . A quality program affects a child in a positive and life-affirming way" (quoted in Tebbs, 1996, p. 80).

PUBLIC POLICIES related to maternal and child health, paid family leave, child care, and early childhood education have the potential to either undermine or support a child's future. Fred Rogers (2003), the longtime and beloved host of the children's television program *Mr. Rogers' Neighborhood,* offered this advice with respect to how a society can shape that future: "In every neighborhood, all across our country, there are good people insisting on a good start for the young, and doing something about it" (p. 155).

MEANING-MAKING THROUGH INFANTS' EYES

Infants arrive at birth biologically prepared and strongly motivated to seek the companionship of others. The mutually satisfying connections that result establish a deep sense of belonging. This deep sense of belonging forms the central core of attachment and fosters healthy development. As illustrated in Chapter 12, the absence of this sense of belonging undermines health, both mental and physical, and is increasingly being seen as the root cause of many societal ills.

It is through the dynamics of everyday experiences that infants sense that they belong and that they make meaning of all they encounter. In his book *Diary of a Baby,* researcher Daniel Stern (1998) applies his study of the role of dynamics within parent–infant interactions to illustrate how babies perceive experiences. His work gives voice to infants, as illustrated in this excerpt describing Joey, just a few weeks old:

> Joey experiences objects and events mainly in terms of *feelings* they evoke in him, and the opportunities for action they offer him. He does not experience them as objects in and of themselves. When his parents call him "honey," he doesn't know that *honey* is a word and refers to him. He doesn't even particularly notice it as a sound distinct from a touch or a light. But he attends carefully to how the sound flows over him. He feels its glide, smooth and easy, soothing him; or its friction, turbulent and stirring him up, making him more alert. Every experience is like that, having its own special feeling tone—for infants as for adults. But we pay less attention to it. Our sense of being is not focused on it as Joey's is. (p. 13)

Stern also describes how Joey sees the inanimate world, in this depiction of the perceptions of the just-awakened 6-week-old as he stares at a patch of sunlight on the wall near his crib:

> A space glows over there. A gentle magnet pulls to capture. The space is growing warmer and coming to life. Inside it, forces start to turn around one another in a slow dance. The dance comes closer and closer. Everything rises to meet it. It keeps coming. But it never arrives. The thrill ebbs away. (p. 18)

Stern interprets this moment:

> At six weeks of age, he can see quite well, though not yet perfectly. He is already aware of different colors, shapes, and intensities. And he has been born with strong preferences about what he wants to look at, about what pleases him . . . intensity and contrast top the list. . . . Joey is . . . drawn to areas enclosed in a clearly marked frame. The edges of the square sun-patch catch his eye at the line where lighter and darker wall meet. In a sense, [the intensity of] the sunlight pulls, and the edges capture. . . . Even at this young age, Joey is able to calculate distances and quadrants of space. Soon he will divide all space into two distinct areas: a near world within the reach of his extended arm, and a far world beyond it. (p. 18)

Everyday experiences are central to how infants and toddlers grow and how they come to know the world of objects, people, and events. These experiences may appear to be simply moments of play, but in truth they are moments when infants and toddlers make meaning about people, objects, and events, building on their biological expectation to get to know and to figure out the world they encounter (Figure 13.6). As researcher Ed Tronick (2015) explains:

FIGURE 13.6. Making Meaning

Photograph by Jillian Rich

> The primary process for making meaning . . . involves the bringing together of two (or more) meaning-making beings—the child and the adult—into a dyadic communicative process, a process that cannot exist in only one of them. And out of their dyadic engagement, new meanings are co-created. . . . And that is the whole point—to grow the child. (p. 168)

It is this, then, that infants ask of us—as parents, teachers, social workers, health-care workers, or policy makers—to help them grow, to support their biological expectation to thrive, but also to treat them with playful, human respect (Trevarthen, 2016), and when the opportunity presents itself, to be their faithful traveling companion (Rinaldi, 2006) in their dynamic search for meaning.

Afterword

INFANT DEVELOPMENT comes alive in this book. Mary Jane Maguire-Fong and Marsha Peralta present us with a review of what we have come to know about infants over the past 50 or more years in a dynamic manner that more than captures the excitement of our growing understanding. What they present confronts the founding ideas of our field as described in a paper I wrote for a special issue of the *American Psychologist* and have used as part of the curriculum in my Infant Mental Health Fellowship Program at the University of Massachusetts Boston:

> James's infant lived in a world characterized by "blooming buzzing confusion" (James, 1890, p. 488), and Freud's infant was either in a state of tension seeking release or quiescence. . . . Watson went so far as to suggest that infants' mental life was a figment of the adult imagination. . . . In these historical views, infants could not have mental health problems because they had no mental life. But these classical theorists were, well, colossally wrong: wrong only in the way colossal thinkers can be. (Tronick & Beeghly, 2011, p. 107)

Certainly, it would be unfair for Maguire-Fong and Peralta or anyone else to have to challenge these luminaries. But their book, like my article, *is* a challenge. I have to believe or at least hope that James, Freud, and Watson would find the information and perspective in this book revelatory and that they would welcome it. For me the book makes clear that almost everything I knew to be "absolutely true" when I was in training and doing my first studies has been, shall I say, transformed. Take the challenge of Maguire-Fong and Peralta's key threads—connection, participation, belonging, meaning-making, and companionship—and their central question: "What do babies ask of us?" Babies asking us! Well, maybe one or the other of the colossal thinkers would be rolling over in his grave. Be that as it may, Maguire-Fong and Peralta do ask the question and they give us appreciation of what the answers might be with respect to practice and policy. Just as importantly they do not shy away from the complexity that is inherent in these threads. Rather, they address some of the organizing processes or principles that for me underlie these concepts.

Clearly the threads of connection, belonging, meaning-making, and companionship are interconnected and integrated in the infant. Each is essential for the functioning and development of the infant, and each affects the other. When a thread is absent, the infant will fail, their functioning dysregulated and their experience of being in the world disrupted, disturbed, and fractured. Why are these processes so critical? One answer of course is that we evolved as a meaning-making, socially connected species. This is true enough, but what matters is what the infant is doing now, in this moment or the next moment. Indeed, there are so many ways that humans interact with infants in the world now. The Quechua totally wrap their tightly swaddled infants in a protective cocoon of blankets and carry them on their backs for several months. The Efe carry their infants on their hips or in slings fully exposed to the world. The Gusii do not engage in face-to-face play with their infants. Many Americans do, but they also leave their infants alone with toys for long periods of time and they have them sleep alone. And there are many other ways of being with babies.

I think a more useful answer to the criticality of the processes identified by Maguire-Fong and Peralta comes from the principles of dynamic open systems. As with all biological systems, humans are a hierarchy of subsystems in which causal events travel bidirectionally (top down and bottom up) among the subsystems. Continuously and constantly engaged with the surrounding world, these systems operate in real time, with change being nonlinear, and outcomes becoming causes. The most fundamental characteristic of open systems—the governing principle—is that they must gain energy to maintain their organization and to expand their coherence and complexity. Perhaps a useful way to think of the infant as a system is as a Resource Acquisition Device (RAD). This concept may be much too mechanical, but just ask exhausted parents about the constancy of demands from the infant; so maybe it isn't.

As is made obvious in this book, infants act like systems, like RADS. They are active, always engaged, always expanding and growing, always demanding. They gain energy through connection with others, participation in the world, belonging and companionship, and making meaning of it all. Each of the threads identified by Maguire-Fong and Peralta is a context or a process for gaining energy. But while energy is necessary, it is not enough even for a RAD; infants surely demand more. They demand a necessary resource in the form of meaningful information about the world of things and people. Meaningful information makes it possible for the infant to find and then appropriate those resources to grow and expand itself. The studies of Spitz and Bowlby demonstrate that energy is not enough. Perhaps the most important resource for the infant is connection with others who control the energy and information the infant needs to grow and develop. When information already incorporated by the infant is integrated with information from another person, a larger dyadic system is created. In this dyadic system—a dyadic state of consciousness—new meaning is co-created that did not exist in the infant before. The infant—the RAD—grows and expands.

Most important to this process are people. As Vygotsky recognized, people contain more information than objects. Thus, while infants are oriented to the world of things, they are more oriented to the world of people. Less predictable than objects, people are more difficult to engage, but they offer more resources to the infant when communication is successful.

Maguire-Fong and Peralta know this when they frame the question "What do babies ask of us?" And they provide an answer—connection, participation, belonging, meaning-making, and companionship. In fulfilling these "asks" we fulfill systems principles, that is, the infant's need for energy and meaningful information for growth and development. And growing is what infants are about.

Ed Tronick
*Distinguished University Professor,
University of Massachusetts Boston*
*Research Associate, Department of Newborn
Medicines, Harvard Medical School*
*Chief Faculty, Infant–Parent Mental Health
Fellowship Certificate Program,
University of Massachusetts Boston*

References

Adachi, K., Shimada, M., & Usui, A. (2003). The relationship between the parturient's positions and perceptions of labor pain intensity. *Nursing Research, 52*(1), 47–51.

Adolph, K. E., & Berger, S. A. (2006). Motor development. In W. Damon & R. Lerner (Series Eds.) & D. Kuhn & R. S. Siegler (Vol. Eds.), *Handbook of child psychology: Vol. 2. Cognition, perception, and language* (6th ed., pp. 161–213). New York, NY: Wiley.

Adolph, K. E., & Berger, S. (2015). Physical and motor development. In M. H. Bornstein & M. E. Lamb (Eds.), *Developmental science: An advanced textbook* (7th ed., pp. 261–334). New York, NY: Psychology Press.

Adolph, K. E., Cole, W. G., Komati, M., Garciaguirre, J. S., Badaly, D., Lingeman, J. M., et al. (2012). How do you learn to walk? Thousands of steps and hundreds of falls per day. *Psychological Science, 23,* 1387–1394.

Adolph, K. E., & Joh, A. S. (2011). How infants get into the act. In A. Slater & M. Lewis (Eds.), *Introduction to infant development* (2nd ed., pp. 63–80). New York, NY: Oxford University Press.

Adolph, K. E., Karasik, L. B., & Tamis-LeMonda, C. S. (2010). Motor skills. In M. H. Bornstein (Ed.), *Handbook of cultural developmental science* (pp. 61–88). New York, NY: Taylor and Francis.

Adolph, K. E., & Robinson, S. R. (2013). The road to walking: What learning to walk tells us about development. In P. Zelazo (Ed.), *Oxford handbook of developmental psychology* (pp. 403–443). New York, NY: Oxford University Press.

Adolph, K. E., & Robinson, S. R. (2015). Motor development. In R. M. Lerner (Series Ed.) & L. Liben & U. Muller (Vol. Eds.), *Handbook of child psychology and developmental science: Vol. 2. Cognitive processes* (7th ed., pp. 113–157). New York, NY: Wiley.

Agnetta, B., & Rochat, P. (2004). Imitative games by 9-, 14-, and 18-month-old infants. *Infancy, 6,* 1–36.

Ainsworth, M., Blehar, M., Waters, E., & Wall, S. (1978). *Patterns of attachment: A psychological study of the strange situation.* Hillsdale, NJ: Erlbaum.

Akhtar, N., Dunham, F., & Dunham, P. J. (1991). Directive interactions and early vocabulary development: The role of joint attentional focus. *Journal of Child Language, 18,* 41–49.

Alderete, T. L., Autran, C., Brekke, B. E., Knight, R., Bode, L., Goran, M. I., et al. (2015). Associations between human milk oligosaccharides and infant body composition in the first 6 mo of life. *The American Journal of Clinical Nutrition, 102*(6), 1381–1388.

Als, H. (2007, July). *Caring for the preterm infant: Earliest brain development and experience.* Paper presented at the 43rd annual meeting of the Japanese Perinatal and Neonatal Association, Tokyo, Japan.

American Academy of Pediatrics. (2012). Policy statement: Breastfeeding and the use of human milk. *Pediatrics, 129*(3), e827–e841.

American Academy of Pediatrics Task Force on Sudden Infant Death Syndrome. (2016). SIDS and other sleep-related infant deaths: Recommendations for a safe infant sleeping environment. *Pediatrics, 138,* e20162938.

American College of Obstetricians and Gynecologists. (2013). Weight gain during pregnancy. Committee Opinion No. 548. *Obstetrics and Gynecology, 121,* 210–212.

American College of Obstetricians and Gynecologists. (2016). Practice Bulletin No. 165: Prevention and management of obstetric lacerations at vaginal delivery. *Obstetrics & Gynecology, 128,* e1–e15.

American College of Obstetricians and Gynecologists. (2017a). Approaches to limit intervention during labor and birth. Committee Opinion No. 687. *Obstetrics and Gynecology, 129,* e20–e28.

American College of Obstetricians and Gynecologists. (2017b). Delayed umbilical cord clamping after birth. Committee Opinion No. 684. *Obstetrics and Gynecology, 129,* e5–e10.

American College of Obstetricians and Gynecologists. (2017c). Optimizing support for breastfeeding as part of obstetric practice. Committee Opinion No. 658. *Obstetrics and Gynecology, 127,* e86–e92.

Amis, D. (2014). Healthy birth practice #1: Let labor begin on its own. *The Journal of Perinatal Education, 23*(4), 178–187.

Anders, T. F., Goodlin-Jones, B. L., & Zalenko, M. (1998). Infant regulation and sleep–wake state development. *Zero to Three, 19*(2), 5–8.

Anders, T., Sadeh, A., & Appareddy, V. (1995). Normal sleep in neonates and children. In R. Ferber & M. H. Kryger (Eds.), *Principles and practice of sleep medicine in the child* (pp. 7–18). Philadelphia, PA: Saunders.

Anderson, R. M. (1995). Revisiting the behavioral model and access to medical care: Does it matter? *Journal of Health and Social Behavior, 36,* 1–10.

Antell, S. E., & Keating, D. P. (1983). Perception of numerical invariance in neonates. *Child Development, 54,* 695–701.

Baby-Friendly USA. (2018). *The ten steps to successful breastfeeding* [Fact sheet]. Available at https://www.babyfriendlyusa.org/about-us/10-steps-and-international-code

Badanes, L. S., Dmitrieva, J., & Watamura, S. E. (2012). Understanding cortisol reactivity across the day at child care: The potential buffering role of secure attachments to caregivers. *Early Childhood Research Quarterly, 27,* 156–165.

Bahl, V. (2015). Toxicological evaluation of thirdhand smoke using in-vitro models. Doctoral dissertation, University of California, Riverside. Available at https://escholarship.org/uc/item/0b6419mw

Baillargeon, R., Spelke, E. S., & Wasserman, S. (1985). Object permanence in five-month-old infants. *Cognition, 20,* 191–208.

Ball, H. L. (2006). Night-time infant care: Cultural practice, evolution, and infant development. In P. Liamputtong (Ed.), *Childrearing and infant care issues: A cross-cultural perspective* (pp. 47–61). Melbourne, Australia: Nova.

Ball, H. L., & Klingaman, K. (2007). Breastfeeding and mother–infant sleep proximity: Implications for infant care. In W. R. Trevathan, E. O. Smith, & J. J. McKenna (Eds.), *Evolutionary medicine and health: New perspectives* (pp. 226–241). New York, NY: Oxford University Press.

Ball, H. L., & Russell, C. K. (2012). Nighttime nurturing: An evolutionary perspective on breastfeeding and sleep. In D. Narvaez, J. Panksepp, A. N. Schore, & T. R. Gleason (Eds.), *Evolution, early experience and human development: From research to practice and policy* (pp. 241–261). New York, NY: Oxford University Press.

Ball, H. L., Ward-Platt, M. P., Howel, D., & Russell, C. (2011). Randomised trial of sidecar crib use on breastfeeding duration (NECOT). *Archives of Disease in Childhood, 96,* 360–364.

Bartocci, M., Winberg, J., Ruggiero, C., Bergqvist, L. L., Serra, G., & Lagercrantz, H. (2000). Activation of olfactory cortex in newborn infants after odor stimulation: A functional near-infrared spectroscopy study. *Pediatric Research, 48*(1), 18–23.

Bateson, M. C. (1979). The epigenesis of conversational interaction: A personal account of research development. In M. Bullowa (Ed.), *Before speech: The beginning of human communication* (pp. 63–77). London, UK: Cambridge University Press.

Bayley, N. (1969). *Bayley Scales of Infant Development* (1st ed.). New York, NY: Psychological Corporation.

Bayley, N. (2006). *Bayley Scales of Infant and Toddler Development administration manual.* San Antonio, TX: Harcourt Assessment.

Beatty, T., Stranger, C., Beatty, N., & Gerber, M. (Producers). (1984). *Seeing infants with new eyes* [DVD]. Los Angeles, CA: Resources for Infant Educarers.

Beebe, B. (2014). My journey in infant research and psychoanalysis: Microanalysis, a social microscope. *Psychoanalytic Psychology, 31,* 4–25.

Beebe, B., Cohen, P., & Lachmann, F. (2016). *The mother–infant interaction picture book: The origins of attachment.* New York, NY: Norton.

Behne, T., Carpenter, M., Call, J., & Tomasello, M. (2005). Unwilling versus unable: Infants' understanding of intentional action. *Developmental Psychology, 41*(2), 328–337.

Bergman, J., & Bergman, N. (2013). Whose choice? Advocating birthing practices according to baby's biological needs. *The Journal of Perinatal Education, 22*(1), 8–13.

Bergman, N. J. (2014). The neuroscience of birth—and the case for Zero Separation. *Curationis, 37*(2), 1–4.

Blunden, S. L., Thompson, K. R., & Dawson, D. (2011). Behavioural sleep treatments and night time crying in infants: Challenging the status quo. *Sleep Medicine Reviews, 15,* 327–334.

Bly, L. (1994). *Motor skills acquisition in the first year.* San Antonio, TX: Therapy Skill Builders.

Bode, L. (2012). Human milk oligosaccharides: Every baby needs a sugar mama. *Glycobiology, 22,* 1147–1162.

Bohren, M. A., Hofmeyr, G. J., Sakala, C., Fukuzawa, R. K., & Cuthbert, A. (2017). Continuous support for women during childbirth. *Cochrane Database of Systematic Reviews,* Issue 7, Art. No. CD003766.

Bowlby, J. (1982). *Attachment and loss: Vol. 1. Attachment* (2nd ed.). New York, NY: Basic Books.

Brandt, K. (2014). Core concepts in infant–family and early childhood mental health. In K. Brandt, B. Perry, S. Seligman, & E. Tronick (Eds.), *Infant and early childhood mental health: Core concepts and clinical practice* (pp. 1–20). Washington, DC: American Psychiatric Publishing.

Brandt, K., Perry, B., Seligman, S., & Tronick, E. (2014). *Infant and early childhood mental health: Core concepts and clinical practice.* Washington, DC: American Psychiatric Publishing.

Bråten, S. (2007). Altercentric infants and adults: On the origins and manifestations of participant perception of others' acts and utterances. In S. Bråten (Ed.), *On being moved: From mirror neurons to empathy* (pp. 111–136). Amsterdam, The Netherlands: John Benjamins Publishing.

Brazelton, T. B. (with Sparrow, J.). (2006). *Touchpoints, birth to 3: Your child's emotional and behavioral development.* Cambridge, MA: DeCapo Press.

Brazelton, T. B., Koslowski, B., & Main, M. (1974). The origins of reciprocity. In M. Lewis & L. Rosenblum (Eds.), *The effect of the infant on its caregiver* (pp. 49–70, 137–154). New York, NY: Wiley-Interscience.

Bruner, J. (1972). Nature and uses of immaturity. *American Psychologist, 27,* 28–60.

Bruner, J. (1975). From communication to language: A psychological perspective. *Cognition, 3,* 255–287.

Bruner, J. (1990). *Acts of meaning.* Cambridge, MA: Harvard University Press.

Bruner, J. (2002). *Making stories.* New York, NY: Farrar, Straus, & Giroux.

Buckley, S. J. (2015). *Hormonal physiology of childbearing: Evidence and implications for women, babies, and maternity care.* Washington, DC: National Partnership for Women & Children.

Bystrova, K., Widstrom, A. M., Matthiesen, A. S., Ransjo-Arvidson, A. B., Welles-Nystrom, B., Wassbert, C., et al. (2003). Skin-to-skin contact may reduce negative consequences of "the stress of being born." *Acta Paediatrica, 92*(3), 320–326.

California Department of Education. (2012). *California infant/toddler curriculum framework.* Sacramento, CA: Author.

California Department of Education. (2016). *The integrated nature of learning.* Sacramento, CA: Author.

Center for Youth Wellness. (2014). *The science: Decades of scientific investigation guides our work to solve this public health crisis.* Available at https://centerforyouthwellness.org/the-science/

Centers for Disease Control. (2016). 2016 Breastfeeding report card. Available at https://www.cdc.gov/breastfeeding/pdf/2016breastfeedingreportcard.pdf

Chahin, E. (with Tardos, A.). (2017). *In loving hands: How the rights for young children living in children's homes offer hope and happiness in today's world.* San Bernadino, CA: Exlibris.

Chitty, J. (2016). *Working with babies.* Boulder, CO: Polarity Press.

Cito, G., Luisi, S., Mezzesimi, A., Cavicchioli, C., Calonaci, G., & Petraglia, F. (2005). Maternal position during non-stress test and fetal heart rate patterns. *Acta Obstetrica et Gynecologica Scandinavica, 84,* 335–338.

Clements, D. H. (2004). Major themes and recommendations. In D. H. Clements & J. Samara (Eds.), *Engaging young children in mathematics: Standards for early childhood educators* (pp. 7–77). Mahwah, NJ: Erlbaum.

Cloud, J. (2010, January 6). Why your DNA isn't your destiny. *Time.* Available at http://content.time.com/time/magazine/article/0,9171,1952313,00.html

Conde-Agudelo, A., Belizán, J. M., & Diaz-Rossello, J. (2011). Kangaroo mother care to reduce morbidity and mortality in low birthweight infants. *Cochrane Database of Systematic Reviews,* Issue 3, Art. No. CD002771.

Condon, L. W., & Sander, L. W. (1974). Neonate movement is synchronized with adult speech: Interactional participation and language acquisition. *Science, 183,* 99–101.

Cooper, D. (2015). *Raising the minimum wage to $12 by 2020 would lift wages for 35 million American workers.* EPI Briefing Paper #405. Washington, DC: Economic Policy Institute. Available at http://s4.epi.org/files/2015/raising-the-minimum-wage-to-12-dollars-by-2020-would-lift-wages-for-35-million-american-workers.pdf

Cunningham, F. G., Leveno, K. J., Bloom, S. L., Spong, C. Y., Dashe, J. S., Hoffman, B. L., et al. (2018). *Williams obstetrics* (25th ed.). New York, NY: McGraw-Hill.

Dana, D. (2018). *The polyvagal theory in therapy: Engaging the rhythm of regulation.* New York, NY: Norton.

Darwin, C. (1877). A biographical sketch of an infant. *Mind: A Quarterly Review of Psychology and Philosophy, 2,* 285–294. Available at http://www.mpi.nl/publications/escidoc-2309887

Davis, K. L., & Panksepp, J. (2018). *The emotional foundations of personality: A neurobiological and evolutionary approach.* New York, NY: Norton.

de Boysson-Bardies, B. (2001). *How language comes to children: From birth to two years.* Cambridge, MA: MIT Press.

DeCasper, A., & Spence, M. (1986). Prenatal maternal speech influences newborn's perception of speech sounds. *Infant Behavior and Development, 9,* 133–150.

DeCasper, A., & Spence, M. (1991). Auditorially mediated behavior during the perinatal period: A cognitive view. In M. J. S. Weiss & P. R. Zelazo (Eds.), *Newborn attention: Biological constraints and the influence of experience* (pp. 142–176). Stamford, CT: Ablex.

Declercq, E. R., Sakala, C., Corry, M. P., & Applebaum, S. (2013). *Listening to mothers III: Report of the second national U.S. survey of women's childbearing experiences.* New York, NY: Childbirth Connection.

Demetriou, H., & Hay, D. F. (2004). Toddlers' reactions to the distress of familiar peers: The importance of context. *Infancy, 6,* 299–318.

Devane, D., Lalor, J. G., Daly, S., McGuire, W., Cuthbert, A., & Smith, V. (2017). Cardiotocography versus intermittent auscultation of fetal heart on admission to labour ward for assessment of fetal wellbeing. *Cochrane Database of Systematic Reviews,* Issue 1, Art. No. CD005122.

de Vries, J. I. P., & Hopkins, B. (2005). Fetal movements and postures: What do they mean for postnatal development? In B. Hopkins & S. P. Johnson (Eds.), *Prenatal development of postnatal functions* (pp. 177–220). Westport, CT: Praeger.

de Vries, J. I. P., Visser, G. H. A., & Prechtl, H. F. R. (1982). The emergence of fetal behavior. I. Quantitative aspects. *Early Human Development, 7,* 301–322.

de Vries, J. I. P., Visser, G. H. A., & Prechtl, H. F. R. (1985). The emergence of fetal behavior. II. Quantitative aspects. *Early Human Development, 12,* 99–120.

Dieterich, C. M., Felice, J. P., O'Sullivan, E., & Rasmussen, K. M. (2013). Breastfeeding and health outcomes for the mother–infant dyad. *Pediatric Clinics of North America, 60,* 31–48.

Dietert, R., & Dietert, J. (2012). The completed self: An immunological view of the human micro-biome super organism and risk of chronic diseases. *Entropy, 14*(11), 2036–2065.

Donkin, I., & Barres, R. (2018). Sperm epigenetics and influence of environmental factors. *Molecular Metabolism, 14,* 1–11. Available at https://www.sciencedirect.com/science/article/pii/S2212877818301042

Douglas, P. S., & Hill, P. S. (2013). Behavioral sleep interventions in the first six months of life do not improve outcomes for mothers or infants: A systematic review. *Journal of Developmental & Behavioral Pediatrics, 34,* 497–507.

Eckerman, C., & Rheingold, H. L. (1974). Infants' exploratory responses to toys and people. *Developmental Psychology, 10,* 255–259.

Eimas, P., & Quinn, P. (1994). Studies on the formation of perceptually-based basic-level categories in young infants. *Child Development, 65,* 903–917.

Eisenberg, R. B. (1976). *Auditory competencies in early life: The roots of communicative behavior.* Baltimore, MD: University Park Press.

Ellis, W., & Dietz, W. (2017). A new framework for addressing adverse childhood and community experiences: The building community resilience (BCR) model. *Academic Pediatrics, 17,* S86–S93. DOI: 10.1016/j.acap.2016.12.011.

Fantz, R. L., & Miranda, S. B. (1975). Newborn infant attention to form of contour. *Child Development, 46,* 224–228.

Feldman, R. (2007). Parent–infant synchrony and the construction of shared timing; physiological precursors, developmental outcomes, and risk conditions. *Journal of Child Psychology and Psychiatry, 48,* 329–354.

Felitti, V. J., Anda, R. F., Nordenberg, M., Williamson, D., Spitz, A., Edwards, V., et al. (1998). Relationship of childhood abuse and household dysfunction to many of the leading causes of death in adults: The adverse childhood experiences (ACE) study. *American Journal of Preventive Medicine, 14*(4), 245–258.

Fenson, L., Dale, P., Reznick, J., Bates, E., Thal, D., & Pethick, S. (1994). Variability in early communicative development. *Monographs of the Society for Research in Child Development, 59,* 1–185.

Ferjan Ramírez, N., Ramírez, R. R., Clarke, M., Taulu, S., & Kuhl, P. K. (2017). Speech discrimination in 11-month-old bilingual and monolingual infants: A magnetoencephalography study. *Developmental Science, 20,* e12427.

Fernald, A. (1985). Four-month-old infants prefer to listen to motherese. *Infant Behavior and Development, 8,* 181–195.

Fernald, A. (1992). Meaningful melodies in mothers' speech to infants. In H. Papousek, U. Jurgens, & M. Papousek (Eds.), *Nonverbal vocal communication: Comparative and developmental approaches* (pp. 262–282). Cambridge, UK: Cambridge University Press.

Fernald, A. (1993). Approval and disapproval: Infant responsiveness to vocal affect in familiar and unfamiliar languages. *Child Development, 64,* 657–674.

Fernald, A., Marchman, V. A., & Weisleder, A. (2013). SES differences in language processing skill and vocabulary are evident at 18 months. *Developmental Science, 16,* 234–248.

Field, T. M. (1981). Infant gaze aversion and heart rate during face-to-face interactions. *Infant Behavior and Development, 4*(1), 307–315.

Field, T. (1998). Maternal depression effects on infants and early interventions. *Preventive Medicine, 27,* 200–203.

Field, T. M., Woodson, R., Greenberg, R., & Cohen, D. (1982). Discrimination and imitation of facial expressions by neonates. *Science, 218,* 179–181.

Fogel, A. (2009a). *Infancy: Infant, family, and society* (5th ed.). Cornwall-on-Hudson, NY: Sloan.

Fogel, A. (2009b). *The psychophysiology of self-awareness.* New York, NY: Norton.

Fogel, A. (2015). *Infant development: A topical approach.* Cornwall-on-Hudson, NY: Sloan.

Forman, D., Videbech, P., Hedegaard, M., Dalby, J., & Secher, N. J. (2000). Post-partum depression: Identification of women at risk. *International Journal of Obstetrics and Gynecology, 107*(10), 1210–1217.

For Our Babies. (2018). *Getting it right for our babies* [Infographic]. Available at https://forourbabies.org/

Galland, B. C., Taylor, B. J., Elder, D. E., & Herbison, P. (2012). Normal sleep patterns in infants and children: A systematic review of observational studies. *Sleep Medicine Reviews, 16,* 213–222.

Gaskin, I. M. (2003). *Ina May's guide to childbirth.* New York, NY: Bantam Dell.

Gerber, M. (2002). *Dear parent: Caring for infants with respect* (J. Weaver, Ed., 2nd ed.). Los Angeles, CA: Resources for Infant Educarers.

Gergely, G., Bekkering, H., & Kiraly, I. (2002). Developmental psychology: Rational imitation in preverbal infants. *Nature, 415,* 755.

Gerhardt, K. J., Pierson, L. L., & Abrams, R. M. (1996). Fetal response to intense sounds. In A. Axelsson, H. Borchgrevink, R. Hamernik, P. A. Hellstrom, D. Henderson, & R. J. Salvi (Eds.), *Scientific basis of noise-induced hearing loss* (pp. 229–240). New York, NY: Thieme.

Gertner, S., Greenbaum, C. W., Sadeh, A., Dolfin, Z., Sirota, L., & Ben-Nun, Y. (2002). Sleep–wake patterns in preterm infants and 6 month's home environment: Implications for early cognitive development. *Early Human Development, 68,* 93–102.

Gilkerson, L., & Klein, R. (2008). *Early development and the brain: Teaching resources for educators.* Washington, DC: Zero to Three.

Ginsburg, H. P., & Opper, S. (1988). *Piaget's theory of intellectual development* (3rd ed.). New York, NY: Pearson.

Goer, H., & Romano, A. (2012). *Optimal care in childbirth: The case for a physiologic approach.* Seattle, WA: Classic Day.

Goldman, B. D., & Ross, H. S. (1978). Social skills in action: An analysis of early peer games. In J. Glick & K. A. Clarke-Stewart (Eds.), *Social and cognitive development: Vol. 1. The development of social understanding* (pp. 177–212). New York, NY: Gardner Press.

Golinkoff, R. M., Can, D. D., Soderstrom, M., & Hirsh-Pasek, K. (2015). (Baby)Talk to me: The social context of infant-directed speech and its effects on early language acquisition. *Current Directions in Psychological Science, 24*(5), 339–344.

Gonzalez-Mena, J., & Eyer, D. W. (2012). *Infants, toddlers, and caregivers.* Columbus, OH: McGraw-Hill.

Gopnik, A. (2009). *The philosophical baby: What children's minds tell us about truth, love, and the meaning of life.* New York, NY: Farrar, Straus, & Giroux.

Gopnik, A., Meltzoff, A. N., & Kuhl, P. K. (1999). *The scientist in the crib: What early learning tells us about the mind.* New York, NY: Harper Collins.

Gratier, M., & Trevarthen, C. (2013). Musical narrative and motives for culture in mother–infant vocal interaction. *Journal of Consciousness Studies, 15*(10–11), 122–158.

Gray, P. (2013). The value of a play-filled childhood in development of the hunter-gatherer individual. In D. Narvaez, J. Panksepp, A. N. Schore, & T. R. Gleason (Eds.). *Evolution, early experience and human development: From research to practice and policy* (pp. 352–370). New York, NY: Oxford University Press.

Green, J., Pickles, A., Pasco, G., Bedford, R., Wan, M. W., & Elsabbagh, M. (2017). Randomised trial of a parent-mediated intervention for infants at high risk for autism: Longitudinal outcomes to age 3 years. *The Journal of Child Psychology and Psychiatry, 58*(12), 1330–1340.

Greenspan, S., & Wieder, S. (2006). *Engaging autism: Using the Floortime approach to help children relate, communicate, and think.* Cambridge, MA: DeCapo.

Gunnar, M. R., Kryzer, E., Van Ryzin, M. J., & Phillips, D. A. (2010). The rise in cortisol in family day care: Associations with aspects of care quality, child behavior, and child sex. *Child Development, 81*(3), 853–870.

Gupta, J. K., & Nikodem, V. C. (2000). Woman's position during second stage of labour. *Cochrane Database of Systematic Reviews,* Issue 2, Art. No. CD002006.

Gura, T. (2014). Nature's first functional food. *Science, 345,* 747–749.

Haight, W. L., & Miller, P. J. (1993). *SUNY series, children's play in society. Pretending at home: Early development in a sociocultural context.* Albany, NY: State University of New York Press.

Hamlin, J. K., & Wynn, K. (2012). Young infants prefer prosocial to antisocial others. *Cognitive Development, 26*(1), 30–39.

Hamlin, J. K., Wynn, K., & Bloom, P. (2010). Three-month-olds show a negativity bias in their social evaluations. *Developmental Science, 13,* 923–929.

Hamlin, J. K., Wynn, K., Bloom, P., & Mahajan, N. (2011). How infants and toddlers react to antisocial others. *Proceedings of the National Academy of Sciences USA, 108,* 19931–19936.

Harmon, T., & Wakeford, A. (2017). *Your baby's microbiome.* White River Junction, VT: Chelsea Green.

Harris, J., Golinkoff, R. M., & Hirsh-Pasek, K. (2011). Lessons from the crib for the classroom: How children really learn vocabulary. In S. B. Neuman & D. K. Dickinson (Eds.), *Handbook of early literacy research* (pp. 49–66). New York, NY: Guilford Press.

Hart, B., & Risley, T. R. (1995). *Meaningful differences in the everyday experiences of young American children.* Baltimore, MD: Brookes.

Hastie, C., & Fahy, K. M. (2009). Optimising psychophysiology in third stage of labour: Theory applied to practice. *Women and Birth, 22,* 89–96.

Hauser-Cram, P., Nugent, J. K., Thies, K. M., & Travers, J. F. (2014). *The development of children and adolescents.* Hoboken, NJ: Wiley.

Hay, D. F., Castle, J., & Davies, L. (2000). Toddlers' use of force against familiar peers: A precursor of more serious aggression? *Child Development, 71,* 457–467.

Hay, D. F., Castle, J., Davies, L., Demetriou, H., & Stimson, C. A. (1999). Prosocial action in very early childhood. *Journal of Child Psychology and Psychiatry, 40,* 905–916.

Hay, D. F., Nash, A., & Pedersen, J. (1983). Interaction between six-month-old peers. *Child Development, 54,* 557–562.

Hay, D., & Ross, H. S. (1982). The social nature of early conflict. *Child Development, 53,* 105–111.

Henderson, J. M. T., France, K. G., Owens, J. L., & Blampied, N. M. (2010). Sleeping through the night: The consolidation of self-regulated sleep across the first year of life. *Pediatrics, 126,* e1081–e1087.

Hepper, P. (2003). Prenatal psychological and behavioural development. In J. Valsiner & K. J. Connolly (Eds.), *Handbook of developmental psychology* (pp. 91–113). Thousand Oaks, CA: Sage.

Hewlett, B. S. (1991). *Intimate fathers: The nature and context of Aka Pygmy paternal infant care.* Ann Arbor, MI: University of Michigan Press.

Heyman, M. B., Abrams, S. A., American Academy of Pediatrics [AAP] Section on Gastroenterology, Hepatology, and Nutrition, & AAP Committee on Nutrition. (2017). Fruit juice in infants, children, and adolescents: Current recommendations. *Pediatrics, 139*(6), e20170967.

Hinde, K. (2013). Lactational programming of infant behavioral phenotype. In K. B. H. Clancy, K. Hinde, & J. N. Rutherford (Eds.), *Building babies: Primate development in proximate and ultimate perspective.* New York, NY: Springer Science+Business Media.

Hinde, K., & German, J. B. (2012). Food in an evolutionary context: Insights from mother's milk. *Journal of the Science of Food and Agriculture, 92,* 2219–2223.

Hofer, M. A. (1994). Early relationships as regulators of infant physiology and behavior. *Acta Paediatrica, 397,* 9–18.

Hopkins, B., & Westra, T. (1988). Maternal handling and motor development: An intracultural study. *Genetic, Social, and General Psychology Monographs, 114,* 379–408.

Hupbach, A., Gomez, R. L., Bootzin, R. R., & Nadel, L. (2009). Nap-dependent learning in infants. *Developmental Science, 12,* 1007–1012.

Hyde, D. C., & Spelke, E. S. (2011). Neural signatures of number processing in human infants: Evidence for two core systems underlying numerical cognition. *Developmental Science, 14,* 360–371.

Improving Birth Coalition. (2018). *Mother-friendly childbirth initiative.* Available at http://www.motherfriendly.org/MFCI

Institute of Medicine (U.S.) & National Research Council (U.S.). (2015). *Transforming the workforce for children birth through age 8: A unifying foundation.* Washington, DC: National Academies Press.

Izard, V., Dehaene-Lambertz, G., & Dehaene, S. (2008). Distinct cerebral pathways for object identity and number in human infants. *PLoS Biology, 6*(2), e11.

Jaffe, J., Beebe, B., Feldstein, S., Crown, C. L., Jasnow, M. D., Rochat, P., et al. (2001). Rhythms of dialogue in infancy: Coordinated timing in development. *Monographs of the Society for Research in Child Development, 66*(2), 1–149.

James, W. (1890). *The principles of psychology.* New York, NY: Henry Holt.

Johnson, N., Johnson, V., & Gupta, J. (1991). Maternal positions during labor. *Obstetric and Gynecological Survey, 46,* 428–434.

Johnson, S. C., Dweck, C. S., & Chen, F. S. (2007). Evidence for infants' internal working models of attachment. *Psychological Sciences, 18*(6), 501–502.

Johnson, S. P., Amso, D., & Slemmer, J. A. (2003). Development of object concepts in infancy: Evidence for early learning in an eye tracking paradigm. *Proceedings of the National Academy of Sciences USA, 100,* 10568–10573.

Jones, E., & Reynolds, G. (2011). *The play's the thing: Teachers' roles in children's play.* New York, NY: Teachers College Press.

Jones, L., Othman, M., Dowswell, T., Alfierevic, Z., Gates, S., Newborn, M., et al. (2012). Pain management for women in labour: An overview of systematic reviews. *Cochrane Database of Systematic Reviews,* Issue 3, Art. No. CD009234.

Kálló, E., & Balog, G. (2005). *The origins of free play.* Budapest, Hungary: Pikler-Loczy Association.

Kamii, C. (2014). Kindergarten through Grade 1: Direct versus indirect teaching of number concepts for ages 4 to 6: The importance of thinking. *YC Young Children, 69*(5), 72–77.

Karasik, L. B., Adolph, K. E., Tamis-LeMonda, C. S., & Zuckerman, A. (2012). Carry on: Spontaneous object carrying in 13-month-old crawling and walking infants. *Developmental Psychology, 48,* 389–397.

Karasik, L. B., Tamis-LeMonda, C. S., & Adolph, K. E. (2011). Transition from crawling to walking and infants' actions with objects and people. *Child Development, 82,* 1199–1209.

Kisilevsky, B. S., & Hains, S. M. (2011). Onset and maturation of fetal heart rate response to the mother's voice over late gestation. *Developmental Science, 14,* 214–223.

Kisilevsky B., Hains, S., Lee, K., Xie, X., Huang, H., Ye, H., et al. (2003). Effects of experience on fetal voice recognition. *Psychological Science, 14,* 220–224.

Klaus, M., Kennell, J., & Klaus, P. (2012). *The doula book: How a trained labor companion can help you have a shorter, easier, and healthier birth* (2nd ed.). Boston, MA: Da Capo Press.

Kugiumutzakis, G. (1999). Genesis and development of early infant mimesis to facial and vocal models. In J. Nadel & G. Butterworth (Eds.). *Imitation in infancy* (pp. 36–59). Cambridge, UK: Cambridge University Press.

Kuhl, P. K. (2000). A new view of language acquisition. *Proceedings of the National Academy of Sciences USA, 97,* 11850–11857.

Kuhl P. K. (2007). Is speech learning 'gated' by the social brain? *Developmental Science, 10,* 110–120.

Kuhl, P. K. (2011). Brain mechanisms underlying the critical period for language: Linking theory and practice. *Human Neuroplasticity and Education, Pontifical Academy of Sciences, Scripta Varia, 117,* 33–59.

Kuhl, P. K., & Rivera-Gaxiola, M. (2008). Neural substrates of language acquisition. *Annual Review of Neuroscience, 31,* 511–534.

Kuhl, P. K., Tsao, F., & Liu, H. (2003). Foreign-language experience in infancy: Effects of short-term exposure and social interaction on phonetic learning. *Proceedings of the National Academy of Sciences USA, 100,* 9096–9191.

Ladefoged, P. (2001). *Vowels and consonants: An introduction to the sounds of languages.* Oxford, UK: Blackwell Publishers.

Lagercrantz, H., & Bistoletti, H. (1977). Catecholamine release in the newborn infant at birth. *Pediatric Research, 11*(8), 889–893.

Lally, J. R. (2009). The science and psychology of infant–toddler care: How an understanding of early learning has transformed child care. *Zero to Three, 3*(2), 47–53.

Lally, J. R. (2011). A developmental approach to the socialization, guidance, and discipline of infants and toddlers. In J. R. Lally (Ed.), *Infant–toddler caregiving: A guide to social–emotional growth and socialization* (2nd ed., pp. 33–39). Sacramento, CA: California Department of Education.

Lally, J. R. (2013). *For our babies: Ending the invisible neglect of America's infants.* New York, NY: Teachers College Press; San Francisco, CA: WestEd.

Lawrence, R., & Lawrence, R. (2015). *Breastfeeding: A guide for the medical profession.* Maryland Heights, MI: Elsevier.

Lester, B. M. (2005). *Why is my baby crying? The parent's survival guide for coping with crying problems and colic.* New York, NY: Harper.

Lester, B. M. (2010). Transforming the research landscape. In B. M. Lester & J. D. Sparrow (Eds.), *Nurturing children and families: Building on the legacy of T. Berry Brazelton.* West Sussex, UK: Wiley-Blackwell.

Lester, B. M., & Sparrow, J. D. (Eds.). (2010). *Nurturing children and families: Building on the legacy of T. Berry Brazelton.* West Sussex, UK: Wiley-Blackwell.

LeVine, R. A., Dixon, S., LeVine, S., Richman, A., Leiderman, P. H., Keefer, C. H., et al. (1994). *Child care and culture: Lessons from Africa.* New York, NY: Cambridge University Press.

Lif Holgerson, P., Harnevik, L., Hernell, O., Tanner, A. C. R., & Johansson, I. (2011). Mode of birth delivery affects oral microbiota in infants. *Journal of Dental Research, 90,* 1183–1188.

Lillas, C. (2014). The neurorelational framework in infant and early childhood mental health. In K. Brandt, B. Perry, S. Seligman, & E. Tronick (Eds.), *Infant and early childhood mental health: Core concepts and clinical practice* (pp. 85–96). Washington, DC: American Psychiatric Publishing.

Lillas, C., & Turnbull, J. (2009). *Infant/child mental health, early intervention, and relationship-based therapies.* New York, NY: Norton.

Lipton, B. (2005). *The biology of belief: Unleashing the power of consciousness.* Santa Rosa, CA: Mountain of Love/Elite Books

Liu, H., Kuhl, P. K., & Tsao, F. (2003). An association between mothers' speech clarity and infants' speech discrimination skills. *Developmental Science, 6,* F1–F10.

Lothian, J. A. (2014). Healthy birth practice #4: Avoid interventions unless they are medically necessary. *The Journal of Perinatal Education, 23*(4), 198–206.

Lu, M. C., & Halfon, N. (2003). Racial and ethnic disparities in birth outcomes: A life-course perspective. *Maternal and Child Health Journal, 7*(1), 13–30.

Luchinger, A. B., Hadders-Algra, M., Colette, M. V., & de Vries, J. I. P. (2008). Fetal onset of general movements. *Pediatric Research, 63,* 191–195.

Ludy-Dobson, C., & Perry, B. (2013). The role of healthy relational interactions in buffering the impact of childhood trauma. In E. Gil (Ed.), *Working with children to heal interpersonal trauma: The power of play* (pp. 26–43). New York, NY: Guilford.

MacLean, P. (1990). *The triune brain in evolution: Role in paleocerebral function.* New York, NY: Plenum.

Maguire-Fong, M. J. (2006). Respectful teaching with infants and toddlers. In J. R. Lally, P. L. Mangione, & D. Greenwald (Eds.), *Concepts for care: 20 Essays on infant/toddler development and learning* (pp. 117–122). San Francisco, CA: WestEd.

Maguire-Fong, M. J. (2015). *Teaching and learning with infants and toddlers: Where meaning-making begins.* New York, NY: Teachers College Press.

Mahler, K. (2017). *Interoception: The eighth sensory system.* Lenexa, KS: AAPC Publishing.

Mangione, P. L., Lally, J. R., & Signer, S. (1990). *The ages of infancy: Caring for young, mobile, and older infants* [DVD booklet]. Sacramento, CA: CDE Press.

March of Dimes. (2016). *Alcohol during pregnancy* [Fact sheet]. Available at https://www.marchofdimes.org/alcohol-during-pregnancy.aspx

March of Dimes, PMNCH, Save the Children, & WHO. (2012). *Born too soon: The global action report on preterm birth* (C. P. Howson, M. V. Kinney, & J. E. Lawn, Eds.). Geneva, Switzerland: World Health Organization.

Martin, J. A., Hamilton, B. E., Osterman, M. J. K., Driscoll, A. K., & Drake, P. (2018). Births: Final data for 2016. *National Vital Statistics Reports, 67*(1). Hyattsville, MD: National Center for Health Statistics.

McCrink, K., & Wynn, K. (2004). Large-number addition and subtraction by 9-month-old infants. *Psychological Science, 15,* 776–781.

McKenna, J. (1990). Evolution and sudden infant death syndrome (SIDS): Part 1: Infant responsivity to parental contact. *Human Nature, 1*(2), 145–177.

McKenna, J. J. (2016). *Sleeping with your baby.* Washington, DC: Platypus Media.

McKenna, J. J., Ball, H., & Gettler, L. (2007). Mother–infant cosleeping, breastfeeding and sudden infant death syndrome: What biological anthropology has discovered about normal infant sleep and pediatric sleep medicine. *American Journal of Physical Anthropology, 134,* 133–161.

Meltzoff, A. N., Kuhl, P. K., Movellan, J., & Sejnowski, T. J. (2009). Foundations for a new science of learning. *Science, 325,* 284–288.

Meltzoff, A. N., & Moore, M. K. (1977). Imitation of facial and manual gestures by human neonates. *Science, 198,* 75–78.

Middlemiss, W., Granger, D. A., Goldberg, W. A., & Nathans, L. (2012). Asynchrony of mother–infant hypothalamic-pituitary-adrenal axis activity following extinction of infant crying responses induced during the transition to sleep. *Early Human Development, 88*(4), 227–232.

Mireault, G. C., & Crockenberg, S. C. (2016) Social referencing. In D. Couchenour & J. K Chrisman (Eds.), *The SAGE encyclopedia of contemporary early childhood education* (pp. 1241–1242). Thousand Oaks, CA: SAGE.

Mirmiran, M., & Lunshof, S. (1996). Perinatal development of human circadian rhythms. *Progress in Brain Research, 111,* 217–226.

Mirmiran, M., Maas, Y. G. H., & Ariagno, R. L. (2003). Development of fetal and neonatal sleep and circadian rhythms. *Sleep Medicine Reviews, 7,* 321–334.

Mitchell, E. A., Taylor, B. J., Ford, R. P., Stewart, A., Becroft, D. M., Thompson, J. M., et al. (1992). Four modifiable and other major risk factors for cot death: The New Zealand study. *Journal of Paediatric Child Health, 28*(Supplement 1), S3–S8.

Montagu, A. (1994). *Touch the future. Ashley Montagu on being human: A conversation with Michael Mendizza.* Available at https://ttfuture.org/files/2/members/int_montague.pdf

Moon, C., Lagercrantz, H., & Kuhl, P. (2013). Language experienced *in utero* affects vowel perception after birth: A two-country study. *Acta Paediatrica, 102*(2), 156–160.

Moon, C., Panneton-Cooper, R., & Fifer, W. E. (1993). Two-day-olds prefer their native language. *Infant Behavior and Development, 16,* 495–500.

Moore, E. R., Anderson, G. C., Bergman, N., & Dowswell, T. (2012). Early skin-to-skin contact for mothers and their healthy newborn infants. *Cochrane Database of Systematic Reviews,* Issue 5, Art. No. CD003519.

Moore, K. L., & Persaud, T. V. N. (1993). *The developing human: Clinically oriented embryology* (5th ed.). Philadelphia, PA: W. B. Saunders.

Morgan, P. L., Farkas, G., Hillemeier, M. M., Scheffner Hammer, C. S., & Maczuga, S. (2015). 24-Month-old children with larger oral vocabularies display greater academic and behavioral functioning at kindergarten entry. *Child Development, 86,* 1351–1370.

Mosko, S., Richard, C., & McKenna, J. (1997). Infant arousals during mother–infant bed-sharing: Implications for infant sleep and sudden infant death syndrome research. *Pediatrics, 100,* 841–849.

Muir, F., & Field, J. (1979). Newborn infants orient to sounds. *Child Development, 50,* 431–436.

Muir, F., & Hains, S. (1999). Young infants' perception of adult intentionality: Adult contingency and eye direction. In P. Rochat (Eds.), *Early social cognition: Understanding others in the first months of life* (pp. 155–187). Mahwah, NJ: Erlbaum.

Mundy, P., Block, J., Vaughan Van Hecke, A., Delgadoa, C., Venezia Parlade, M., & Pomares, Y. (2007). Individual differences and the development of infant joint attention. *Child Development, 78,* 938–954.

Myatt, L. (2006). Placental adaptive responses and fetal programming. *Journal of Physiology, 572*(1), 25–30.

Nagy, E., & Molnar, P. (2004). *Homo imitans* or *Homo provocans*? Human imprinting model of neonatal imitation. *Infant Behavior and Development, 27,* 54–63.

National Association for the Education of Young Children. (2009). *Developmentally appropriate practices in early childhood programs serving children from birth to age 8.* Washington, DC: Author.

National Partnership for Women & Families. (2015). *The hormonal cascade of childbearing* [Fact sheet]. Available at http://www.nationalpartnership.org/research-library/maternal-health/hormonal-cascade-of-childbearing.pdf

National Partnership for Women & Families. (2017). *New professional recommendations to limit labor and birth interventions: What pregnant women need to know* [Fact sheet]. Available at http://www.nationalpartnership.org/research-library/maternal-health/professional-recommendations-to-limit-labor-and-birth-interventions.pdf

National Research Council. (2000). *Eager to learn: Educating our preschoolers* (B. T. Bowman, M. S. Donovan, & M. S. Burns, Eds.). Committee on Early Childhood Pedagogy, Commission on Behavioral and Social Sciences and Education. Washington, DC: National Academies Press.

Nazzi, T., Bertoncini, J., & Mehler, J. (1998). Language discrimination by newborns: Toward an understanding of the role of rhythm. *Journal of Experimental Psychology, 24,* 756–766.

Nelson, E. E., & Panksepp, J. (1998). Brain substrates of infant–mother attachment: Contributions of opioids, oxytocin, and norepinephrine. *Neuroscience and Biobehavioral Reviews, 22*(3), 437–452.

Nelson, J. M., Li, R., & Perrine, C. G. (2015). Trends of US hospitals distributing infant formula packs to breastfeeding mothers, 2007 to 2013. *Pediatrics, 135*(6), 1051–1056.

Newell, K. M., Scully, D. M., McDonald, P. V., & Baillargeon, R. (1989). Task constraints and infant grip configurations. *Developmental Psychobiology, 22,* 817–831.

Nilsson, L., & Hamberger, L. (1990). *A child is born.* New York, NY: Delacorte Press.

Northstone, K., Nethersole, F., & Avon Longitudinal Study of Pregnancy and Childhood Study Team. (2001). The effect of age of introduction to lumpy solids on foods eaten and reported feeding difficulties at 6 and 15 months. *Journal of Human Nutrition and Dietetics, 14,* 43–54.

Nugent, J. K., Keefer, C. H., Minear, S., Johnson, L. C., & Blanchard, Y. (2007). *Understanding newborn behavior and early relationships: The newborn behavioral observations (NBO) system handbook.* Baltimore, MD: Paul H. Brookes.

O'Donohue, J. (1997). *Anam cara: A book of Celtic wisdom.* New York, NY: HarperCollins.

O'Donohue, J. (2008). *To bless the space between us.* New York, NY: Doubleday.

Ondeck, M. (2014). Healthy birth practice #2: Walk, move around, and change positions throughout labor. *The Journal of Perinatal Education, 23*(4), 188–193.

Panksepp, J. (2013). How primary-process emotional systems guide child development: Ancestral regulators of human happiness, thriving, and suffering. In D. Narvaez, J. Panksepp, A. N. Schore, & T. R. Gleason (Eds.), *Evolution, early experience and human development: From research to practice and policy* (pp. 74–94). New York, NY: Oxford University Press.

Pannaraj, P. S., Li, F., Cerini, C., Bender, J. M., Yang, S., Rollie, A., et al. (2017). Association between breast milk bacterial communities and establishment and development of the infant gut microbiome. *Journal of the American Medical Association, Pediatrics, 171*(7), 647–654.

Papousek, H., & Papousek, M. (1977). Mothering and cognitive head start: Psychobiological considerations. In H. R. Schaffer (Ed.), *Studies in mother–infant interaction: The Loch Lomond Symposium* (pp. 63–85). London, UK: Academic Press.

Papousek, H., & Papousek, M. (1989). Intuitive parenting: Aspects related to educational psychology. *European Journal of Psychology of Education, IV,* 201–210.

Papousek, M., & von Hofacker, N. (1995). Persistent crying and parenting: Search for a butterfly in a dynamic system. *Early Development and Parenting, 4*(4), 209–224.

Parmelee, A., Wenner, W. H., & Schultz, H. R. (1964). Infant sleep patterns: From birth to 16 weeks of age. *Pediatrics, 65,* 576–582.

Pawl, J. (2006). Being held in another's mind. In J. R. Lally, P. L. Mangione, & D. Greenwald (Eds.), *Concepts for care: 20 essays on infant/toddler development and care* (pp. 1–4). San Francisco, CA: WestEd.

Pawl, J., & St. John, M. (1998). *How you are is as important as what you do.* Washington, DC: Zero to Three.

Peireno, P., Algarín, C., & Uauy, R. (2003). Sleep–wake states and their regulatory mechanisms throughout early human development. *Journal of Pediatrics, 143,* 70–79.

Pembrey, M., Saffery, R., & Bygren, L. O. (2014). Human transgenerational responses to early-life experience: Potential impact on development, health and biomedical research. *Journal of Medical Genetics, 51*(9), 563–572.

Perry, B. (1997). Incubated in terror: Neurodevelopmental factors in the "cycle of violence." In J. Osofsky (Ed.), *Children in a violent society* (pp. 124–149). New York, NY: Guilford Press.

Perry, B. (2014a). *Helping traumatized children: A brief overview for caregivers.* Houston, TX: The Child Trauma Academy.

Perry, B. (2014b). The neurosequential model of therapeutics: Application of a developmentally sensitive and neurobiology informed approach to clinical problem solving in maltreated children. In K. Brandt, B. Perry, S. Seligman, & E. Tronick (Eds.), *Infant and early childhood mental health: Core concepts and clinical practice* (pp. 21–53). Washington, DC: American Psychiatric Publishing.

Perry, B., Pollard, R. A., Blakley, T. L., Baker, W. L., & Vigilante, D. (1995). Childhood trauma, the neurobiology of adaptation, and "use-dependent" development of the brain: How "states" become "traits." *Infant Mental Health Journal, 16*(4), 271–287.

Petitto, L. A., Holowka, S., Sergio, L. E., Levy, B., & Ostry, D. J. (2004). Baby hands that move to the rhythm of language: Hearing babies acquiring sign languages babble silently on the hands. *Cognition, 93,* 43–73.

Piaget, J. (1952). *The origins of intelligence in children.* New York, NY: International Universities Press.

Pikler, E. (1988). Give me time: The independent motor development of the infant up to free walking. *Pikler Institute training material* (pp. 31–43). Budapest, Hungary: Emmi Pikler International Public Foundation.

Pikler, E. (1994). Emmi Pikler, 1902–1984: Excerpts from "Peaceful babies—Contented mothers." *Sensory Awareness Foundation Bulletin, 14,* 5–24.

Porcaro, C., Zappasodi, F., Barbati, G., Salustri, C., Pizzella, V., Rossini, P. M., et al. (2006). Fetal auditory responses to external sounds and mother's heart beat: Detection improved by independent component analysis. *Brain Research, 1101,* 51–58.

Porges, S. (2011). *The polyvagal theory: Neurophysiological foundations of emotions, attachment, communication, self-regulation.* New York, NY: Norton.

Porges, S. W., & Furman, S. A. (2011). The early development of the autonomic nervous system provides a neural platform for social behavior: A polyvagal perspective. *Infant and Child Development, 20*(1), 106–118.

Porter, R. H. (1998). Olfaction and human kin recognition. *Genetica, 104*(3), 259–263.

Powell, B., Cooper, G., Hoffman, K., & Marvin, B. (2013). *The circle of security intervention: Enhancing attachment in early parent–child relationships.* New York, NY: Guilford Press.

Pratt, C. (1948). *I learn from children: An adventure in progressive education.* New York, NY: Simon & Schuster.

Provasi, J., Anderson, D. I., & Barbu-Roth, M. (2014). Rhythm perception, production, and synchronization during the perinatal period. *Frontiers in Psychology, 5,* 1–16.

Ramirez-Esparza, N., Garcia-Sierra, A., & Kuhl, P. (2017). Look who's talking NOW! Parentese speech, social context, and language development across time. *Frontiers in Psychology, 8,* 1–12.

Reddy, U. M., Bettegowda, V. R., Dias, T., Yamada-Kushnir, T., Ko, C.-W., & Willinger, M. (2011). Term pregnancy: A period of heterogeneous risk for infant mortality. *Obstetrics & Gynecology, 117*(6), 1279–1287.

Reddy, V. (2008). *How infants know minds.* Cambridge, MA: Harvard University Press.

Renfrew, M. J., McFadden, A., Bastos, M. H., Campbell, J., Channon, A. A., Cheung, N. F., et al. (2014). Midwifery and quality care: Findings from a new evidence-informed framework for maternal and newborn care. *Lancet, 384,* 1129–1145.

Rheingold, H. L., Hay, D. F., & West, M. J. (1976). Sharing in the second year of life. *Child Development, 47,* 1148–1158.

Rinaldi, C. (2006). Creativity, shared meaning, and relationships. In J. R. Lally, P. L. Mangione, & D. Greenwald (Eds.), *Concepts for care* (pp. 21–23). San Francisco, CA: WestEd.

Rivkees, S. A. (2003). Developing circadian rhythmicity in infants. *Pediatrics, 112*(2), 373–381.

Rochat, P. (1992). Self-sitting and reaching in 5- to 8-month-old infants: The impact of posture and its development on early eye–hand coordination. *Journal of Motor Behavior, 24,* 210–220.

Rochat, P. (2001). *The infant's world.* Cambridge, MA: Harvard University Press.

Rochat, P., & Goubet, N. (1995). Development of sitting and reaching in 5-to 6-month-old infants. *Infant Behavior and Development, 18,* 53–68.

Rogers, F. (1994). *You are special: Words of wisdom for all ages from a beloved neighbor.* New York, NY: Penguin Books.

Rogers, F. (1997, September). *Ten seconds of silence* [Lifetime Achievement Award speech]. Emmy Awards, Pasadena Civic Auditorium, Pasadena, CA.

Rogers, F. (2002). *You are special: Neighborly wit and wisdom from Mister Rogers.* Philadelphia, PA: Running Press.

Rogers, F. (2003). *The world according to Mr. Rogers: Important things to remember.* New York, NY: Hyperion.

Rogers, S., Dawson, G., & Vismara, L. A. (2012). *An early start for your child with autism: Using everyday activities to help children connect, communicate, and learn.* New York, NY: Guilford Press.

Rogers, S. J., Estes, A., Lord, C., Vismara, L., Winter, J., Fitzpatrick, A., et al. (2012). Effects of a brief Early Start Denver Model (ESDM)-based parent intervention on toddlers at risk for autism spectrum disorders: A randomized controlled trial. *Journal of the American Academy of Child and Adolescent Psychiatry, 51*(10), 1052–1065.

Rogers, S. J., Vismara, L., Wagner, A. L., McCormick, C., Young, G., & Ozonoff, S. (2014). Autism treatment in the first year of life: A pilot study of Infant Start: A parent-implemented intervention for symptomatic infants. *Journal of Autism and Developmental Disorders, 44,* 2981–2995.

Rogoff, B. (2003). *The cultural nature of human development.* New York, NY: Oxford University Press.

Rogoff, B. (with Gonzalez, C. P., Quiacain, C. C., & Quiacain, J. C.). (2011). *Developing destinies: A Mayan midwife and town.* New York, NY: Oxford University Press.

Roitman, J. D., Brannon, E. M., & Platt, M. L. (2007). Monotonic coding of numerosity in macaque lateral intraparietal area. *PLoS Biology, 5*(8), e208.

Romano, A. M., & Lothian, J. A. (2008). Promoting, protecting, and supporting normal birth. *Journal of Obstetric, Gynecologic, & Neonatal Nursing, 37*(1), 94–105.

Ross, H. E., & Young, L. J. (2009). Oxytocin and the neural mechanisms regulating social cognition and affiliative behavior. *Frontiers in Neuroendocrinology, 30*(4), 534–547.

Ross, H. S. (1982). The establishment of social games among toddlers. *Developmental Psychology, 18,* 509–518.

Ross, H. [S.], Vickar, M., & Perlman, M. (2010). Early social cognitive skills at play in toddlers' peer interactions. In J. G. Bremner & T. D. Wachs (Eds.), *The Wiley-Blackwell handbook of infant development: Vol. 1. Basic research* (2nd ed., pp. 510–531). West Sussex, UK: Wiley-Blackwell.

Rossmanith, N., Costall, A., Reichelt, A. F., Lopez, B., & Reddy, V. (2014). Jointly structuring triadic spaces of meaning and action: Book sharing from 3 months on. *Frontiers in Psychology, 5,* 1–22.

Rowe, M. L., & Goldin-Meadow, S. (2009). Early gesture selectively predicts later language learning. *Developmental Science, 12,* 182–187.

Ruhm, C. (2017). *A national paid parental leave policy for the United States.* Washington, DC: Hamilton Project, Brookings Institution.

Sadacharan, R., Grossman, X., Sanchez, E., & Merewood, A. (2011). Trends in U.S. hospital distribution of industry-sponsored infant formula sample packs. *Pediatrics, 128*(4), 702–705.

Saffran, J. R., Aslin, R. N., & Newport, E. L. (1996). Statistical learning by 8-month-old infants. *Science, 274*(5294), 1926–1928.

Sandall, J., Soltani, H., Gates, S., Shennan, A., & Devane, D. (2016). Midwife-led continuity models versus other models of care for childbearing women. *Cochrane Database of Systematic Reviews,* Issue 4, Art. No. CD004667.

Sander, L. (2008). *Living systems, evolving consciousness, and the emerging person: A selection of papers from the life work of Louis Sander.* New York, NY: Analytic Press/Taylor & Francis.

Sandman, C. A., & Davis, E. P. (2012). Neurobehavioral risk is associated with gestational exposure to stress hormones. *Expert Review of Endocrinology and Metabolism, 7*(4), 445–459.

Satter, E. (2000). *Child of mine: Feeding your child with love and good sense.* Boulder, CO: Bull Publishing.

Schofield, T., Lee, R., & Merrick, M. (2013). Safe, stable, nurturing relationships as a moderator of intergenerational continuity of child maltreatment: A meta-analysis. *Journal of Adolescent Health, 53,* S32–S38.

Schore, A. N. (2001). The effects of relational trauma on right brain development, affect regulation, and infant mental health. *Infant Mental Health Journal, 22,* 201–269.

Schrijver, K., & Schrijver, I. (2015). *Living with the stars: How the human body is connected to the life cycles of the earth, the planets, and the stars.* Oxford, UK: Oxford University Press.

Schwarz, E. B., Ray, R. M., Stuebe, A. M., Allison, M. A., Ness, R. B., Freiberg, M. S., et al. (2009). Duration of lactation and risk factors for maternal cardiovascular disease. *Obstetrics & Gynecology, 113*(5), 974–982.

Seidman, D. (1998). Postpartum psychiatric illness: The role of the pediatrician. *Pediatrics in Review, 19*(4), 128–131.

Shonkoff, J. P., Boyce, W. T., & McEwen, B. S. (2009). Neuroscience, molecular biology, and the childhood roots of health disparities: Building a new framework for health promotion and disease prevention. *Journal of the American Medical Association, 301*(21), 2252–2259.

Siegel, D. J. (2015). *The developing mind: How relationships and the brain interact to shape who we are* (2nd ed.). New York, NY: Guilford Press.

Siegel, D. J., & Hartzell, M. (2013). *Parenting from the inside out: How a deeper self-understanding can help you raise children who thrive.* New York, NY: Penguin Group.

Simkin, P. (2013). *The birth partner: A complete guide to childbirth for dads, doulas, and other labor companions* (4th ed.). Beverly, MA: Harvard Commons Press.

Slater, A., & Lewis, M. (2011). *Introduction to infant development.* New York, NY: Oxford University Press.

Smitsman, A. W., & Corbetta, D. (2010). Action in infancy—Perspectives, concepts, and challenges. In J. G. Bremmer & T. D. Wachs (Eds.), *Handbook of infant development: Vol. 1* (2nd ed., pp. 167–203). Oxford, UK: Wiley-Blackwell.

Søndergaard, C., Olsen, J., Friis-Haschè, E., Dirdal, M., Thrane, N., & Toft Sørensen, H. (2003). Psychosocial distress during pregnancy and the risk of infantile colic: A follow-up study. *Acta Paediatrica, 92,* 811–816.

Sroufe, L. A., Egeland, B., Carlson, E. A., & Collins, W. A. (2009). *The development of the person: The Minnesota study of risk and adaptation from birth to adulthood.* New York, NY: Guilford Press.

Stern, D. N. (1971). A microanalysis of the mother–infant interaction. *Journal of the American Academy of Child and Adolescent Psychiatry, 10,* 501–507.

Stern, D. N. (1998). *Diary of a baby.* New York, NY: Basic Books.

Stern, D. N. (2000). *The interpersonal world of the infant: A view from psychoanalysis and developmental psychology* (2nd ed.). New York, NY: Basic Books.

Stern, D. N. (2010). A new look at parent–infant interaction: Infant arousal dynamics. In B. M. Lester & J. D. Sparrow (Eds.), *Nurturing children and families: Building on the legacy of T. Berry Brazelton* (pp. 73–82). West Sussex, UK: Wiley-Blackwell.

Sullivan, L. M., & Brumfield, C. (2016). *The first 1,000 days: Nourishing America's future.* Washington, DC: 1,000 Days.

Sumner, G., & Spietz, A. (1994). *Caregiver/parent–child interaction feeding manual.* Seattle, WA: University of Washington, School of Nursing, NCAST-AVENUW.

Tamis-LeMonda, C. S., & Bornstein, M. H. (1994). Specificity in mother–toddler language-play relations across the second year. *Developmental Psychology, 30,* 283–292.

Tarullo, A. R., Balsam, P. D., & Fifer, W. P. (2011). Sleep and infant learning. *Infant and Child Development, 20,* 35–46.

Tebbs, K. P. (1996). *Thoughtful reflections for future directions: The Los Angeles County child care oral history.* Los Angeles, CA: Los Angeles County Child Care Advisory Board.

Thiessen, E. D., & Saffran, J. R. (2003). When cues collide: Use of stress and statistical cues to word boundaries by 7- to 9-month-old infants. *Developmental Psychology, 39,* 706–716.

Thurow, R. (2016). *The first 1,000 days: A crucial time for mothers and children—and the world.* New York, NY: PublicAffairs.

Tincoff, R., & Jusczyk, P. W. (1999). Some beginnings of word comprehension in 6-month-olds. *Psychological Science, 10,* 172–175.

Tomasello, M. (2009). *Why we cooperate.* Cambridge, MA: MIT Press.

Tomasello, M., & Farrar, J. (1986). Joint attention and early language. *Child Development, 57,* 1454–1463.

Transforming Maternity Care Symposium Steering Committee. (2010). Blueprint for action: Steps toward a high-quality, high-value maternity care system. *Women's Health Issues, 20,* S18–S49.

Trevarthen, C. (1999). Musicality and the intrinsic motive pulse: Evidence from human psychobiology and infant communication. In *Rhythms, musical narrative, and the origins of human communication. Musicae Scientiae, Special Issue, 1999-2000* (pp. 157–213). Liège, Belgium: European Society for the Cognitive Sciences of Music.

Trevarthen, C. (2004). Learning about ourselves, from children: Why a growing human brain needs interesting companions. *Research and Clinical Center for Child Development, Annual Report, 26,* 9–44.

Trevarthen, C. (2005). Stepping away from the mirror: Pride and shame in adventures of companionship—Reflections on the nature and emotional needs of infant intersubjectivity. In C. S. Carter, L. Ahnert, K. E. Grossman, S. B. Hrdy, M. E. Lamb, S. W. Porges, et al. (Eds.), *Attachment and bonding: A new synthesis* (pp. 55–83). Dahlem Workshop Report 92. Cambridge, MA: MIT Press.

Trevarthen, C. (2011). What is it like to be a person who knows nothing? Defining the active intersubjective mind of a newborn human being. *Infant and Child Development, 20,* 119–135.

Trevarthen, C. (2015). Awareness of infants: What do they, and we, seek? *Psychoanalytic Inquiry, 34,* 395–416.

Trevarthen, C. (2016, January). *Pre-birth to three: Interview with Professor Colwyn Trevarthen—Companionable relationships* [Online multimedia resource created to accompany the "Pre-Birth to Three: Positive Outcomes for Scotland's Children and Families" guidance]. Available at https://www.youtube.com/watch?v=pW42_wYNGWk

Trevarthen, C. (2017). Play with infants: The impulse for human story-telling. In T. Bruce, P. Hakkarainen, & M. Bredikyte (Eds.), *The Routledge international handbook of play in early childhood* (pp. 198–215). Abingdon, UK: Routledge.

Trevarthen, C., & Aitkin, K. J. (2001). Infant intersubjectivity: Research, theory, and clinical applications. *Journal of Child Psychology and Psychiatry, 42,* 3–48.

Trevarthen, C., & Delafield-Butt, J. (2017). Intersubjectivity in the imagination and feelings of the infant: Implications for education in the early years. In E. J. White & C. Dalli (Eds.), *Under-three year olds in policy and practice. Policy and pedagogy with under-three year olds: Cross-disciplinary insights and innovations* (pp. 17–39). Singapore: Springer.

Trevarthen, C., & Hubley, P. (1978). Secondary intersubjectivity: Confidence, confiding and acts of meaning in the first year. In A. Lock (Ed.), *Action, gesture and symbol* (pp. 183–229). London, UK: Academic Press.

Trevarthen, C., & Malloch, S. (2002). Musicality and music before three: Human vitality and invention shared with pride. *Zero to Three, 23,* 10–18.

Tronick, E. (1989). Emotions and emotional communication in infants. *American Psychologist, 44*(2), 112–119.

Tronick, E. (2007). *The neurobehavioral and social-emotional development of infants and children.* New York, NY: Norton.

Tronick, E. (2015). Afterword. In M. J. Maguire-Fong, *Teaching and learning with infants and toddlers: Where meaning-making begins* (p. 168). New York, NY: Teachers College Press.

Tronick, E., & Beeghly, M. (2011). Infants' meaning-making and the development of mental health problems. *American Psychologist, 66*(2), 107–119.

Tsiaras, A. (2002). *From conception to birth.* New York, NY: Doubleday.

Turati, C., Simion, F., Milani, I., & Umiltà, C. (2002). Newborns' preference for faces: What is crucial? *Developmental Psychology, 38,* 875–882.

United Nations Human Rights Office of the High Commissioner. (2018). *Joint statement by the UN Special Rapporteurs on the Right to Food, Right to Health, the Working Group on Discrimination Against Women in Law and in Practice, and the Committee on the Rights of the Child in support of increased efforts to promote, support and protect breast-feeding.* Geneva, Switzerland: Author. Available at https://www.ohchr.org/EN/NewsEvents/Pages/DisplayNews.aspx?NewsID=20871

United Nations Population Fund, International Confederation of Midwives, & World Health Organization. (2014). *The state of the world's midwifery 2014: A universal pathway. A woman's right to health.* New York, NY: United Nations.

United States Department of Health and Human Services. (2011). *The Surgeon General's call to action to support breastfeeding.* Washington, DC: U.S. Department of Health and Human Services, Office of the Surgeon General.

van der Kolk, B. (2014). *The body keeps the score: Brain, mind, and body in the healing of trauma.* New York, NY: Penguin/Random House.

Varrassi, G., Bazzano, C., & Edwards, W. T. (1989). Effects of physical activity on maternal beta-endorphin levels and perception of labor pain. *American Journal of Obstetrics and Gynecology, 160*(3), 707–712.

Victora, C. G., Barros, A. J. D., Franca, G. V. A., Horton, S., Krasevec, J., Murch, S., et al. (2016). Breastfeeding in the 21st century: Epidemiology, mechanisms, and lifelong effect. *The Lancet, 387,* 475–489.

Voegtline, K. M., Costigan, K. A., Pater, H. A., & DiPietro, J. A. (2013). Near-term fetal response to maternal spoken voice. *Infant Behavior and Development, 36*(4), 526–533.

Volpe, L. E., Ball, H. L., & McKenna, J. J. (2013). Nighttime parenting strategies and sleep-related risks to infants. *Social Science and Medicine, 79,* 92–100.

von Hof, P., van der Kamp, J., Caljouw, S. R., & Savelsbergh, G. J. P. (2005). The confluence of intrinsic and extrinsic constraints on 3- to 9-month-old infants' catching behavior. *Infant Behavior & Development, 28,* 179–193.

von Hofsten, C., & Ronnqvist, L. (1988). Preparation for grasping an object: A developmental study. *Journal of Experimental Psychology: Human Perception and Performance, 14,* 610–621.

Wadhwa, P. D., Entringer, S., Buss, C., & Lu, M. C. (2011). The contribution of maternal stress to preterm birth: Issues and considerations. *Clinics in Perinatology, 36*(3), 351–382.

Wall, G. (2013). *Outcomes of breastfeeding.* Available at http://www.llli.org/docs/cbi/outcomes_of_breastfeeding_jan_2013.pdf

Wambach, K., & Riordan, J. (Eds.). (2016). *Breastfeeding and human lactation* (5th ed.). Burlington, MA: Jones & Bartlett Learning.

Wambach, K., & Watson Genna, C. (2016). Anatomy and physiology of lactation. In K. Wambach & J. Riordan (Eds.), *Breastfeeding and human lactation* (5th ed., pp. 79–120). Burlington, MA: Jones & Bartlett Learning.

Warneken, F. (2013). The development of altruistic behavior: Helping in infants and chimpanzees. *Social Research, 80,* 431–442.

Warneken, F., Hare, B., Melis, A. P., Hanus, D., & Tomasello, M. (2007). Spontaneous altruism by chimpanzees and young children. *PLoS Biology, 5,* 1414–1420.

Warneken, F., & Tomasello, M. (2006). Altruistic helping in human infants and young chimpanzees. *Science, 311,* 1301–1303.

Warneken, F., & Tomasello, M. (2007). Helping and cooperation at 14 months of age. *Infancy 11,* 271–294.

Warneken, F., & Tomasello, M. (2008). Extrinsic rewards undermine altruistic tendencies in 20-month-olds. *Developmental Psychology, 44,* 1785–1788.

Weinberg, M. K., & Tronick, E. Z. (1998). Emotional characteristics of infants associated with maternal depression and anxiety. *Pediatrics, 102*(5), 1298–1304.

Weinstein, A. D. (2016). *Prenatal development and parents' lived experiences: How early events shape our psychophysiology and relationships.* New York, NY: Norton.

Wendell, A. D. (2013). Overview and epidemiology of substance abuse in pregnancy. *Clinical Obstetrics and Gynecology, 56*(1), 91–96.

Whitebook, M., Austin, L. J. E., & Amanta, F. (2015). *Addressing infant-toddler teacher compensation.* Washington, DC: Administration for Children & Families.

Whitebook, M., Howes, C., & Phillips, D. (1989). *The national child care staffing study: Who cares? Child care teachers and the quality of care in America. Executive summary.* Oakland, CA: Child Care Employee Project.

Whitebook, M., Phillips, D., & Howes, C. (2014). *Worthy work, STILL unlivable wages: The early childhood workforce 25 years after the National Child Care Staffing Study. Executive summary.* Berkeley, CA: Center for the Study of Child Care Employment, University of California, Berkeley.

Wiessinger, D., West, D., & Pitman, D. (2010). *The womanly art of breastfeeding* (8th ed.). New York, NY: Ballantine Books.

Winnicott, D. W. (1964). *The child, the family and the outside world.* Harmondsworth, UK: Penguin Books.

Winnicott, D. W. (1965). *The maturational processes and the facilitating environment: Studies in the theory of emotional development.* Madison, CT: International Universities Press.

Witherington, D. C. (2005). The development of prospective grasping control between 5 and 7 months: A longitudinal study. *Infancy, 7,* 143–161.

Wolff, P. H. (1966). *The causes, controls, and organization of behavior in the neonate.* New York, NY: International Universities Press.

World Health Organization. (1988). *International code of marketing of breastmilk substitutes.* Geneva, Switzerland: Author.

World Health Organization. (2003). *Global strategy for infant and young child feeding.* Geneva, Switzerland: Author.

World Health Organization. (2007). *Safe preparation, storage and handling of powdered infant formula: Guidelines* [Brochure]. Geneva, Switzerland: Author.

World Health Organization. (2014a). *Every newborn: An action plan to end preventable deaths.* Geneva, Switzerland: Author.

World Health Organization. (2014b). *WHO guideline: Delayed umbilical cord clamping for improved maternal and infant health and nutrition outcomes.* Geneva, Switzerland: Author.

World Health Organization. (2015). *WHO statement on caesarean section rates.* Geneva, Switzerland: Author.

World Health Organization. (2016). *Infant and young child feeding: Fact sheet* [Brochure; updated September 2016]. Available at http://www.who.int/mediacentre/factsheets/fs342/en/

World Health Organization. (2017a). *Guideline: Protecting, promoting and supporting breastfeeding in facilities providing maternity and newborn services.* Geneva, Switzerland: Author. Available at http://apps.who.int/iris/handle/10665/259386

World Health Organization. (2017b). *Guiding principles for complementary feeding of the breastfed child.* Washington, DC: Pan American Health Organization/WHO. Available at http://www.who.int/nutrition/publications/guiding_principles_compfeeding_breastfed.pdf

World Health Organization. (2017c). *Managing complications in pregnancy and childbirth: A guide for midwives and doctors* (2nd ed.). Geneva, Switzerland: Author.

World Health Organization. (2018a). *Every Newborn Action Plan: Saving the lives of the 3 million women and newborns who die each year* [Info-graphic]. Available at http://www.who.int/maternal_child_adolescent/newborns/every-newborn/investing-saves-women-newborns.jpg?ua=1

World Health Organization. (2018b). *WHO recommendations: Intrapartum care for a positive childbirth experience.* Geneva, Switzerland: Author.

World Health Organization & United Nations Children's Fund. (2014). *Global nutrition targets 2025: Breastfeeding policy brief 14.7.* Geneva, Switzerland: WHO.

World Health Organization & United Nations Children's Fund. (2016). *Guideline: Updates on HIV and infant feeding.* Geneva, Switzerland: Author.

Wynn, K. (1992). Addition and subtraction by human infants. *Nature, 358,* 749–750.

Xu, F., & Garcia, V. (2008). Intuitive statistics by 8-month-old infants. *Proceedings of the National Academy of Sciences USA, 105,* 5012–5015.

Xu, F., & Spelke, E. S. (2000). Large number discrimination in 6-month-old infants. *Cognition, 74*(1), 1–11.

Zahn-Waxler, C., Radke-Yarrow, M., Wagner, E., & Chapman, M. (1992). Development of concern for others. *Developmental Psychology, 28,* 126–136.

Zero to Three. (2017). *The basics of infant and early childhood mental health: A briefing paper.* Washington, DC: Zero to Three. Available at https://www.zerotothree.org/resources/1951-the-basics-of-infant-and-early-childhood-mental-health-a-briefing-paper

Index

Abrams, R. M., 86
Abuse, 139, 140, 142, 143
Acceptable behavior, house rules on, 125, 131–133
Active (light) sleep, 51, 63, 64–65, 69
Adachi, K., 32
Adaptation in prenatal development, 23
Adolph, K. E., 86, 87, 88, 90, 91, 92, 93, 94
Adverse childhood experiences, 25, 139–140, 141, 142
Adversity, coping with, 123, 134–145
Affect attunement, 3
Afferent arc, 56
Affordability of infant care, 156, 157
Age
  of fetal viability, 17
  gestational, 17–19
  and language development, 84–85
  and motor development, 89, 90, 91, 92, 93, 94
Agnetta, B., 129
Ainsworth, M., 2, 49
Aitkin, K. J., 4
Aka Pygmy community, 126
Akhtar, N., 84
Alcohol use in pregnancy, 24
Alderete, T. L., 58
Alert state, 50–52, 138
Algarín, C., 69
Als, H., 136
Altero-centric infants, 4
Altruistic behavior, 130–131
Alveoli of mammary glands, 57
Amanta, F., 155
American Academy of Pediatrics, 58, 150, 152
  Task Force on Sudden Infant Death Syndrome, 65–66, 67
American College of Obstetricians and Gynecologists, 17–19, 32, 36, 38, 39, 40, 41, 42, 45, 152
Amis, D., 28
Amniotic fluid, 17, 29, 34, 39, 87
Amniotic membrane, 34, 46
Amniotic sac, 12, 34, 39, 47
Amniotomy, 39, 42
Amso, D., 86
Amygdala, 21, 22
  in newborn, 47
  trauma affecting, 140, 143
Anders, T., 64
Anderson, D. I., 73
Anderson, G. C., 36
Anderson, R. M., 147
Anemia, iron deficiency, 36, 58
Anesthesia in labor and delivery, 35, 39–40, 41, 67, 148
Anger, 132, 133
Animal studies
  on object perception, 106
  on perinatal oxytocin, 28
  on play, 95, 96
  on sleep and brain development, 64
Antell, S. E., 106
Appareddy, V., 64
Applebaum, S., 39
Apraxia, 84–85
Ariagno, R. L., 64
Arousal, 139
  cues of, 3, 50, 51
  prenatal cocaine exposure affecting, 25
  regulation of, 3, 6, 25, 135, 136, 138
  in sleep-wake cycle, 64, 65, 69
  states of, 136, 137
Aslin, R. N., 107
Attachment, 2, 49–50, 96
  limbic region in, 21
  paid parental leave time for, 154
  postpartum depression affecting, 153
  prenatal stress exposure affecting, 26
  social referencing in, 128
Attention of infant, 73, 127–128
  in alert state, 50–52
  gaze in, 76, 104, 127–128
  in habituation, 106, 107, 108
  to infant-directed speech, 79
  and joint attention, 127–128
  to objects, 104, 105, 107
  orientation of head in, 76
  parent language in response to, 84
  pointing gesture in, 128
  reaching in, 78
  regulation of, 137
Attunement, interactive, 3, 4
Austin, L. J. E., 155
Autism, 102–103
Autonomic nervous system, 20
  in neuroception, 21
  parasympathetic, 48, 49, 50, 69, 138
  and social engagement system, 48–49
  in stress response, 138
  sympathetic, 48, 49, 50, 138
Autonomy of children, cultural influences on, 126
Avoidant behavior of newborn, 50, 51
Avon Longitudinal Study of Pregnancy and Childhood Study Team, 60
Axons, 20

Babbling, 79, 85
  of deaf infants, 80
Baby-Friendly Hospitals Initiative, 152
Baby-friendly policies, 146–159
  affordable and quality infant care in, 155–157
  mother-baby care in, 148–154
  paid family leave in, 151, 154
  pre-conception, 146–147
  in pregnancy, 147–148
Back to Sleep campaign, 67
Bacteria in microbiome, 46, 47, 58
Badanes, L. S., 156
Bahl, V., 24
Baillargeon, R., 89, 104
Baker, W. L., 5
Ball, H. L., 65, 66, 67, 68, 69
Balog, G., 113, 114, 116, 117, 118, 119
Balsam, P. D., 64
Barbu-Roth, M., 73
Barres, R., 23
Bartocci, M., 47
Bateson, M. C., 79
Bayley, N., 90, 91, 92, 93
Bayley Mental Development Index, 64
Bayley Scales of Infant Development, 93–94
Beebe, B., 2–3, 74, 75, 76, 78
Beeghly, M., 161
Behavior
  clear limits on, 132, 133
  house rules on, 125, 131–133
  limited choice offered on, 132–133
  redirection of, 132, 133
  trauma affecting, 142–143
Behaviorism, 67
Behne, T., 129
Bekkering, H., 129
Belizán, J. M., 45
Belonging, 4–5, 123, 125–133, 158
Berger, S. A., 86, 87, 91, 93
Bergman, J., 45
Bergman, N., 36, 45, 46, 47
Bertoncini, J., 74
Bilingualism, 82
Birth, 27–42. *See also* Labor and delivery
Birthing centers, 32, 37
  breastfeeding support in, 152
  optimal maternal care in, 148
Birth weight, 17, 18, 149
  low, 18, 24, 25, 149
Bistoletti, H., 47
Blakley, T. L., 5
Blampied, N. M., 63
Blanchard, Y., 50
Blank slate (tabula rasa), 2, 6
Blastocyst, 16
Blehar, M., 2
Bloom, P., 130
Blunden, S. L., 69
Bly, L., 87, 88
Bode, L., 58
Bohren, M. A., 38
Bootzin, R. R., 64
Bornstein, M. H., 50
Bottle feeding of infants, 58–59, 67, 152
  compared to breastfeeding, 58–59, 152
  marketing of formula for, 152
Bowlby, J., 2
Boyce, W. T., 23
Brain
  in autism, 103
  in emotions, 21, 22, 96

in interoception, 135
language areas in, 79–80, 82
in newborn, 47, 64–65, 67
in object perception, 106, 107
in play, 95
prenatal development of, 17, 19–23, 73
regions of, 21–22
in regulation system, 136
in sleep patterns, 64–65, 67
in stress response, 21, 22, 138
trauma affecting, 140, 141–142, 145
Brainstem, 21, 22
in newborn, 64
and social engagement system, 48
Brandt, K., 135
Brannon, E. M., 106
Bråten, S., 4
Braxton-Hicks contractions, 31
Brazelton, T. B., 6, 53, 76
Breastfeeding, 54–58, 59, 60–61
colostrum in, 55–56
compared to formula feeding, 58–59, 152
complementary food with, 59–60
microbiome in, 47, 56, 58
oxytocin in, 27, 28, 45, 48, 56, 57, 58
paid parental leave time in, 154
prolactin in, 27, 29, 48, 55, 56–57
protective benefits of, 56, 58, 152, 153
rooting reflex in, 45, 55
schedule in, 57
and sleep patterns, 66, 68
suckling reflex in, 36, 45, 48, 54, 55
support of, 148, 149, 150–153
synchrony in, 3, 54–59
Breast milk, 54–58, 59
and complementary foods, 59–60
composition of, 54, 55–56, 57, 58, 60–61
formula substitutes for, 58–59, 67, 152
production of, 54, 56–57
protective factors in, 56, 58, 152, 153
Breathing, rhythmic, for calming, 145
Breech position, 30
Broca's area, 79–80
Brumfield, C., 146, 150, 152, 153, 154
Bruner, J., 5, 85, 95, 102, 125, 127
Buckley, S. J., 27, 29, 39
Buss, C., 17
Bygren, L. O., 13
Bystrova, K., 46

California Department of Education, 155
Caljouw, S. R., 90
Call, J., 129
Can, D. D., 79
Cardiovascular system
adverse childhood experiences affecting, 140
prenatal development of, 16, 17
CARE/Nurturance system, 96
Caring, altruistic behavior in, 130–131
Carlson, E. A., 143
Carpenter, M., 129
Castle, J., 129, 130
Catecholamines, 28, 29, 32, 35, 45
Categorization of objects by infants, 104, 107–108
in play, 111–112
Causality, infant knowledge of, 105–106, 108
of mobile infants, 115–116
of older infants, 118–119
of young infants, 112–113
Cells, 11, 12, 13
glial, 20
neurons, 12, 13, 20–21
nucleus of, 12, 13
reproductive, 12, 13, 14–15, 23
somatic, 12, 13
Centers for Disease Control, 139, 150
Central nervous system, 19–23. *See also* Brain
Cerebral cortex, 21, 22, 64
Certification
of doulas, 37
of early childhood teachers, 155–156, 157
Cervix, uterine, 15, 28, 31–36
dilation of, 31, 32, 34, 35, 41
effacement of, 31, 32
ripening of, 31
Cesarean delivery, 30, 39, 40–41, 47
Chahin, E., 61
Chapman, M., 130
Chen, F. S., 50
Child care programs, 155–157
in return to work of parent, 154
teacher preparation and certification in, 155–156, 157
Chitty, J., 134
Choice, limited, on behavior, 132–133
Choking hazard from play materials, 110
Chromosomes, 11, 12
Circadian rhythms, 54, 65, 68
Cito, G., 73
Clarke, M., 82
Classification of objects, 107–108
by mobile infants, 114–115
by older infants, 118
by young infants, 111–112
Clear limits on behavior, 132, 133
Clements, D. H., 107, 120
Cloud, J., 13
Cocaine use in pregnancy, 25
Cognitive development, fetal alcohol exposure affecting, 24
Cohen, D., 74
Cohen, L., 134
Cohen, P., 74
Colette, M. V., 86
Colic, 52
Collins, W. A., 143
Colostrum, 55–56
Communication
in autism, 102–103
competency of newborns in, 6
emotions expressed in, 76–78
facial expressions in, 74–75, 76–77, 129
infant-directed speech in, 78–79, 80, 83–84, 96
in joint attention, 127–128
language development in, 73–85
modes of, 76–78
moments of meeting in, 7
musicality of interactions in, 75–76, 85
parent response to crying in, 67, 136
pointing gesture in, 128
protoconversations in, 79
reaching in, 78
reading nonverbal cues in, 50–52, 53
in respectful newborn care, 52–53
sensitivity and responsiveness of infants to, 7
shared stories in, 85
in social play, 96–97, 102
synchrony in, 74–76, 78
touch in, 78
Companionship, 1, 6–7, 73, 135–138
in autism, 103
expectations of infants for, 45, 96, 103, 135
joint attention in, 127–128
panic of infant in separation from, 96
play in, 95, 96–97, 99, 100
postpartum depression affecting, 153
regulatory companions in, 136–137
sharing in, 129–130
Compensation of early childhood teachers, 155, 156, 157
Conception, 11, 14–15, 16
Conde-Agudelo, A., 45
Condon, L. W., 7, 75
Conflicts in play, 129–130, 131
Contractions, uterine, 27, 28–29, 31–36, 38, 39–40
frequency of, 34
intensity of, 34, 38
oxytocin in, 27, 28, 32, 35, 36, 39, 40, 45, 58
in prelabor, 30–31
Cooper, D., 156
Cooper, G., 50
Coping with adversity, 123, 134–145
Corbetta, D., 93
Co-regulation, 3, 69, 136
Correspondence between infant and caregiver, 74–75, 76. *See also* Synchrony
Corry, M. P., 39
Cortex, cerebral, 21, 22, 64
Cortisol, 28, 29, 69, 150
Co-sleeping of infant and caregiver, 65–66, 67, 68
Costall, A., 98
Costigan, K. A., 74
Cost of care for infants and young children, 156
Cow's milk, 61
Crawling, motor development for, 92, 93, 94
Creeping movement, 92
Crockenberg, S. C., 128
Crowning, 36
Cruising by infants, 92
Crying of infants, 50, 51, 52
in colic, 52
in feeding, 59
parent response to, 67, 136
in sleep–wake cycle, 64, 66, 69
Cues in infant communication, 50–52, 53
on engagement/disengagement. *See* Engagement/disengagement cues
in feeding, 59, 61–62
Cultural influences
on learning, 125–126
on motor development, 93–94
on sleeping arrangements, 66–67, 68, 70
Cunningham, F. G., 30, 46
Curriculum in early childhood education, 155
Cuthbert, A., 38

Dalby, J., 153
Dana, D., 136
Darwin, C., 99
Davies, L., 129, 130
Davis, E. P., 23
Davis, K. L., 96
Dawson, D., 69
Dawson, G., 102, 103
Deafness, language development in, 80
de Boysson-Bardies, B., 80
DeCasper, A., 73, 74
Declercq, E. R., 39, 40
Deep (quiet) sleep, 51, 63, 64, 65, 69
Dehaene, S., 107
Dehaene-Lambertz, G., 107
Delafield-Butt, J., 3, 6
Delays, developmental
in language development, 84, 85
in motor development, 94
Delivery. *See* Labor and delivery
Demetriou, H., 129, 130
Dendrites, 20, 21
Depression of parent
postpartum, 49, 153
social referencing of infant in, 129
Devane, D., 40, 148
de Vries, J. I. P., 86, 87
Diaper changing, respectful, 52, 53
Diarrhea, 58, 60, 153
Diary of a Baby (Stern), 158
Diaz-Rossello, J., 45
Diet
epigenetic influences of, 13, 23
of infants. *See* Feeding of infants
Dieterich, C. M., 58, 67
Dietert, J., 47

Dietert, R., 47
DiPietro, J. A., 74
Disengagement cues. *See* Engagement/disengagement cues
Dmitrieva, J., 156
DNA, 12
Donkin, I., 23
Douglas, P. S., 69
Doulas, 37–38
Dowswell, T., 36
Drake, P., 41
Driscoll, A. K., 41
Drowsiness of infant, 51, 64
Drug use in pregnancy, 24–26
Dunham, F., 84
Dunham, P. J., 84
Dweck, C. S., 50

Early interventions in autism, 102–103
Early-term birth, 18
Eckerman, C., 100
Economic insecurity of early childhood teachers, 156, 157
Ectoderm, 16
Education in infancy and early childhood, 155–156
  contexts for learning in, 155
  curriculum in, 155
  teacher preparation and certification in, 155–156
Effacement, cervical, 31, 32
Egeland, B., 143
Egg. *See* Ovum
Egocentric stage of development, 3
Eimas, P., 107
Eisenberg, R. B., 73
Elder, D. E., 63
Embodied self, 134–135
Embryonic development, 15, 16–17
Emergent self, 2, 134–135
Emotions, 135
  caring feelings in, 130–131
  facial expressions of, 76–77, 129
  limbic region in, 21, 22
  neural systems in, 96
  regulation of, 135, 136, 137
  social referencing of, 128–129
  tempers, tantrums, and strong feelings in, 133
  trauma affecting, 142–143
Employment
  as early childhood teacher, compensation in, 155, 156, 157
  paid parental leave from, 151, 154, 157
Endoderm, 16
Endorphins, 27–28, 29, 32, 48
Engagement, social, 48–49, 50. *See also* Social engagement system
Engagement/disengagement cues, 50–52
  in feeding, 59
  gaze in, 76
  head orientation in, 76
  in listening to reading, 98
  reaching in, 78
Entringer, S., 17
Environmental influences
  cultural. *See* Cultural influences
  epigenetics in. *See* Epigenetics
  in prenatal development, 11, 12–13, 22–26
Epidemiology, 12
Epidural anesthesia in labor, 35, 39–40, 41, 148
Epigenetics, 12–13
  in females, 13, 23, 146, 147
  in males, 13, 23, 146
  sensitive periods in, 13, 146
  and social experiences, 95–96
Epigenome, 12, 13, 95–96
Epinephrine, 28, 46
Episiotomy, 39, 40, 42, 148
Estes, A., 103
Estrogen, 28, 55, 56
Ethology, 2
Executive function, 82
Exercise during pregnancy, 29
Expectations of family, house rules on, 125, 131–133
Expectations of infants, 125
  and attachment, 49–50
  for belonging, 4–5
  at birth, 4, 45
  for care, 1, 4–5, 45, 49–50, 96
  for companionship, 45, 96, 103, 135
  in language development, 76
  in learning and meaning-making, 155, 158
  in motor development, 93
  in neonatal period, 4, 45
  on numbers, 107
  in play, 96, 97, 98, 103
  on spatial relations, 104–105, 106
  violation of expectations experiment on, 104–105, 107
Exploration in motor development, 97–98
Expressive language development, 84, 85
Extrusion reflex of newborn, 55, 60
Eye movements in sleep, 51, 63, 64
Eyer, D. W., 53

Facial expressions, 6
  emotions communicated in, 76–77, 129
  imitation of, 5, 74
  in postpartum depression, 153
  in social engagement system, 49
  and social referencing, 128
  in Still Face experiment, 49, 129
  synchrony in, 2–3, 4, 74–75
Fahy, K. M., 37
Fallopian tubes, 12, 14, 15
Family
  culture of, 123
  expectations and house rules of, 125, 131–133
  foods eaten in, 60, 61
  and household dysfunction, 139
  of newborn, 36, 37, 42
  as personal support during labor, 37
  in social context of development, 134
  socioeconomic status of, 82–83
Family and Medical Leave Act, 154
Famine, epigenetic influences of, 13
Fantz, R. L., 73
Farkas, G., 83
Farrar, J., 84
Fathers, epigenetic influences on, 13, 23, 146
Fat in breast milk, 57
Feeding of infants, 54–62
  active participation of infants in, 55, 59, 61–62
  breastfeeding in. *See* Breastfeeding
  complementary food in, 59–61
  in crib, concerns in, 59
  formula in, 58–59, 67, 152
  readiness of infant for, 59
  responsiveness to infant cues in, 59, 61–62
  safety in, 59, 60
  schedule of, 57, 60, 67
  and sleep patterns, 63, 64, 66, 68
Feldman, R., 52, 54, 69
Felice, J. P., 58
Fenson, L., 84
Ferjan Ramírez, N., 82
Fernald, A., 77, 78, 79, 82, 83
Fertility, 14–15
Fetus, 15, 17
  age of viability for, 17
  alcohol exposure of, 24
  birth of. *See* Labor and delivery
  environmental influences on, 23–26
  monitoring of, 40, 42, 73
  movements of, 17, 22, 86–87
  nervous system of, 20–23
  respiratory system of, 19, 29
  response to maternal voice, 73–74
  sleep of, 65
  undernutrition of, 150
Field, J., 73
Field, T. M., 74, 76, 153
Fifer, W. E., 74
Fifer, W. P., 64
Fight–flight response, 21, 28, 138
Fogel, A., 13, 15, 16, 17, 21, 22, 24, 25, 26, 50, 52, 135, 138, 141
Foods for infants, 59–61
Forman, D., 153
Formula feeding of infants, 58–59, 67, 152
  compared to breastfeeding, 58–59, 152
  marketing of products for, 152
For Our Babies (Lally), 154
France, K. G., 63
Fruit juice, 61
Frustration of infant, 132, 133
Fukuzawa, R. K., 38
Full-term birth, 18, 36
Furman, S. A., 49, 69

Galland, B. C., 63
Games, interactive, 96–99
  of imitation and pretense, 101–102
  with objects, 97–99
  with peers, 100
Gametes, 12, 13, 14–15, 23
Garcia, V., 107
Garcia-Sierra, A., 79
Gaskin, I. M., 32, 39
Gates, S., 148
Gaze
  communication in, 76
  in joint attention, 127–128
  at objects, 104
Generational transmission
  of epigenetic changes, 13, 146, 147
  of microbiome, 47
Genes, 11, 12
Genetic factors
  in autism, 103
  and epigenetics. *See* Epigenetics
  in play, 95–96
  in prenatal development, 11, 12–13, 23
Genome, 12
Gerber, M., 52, 91, 110, 131
Gergely, G., 129
Gerhardt, K. J., 86
German, J. B., 55
Germinal phase of prenatal development, 15–16
Gertner, S., 64
Gestational age, 17–19
Gestures, communicative
  pointing in, 128
  and vocabulary development, 84
Gettler, L., 65
Gilkerson, L., 17, 24, 25
Ginsburg, H. P., 3
Glial cells, 20
Goer, H., 36, 37, 40, 148, 149
Goldberg, W. A., 69
Goldin-Meadow, S., 84
Goldman, B. D., 101
Golinkoff, R. M., 79, 81
Gomez, R. L., 64
Gonadotropin, human chorionic, 16
Gonzalez-Mena, J., 53
Goodlin-Jones, B. L., 64
Gopnik, A., 1, 80, 107
Goubet, N., 88
Granger, D. A., 69
Grasping by infants, 88–90
  feeding in, 60
  palmar, 89, 111
  pincer, 89, 111

of play objects, 110–111, 112
tactile communication in, 78
Gratier, M., 85
Gray, P., 102
Green, J., 103
Greenberg, R., 74
Greenspan, S., 103
Grossman, X., 152
Growth factor in colostrum, 56
Gunnar, M. R., 156
Gupta, J. K., 36
Gura, T., 58, 152

Habituation, 106, 107, 108
Hadders-Algra, M., 86
Haight, W. L., 100
Hains, S., 74, 97
Halfon, N., 149, 150
Hamberger, L., 87
Hamilton, B. E., 41
Hamlin, J. K., 130
Hanus, D., 131
Hare, B., 131
Harmon, T., 47
Harnevik, L., 47
Harris, J., 81, 84
Hart, B., 83
Hartzell, M., 21
Hastie, C., 37
Hauser-Cram, P., 13, 14, 15, 17, 20
Hay, D. F., 129, 130
Head of infant
crowning of, in delivery, 36
orientation of, as engagement cue, 76
Healing from trauma, 143–145
Hearing, 73
language development with impairment of, 80, 84
prenatal development of, 73–74
Heart
adverse childhood experiences affecting, 140
prenatal development of, 16, 17
Heart rate, fetal
monitoring of, during labor, 40, 42
in response to rhythmic stimulation, 73
Hedegaard, M., 153
Helpful behavior, 130–131
Hemorrhage, postpartum, 39, 45, 58
Henderson, J. M. T., 63
Hepper, P., 87
Herbison, P., 63
Hernell, O., 47
Hewlett, B. S., 126
Heyman, M. B., 61
Hide and seek game, 138–139
Hill, P. S., 69
Hillemeier, M. M., 83
Hinde, K., 54, 55
Hippocampus, 21, 22, 140
Hirsh-Pasek, K., 79, 81
Hiteshew, B., 157
HIV infection, breastfeeding in, 58
Hofer, M. A., 47
Hoffman, K., 50
Hofmeyr, G. J., 38
Holowka, S., 80
Hopkins, B., 87, 94
Hormones
in labor and delivery, 27–29, 32, 35, 36, 39, 40
in lactation and breastfeeding, 28, 29, 48, 55, 56–57, 58
and newborn care, 45–46, 47, 48
in pregnancy, 16
in stress response, 23, 26, 69, 138, 150
Hospital setting
breastfeeding support in, 152
delivery in, 32, 37, 39, 40, 47, 67, 148, 149
optimal maternal care in, 148
premature infants in, 19, 22
separation of newborn and mother in, 47, 67
sleep training and infant stress in, 69
House rules, 125, 131–133
Howel, D., 65
Howes, C., 156
Hubley, P., 98
Human chorionic gonadotropin (HCG), 16
Humor, 99–100
Hupbach, A., 64
Hyde, D. C., 107

Imitation
of facial expressions, 5, 74
learning in, 126
in play, 5, 100, 101
of vocal sounds, 74
Immune system
adverse childhood experiences affecting, 140
breastfeeding benefits for, 152
of newborn, 47, 56, 58
Implantation, 16
Improving Birth Coalition, 148, 149
Infant-directed speech, 78–79, 80, 83–84, 96
Infant–parent mental health, 135–136
Insecure attachment, 49–50
Institute of Medicine, 155
Intelligence at birth, 6
Intentions of others, infant awareness of, 129
Interactive games. *See* Games, interactive
International Code of Marketing of Breastmilk Substitutes (WHO), 152
International Confederation of Midwives, 148
Interoception, 135, 138, 141, 144
Intersubjectivity, 4
Intuitive parenting, 96
Iron deficiency anemia, 36, 58
Izard, V., 107

Jaffe, J., 79
James, W., 161
Joh, A. S., 88, 90, 92, 93
Johansson, I., 47
Johnson, L. C., 50
Johnson, N., 36
Johnson, S. C., 50
Johnson, S. P., 86
Johnson, V., 36
Joint attention, 127–128
Jones, E., 155
Jones, L., 38
Jusczyk, P. W., 83

Kálló, E., 113, 114, 116, 117, 118, 119
Kamii, C., 108, 131
Karasik, L. B., 86, 93
Keating, D. P., 106
Keefer, C. H., 50
Kennell, J., 17
Kiraly, I., 129
Kisilevsky, B. S., 74
Klaus, M., 17, 37
Klaus, P., 17
Klein, R., 17, 24, 25
Klingaman, K., 68
Koslowski, B., 76
Kryzer, E., 156
Kugiumutzakis, G., 74
Kuhl, P., 73, 79, 80, 81, 82, 107

Labor and delivery, 27–42
anesthesia in, 35, 39–40, 41, 67, 148
birth weight in, 17, 18, 24, 25, 149
breech position in, 30
continuous personal support in, 37–38, 42
crowning in, 36
and experience of baby at birth, 4
family stories about, 42
fetal monitoring in, 40, 42
fetal positions in, 30, 33, 35, 39
gestational age in, 17–18
in hospital setting, 32, 37, 39, 40, 47, 67, 148, 149
induction of, 39
maternal positions in, 32, 34, 35–36, 38, 40
maternal pushing effort in, 35, 36, 40
medically necessary interventions in, 38, 39
medical-management model of, 149
microbiome in, 46–47
normalcy of, 149
optimal care in, 36–42, 148–149
physiologic care in, 37, 149
placenta delivery in, 36
policy recommendations on, 40–42
and prelabor, 30–31
premature, 17–19. *See also* Prematurity
preparation for, 28–29
progression of, 41
routine interventions avoided in, 38–40, 41, 42
sanctum for, 37
spontaneous onset of, 27, 28, 29, 39
stages of, 31–36
Lachmann, F., 74
Lactation, 54–59. *See also* Breastfeeding
Lactobacillus bacteria, 46
Ladefoged, P., 80
Lagercrantz, H., 47, 73
Lally, J. R., vii–viii, 53, 92, 131, 147, 154, 155, 156, 157
Language development, 22, 71, 73–85
anticipating language patterns in, 79–80
awareness of foreign languages in, 74, 80
babbling in, 79, 80, 85
brain areas in, 79–80, 82
categorization skills in, 108
delays in, 84, 85
expectation of contingency in, 76
fetal responses in, 73–74
first words in, 84
in hearing impairment, 80, 84
infant-directed speech in, 79, 80, 83–84, 96
initial conversations in, 74–75, 76
joint attention in, 128
listening to reading in, 98
milestones in, 84–85
modes of communication in, 76–78
musicality of interactions in, 75–76, 85
narratives in, 85
native language sounds in, 80
number concepts in, 107
phonological awareness in, 81
processing time in, 83
protoconversations in, 79, 85
reading in, 81, 82–84, 98
shared stories in, 85
social context of, 80, 81–82, 99
socioeconomic factors affecting, 82, 83
synchrony of infant and caregiver in, 74–76, 78
vocabulary growth in, 82–84
word recognition in, 80–81
Language disorders, 84
Latent phase of labor, 31–32
Late-term birth, 18
Laughter of infants, 99–100
Lawrence, R. A., 56
Lawrence, R. M., 56
Learning, 125–127
about objects, 71, 104–122
about people, 71, 95–103
cultural differences in, 125–126
fetal alcohol exposure affecting, 24
imitation in, 126
of language, 80, 81–82
by listening-in, 126
meaning making in. *See* Meaning making
in play, 71, 95–103, 121–122, 155
to read, 81

Learning (*contd.*)
in respectful newborn care, 52–53
sleep affecting, 64
in virtual participation, 5
Lee, R., 140
Lester, B. M., 5, 6, 52
Letdown reflex, 56, 57
LeVine, R. A., 125
Levy, B., 80
Lewis, M., 28
Li, R., 152
Life-course perspective on maternal care, 149–150
Lif Holgerson, P., 47
Light (active) sleep, 51, 63, 64–65, 69
Lightening, 30
Lillas, C., 136, 137–138
Limbic region, 21–22, 48
Limited choice on behavior, 132–133
Lipton, B., 13
Liu, H., 79, 81
Locomotion, motor development for, 91–93, 94
Logicomathematical knowledge, 108
Lopez, B., 98
Lothian, J. A., 32, 35, 39
Low birth weight, 18, 24, 25, 149
Lu, M. C., 17, 149, 150
Luchinger, A. B., 86
Ludy-Dobson, C., 21, 23
Lungs, prenatal development of, 28, 29, 39, 87
Lunshof, S., 54

Maas, Y. G. H., 64
MacLean, P., 21
Maczuga, S., 83
Maguire-Fong, M. J., 109, 132, 155, 156
Mahajan, N., 130
Mahler, K., 135
Main, M., 76
Make-believe play, 120–121
Malloch, S., 78, 96
Mammary glands, 56–57
Mangione, P. L., 92
Marchman, V. A., 82
March of Dimes, 18, 24, 148
Marijuana use in pregnancy, 24–25
Marketing of infant formula, 152
Martin, J. A., 41
Marvin, B., 50
Maternal and Child Health programs, 148
McCrink, K., 106
McDonald, P. V., 89
McEwen, B. S., 23
McKenna, J. J., 65, 66, 67, 68, 69, 70
Meaning making, 1, 5–6, 7, 71–122, 158–159
language development in, 71, 73–85
learning about objects in, 71, 104–122
learning about people in, 71, 95–103
limbic region in, 22
motor development in, 71, 86–94
play in, 71, 95–103
Meconium, 56
Medical-management model of care, 149
Mehler, J., 74
Melis, A. P., 131
Meltzoff, A. N., 3, 74, 80, 82, 107
Memory
limbic region in, 21, 22
sleep affecting, 64
Menstrual cycle, 14, 15
in breastfeeding, 57, 58
Mental health of infants, 153–154
and parents, 135–136
Merewood, A., 152
Merrick, M., 140
Mesoderm, 16
Microbiome, 46–47, 56, 58
Middlemiss, W., 69
Midwives, 147–148
Milani, I., 73
Miller, P. J., 100
Minear, S., 50
Minerals, dietary, 61
Miranda, S. B., 73
Mireault, G. C., 128
Mirmiran, M., 54, 64, 65
Misbehavior
house rules on, 125, 131–133
tantrums in, 133
Mobile infants. *See also* Toddlers
motor development of, 91–93, 94
play of, 109, 114–117
social referencing of, 128
Molnar, P., 74
Montagu, A., 45
Moon, C., 73, 74
Moore, E. R., 36, 46
Moore, K. L., 87
Moore, M. K., 3, 74
Morgan, P. L., 83
Morula, 16
Mosko, S., 65
Mother-Friendly Childbirth Initiative, 148
Mothers, 147–153
attachment of infant to, 2. *See also* Attachment
breastfeeding by. *See* Breastfeeding
depression of, postpartum, 49, 153
epigenetic influences on, 13, 23, 146, 147
fetal response to voice of, 73–74
first meeting with newborn, 36, 40, 47, 48
in labor and delivery, 27–42
life-course perspective on care of, 149–150
medical-management model on care of, 149
microbiome of, 46–47
optimal care of, 148–149
physiologic model on care of, 149
pregnancy of. *See* Pregnancy
responsive "good-enough" care provided by, 2
separation from newborn, 36, 47, 67
Motility of sperm, 12, 15
Motor development, 71, 86–94
assessment of, 93–94
crawling in, 92, 93, 94
cultural influences on, 93–94
delays in, 94
exploration in, 97–98
and feeding, 60, 61
fetal movements in, 17, 22, 86–87
formal skills training in, 94
freedom to move in, 91, 93
grasping in. *See* Grasping by infants
locomotion in, 91–93
of newborns, 87–88
and play, 86, 97–98, 110–111, 112, 114–117, 118
reaching in. *See* Reaching by infants
rolling over in, 90
sequence of, 93, 94
sitting up in, 88, 90–91, 94
social context of, 93–94
walking in, 91, 92–93, 94
Movellan, J., 82
Muir, F., 73, 97
Multiple language learning, 82
Mundy, P., 128
Muscle development. *See* Motor development
Mutual regulation of infant and caregiver, 49
Myatt, L., 17
Myelination, 20

Nadel, L., 64
Nagy, E., 74
Narratives, 85
Nash, A., 130
Nathans, L., 69
National Academies of Sciences, Engineering, and Medicine, 155
National Association for the Education of Young Children, 155
National Child Traumatic Stress Network, 142
National Partnership for Women and Families, 148
National Research Council, 155, 156
Native language sounds, infant detection of, 80
Nature
genes in. *See* Genetic factors
and nurture interactions, 11
Nazzi, T., 74
Neglect, 139, 140, 142, 143
Nelson, E. E., 47
Nelson, J. M., 152
Neocortex, 22
Nervous system
brain in. *See* Brain
breathing activities calming, 145
in emotions, 21, 22, 96
in play, 95, 96
prenatal development of, 16, 17, 19–23, 73, 87
regulatory processes of, 136
in stress response, 138
trauma affecting, 140, 141–142, 145
Nethersole, F., 60
Neural tube, 19, 20
Neuroception, 21, 48, 135
Neurogenesis, 12, 20
Neurons, 12, 13, 20–21
Neurotransmitters, 20–21
Newborns, 4, 43–70
attachment of, 49–50
communication competency of, 6
expectations of, 4, 45
feeding of, 54–62
inconsistent or unreliable care of, 49
maternal depression affecting, 49, 153
microbiome of, 46–47
movements of, 87–88
mutual regulation in, 49
optimal care of, 46
paid parental leave for care of, 154
respectful interactions with, 52–53
responsive interactions with, 50–53
safety of, 47–50
separation from mother, 36, 47, 67
skin-to-skin contact for, 45–46, 47, 136
sleep of, 54, 63–70, 137
social engagement system of, 48–49, 50
stress of, 49, 50, 52, 136
substance use of parents affecting, 25–26
synchrony between caregiver and, 50, 54–70
trauma affecting, 142
Newell, K. M., 89
Newport, E. L., 107
Night, infant sleeping through, 64, 68–70
training of infant for, 64, 69
Nikodem, V. C., 36
Nilsson, L., 87
Nonverbal communication. *See also* Communication
gestures in, 84, 128
reading cues in, 50–52, 53
synchrony in, 74–75
and vocabulary development, 84
Noradrenalin, 47
Northstone, K., 60
Nucleus of cells, 12, 13
Nugent, J. K., 13, 50, 63, 64, 78, 105
Number concept, 106–107, 108
of mobile infants, 116–117
of older infants, 120
of young infants, 114
Numerosity, 106
Nursery rhymes, 79, 96, 97
Nurture
environmental influences in. *See* Environmental influences
and nature interactions, 11

Nutrition
epigenetic influences of, 13, 23
of infants. *See* Feeding of infants

Obesity, 58
Objects
categorization of, 104, 107–108, 111–112
classification of. *See* Classification of objects
interactive games with, 97–99
joint attention to, 127–128
learning about, 71, 104–122
number of, 106–107, 114, 116–117, 120
permanence of, 104
play with, 97–99, 102, 108–122
spatial relations of, 104–106, 113–114, 116, 119, 120
Obstetricians, 147
O'Donohue, J., 45, 73, 134
Older infants, play of, 109, 118–121
Oligosaccharides in breast milk, 58
Ondeck, M., 40
1,000 Days initiative, 54, 146
Oocytes, 12, 14
Opioid use in pregnancy, 25
Opper, S., 3
Optimal care, 135
in labor and delivery, 36–42, 148–149
of newborn, 46
Osterman, M. J. K., 41
Ostry, D. J., 80
O'Sullivan, E., 58
Ovaries, 12, 14
Ovulation, 14, 15
in breastfeeding, 57
Ovum (ova), 12, 14, 15
epigenetic changes affecting, 13, 23, 146
lifetime number of, 14
prenatal development of, 13, 14, 146
in puberty, 14
Owens, J. L., 63
Oxygen supply of fetus and infant, 24
in labor and delivery, 28, 29, 32, 34
Oxytocin
and attachment, 27, 48
and endorphins, 29, 32
epidural anesthesia affecting, 35, 40
fetal, 28–29, 32
in lactation and breastfeeding, 27, 28, 45, 48, 56, 57, 58
and Pitocin, 39
and postpartum hemorrhage, 39, 45, 58
skin-to-skin contact releasing, 45–46
and uterine contractions, 27, 28, 32, 35, 36, 39, 40, 45, 58

Paid family leave, 151, 154, 157
Pain
in labor, 27, 29, 30, 32, 34, 36, 38, 39–40
postpartum, 40
Palmar grasp, 89, 111
PANIC/Sadness system, 96
Panksepp, J., 47, 95, 96
Pannaraj, P. S., 47
Panneton-Cooper, R., 74
Papousek, H., 74, 96
Papousek, M., 52, 74, 96
Parasympathetic nervous system, 48, 138
of newborn, 49, 50
in sleep training of infant, 69
Parmelee, A., 63
Participation of infants, 1, 2–4
in diaper changing, 52, 53
in feeding and meals, 55, 59, 61–62
learning in, 5, 126
in nonverbal social dialogue, 74
in respectful interactions, 52–53
in shared reading, 98
Partnership for Maternal, Newborn and Child Health (PMNCH), 18
Pater, H. A., 74
Pawl, J., 6, 62, 96
Pedersen, J., 130
Peek-a-boo game, 97
Peers
conflicts with, 129–130
playing with, 100, 101, 129
sharing with, 129
Peireno, P., 69
Pelvic bones in labor and birth, 33, 35, 39
Pembrey, M., 13
Perinatal period, 27–42
first meeting of mothers and newborn in, 36, 40, 47, 48
labor and delivery in. *See* Labor and delivery
microbiome in, 46–47
newborn care in. *See* Newborns
optimal care in, 36–42, 148–149
physiologic care in, 37, 149
prelabor in, 30–31
separation of mother and newborn in, 36, 47, 67
Peripheral nervous system, prenatal development of, 19, 20
Perlman, M., 101
Perrine, C. G., 152
Perry, B., 5, 6, 21, 23, 49, 50, 134, 135, 140, 141, 143, 144
Persaud, T. V. N., 87
Petitto, L. A., 80
Phillips, D. A., 156
Phonemes in language development, 80
Phonological awareness, 81
Physiological regulation, 21, 22, 65, 137
Physiologic care, perinatal, 37, 149
Piaget, J., 3, 5, 87, 104, 131
Pierson, L. L., 86
Pikler, E., 52, 61, 86, 91
Pikler Institute, 61, 62
Pincer grasp, 89, 111
Pitman, D., 57
Pitocin, 39, 40
Pituitary gland
fetal, 29
in labor, 32, 40
in lactation and breastfeeding, 55, 56, 58
in menstrual cycle, 14
Placenta, 12, 16–17
delivery of, 36
Platt, M. L., 106
Play, 71, 95–103
in autism interventions, 102–103
as biological urge, 95–96
conflicts in, 129–130, 131
face-to-face, 5, 49
house rules in, 131
humor and affection in, 99–100
imitation in, 5, 100, 101
interactive games in. *See* Games, interactive
learning in, 71, 95–103, 121–122, 155
of mobile infants, 109, 114–117
and motor development, 86, 97–98, 110–111, 112, 114–117, 118
with objects, 97–99, 102, 108–122
of older infants, 109, 118–121
with peers, 100, 101
pretend. *See* Pretend play
recommended materials and objects in, 109–122
rough-and-tumble, 102
sharing in, 129–130
social, 96–102
Still Face experiment in, 49, 129
sympathetic interactions in, 96
in trauma interventions, 145
of young infants, 109, 110–114
PLAY/Joy system, 96
Pointing gesture, 128
Pollard, R. A., 5
Porcaro, D., 73
Porges, S., 21, 48, 49, 69
Porter, R. H., 47
Postpartum depression, 49, 153
Postpartum hemorrhage, 39, 45, 58
Post-term birth, 18
Powell, B., 50, 140
Pratt, C., 125
Prechtl, H. F. R., 87
Pre-conception period, 14
baby-friendly policies in, 146–147
epigenetic influences in, 12–13, 23, 146, 147
Prefrontal cortex, 21, 22, 140
Pregnancy
environmental influences in, 11, 12–13, 22–26
exercise in, 29
health care during, 147–148, 150
labor and delivery in, 27–42
maternal weight in, 19
medical-management model of care in, 149
phases of prenatal development in, 15–17
physiologic care in, 37, 149
reducing risk factors in, 147
stress in, 23, 26, 52, 136, 147, 150
trimesters of, 16
urine test for, 16
Prehension, 89, 108
Prelabor, 30–31
Prematurity, 17–19, 149, 150
age of viability in, 17
global campaign on, 18
health problems in, 19
language development in, 85
in maternal alcohol use, 24
skin-to-skin care in, 46
social engagement system in, 49
Prenatal care, 147–148, 150
Prenatal development, 11–26
age of viability in, 17
co-regulation in, 136
as dynamic process, 15
environmental influences on, 11, 12–13, 22–26
genetic factors in, 11, 12–13, 23
life-course perspective on, 149–150
movement in, 86–87
nature and nurture in, 11
of nervous system, 16, 17, 19–23, 73, 87
of ova, 13, 14, 146
phases of, 15–17
reducing risk factors in, 147
terminology related to, 12
touch in, 78
Pre-reaching, 88
Pretend play, 100–101, 102, 108–109
of mobile infants, 117
of older infants, 120–121
symbolic representation in, 117, 120–121
Primitive streak, 19, 20
Progesterone in pregnancy, 15, 28, 55, 56
Prolactin, 27, 29, 48, 55, 56–57
Protoconversations, 79, 85
Provasi, J., 73
Pruning, synaptic, 21
Puberty, 13, 14, 146
Public policies, 157

Quality of infant and child care, 155–157
Quickening, 17, 87
Quiet (deep) sleep, 51, 63, 64, 65, 69
Quinn, P., 107

Radke-Yarrow, M., 130
Ramírez, R. R., 82
Ramirez-Esparza, N., 79
Rapid-eye-movement (REM) sleep, 51, 63, 64

Rasmussen, K. M., 58
Reaching by infants, 88–90
  communication in, 78
  goal-directed, 88, 89
  for play objects, 112
Reading, 81, 82–84
  infant listening to, 98
Receptive language development, 84
Reddy, U. M., 19
Reddy, V., 3, 96, 98, 99, 100
Redirection of behavior, 132, 133
Regulation, 136–138
  of arousal, 3, 6, 25, 135, 136, 138
  attentional, 137
  companions in, 136–137
  and co-regulation, 3, 69, 136
  emotional, 135, 136, 137
  physiological, 21, 22, 65, 137
  responsive care in, 137–138
  self-regulation in. *See* Self-regulation and self-soothing
Reichelt, A. F., 98
Relaxation techniques
  in labor, 34, 38
  for young children, rhythmic breathing in, 145
Renfrew, M. J., 148
Representational play
  of mobile infants, 117
  of older infants, 120–121
Reproductive cells, 12, 13, 14–15, 23
Research techniques, microanalysis of film and video in, 2
Resources, in trauma and repair, 137
Resources for Infant Educarers (RIE), 52
Respectful interactions, 52–53
  in diapering, 52, 53
  in feeding, 61–62
  limited choice offered in, 132–133
Respiratory system
  infections of, 153
  in prematurity, 19
  prenatal development of, 19, 28, 29, 39, 87
  in sleep of infant, 65–66
  in sudden infant death syndrome, 66
Responsive interactions, 2, 50–53, 137–138
  in diapering, 52, 53
  in feeding, 59, 61–62
  in play, 97
  reading cues and states in, 50–52
  in secure attachment of infant, 50
Restitution movement in labor, 33
Reynolds, G., 155
Rheingold, H. L., 100, 129
Richard, C., 65
Rinaldi, C., 7, 104, 159
Riordan, J., 59
Ripening, cervical, 31
Risley, T. R., 83
Rivera-Gaxiola, M., 80, 81
Rivkees, S. A., 69
Robinson, S. R., 87, 92, 93, 94
Rochat, P., 88, 104, 105, 106, 108, 127, 129
Rogers, F., 27, 73, 95, 146, 147, 157
Rogers, S., 102, 103
Rogoff, B., 5, 125, 126
Roitman, J. D., 106
Rolling over movement, 90–91
Romano, A., 32, 35, 36, 37, 39, 40, 148, 149
Ronnqvist, L., 90
Rooting reflex, 45, 55
Ross, H. E., 47
Ross, H. S., 101, 129
Rossmanith, N., 98
Rough-and-tumble play, 102
Rowe, M. L., 84
Ruhm, C., 154
Rules of acceptable behavior, 131–133
Russell, C., 65, 67
Sadacharan, R., 152
Sadeh, A., 64
Safety
  in birth sanctum, 37
  in feeding of infants, 59, 60
  in newborn care, 47–50
  of play materials, 109, 110
  in sleep, 64, 65–66, 67–68
Saffery, R., 13
Saffran, J. R., 79, 107
St. John, M., 6, 62
Sakala, C., 38, 39
Sanchez, E., 152
Sandall, J., 148
Sander, L. W., 7, 75
Sandman, C. A., 23
Satter, E., 60
Savelsbergh, G. J. P., 90
Save the Children, 18
Scheffner Hammer, C. S., 83
Schofield, T., 140
Schore, A. N., 136
Schrijver, I., 11
Schrijver, K., 11
Schwarz, E. B., 153
Schulz, H. R., 63
Scully, D. M., 89
Secher, N. J., 153
Secondhand smoke, 24
Second language learning, 82
Secure attachment, 49–50
Sejnowski, T. J., 82
Seidman, D., 153
Self
  embodied, 134–135
  emerging sense of, 2, 134–135
Self-regulation and self-soothing, 50, 59, 69, 135
  gaze aversion in, 76
  regulatory companions in development of, 136–137
  touch in, 78
Seligman, S., 135
Semen, 14
Sensitive periods in development, 150
  environmental exposures in, 24
  sex differences in, 13, 146
Sensori-motor stage, 3, 5
Sensory proximity of infant and caregiver
  in skin-to-skin contact, 36, 45–46, 47, 136
  in sleep, 65–66, 67, 68
Separation of newborn and mother, 36, 47, 67
Sergio, L. E., 80
Sex differences in epigenetic influences, 13, 23, 146
Shared reading, 98
Sharing, 100, 129–130
  conflicts in, 129–130, 131
Shennan, A., 148
Shimada, M., 32
Shonkoff, J. P., 23
Siegel, D. J., 21, 22, 135, 144
Signer, S., 92
Simion, F., 73
Simkin, P., 29, 32, 34, 35, 38, 41
Sitting up movement, 88, 91, 94
Skin-to-skin contact in newborn care, 36, 45–46, 47, 136
Slater, A., 28
Sleep, 63–70
  co-sleeping of infant and caregiver in, 65–66, 67, 68
  cultural influences on, 66–67, 68, 70
  daily hours of, 63, 64
  deep (quiet), 51, 63, 64, 65, 69
  and feeding times, 63, 64, 66, 68
  of fetus, 65
  light (active), 51, 63, 64–65, 69
  positioning of infant in, 67
  rapid-eye-movement (REM), 51, 63, 64
  safety in, 64, 65–66, 67–68
  sensory proximity of infant and caregiver in, 65–66, 67, 68
  stages of, 63, 64
  states of, 50, 51, 63
  sudden infant death syndrome in, 65–66, 67–68, 69
  through night, 64, 68–70
  training of infant for, 64, 69
  and wake cycle of newborn, 64, 65, 137
Slemmer, J. A., 86
Small-for-gestational age, 18
Smiling, 3, 76–77, 99
Smitsman, A. W., 93
Smoke exposure, 13, 24–25, 67
Snacks, 60
Social context of development, 134, 135
  infant–parent mental health in, 135–136
  of language, 80, 81–82, 99
Social-conventional knowledge, 131
Social engagement system, 48–49, 50, 96, 138
  cues on. *See* Engagement/disengagement cues
  in healing from trauma, 144–145
  joint attention in, 128
Social play, 96–102
Social referencing, 128–129
Socioeconomic factors in vocabulary size, 82, 83
Soderstrom, M., 79
Soltani, H., 148
Somatic cells, 12, 13
Somatic nervous system, 20
Søndergaard, C., 52
Sparrow, J. D., 6
Spatial relations knowledge, 104–106, 108
  of mobile infants, 116
  of older infants, 119, 120
  of young infants, 113–114
Speech
  disorders of, 84–85
  first words in, 84
  infant awareness of foreign words in, 74, 80
  infant-directed, 78–79, 80, 83–84, 96
  language processing time in response to, 83
  native language sounds in, 80
  recognition of words in, 80–81
Spelke, E. S., 104, 106, 107
Spence, M., 73, 74
Sperm, 12, 14, 15
  epigenetic changes affecting, 13, 23, 146
  lifetime number of, 14
  motility of, 12, 15
  in puberty, 13, 14, 146
Spermatogenesis, 12, 14
Spermatozoa, 12, 14, 15
Spietz, A., 50, 51
Spinal cord, prenatal development of, 19
Sroufe, L. A., 143
Standing position, motor development for, 92, 93
States, 50, 51, 136
  in sleep, 50, 51, 63
  and traits, 49
Stern, D., 3, 5–6, 76, 158
Still Face experiment, 49, 129
Stimson, C. A., 129
Stimulation of infant
  attention in, 50–52
  sensitivity in, 52
Stranger anxiety, 100
Stress
  autonomic nervous system in, 138
  brain in response to, 21, 22, 138
  crying of infant in, 52
  healing from, 143–145
  impact of, 140–141
  of infant in maternal depression, 153
  of newborn, 49, 50, 52, 136

of parents, 145, 150
in pregnancy, 23, 26, 52, 136, 147, 150
regulation system in, 136, 137
in sleep–wake cycle of infant, 65, 66, 69
and sudden infant death syndrome, 66
Stress hormones, 138, 150
prenatal exposure to, 23, 26
in sleep training of infant, 69
Subitizing skill, 107, 120
Substance use, 24–26
Suckling reflex, 36, 45, 48, 54, 55
Sudden infant death syndrome (SIDS), 65–66, 67–68
breastfeeding reducing incidence of, 153
in opioid-exposed infants, 25
Sullivan, L. M., 146, 150, 152, 153, 154
Sumner, G., 50, 51
Surprising events, infant response to, 105
Swallowing reflex, 55
Symbolic representation
of mobile infants, 117
of older infants, 120–121
Sympathetic interactions of parent and infant, 96
Sympathetic nervous system, 48, 49, 50, 138
Synapses, 12, 20, 21
Synaptogenesis, 12, 20
Synchrony, 54–70
biological, 3, 54
in communication, 74–76, 78
in co-regulation, 136
in facial expressions, 2–3, 4, 74–75
in feeding and meals, 3, 54–63
physiological, 3, 27, 43, 57, 65
in play, 97
in sleep patterns, 3, 54, 63–70
in social exchanges, 50

Tabula rasa (blank slate), 2
Tamis-LeMonda, C. S., 50, 86, 93
Tanner, A. C. R., 47
Tantrums, 133
Tarullo, A. R., 64
Taulu, S., 82
Taylor, B. J., 63
Teachers of infants and young children, 155–157
compensation of, 155, 156, 157
economic insecurity of, 156, 157
preparation and certification of, 155–156, 157
Teasing, 99, 100, 129
Tebbs, K. P., 157
Teeth of infants, 59, 60, 61
Temperature, and spermatogenesis, 14
Tense–freeze response, 138
Term birth, 18
Term of pregnancy, 12, 18
Testicles, 12
Thies, K. M., 13
Thiessen, E. D., 79
Thirdhand smoke, 24
Thompson, K. R., 69
1,000 Days initiative, 54, 146
Thurow, R., 146, 152
Tincoff, R., 83
Tobacco smoking, 13, 24, 67
Toddlers
autism intervention in, 103
caring by, 130
causality in object play of, 119
classification in object play of, 114, 118
egocentric development in, 3
house rules on behavior of, 131, 132
imitation by, 100, 101, 126
language development in, 83, 107
learning by, 126, 155, 158
motor development in, 86, 91, 92–93
number concept of, 120
peer interactions of, 100, 101
pretend play of, 101
rough-and-tumble play of, 102
sharing by, 100, 129–130, 131
social referencing by, 128
teachers working with, 155, 156, 157
trauma affecting, 142, 144, 145
Tollner, T., 15
Tomasello, M., 84, 128, 129, 130, 131, 133
Touch
communication in, 78
and skin-to-skin contact in newborn care, 36, 45–46, 47, 136
Touchpoints program, 6
Toxin exposure
pre-conception, 23, 146
in pregnancy, 23, 24
Toys and playthings, 109–122
for mobile infants, 114–117
for older infants, 118–121
safety of, 109, 110
sharing of, 129–130, 131
for young infants, 110–114
Training of infants
cultural influences on, 125
on motor skills, 94
on sleep–wake cycle, 64, 69
Traits, states becoming, 49
Transforming Maternity Care Symposium Steering Committee, 148
Transgenerational transmission
of epigenetic changes, 13, 146, 147
of microbiome, 47
Transition phase of labor, 34–35
Trauma, 138–145
in adverse childhood experiences, 139–140
behavioral expressions of, 142–143
conscious awareness of response to, 142
healing from, 143–145
impact of, 140–143
individual differences in response to, 141
interventions in, 143–145
physical expressions of, 141–142
resources in, 137
social engagement system in, 144–145
supportive and nurturing adults in recovery from, 144
Travers, J. F., 13
Trevarthen, C., 3, 4, 5, 6, 73, 74, 75–76, 78, 79, 85, 95, 96, 98, 100, 159
Trimesters of pregnancy, 16
Tronick, E., 2, 5, 7, 49, 129, 135, 153, 158, 161–162
True Self, 135
Tsao, F., 79, 81
Tsiaras, A., 19
Turati, C., 73
Turnbull, J., 136, 137–138

Uauy, R., 69
Umbilical cord, 12
Umiltà, C., 73
UNICEF, 58, 150, 152
United Nations, 148
Children's Fund, 58
Human Rights Office of the High Commissioner, 150
Population Fund, 148
United States Department of Health and Human Services, 151
Usui, A., 32
Uterus, 12
cervix of. *See* Cervix, uterine
contractions of. *See* Contractions, uterine
in menstrual cycle, 14
in pregnancy, 14, 15, 16, 17, 28
sperm entering, 15

Vaginal delivery, 30–42
microbiome in, 46–47
in midwife-led care, 148
van der Kamp, J., 90
van der Kolk, B., 21, 22, 135, 140, 141, 142, 143, 144
Van Ryzin, M. J., 156
Vestibular system, prenatal development of, 73
Vickar, M., 101
Victora, C. G., 153
Videbech, P., 153
Vigilante, D., 5
Vismara, L. A., 102
Visser, G. H. A., 87
Vitality, 5–6
Vocabulary growth in language development, 82–84
Voegtline, K. M., 74
Voice
fetal response to, 73–74
in infant-directed speech, 79
infant response to, 73, 75–76, 77
Volpe, L. E., 68
von Hof, P., 90
von Hofacker, N., 52
von Hofsten, C., 90

Wadhwa, P. D., 17, 19
Wagner, E., 130
Wakeford, A., 47
Walking, motor development for, 91, 92–93, 94
Wall, G., 58, 61
Wall, S., 2
Wambach, K., 55, 59
Ward-Platt, M. P., 65
Warneken, F., 130, 131, 133
Wasserman, S., 104
Watamura, S. E., 156
Waters, E., 2
Watson Genna, C., 55
Wear and tear, cumulative, in life-course perspective, 150
Weight
at birth, 17, 18, 24, 25, 149
maternal, in pregnancy, 19
Weinberg, M. K., 153
Weinstein, A. D., 15, 23
Weisleder, A., 82
Wendell, A. D., 25
Wenner, W. H., 63
Wernicke's area, 79–80
West, D., 57
West, M. J., 129
Westra, T., 94
Whitebook, M., 155, 156, 157
Wieder, S., 103
Wiessinger, D., 57
Winnicott, D. W., 1–2, 95, 134–135
Witherington, D. C., 90
Wolff, P. H., 50
Woodson, R., 74
Word recognition in language development, 80–81
and vocabulary growth, 82–84
World Health Organization, 18, 31, 36, 37, 38, 40, 41, 42, 45, 58, 59, 60, 148, 150, 152
Wynn, K., 106, 107, 130

Xu, F., 106, 107

Young, L. J., 47
Young infants, play of, 109, 110–114

Zahn-Waxler, C., 130
Zalenko, M., 64
Zero to Three, 154
Zona pellucida, 12
Zuckerman, A., 86
Zygotes, 15–16

About the Authors

MARY JANE MAGUIRE-FONG is faculty emerita in Early Childhood Education at American River College in Sacramento, California. She has served as faculty for the Program for Infant Toddler Care and holds an Infant–Parent Mental Health Certificate from the University of Massachusetts. She is the author of *Teaching and Learning with Infants and Toddlers: Where Meaning-Making Begins* (2015) and a contributing author for the California Department of Education Infant–Toddler and Preschool Curriculum Frameworks.

MARSHA PERALTA is a professor of early childhood education at Folsom Lake College and previously at Pacific Oaks College. She has degrees in psychology and human development and she holds an Infant–Parent Mental Health Certificate from the University of Massachusetts. Prior to teaching, she worked with infants and their families, drawing on extensive training in somatic psychology, trauma resolution, interpersonal neurobiology, and pre- and perinatal psychology.